MW01641810

בעזהי"ת

MASTERS OF THE MESORAH: EARLY RISHONIM

Other Volumes in the Hashkafah Series, by Rabbi Zechariah Fendel

Anvil of Sinai
[4th edit.] An in-depth analysis of fundamental Torah concepts

Challenge of Sinai
[2nd edit.] A Torah approach to a wide range of contemporary problems

The Ethical Personality
Torah ethics; with "Iggeres haRamban," and "Iggeres haMussar" of Rav Yisroel Salanter

The Halacha and Beyond
[2nd edit.] Fiscal-ethical responsibilities, and the bitachon concept

Legacy of Sinai
[4th edit.] History of Torah transmission, Creation through 4800 [1040 C.E.]

Masters of the Mesorah: Early Rishonim
[2nd edit.] History of Torah transmission, Geonim through Early Rishonim [900-1300 C.E.]

Masters of the Mesorah: Later Rishonim
[2nd edit.] History of Torah transmission, Closing centuries of Rishonim [1100-1575 C.E.]

Seasons of Majesty: Days of Awe; Days of Joy
Hashkafah insights: Rosh Hashanah, Yom Kippur, Sukkos, and Simchas Torah

Seasons of Splendor: Shabbos and the Mo'adim
Hashkafah insights: Shabbos, Pesach, and Shavu'os

The Torah Ethic
[3rd edit.] The Torah ethic of "Bein adam la-chavero," with "Ethical Bequest of Rambam"

Torah Faith: The Thirteen Principles
[2nd edit.] The 13 Principles of Torah Faith; including relevant Holocaust narratives

Chanukah: Season of Valor
A hashkafah-mussar perspective

Purim: Season of Miracles
A hashkafah-mussar perspective

Charting the Mesorah
Vol. I: Creation through Geonim, 1-4800 [1040 C.E.]
Vol. II: Early and Later Rishonim, 900-1575 C.E.
Original Charts, Maps, Tables, and Overview of Torah transmission.

בעזהי"ת

ראשונים כמלאכים

אם ראשונים בני מלאכים, אנו בני אנשים. [שבת קיב:]

If the earlier Torah masters are regarded as Angels,
then we may be regarded as human beings. [Shabbos 112b.]

In His munificent benevolence,
the Almighty implanted seeds of Torah learning
in the far-flung communities of the Diaspora.
Nurtured and sustained in foreign soil,
these seeds grew into mighty cedars
and magnificent citadels of Torah learning,
which brought the light of Torah
to all corners of the Diaspora.
[See Historical Overview, p. 9]

MASTERS OF THE MESORAH: EARLY RISHONIM

by Rabbi Zechariah Fendel

A History of Torah Transmission
with World Backgrounds:
From the Geonic Era, through the
Era of the Early Rishonim [900-1300 C.E.]

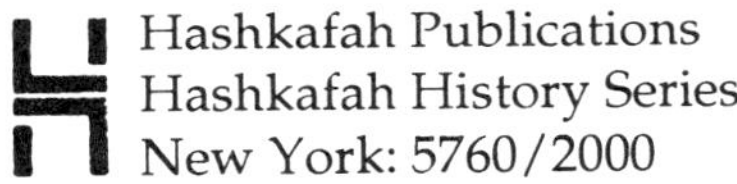

Hashkafah Publications
Hashkafah History Series
New York: 5760/2000

First edition, 1990
Second revised edition, 2000

68-61 Selfridge Street
Forest Hills, NY 11375
(718) 261-6076

Library of Congress Catalogue Number: 90—083669

ISBN: 1—879061—01-5

כל הספרים שלנו הקודמים הופיעו בהסכמה זו
מכבוד הגאון האדיר ושר התורה,
אור ישראל, ועמוד ההוראה
רשכבה״ג מורנו ורבנו מרן ר׳ משה פיינשטיין, זצוק״ל

RABBI MOSES FEINSTEIN
455 F. D. R. DRIVE
NEW YORK, N. Y. 10002
OREGON 7-1222

משה פיינשטיין
ר״מ תפארת ירושלים
בנוא יארק

בע״ה

הנה ידידי הנכבד מאד ירא שמים ובעל רעיונות נשגבים בדרך התורה והאמונה הטהורה המסורה לנו, הרה״ג מו״ה ר׳ זכריה פענדעל שליט״א, כתב רעיונותיו והשקפותיו בתורה ובמדות הטובות עלי ספר בשפת האנגלית המדוברת לאחינו בני ישראל שבמדינתנו ארצות הברית, שכעת רוב אחב״י נמצאים עד גאולתנו ע״י משיח צדקנו בקרוב בעה״י, שהוא לעורר לתורה הקדושה ולאמונה טהורה בהשי״ת ולהתנהג בדרך הישר כפי שנצטווינו.

ואף שאני בעצמי מכיר את הר״ר זכריה שליט״א המחבר בצדקתו וישרתו לטובה וכוונתו הטובה, שלחתי את חבורו לבני הגדולים בתורה היראים והשלמים, שהם ראו הרבה ענינים ומסרו לי איך שדבריו נכונים במאמרים חשובים לאהבת התורה ויראת שמים טהורה, אשר על כן אני מברכו שיצליח ויקרב בספרו את לבות הצעירים לאהבת התורה ויראת השם וטהרת המדות. וע״ז באתי על החתום בט״ו כסלו תשל״ז בנוא יארק.

נאום משה פיינשטיין

הסכמה מכבוד מורנו ורבנו
הרב הגאון ר׳ חיים פנחס שיינבערג, שליט״א
ראש ישיבת „ישיבה תורה אור״ ודיין דקרית מטרסדורף

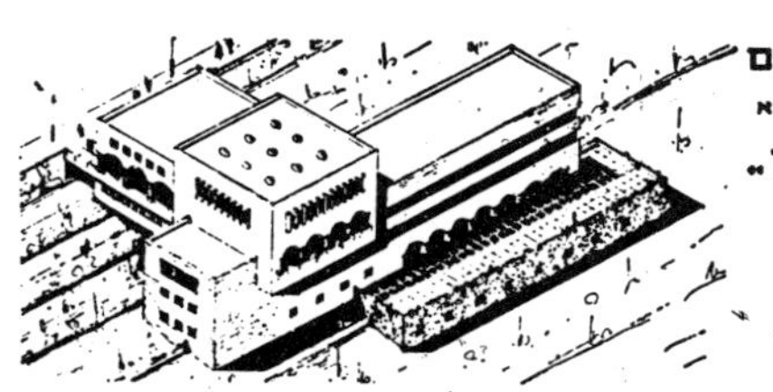

ישיבת „תורה-אור" בעיה"ק ירושלים
בנשיאות מרן הרב הגאון רבי חיים פנחס שיינברג שליט"א
„TORAH–ORE" SEMINARY
The American Seminary in Israel
Kiryath Mattersdorf - קרית מטרסדורף
TEL. 523049 טלפון ★ P. O. B. 15008 .ת. ד
JERUSALEM, ISRAEL

בואו ונחזיק טובה לידידנו היקר הדגול מרבבה בתורתו וברוחו כבוד הרב ר׳ זכריה פענדעל נ״י, שאני מכירו כבר מכמה שנים כירא שמים ובן תורה אמיתי מאז למד אצלנו, עוד טרם נתייסדה ישיבתנו, והיה מתלמידינו החשובים. שבכר מאז הקדיש שנים הרבה להרבצת התורה בין תלמידי הישיבות, וכבר העמיד תלמידים הרבה על ידי השיעורים שלו ושיחותיו המוסריות, ועל ידי פעולותיו הפוריות שיגע ביגיעה רבה לקרב לבבות התלמידים לתורה וליראה.

והרי עכשו עמל והשקיע כחו בדבר חשוב מאד לצרף וללבן כמה דברים הנוגעים ליסודות הדת ולעניני מוסר על פי האמת, ממקורות הקדושות הנובעים מדברי חז״ל, אשר הם מעוררים לחבב את התורה והמצוה על שומריהן, ויועילו לבצר את חומת הדת.

ותקותנו ותפלתנו שיצליח להמשיך את הלבבות של התלמידים לאהבת התורה ולחיזוק האמונה, ולקרב לבם אל אבינו שבשמים, שעל ידי זה נזכה לגאולה שלמה במהרה בימינו אמן.

ואסיים בברכת הצלחה בכל הענינים שלו כעתירת נפש ידידו הדו״ש, פה עיר הקדש, ירושלים תובב״א, ר״ח כסלו, תשל״ז.

נאום חיים פנחס שיינבערג

Table of Contents

Introduction xi

Preface 1

Historical Overview 8

I. Origins of the Early Schools 29

"The sun rises and the sun sets" / Origins of Sephardic Jewry / The Arabian-Muslim conquest / Links with the Babylonian Academies / R. Chisdai Ibn Shaprut / The Khazar Kingdom / The early Hebrew lexicographers / A milestone in Hebrew grammar / The *Arba'ah Shevuyyim* / From Lucca to Mayence / Origins of the Italian School / The Early Ashkenazic School / Development of the Sephardic School / The Rosh Hashanah *Mussaf* controversy / Convergence of the Babylonian and Eretz Yisroel Schools / The guiding hand of Divine Providence

II. The Early Sephardic Torah Masters 59

R. Moshe and R. Chanoch / R. Shmuel haNagid: Scholar, statesman, poet, benefactor / R. Shemariah in Alexandria / The North African Torah Center / R. Chananel b. R. Chushiel / R. Nissim b. Yaakov of Kairouan / Origins of the Italian Jewish community / The Scroll of Achima'atz / The Ten Italian Martyrs / Early Italian Torah Masters / R. Nasan b. Yechiel: Ba'al haAruch / R. Yitzchak of Siponto / *Tosafos Rid* / The Anavim Family / *Shibolei haLeket* / The benevolent Carolingian Kings / R. Amnon: *U'nesaneh Tokef* / The Early Provencal School / R. Moshe haDarshon of Narbonne Roots of Anti-Semitism and Holocaust: / 5 Centuries of Torah leadership.

III. The Rif, Contemporaries and Disciples 95

The Five Yitzchaks / R. Yitzchak Alfasi [the Rif] / *Hilchos Rav Alfas* / The *Talmud Yerushalmi* vis-a-vis the *Talmud Bavli* / The "Armor-Bearers" of the Rif / The Ri Migash / The Almohad Invasion / An unexpected haven / *Olam Kattan* / R. Bachya Ibn Paquda: The *Chovos haLevavos* / Poet and philosopher: R. Yehudah haLevi / Ode to Zion / *Sefer HaKuzari* / The historical imperative of Torah faith / An exposition of fundamental Torah concepts / R. Avraham Ibn Ezra: Prolific scholar and poet / The world travelers / Ravad I: The *Sefer haKabbalah* / Strengthening the Mesorah / Martyred *Al Kiddush HaShem* / A sapling planted in Spain

IV. Rambam: Prince of Torah 131

The trials and tribulations of R. Maimon / Rambam: Prince of Torah / A prolific pen / *Sefer haMa'or* / The *Yad haChazakah* / The 14 *sefarim* of the *Yad* / A monumental halachic edifice / The *Moreh Nevuchim* / Vindication of the Rambam's *Moreh* / The Thirteen Principles of Torah Faith / *Iggeres haShmad* and *Iggeres Teiman* / Man of impeccable integrity . . . / . . . and of great humility / "Follow in my footsteps" / A life of hardship and suffering / Words of faith and hope / "Among all the exiles, there was none like Moshe" / R. Avraham haNagid b. haRambam / *Sefer haMaspik leOvdei HaShem* / R. Dovid b. Avraham haNagid / Admirers and critics of the Rambam's *Mishneh Torah*

V. The Provencal School 169

Primary architects of the Provencal School / Ravad II: Ba'al haEshkol / R. Moshe b. Yosef b. Mervon haLevi / R. Meshullam of Lunel: Scholar and patron of Torah / R. Aharon b. Meshullam and the Rosh of Lunel / *Sefer haHashlamah* / R. Meir haKohen of Narbonne / The Ravad Ba'al haHasagos: Master of critique / *Hasagos haRavad*: Critical glosses on *Mishneh Torah* / *Ba'alei haNefesh le-haRavad* / *Ruach haKodesh* of the Ravad / R. Zerachiah haLevi, Ba'al haMa'or / "Old wine in new vessels" / Ba'al haIttur

R. Yehonasan haKohen and the Chachmei Lunel /R. Meir of Trinquetaille / R. Nasan of Trinquetaille: *Sefer haEzer* / R. Avraham b. Nasan haYarchi: *Sefer haManhig* / R. Shlomo Min haHar and the Maimonidean controversy / R. David Kimchi: the Radak / The Ibn Tibbon Family: The Translators / Corresponding with the Rambam / R. Menachem b. Shlomo: The Me'iri / *Bais haBechirah* / Infusing the halacha with vitality / R. Avraham min haHar / Ralbag / R. Aharaon haKohen of Lunel: *Orchos Chaim* / The French Expulsion of 1306 / R. Estori haParchi: *Kaftor vaPherach* / The decline of the Provencal School

VI. Franco-German School: Rashi: Teacher of Israel..... 209

Origins of the Mainz Community: The Kalonymos Family / R. Yehudah haKohen Leontin; R. Meshullam b. Kalonymos / R. Shimon haGadol / The Jewish Pope / R. Gershom: "Light of the Exile" / *Akdamos Millin*: A magnificent *piyyut* / *Takanos* of R. Gershom Me'or haGolah / R. Yosef Tov Elem / Rashi's teachers / R. Yaakov b. Yakar / R. Yitzchak b. Yehudah / R. Yitzchak haLevi / Rashi: Teacher of all Israel / A Heavenly blessing / The wall bent inward / Eliyahu haNavi / Beloved by his teachers / The master commentator / An indispensable guide to Talmud / *Parshan Dassa* / An indelible imprint / A personification of Torah / Ravages of the First Crusade / Rashi's "prophecy" / The light glows ever brighter / A father-son relationship / Rashi's *talmidim*

Tables and Time-Line Charts

I. Time-Line Chart: *Mattan Torah* through Geonic Era 25
II. Time-Line Chart: 11th, 12th, 13th Centuries 26
III. Time-Line Chart: 14th and 15th Centuries 27
IV. Time-Line Chart: 16th and 17th Centuries 28
V. Early Sephardic Schools: Post-Geonic Era 58
VI. Early Italian Torah Masters 73
VII. Significant Historical Events of Medieval Period 85
VIII. Sephardic School: From Rif to Rambam 99
IX. Provencal School: Early Torah Masters 187
X. Provencal School: Later Torah Masters 188
XI. Franco-German School: Rashi, Teachers and Disciples 215

Maps

I. The Iberian Peninsula 100
II. Germany, France, and Southern France 216

Indices

Subject Index 247
Sefarim Index 256
Name Index 259
Bibliography and Source Index 267
Glossary of Hebrew Terms 273
Abbreviations 274

This . . . Our Torah!

This, our Torah . . . At Sinai received,
As flames screamed up to the heart of the heavens.
With an oath of fire we pledged our creed,
To cherish forever the Law we were given.

This, our Torah . . . Our guide through the night,
When our sins brought upon us the terrible war.
Gone was our Temple — Gone was the light;
From Zion to Yavneh, we carried G-d's Law.

This, our Torah . . . Where now was her beacon,
When ten Torah masters were felled by the sword?
All hope seemed lost; Yet ne'er did they weaken,
With the *Shema* on their lips, they sanctified the L-rd.

This, our Torah . . . She too rent her garments,
When our people embarked on the long Galus night.
Then, as they wandered, she with them did wander,
From her great Torah masters, came guidance and light.

This, our Torah . . . With our lives did we guard you,
When pressed with conversion by barbaric hordes.
With defiant reply, we chose to uphold you,
"Life is temporal — The soul is the L-rd's."

This, our Torah . . . O' what grief we shared,
When for the Six Million we stood bereaved.
From the nethermost depths, to hope they dared!
From their lips came a song — "I Believe."

This, our Torah . . . Lifeline of our people,
When, homeless, they wandered, in exile to grope.
It was then you, O' Torah, who gave strength to our people,
In your words they found faith, courage, and hope.

This, our Torah . . . Everlasting, eternal,
Who is the man who will not comprehend?
This, our Torah, and for time all-eternal,
Legacy of our children — generations no end.

Z.F.

זאת . . . תורתנו

זאת, תורתנו . . . בסיני קבלנו,
עת בוערת אש עד לב השמים.
אז, שבועת־אש לאלקינו נשבענו,
לא נשכח עולמים מעמד מחנים.

זאת, תורתנו . . . עליך נהרגנו,
עת בעוננו נחרב המקדש.
אז, במר־נפש, בדמעת לבבנו,
מציון ליבנה, העברנו אש דת.

זאת, תורתנו . . . עמך נתיתמנו,
עת בני בליעל שפכו דם קדושים.
אז, על ארזי הלבנון התאבלנו,
בשמע על שפתם, נהרגו — שמחים.

זאת תורתנו . . . גם היא שק חגרה,
עת ראתה עמי בגולה.
אז בנודדם, גם היא עמם נדדה,
אין מקום בגלות לא נשאו התורה.

זאת, תורתנו . . . בדם־נפש שמרנו,
עת קם הצורר להשבית דת קל.
אז — תשובה נוצחת השבנו,
„הגוף מעפר . . . הנפש לקל״.

זאת, תורתנו . . . ראית לחצנו,
עת כאב סבלנו מבלי להאמין.
אז, ביום עברה, נשחטו מליוננו,
ונשמע קול מאבדון . . . „אני מאמין!״

זאת, תורתנו . . . חי־נפש עמנו,
עת נדדו — נפוצו בגולה.
אז, היית את חי־רוח אפנו,
מדבריך נתחזקנו, מצאנו תקוה.

זאת, תורתנו . . . לא יחליף הקל,
מי בן־אדם לא יבין את זאת.
זאת תורתנו . . . תורת ישראל,
מורשת בנינו — לשמור ולעשות.

בעזהי״ת

Introduction

Masters of the Mesorah: Early Rishonim, together with its companion volume, *Masters of the Mesorah: Later Rishonim*, consists of a thoroughly documented study of the highlights of the Torah transmission process during the Medieval Period, in two volumes, covering the eras of the Early and Later *Rishonim* (ca. 900-1575 C.E.). These books, which are a sequel to our earlier work in this series, *Legacy of Sinai* (N.Y., 1981), trace the earliest origins of the establishment of Torah schools in the far-flung communities of North Africa, Italy, Spain, the cities of the Rhine and of Northern France, as well as in the cities of the Provence in Southern France. In so doing, this work underscores the continuity of the transmission process during the period of Torah decentralization, which commenced in the early decades of the tenth century, even before the Babylonian academies of Sura and Pumbedisa ceased to function as central Torah academies for the entire Diaspora in 1038 C.E.

Living Links in the Transmission Process

In sequential units, this study deals with each of these Schools — the Italian School, the North African School, the Sephardic School, the Provencal School, and the Franco-Ashkenazic School — tracing its philosophical leanings, its unique areas of creative literary activity, and its distinctive contributions to all phases of Torah study and halachic development.

While this work is replete with biographical sketches of the outstanding leaders of the transmission process in each generation, these are not presented merely as isolated sketches of great Torah personalities. These leaders are portrayed, rather, as living links in the greater transmission process — linking Rebbe and *talmid*, father and son, colleagues and contemporaries, antagonists and protagonists, as well as important statesmen and Torah benefactors, who provided the political and financial assistance which stimulated the growth and development of each of these great independent Schools of Torah study.

A Cohesive Narrative Approach

Hence, the biographical sketches of the great Torah masters are rendered within the full context of the particular schools they represent, thereby providing the reader with an insight into the unbroken continuum of the transmission process.

Thus, to cite but one example, Ravad III of Posquires (1120-1198), the great master of the Provencal School of Southern France, is portrayed in the context of his interaction with his teachers (e.g. Rabbe Meshullam b. Yaakov of Lunel, Rabbe Moshe b. Yosef b. Mervon haLevi, and Rabbe Avraham b. Yitzchak Ba'al haEshkol, Ravad II of Narbonne), his colleagues (e.g. Rabbe Zerachiah haLevi, Ba'al haMa'or and Rabbe Yitzchak b. Abba Mari of Marseilles, Ba'al haIttur), his great contemporary, the Rambam, and his numerous disciples (e.g. Rabbe Meir b. Yitzchak of Trinquetaille, Rabbe Yehonasan haKohen of Lunel, and the Chachmei Lunel). This unit will thereby provide a broad overview of the distinctive contributions of the Provencal School, which was a dynamic center of creative literary activity for over three centuries, and which included such a diverse array of personalities as the Ibn Tibbon family — the translators; the Kimchi family — the illustrious grammarians and Biblical commentators; and later, Rabbe Menachem b. Shlomo haMe'iri of Perpignon, whose death in 1315 brought this prolific literary era to a close.

From the Pens of the Masters

Where relevant, *Masters of the Mesorah* includes world backgrounds, by making reference to those major events in the world community which had a bearing upon the fortunes and the stability of the Jewish community. *Masters of the Mesorah* is written in the form of an ongoing narrative, weaving these important historical events into the context of the narration, to provide cohesiveness and lucidity.

Masters of the Mesorah includes numerous first-hand citations, drawn from the major works, the letters, and the responsa of many of the *Rishonim* themselves, thereby providing the reader with an appreciation of the stimulating intellectual arguments and the classical literature of these great Torah masters. Selections from the writings of the Rambam, for example, have been culled from the extensive fruits of his prolific pen — from his *Yad haChazakah,* his

Mishnah commentary, his famed *Iggeres Teiman* and *Iggeres haShmad*, his *Moreh Nevuchim*, and even his personal correspondence with Rabbe Shmuel Ibn Tibbon and others, all of which provide the reader with fascinating insights into the halachic, hashkafah, and philosophical writings of this illustrious thinker and leader of Israel. Similarly, brief selections are rendered from the writings of many of the great *Rishonim* cited in this work, such as Rabbeinu Yitzchak Alfasi (Rif), Rashi, Ravad of Posquires, the Radak, the Kuzari, the Chovos haLevavos, the Me'iri, and many others.

These selections will make it possible for the reader to experience first-hand the powerful current of spiritual enrichment and intellectual, moral, and ethical stimulation which emanated from the pens of the great teachers of Israel.

Thus, *Masters of the Mesorah* weaves a vibrant, living tapestry of the mesorah process, infusing the legacy of our *Rishonim* with life and vitality, underscoring the far-reaching significance of their great literary contributions, and pointing always to their primary function as indispensable links in the unbroken continuum of Torah transmission.

It is hoped that this work will prove to be useful for scholar and layman alike. The inclusion of numerous citations from a variety of primary sources, as well as the abundance of footnotes, source references, elaborate indices and bibliographic material, will prove to be invaluable to the scholar and to the teacher of Jewish history, who may wish to supplement the material rendered here with further research and in-depth study. At the same time, the lucid, narrative style, the informative biographical sketches, the numerous chronological tables and time-line charts, as well as the methodical presentation of the various Schools of Torah transmission as distinctive, cohesive units, will be of interest even to those individuals who may have had little prior knowledge of Jewish history.

It is my sincere hope that *Masters of the Mesorah* will provide the reader with a deeper awareness of the rich literary productivity of the *Rishonim*, of their lofty spiritual stature, and of their indispensable role as Masters of the Mesorah, and as vital links in the ongoing process of Torah transmission.

Z.F.

בעזהי״ת

Preface

I shall enter Thy house with ascent offerings; *I shall fulfill my vows to Thee . . .*	אבוא ביתך בעולות; אשלם לך נדרי. . .
Blessed is G-d, *Who has not removed* *My prayer, nor His loving kindness* *From me.* *[Psalms 66:13, 20]*	ברוך אלקים, אשר לא הסיר תפלתי וחסדו מאתי. [תהלים ס״ו: י״ג, כ׳]

With a heart filled with thanksgiving, I express my gratitude to the Almighty for having privileged me to attain yet another milestone in the Hashkafah Library Series, with the publication of *Masters of the Mesorah: Early Rishonim.* It is my hope and prayer that this book may enrich the lives of my fellow Jews by providing them with an awareness of the radiant spiritual stature of our early Torah masters and teachers, the *Rishonim,* "by whose words we live, and whose life-giving waters of Torah sustain us."

Masters of the Mesorah: Early Rishonim, together with its sequel, *Masters of the Mesorah: Later Rishonim,* is a continuation of our earlier work, *Legacy of Sinai,* which traces the history of Torah transmission from Creation through the close of the Geonic era in 1038 C.E. Commencing, as it does, with the incipient stages of the era of Torah decentralization, which began in the late ninth and early tenth centuries, well before the close of the Geonic era, *Masters of the Mesorah* continues to trace the course of Torah transmission throughout the turbulent era of the *Rishonim.* This study of the lives and important literary contributions of our early Torah masters is based upon extensive and painstaking research.

Because of the abundance of material available, it was decided to publish this work in two separate volumes, with Volume I covering the origins of the Early Schools in Italy, Spain, North Africa, Germany, Northern France, and Southern France, through their establishment as independent Torah centers. In this first volume, the history of the Sephardic School has been carried through the deaths of the Rambam (1135-1204) and his descendants, while the history of the Provencal School has been carried beyond the death of the Ravad of Posquires (1120-1198), to its termination in the early 14th century, so that this School might be seen as one integral unit. In regard to the Franco-German School, on the other hand, we have closed the narration in Volume I with the death of Rashi (1040-1105), so that the *Tosafist* School might be seen as an integral unit in Volume II, which will include both the Early and Later *Tosafists* of the twelfth and thirteenth centuries.

Reinforcing Torah Faith

Our primary purpose in having written this history of Torah transmission is to stengthen Torah faith and reinforce *emunah*-values, by providing the reader with an awareness that both our Written and Oral Laws have been transmitted to us in an unbroken chain of Torah scholarship, from Rebbe to *talmid,* from Torah academy to Torah academy, from Sinai to our own day. As Rabbe Avraham ibn Daud (1110-1180) writes at the very outset of his *Sefer haKabbalah,*

> כתבנוהו להודיע לתלמידים כי כל דברי רבותינו ז״ל, חכמי המשנה והתלמוד, כולם מקובלים חכם גדול וצדיק מפי חכם גדול וצדיק, ראש ישיבה וסיעתו מפי ראש ישיבה וסיעתו, מאנשי כנסת הגדולה, שקבלו מהנביאים, זכר כולם לברכה.
>
> We have written this [history of Torah transmission] to inform the students that all the words of our Sages of blessed memory, the Sages of the Talmud and the Mishnah, were all received by one great and exceedingly righteous Sage from another great and exceedingly righteous Sage, by one *Rosh Yeshiva* and his entourage from another *Rosh Yeshiva* and his entourage, from the *Anshei Knesses haGedolah* [the *Sanhedrin* of Ezra, at the beginning of the Second Temple], who, in turn, received it from the Prophets [who received it from Moshe at Sinai].
>
> [Ravad I, Introd. to *Sefer haKabbalah*]

This is reminiscent of the words of the first *mishnah* in *Pirkei Avos*. "Moshe received the Torah at Sinai, and he transmitted it to Joshua, Joshua to the *Zekenim* — the Seventy Elders — the *Zekenim* to the Prophets, and the Prophets to the *Anshei Knesses haGedolah*" [*Avos* 1:1].

It is perhaps with this in mind, too, that the Rambam, in his introduction to his *Mishneh Torah*, renders a concise, sequential account of the forty generations of Prophets and illustrious Torah Sages who stood at the helm of the transmission process in each generation, spanning almost 1800 years, from Moshe Rabbeinu (2448) to Rav Ashi (d. 4187; 427 C.E.) who redacted the Babylonian Talmud. In his introduction to his Mishnah commentary, the Rambam renders a far-more detailed account of the transmission process, as do many *Rishonim* and *Acharonim*, as well. (e.g. Introd. to *Machzor Vitri* on *Pirkei Avos*, and Introd. to Meiri on *Pirkei Avos*.)

It is with this primary purpose in mind that we have approached this arduous and painstaking task as a labor of love — to portray our mesorah as a living mesorah, and as an unbroken continuum of Torah transmission, which has extended from Sinai to our own day. It is to this end, too, that we have cited here numerous brief selections from the words of our *Rishonim*, so that their words might come alive for us again in our own generation, and so that we may learn to recognize the early Torah masters as towering spiritual giants, who have breathed life and vitality into the legacy of Sinai, who have bequeathed to us an unparalleled spiritual heritage, and who have transmitted to us and to all future generations the living mesorah of Sinai.

It has been my sincere aspiration that this thought might permeate the pages of this book, so that our generation of Jews and those who come after us shall learn to appreciate the true radiance and splendor of our Torah heritage, and so that we may learn to recognize the magnificent spiritual stature of the *Gedolei Yisroel* — the guardians and masters of our mesorah throughout all generations. They endured the crucibles of fire and water, blood libels and massacres, incessant pogroms and relentless persecution, and dared to incur the wrath of Kings and nobility, Popes and "holy crusaders," and to withstand banishment and expulsions, public debates and Talmud burnings. Despite all the devious machinations of the enemies of our people, these Torah leaders steadfastly devoted their lives to Torah study and to Torah dissemination, so that they might convey to us and to all future generations the unadulterated Voice of Sinai.

ברוך שבחר בהם ובמשנתם

"Blessed is He who has chosen them,
and their Torah teaching."

A Source of Profound Gratification

I have been deeply gratified to learn that the various books of our Hashkafah Library Series — most of which are in their second or third printing at this time — have been received warmly by many of our fellow Jews, and have made a deep impact upon the lives of many individuals. It is truly heart-warming to read the letters of some of our readers who inform us that one or another of the books in this series "has turned my life around," or "has helped me find the way home again to my magnificent Torah heritage." It is these letters, as well as phone calls to this effect, which have made all the effort and energy expended in this effort worthwhile.

And yet, these books are certainly not only for the uninitiated, or for those of our fellow Jews who have become estranged from our Torah heritage. We have heard from Yeshiva *bachurim,* who regard them as an extension of the mussar *sichos* they hear in their Yeshivos; from Seminary girls who regard them as a series of fundamental hashkafah lectures; from teachers in yeshivos and Seminaries who find in the voluminous source references an invaluable guide for preparation of their lectures and their hashkafah *shiurim.*

Above all, I am profoundly grateful to the Almighty who has enlightened me and who has guided my path in this undertaking, so that many of our fellow Jews have been able to look to these books as a source of personal growth and spiritual enrichment, and as a means of expanding their Torah horizons by providing them with new insights into the eternal values of Torah.

It is my sincere prayer that the Almighty may continue to bless our efforts with success. May these essays serve as a perpetual source of spiritual enrichment and gratification for myriads of our fellow Jews everywhere, and may they instill within them an abiding love and appreciation for authentic Torah values.

May the Almighty grant me strength and wisdom, health, tranquility, patience and understanding, that I may be privileged to witness the publication of other works in the Hashkafah Library Series which will be instrumental in bringing our fellow Jews closer to G-d and to our Torah heritage.

Textual Guidelines and Comments

With but minor revision, textual guidelines for this work are substantially the same as those employed in *Legacy of Sinai.* To facilitate comprehension, pains were taken to differentiate between Scriptural citations and between citations from post-Biblical sources. To this end, all Scriptural citations were set in italic type, while other citations were set in regular type. (In rare instances, italics were used for emphasis or for poetic effect.) Where it was thought that the original Hebrew of any particular citation would add either to the comprehension or to the distinctive flavor of the selection quoted, the Hebrew was included, either directly or in transliteration. Generally, when an unusual Hebrew term was cited for the first time, a translation of the term was included in the text itself to facilitate reading comprehension.

All sources cited are carefully footnoted, and wherever possible, additional cross-references are provided to facilitate further in-depth study. For technical reasons, wherever reference is made to our text, the reference is cited by chapter and footnote number, rather than by page number, despite the fact that almost invariably the reference is to the corresponding text itself.

Exceedingly great care and effort have been lavished upon the Footnotes, the Tables, and the Indices.It is to be hoped that the reader will make ample reference to these notes and to the source materials they contain, and that he will regard them as invaluable supplements to the text itself. Perhaps the reader will find it advisable to make a first, rather cursory reading, with scant reference to the source material, and a second in-depth reading with more attention being paid to the source references. It was in order to facilitate the reader's reference to the source material that pains were taken to include the footnotes on each page rather than at the end of each chapter or of the entire book, although this entailed a great deal of additional tedious and time-consuming work. For this reason, too, all materials contained in the Footnotes, Tables, Time-Line Charts, and Overview have been included in the Index section, where they have been arranged under an elaborate cross-reference system.

A comprehensive Index of Proper Names has also been included, to facilitate immediate reference to the many names contained in the Tables and the Overview, as well as in the text and footnotes themselves. In addition, an elaborate code system was arranged for the Name Index, in order to provide the reader with a maximum amount of information concerning each of the many hundreds of names cited, in the most concise form possible.

The reader will find that the Overview provides much useful information, in summary form. It should be noted that it was, of course, impossible to make all the Charts and Tables of outstanding Torah leaders comprehensive and exhaustive. Unfortunately, due to limitations of time and space, many important names have inadvertently been omitted. Nevertheless, it is believed that these Tables will provide the reader with much valuable information.

Each of the numerous Charts, Tables and Indices which are included in this work, are original contributions which have been painstakingly prepared and researched by the author, so that they might serve as authentic teaching guides for the serious student. Poems and translations of Hebrew texts are likewise original contributions.

In Appreciation

I wish to express my most sincere gratitude and appreciation to a dear friend and patron of Torah, Mr. Henry Schwartz. His warm friendship and his enthusiastic and generous support of the Hashkafah Library Series have been a perpetual source of encouragement, and have contributed greatly to the success of this project. May he and his wife be blessed with many, many years of health, happiness and prosperity. May they continue to see much Torah *nachas* from their sons, Cyrus and Darius, in the years ahead.

I would once again like to extend a sincere *beracha* to my life's partner and אשת חיל, my dear wife, Chava, שתחיה עמו״ש, who has stood by my side with devotion throughout every phase of the preparation of these essays.

כל ברכות התורה לראשה תהיינה, עד תאות גבעות עולם.

May the Almighty grant that we may together be *zocheh* to see much Torah *nachas* from each of our children and grandchildren. May our fondest hopes for each of our children be realized, and may we be privileged to raise them as true *b'nei Torah* and *b'nos Yisroel.* May they each, in turn, build true Torah homes in Israel, permeated with *ahavas haMakom, ahavas haTorah, yir'as Shamayim,* and *ahavas Yisroel* — homes which will radiate joy, warmth, love, and friendship, לשם ולתפארת בישראל.

יהי רצון שתשרה ברכה במעשה ידינו, ונזכה להיות ממזכי הרבים, ויהא זכות הרבים תלוי בנו. ונזכה לראות בנים ובני בנים כשתילי זיתים סביב לשלחננו, עוסקים בתורה ובמצות ועושים רצונו של מקום, מתוך שמחה והרוחה. ולא ימוש ספר התורה הזה מפינו, ומפי זרעינו, ומפי זרע זרעינו, מעתה ועד עולם. „ויהי נעם ה׳ אלקינו עלינו, ומעשה ידינו כוננה עלינו, ומעשה ידינו כוננהו״.

I wish to extend my sincerest appreciation to: Rabbi Yossie Waldman for his meticulous and painstaking proofreading of the entire manuscript; Rabbi Zalman Hillel Fendel and Rabbi Moshe Travitsky, for their valuable suggestions and stimulating comments; Tova, for her diligent efforts in proofreading; Esther, for preparing the index; Shuly, for her valuable art contributions; Esther and Devorah, for their warm support of this project.

May we all go forth together to be מקבל פני משיח צדקנו and to witness הרמת קרן התורה — the elevation of the stature and dignity of Torah, the homecoming of our brethren from the far-flung corners of the Diaspora, and the Redemption of all Israel.

Rabbi Zechariah Fendel

Erev Shavu'os, 5750
Forest Hills, New York

יהי רצון שישלח הקב"ה רפואה שלמה בקרוב
לילד ירחמיאל שאול רפאל בן שרה רבקה זלטה, עמו"ש,
ולילדה חיה אביטל רבקה בת רחל, עמו"ש.

רופא חנם ירפא אותם בקרוב, רפואת הנפש ורפואת הגוף,
בתוך שאר חולי עמו ישראל ברחמים.

Historical Overview: Early Rishonim

מלמד שהראה הקב״ה למשה
כל מה שהיה ועתיד להיות . . .
דור דור ודורשיו,
דור דור ושופטיו,
דור דור ומנהיגיו,
דור דור וצדיקיו.
[במדבר רבה כג, ד]

The Holy One, blessed be He,
Showed Moshe everything that was,
And all that is destined to be . . .
Each generation and its teachers,
Each generation and its judges,
Each generation and its [Torah] leaders,
Each generation and its righteous men.
[Bamidbar Rabbah 23:4]

Historical Overview

The Exile of King Yechoniah

At the time of the first *Churban*, the Jewish people were exiled in separate stages. In the year 3327, King Yechoniah was led into exile together with the nobility and the great Torah scholars. Eleven years later, in the year 3338, the Temple was destroyed, and the mainstream of the Jewish people were led into exile, 850 years after Israel's entry into the Land in the year 2488.

Citing an enigmatic verse in Daniel [9:14], *Chazal* observe that the Almighty benevolently hastened the destruction of the First Temple before its time, while the great Torah scholars who were exiled 11 years earlier with King Yechoniah in 3327 would yet be alive, so that they might teach Torah and build great Torah centers for the multitudes of Jews who were exiled with King Tzidkiyahu at the time of the *Churban*, in 3338. [*Gittin* 88a; *Sanhedrin* 38a.]

The Early Decades

In a similar vein, during the incipient decades of the era of Torah decentralization, the Almighty, in His munificent benevolence and in His inscrutable wisdom, implanted seeds of Torah learning and Torah scholarship in far-flung communities of the Diaspora, even before the glorious era of the *Geonim* came to a close with the death of Rav Hai Gaon, in the year 1038 C.E. These tiny seeds were nurtured and sustained in foreign soil, until they grew into strong saplings, and eventually increased and flourished greatly to become mighty cedars and citadels of Torah learning, which brought the light of Torah to all corners of the Diaspora.

Spanning Six Centuries

In this work we have traced the origins of these early Schools, whose beginnings are often shrouded in obscurity, and we have described their subsequent phenomenal growth and development. In so doing, we have presented the reader with a panoramic view of the uninterrupted process of Torah transmission, as it has continued to weave a beautiful tapestry and to forge an unbroken chain of profound Torah scholarship and incisive erudition, during one of the most trying and turbulent periods in Jewish history.

Spanning, as it does, a period of almost six centuries, from its inception during the decades preceding the close of the Geonic *tekufah* in 1038 C.E. until the compilation of the *Shulchan Aruch* in the year 1555, the era of the *Rishonim* is replete with a degree of prolific literary productivity which is nothing short of amazing. The vast scope and profundity of the literary contributions of the early Torah masters to all areas of Torah literature are truly breathtaking.

Five Primary Schools

While we can hardly hope to do justice to an analytical study of this prolific literary activity with a few strokes of the pen, we will nevertheless attempt to present here a concise overview of the work of the early *Rishonim,* with a cursory analysis of the major contributions of each of the primary Schools of Torah scholarship. For this purpose, we will classify the era of the early *Rishonim* under five primary groups: (a) The Early Italian School; (b) The North African School; (c) The Early Sephardic School; (d) The Provencal School; (e) The Early Franco-German School.

Since this first volume of *Masters of the Mesorah* covers only the first three centuries of the development of these early Schools, we will confine our remarks in this Overview to the contributions of the early Torah masters, who established the foundations of these Schools and who set the tone for their subsequent development. It was they who were the guides and mentors of the myriads of disciples of these Schools, and who thereby left an indelible imprint upon their respective Schools for all future generations.

Influence of the Early Masters

It should be borne in mind that the literary contributions of each of these groups are by no means mutually exclusive in regard to either style or methodology, scope or content. Indeed, they do frequently overlap in regard to each of these areas. Thus, for example, all of these Schools produced major works of Talmudic novellae, important halachic works, and extensive responsa literature.

Nevertheless, there are certain underlying intellectual currents which pervade the major contributions of each of these Schools, and which are indicative of the placement of special emphasis in each School upon a particular approach to Torah study. This influence can often be traced to the early masters, who shaped and molded the distinct character of their respective Schools.

I. THE EARLY ITALIAN SCHOOL: A LINK WITH ERETZ YISROEL

Perhaps the earliest Diaspora Torah center established outside Bavel after the destruction of the Second Temple, was the Italian School. While its earliest origins are shrouded in obscurity, it is presumed that the Italian community, which was under Christian rule, had ties with the Eretz Yisroel Academies rather than with the Babylonian Torah community, which was under Moslem rule. This is confirmed by the Scroll of Achima'atz, which makes reference to links between the Eretz Yisroel School and the Early Italian School in the ninth century.

The Kalonymos, Anavim, and Achima'atz Families . . . Among the earliest Italian scholars known to us were members of the distinguished Kalonymos family, whose descendants were among the thirteenth century Chasidei Ashkenaz. Other distinguished families were the Anavim family and the Achima'atz family. Rabbe Shephatiah, and his son, Rabbe Amittai, composed important *piyyutim* — liturgical poems. In 925, ten Italian Sages were martyred *al Kiddush HaShem,* among them Rabbe Chasdai the Elder, son-in-law of Rabbe Shephatiah.

A Primary Source of Torah Dissemination

It was the Kalonymos family of Lucca, Italy, which established the first Torah academy in Mainz, Germany, during the closing decades of either the ninth or tenth centuries. In the tenth century, the city of Bari, Italy, was the point of departure of the *Arba'ah Shevuyyim,* who were instrumental in establishing important Torah academies in North Africa, Spain, and Alexandria, Egypt. Thus, the early Italian Torah community was a source of Torah dissemination for the entire Diaspora. As Rabbeinu Tam later remarked, *"From Bari shall Torah go forth, and the word of G-d from Otoronto."*

The 10th Century . . . The *Rosh Yeshiva* in Rome in the tenth century was Rabbe Yechiel, who was succeeded by his sons, Rabbe Daniel, Rabbe Avraham, and Rabbe Nasan. Rabbe Matzliach ibn Al-Bazak, a disciple of Rav Hai Gaon, was *dayyan* in Sicily.

The 11th Century . . . In the eleventh century, Rabbe Moshe Kalfo was a leading scholar in the Torah community of Bari, while Rabbe Nasan b. Yechiel (1035-1106) wrote his all-important Talmudic lexicon, the *Aruch,* in Rome, at this time.

The 12th Century . . . In the twelfth century, Rabbe Yitzchak b. Melchizedek wrote a Mishnah commentary on the Orders of *Zera'im* and *Taharos,* which have no *Talmud Bavli* to elucidate them.

Thirteenth Century Italian Scholars

Rabbe Yeshayah of Trani: Elder and Younger . . . The Italian School also produced important works of Torah novellae and definitive halacha. The most illustrious Italian Torah master of the early thirteenth century, Rabbe Yeshayah b. Mali haZaken of Trani (1180-1260), wrote his well-known novellae, *Tosafos Rid,* on many Talmudic tractates, and his *Pesakim,* a work of definitive halacha on the entire Talmud, while his grandson, Rabbe Yeshayah b. Eliyahu the Younger of Trani (Ri'az, d.c. 1280), wrote his *Piskei Halachos* on the entire Babylonian Talmud. Rabbe Yeshayah the Elder corresponded with the French *Tosafist,* Rabbe Yitzchak Or Zaru'a, thereby linking the French and Italian Schools.

Rabbe Yehudah Anav . . . The Italian scholar, Rabbe Yehudah Ya'aleh Anav (1215-1280), wrote a commentary on the Rif and *Shitas Rivavan* on tractate *Shekalim.* Rabbe Yehudah corresponded with the great French *Tosafist,* Rabbe Avigdor haKohen of Vienna, one of the foremost Ashkenazic Torah scholars of his day.

Rabbe Tzidkiyah Anav: The Shibolei haLeket . . . This link between the French and the Italian Schools was accomplished even more directly by Rabbe Yehudah Ya'aleh's disciple, Rabbe Tzidkiyah Anav (fl. 1240), who wrote the *Shibolei haLeket,* an important halachic anthology in which he cites extensively the rulings of the great French *Tosafists,* as well as those of both Sephardic and Italian Torah masters. More than two hundred thirty great Torah scholars are cited by name in this work. Rabbe Tzidkiyah Anav corresponded extensively with his great Ashkenazic contemporary, Maharam Baruch of Rothenburg, who responded with great respect to his halachic questions. In his *Shibolei haLeket,* Rabbe Tzidkiyah Anav writes that he has heard of the tragic burning of twenty-four wagonloads of the Talmud in Paris, in 1242.

Rabbe Binyamin Anav . . . Rabbe Tzidkiah's brother, Rabbe Binyamin haRofei Anav, was also a great Torah scholar. In addition to a number of halachic works, which are no longer extant, he also wrote *piyyutim* and *selichos* which are of great historical significance. Some of the significant historical events which they deal with are: (a) the libelous charges of the the vicious anti-Semite Nicholas Donin [1239]; (b) the Paris Talmud burning [1242]; (c) the Jewish badge [1257]; (d) desecration of *Sifrei Torah* and Jewish graves in Rome [1267].

II. THE NORTH AFRICAN TORAH CENTER

In the early tenth century, there was a vibrant Torah community in Kairouan, North Africa. The community of Kairouan had strong ties to the Babylonian academies, as may be seen in the correspondence between Rabbe Yaakov b. Nissim of Kairouan and Rabbe Sherira Gaon, which elicited Rav Sherira Gaon's well-known historical *Iggeres* in response. When Rabbeinu Chushiel arrived from Italy in ca. 960 C.E., he stood at the head of the Yeshiva of Kairouan. Both his son, Rabbeinu Chananel, and Rabbeinu Nissim b. Yaakov of Kairouan, were his disciples. They also studied under Rav Hai Gaon.

The First Generation of Rabbanim

Rabbeinu Chananel . . . Rabbeinu Chananel (Rach, d. 1055) wrote an important commentary on three *sedarim* of the Talmud, *Mo'ed, Nashim,* and *Nizikin,* as well as on tractates *Berachos* and *Chullin.* His commentary on *seder Mo'ed* and on part of *seder Nezikin* is printed in the margin of the *Vilna Shas.*

When Rabbeinu Chananel makes reference in his Talmudic commentary to the traditions of his teachers, it is believed that he refers to the traditions of his father, Rabbeinu Chushiel, and the great scholars of the Italian School. He does, to be sure, often cite Rav Hai Gaon and other Babylonian *Geonim,* as well.

Rabbeinu Nissim of Kairouan . . . His colleague, Rabbeinu Nissim of Kairouan, also wrote a commentary on the Talmud, *HaMafte'ach,* which is published in the margin of the *Vilna Shas* on tractates *Berachos, Shabbos,* and *Eruvin.*

Rabbeinu Chananel and Rabbeinu Nissim are regarded as having been among the First Generation of *Rabbanim.* They were both teachers of Rabbeinu Yitzchak Alfasi (the Rif).

The Kairouan Jewish community was destroyed by fanatical Arabs during the second half of the eleventh century.

The Alexandria Torah Community

Another of the *Arba'ah Shevuyyim,* Rabbeinu Shemariah b. Elchanan, established an important Torah academy in Alexandria, Egypt. He was succeeded by his son, Rabbe Elchanan. Rabbeinu Shemariah maintained correspondence with both the Babylonian Academies and with the Torah community of Kairouan.

III. THE EARLY SEPHARDIC SCHOOL

Rav Chisdai ibn Shaprut . . . The great benefactor of the Early Sephardic School was the statesman, Rav Chisdai ibn Shaprut, who was in correspondence with the Jewish Khazar King, Joseph. This was the era of the early Hebrew lexicographers, Menachem ibn Saruq (d. 970 C.E.), Dunash ibn Labrat, Yehudah ibn Chiyug, and Yonah ibn Janach (990-1050 C.E.), who were active during the tenth and eleventh centuries.

Rabbeinu Moshe and Rabbeinu Chanoch . . . When Rabbe Moshe b. Chanoch arrived in Cordoba, Rav Chisdai helped him establish an independent Torah academy. Rabbe Moshe was succeeded as *Rosh Yeshiva* by his son, Rabbe Chanoch (d. ca. 1025). Rabbe Moshe and Rabbe Chanoch were the primary architects of the Sephardic School.

Rabbe Shmuel haNagid . . . Rabbe Shmuel haNagid (993-1055), Torah scholar, statesman, and patron of Torah, was a disciple of Rabbe Chanoch. Rabbe Shmuel haNagid, author of *Mavo haTalmud* and *Hilchasa Gavrasa,* was included among the first generation of *Rabbanim,* as were Rabbeinu Chananel and Rabbeinu Nissim of Kairouan.

Second Generation of Rabbanim

The Second Generation of *Rabbanim* consisted of five great Torah scholars, whose names were Yitzchak.

(a) Rabbe Yitzchak b. Yaakov Alfasi (Rif, 1013-1103)
(b) Rabbe Yitzchak b. Yehudah ibn Ghayyas (1038-1089)
(c) Rabbe Yitzchak b. Baruch Albalia (1035-1094)
(d) Rabbe Yitzchak b. Reuven Al-Bargeloni (1043-1100)
(e) Rabbe Yitzchak b. Moshe of Baghdad

The most illustrious scholar among them was Rabbe Yitzchak Alfasi, author of *Hilchos Rav Alfas,* which, it has been said, "was written with *Ru'ach haKodesh.*" His most illustrious disciple was Rabbe Yosef b. Meir haLevi (Ri Migash, 1077-1141), whose profound Talmudic wisdom was "awesome". Among the disciples of Ri Migash was Rabbe Maimon, who later became a *dayyan* in Cordoba. His son, in turn, was the great light of Israel, Rabbe Moshe b. Maimon, the Rambam (1135-1204), author of the *Yad haChazakah* and *Moreh Nevuchim.*

Torah Classics: Chovos haLevavos; Kuzari; Moreh Nevuchim

The Early Sephardic School also produced classical works on Torah philosophy.

(a) **Kuzari,** Rabbe Yehudah haLevi (1075-1141), Torah philosopher and poet
(b) **Chovos haLevavos,** Rabbe Bachya ibn Paquda (fl. 1080)
(c) **Olam Kattan,** Rabbe Yosef ibn Tzaddik (d. 1149, colleague of Rabbe Maimon)
(d) **HaEmunah haRamah,** Rabbe Avraham ibn Daud haLevi (Ravad I, 1110-1180); also wrote the important historical source, *Sefer haKabbalah le-haRavad.*
(e) **Moreh Nevuchim,** Rabbeinu Moshe b. Maimon (Rambam, 1135-1204)
(f) **Ibn Ezra Tanach Commentary,** Rabbe Avraham b. Meir Ibn Ezra (1088-1164); also wrote many other important *sefarim.*

The Rif and the Rambam — An Era of Halachic Codification

Hilchos Rav Alfas . . . The Early Sephardic Schools of the Rif and the Rambam placed great emphasis upon halachic determination and codification. Thus, in his *Hilchos Rav Alfas,* which has been acclaimed as a halachic masterpiece by all subsequent Torah masters, the Rif rewrites large segments of the Talmud, omitting almost all contentious Talmudic discussion and retaining only those Talmudic statements which are halachically relevant, or which are otherwise indicative of a definitive halachic opinion. The *Hilchos Rav Alfas* is regarded as the foremost work of halachic determination of this era.

The Yad haChazakah . . . The Rambam's *Yad haChazakah* is an unsurpassed masterpiece of halachic codification, which covers the entire spectrum of halachic literature contained in both the *Talmud Bavli* and the *Talmud Yerushalmi,* both *Mechiltas,* the *Sifra,* the *Sifrei,* and all known Geonic and post-Geonic literature, until his time. It contains all aspects of Talmudic law, including *Hilchasa liMeshicha* — those halachos which will be relevant only upon the arrival of *Mashiach.*

The *Hilchos Rav Alfas* and the Rambam's *Mishneh Torah,* together comprise two of the three pillars upon which Maran Rav Yosef Caro established his *Shulchan Aruch.*

Rambam's other works . . . In addition to his monumental *Yad haChazakah* and his *Moreh Nevuchim,* the Rambam also wrote the following important *sefarim: Sefer haMitzvos; Sefer haMa'or* — a comprehensive Mishnah commentary; *Iggeres haShmad; Iggeres Teiman.* Among the Rambam's important writings are the comprehensive introductions to various sections of his Mishnah commentary, such as his introduction to the Mishnah [at beginning of *Seder Zera'im*], and his introduction to *Pirkei Avos* — *Shemonah Perakim le-haRambam.*

The Thirteen Ikkarim . . . The Rambam's introduction to *Perek Chelek* includes his formulation of the Thirteen Principles of Torah Faith, which have become a byword in Judaism and are universally regarded as the definitive formulation of the fundamental concepts of Torah faith. In every generation since his time, Jews have submitted to martyrdom and have sanctified the name of G-d with the Rambam's *Ani Ma'amin* on their lips.

In summary form, the Thirteen Principles of Maimonides are as follows:

Our Knowledge of the Creator

1. Existence of an omnipotent Creator
2. Oneness of the Creator
3. Non-corporeality of the Creator
4. Eternity of the Creator [and Creation ex-nihilo]
5. G-d alone must be worshipped

Prophecy and Divine Origin of Torah

6. Truth of Prophecy and of the Prophets
7. Moshe — Greatest of all Prophets
8. Divine Origin of Written and Oral Laws
9. Immutability of Torah

Divine Providence: Reward and Retribution

10. G-d knows all deeds and thoughts of man
11. Reward and Retribution, and *Olam HaBa*
12. Coming of *Mashiach.*
13. *Techiyas haMeisim* — Resurrection

The Rambam was succeeded as *Nagid* of the Jewish community by his son, Rabbe Avraham, who wrote *Sefer haMaspik leOvdei HaShem.* Rabbe Avraham was succeeded, in turn, by his son, Rabbe David, who wrote a *sefer* of sermons, *Midrash Rabbe David haNagid.*

IV. THE PROVENCAL SCHOOL

The Provencal School of Southern France was closer geographically, politically, and to a degree, spiritually, as well, to the Sephardic Torah community than it was to the *Tosafist* School of Northern France and the Franco-German cities of the Rhine. Nevertheless, it was an independent Torah School, whose origins go back to the Babylonian scholar, Rabbe Machir, who settled in Narbonne near the end of the ninth century. He was succeeded by Rabbe Todros and his sons, Rabbe Kalonymos haZaken and Rabbe Moshe the Parnes. Rabbe Moshe haDarshon of Narbonne, whose Torah commentary is cited by Rashi, was *Rosh Yeshiva* in Narbonne at this time. He was the teacher of Rabbe Nasan b. Yechiel of Rome, who wrote the Talmudic lexicon, *HaAruch.*

Three Primary Architects of the Provencal School

The three primary architects of the Provencal School at the beginning of the twelfth century were: Rabbe Avraham b. Yitzchak, Av Bes Din of Narbonne (Ravad II, 1110-1179); Rabbe Moshe b. Yosef b. Mervon haLevi (d. 1165), and Rabbe Meshullam b. Yaakov of Lunel (d. 1170). These were the three primary teachers of the Ravad of Posquires, and of Rabbe Zerachiah haLevi.

Rabbe Avraham b. Yitzchak wrote *Sefer haEshkol,* which is primarily a digest of the *Sefer haIttim* of his teacher, Rabbe Yehudah b. Barzilai, with additional material, as well. Rabbe Moshe haLevi was *Rosh Yeshiva* of the academy of Narbonne. Rabbe Meshullam b. Yaakov, who was an illustrious Torah scholar and a wealthy philanthropist, was a patron of all forms of Torah scholarship. He prevailed upon Rabbe Yehudah ibn Tibbon to embark upon the translation of Rabbe Bachya's *Chovos haLevavos* from Arabic to Hebrew, thereby establishing a bridge of communication between the Sephardic and Provencal Schools of Torah Study.

Sons of Rabbe Meshullam . . . Among the sons of Rabbe Meshullam were Rabbe Asher (Rosh miLunel, cited by *Tosafos, Bava Kamma* 64a, *s.v. Va-yomer*), and Rabbe Aharon (d. 1210), who strongly opposed the efforts of Rabbe Meir b. Todros haLevi of Toledo (Ramah, 1170-1244), to place a ban on the Rambam's *Moreh Nevuchim.* Rabbe Meshullam's grandson, Rabbe Meshullam b. Moshe of Beziers (1175-1250), wrote the *Sefer haHashlamah,* which complements the *Hilchos Rav Alfas* by adding a number of halachos which had been omitted by the Rif.

Rabbe Avraham b. David, Ravad III of Posquires

The most illustrious Torah masters of the Provencal School were Rabbe Avraham b. David of Posquires (Ravad III, Ba'al ha-Hasagos, 1120-1198) and Rabbe Zerachiah haLevi, Ba'al haMa'or (1125-1186). As the name Ba'al haHasagos suggests, the Ravad brought the full scope of his phenomenal Torah erudition to bear upon his critical glosses on the most important halachic works of his time, *Hilchos Rav Alfas,* and the Rambam's *Yad haChazakah.*

In his Glosses on the Rif, the Ravad defends the Rif against the critique of the Ba'al haMa'or, while at the same time, he adds his own critical remarks concerning the words of the great master, although, to be sure, he does so with awe and trepidation.

Hasagos haRavad . . . The Ravad's critical Glosses on the Rambam's *Mishneh Torah* are thorough and comprehensive, covering all 14 sections of this monumental work. It is only in regard to *Hilchos Kidush haChodesh,* — Laws of the Sanctification of the New Moon — that the Ravad expresses the thought that his limited knowledge of astronomy makes him inadequate to comment properly on these particular laws [*Hilchos Kidush haChodesh* 7:7]. Elsewhere, however, the Ravad's comments are so comprehensive that where he does not comment critically and disagree with the Rambam, it is regarded as though the Ravad concurs with the Rambam's opinion.

The very fact that the Ravad expended so much of his valuable time and energy to make critical Glosses on all the fourteen *sefarim* of the Rambam's *Yad haChazakah,* is an indication that he regarded this as a monumental contribution to halachic literature, as he himself indicates when he writes that the Rambam "did a great thing in having gathered the words of the *Talmud Bavli,* the *Yerushalmi,* and the *Tosefta.*" [*Hasagos haRavad, Hilchos K'layim* 6:2.]

There can be little doubt but that the Glosses of the Ravad contributed immensely to the universal acceptance and popularity of the Rambam's *Mishneh Torah,* serving, as they did, as a catalyst which stimulated much thought-provoking comment and debate among all the later Torah masters who wrote voluminous works, such as the *Maggid Mishneh,* the *Kesef Mishneh,* and hundreds of others, in defense and clarification of the words of the Rambam.

Rabbe Zerachiah haLevi, Ba'al haMa'or

At the early age of nineteen, Rabbe Zerachiah wrote his *Sefer haMa'or,* which is an incisive critique of the *Hilchos Rav Alfas,* in two parts: *HaMa'or haGadol,* on the Orders of *Nashim* and *Nezikin;* and *HaMa'or haKattan* on the Order of *Mo'ed* and on the tractates of *Berachos* and *Chullin.* Whereupon, the Ramban later wrote his *Sefer Milchamos HaShem,* in defense of the Rif.

Like the Glosses of the Ravad on the Rambam, the critique of the *Ba'al haMa'or* against the *Hilchos haRif* served as a catalyst which stimulated the Ravad, the Ramban, and many others to hasten to the defense of the great halachic master. This, in turn, enriched our Torah literature immensely, for the words of the Ravad in his Glosses on the Rif, and the Glosses of the Ramban in his *Milchamos HaShem* are a treasure-trove of stimulating Torah arguments and profound erudition.

"Masters of Critique" . . . While, to be sure, the Ravad wrote novellae on the entire Talmud and an important halachic code on *Hilchos Niddah,* both he and his great colleague, Rabbe Zerachiah, Ba'al haMa'or, are best remembered for their provocative and stimulating glosses on the words of the great Torah masters, the Rif and the Rambam. The Ravad and the Ba'al haMa'or were the great "Masters of Critique" of the Provencal School.

Contemporaries and Disciples of the Ravad of Posquires

Rabbe Yitzchak b. Abba Mari of Marseilles... Rabbe Yitzchak b. Abba Mari of Marseilles (1122-1193), a great contemporary of the Ravad, wrote the important halachic code, *Sefer haIttur,* as well as *Me'ah She'arim,* annotations on the Rif which are included in the *Vilna Shas.*

Rabbe Yehonasan haKohen of Lunel... An illustrious disciple of the Ravad and a leader of the *Chachmei Lunel,* Rabbe Yehonasan b. David haKohen wrote a commentary on the Rif. His commentary on tractate *Eruvin* surrounds the Rif in the *Vilna Shas.* Rabbe Yehonasan was in close correspondence with the Rambam, whom he revered greatly. Rabbe Yehonasan prevailed upon Rabbe Shmuel ibn Tibbon to translate the *Moreh Nevuchim* from Arabic into Hebrew.

Rabbe Meir and Rabbe Nasan of Trinquetaille . . . Rabbe Meir b. Yitzchak of Trinquetaille was another illustrious disciple of the Ravad. Rabbe Meir's son, Rabbe Nasan, studied under the great *Tosafist*, Ritzva, in Northern France. He returned to Trinquetaille, and later became one of the primary teachers of the Ramban.

Rabbe Avraham haYarchi . . . Another great disciple of the Ravad was Rabbe Avraham b. Nasan haYarchi (1155-1215), author of *Sefer haManhig*. He traveled widely, and later settled in Toledo, where he sat on the *Bes Din*, together with Rabbe Meir Abulafia of Toledo (Ramah).

Rabbe Shlomo min haHar . . . Rabbe Shlomo of Montpelier was vehemently opposed to the study of philosophy. He was therefore strongly opposed to the Rambam's *Moreh Nevuchim*. He stood at the head of the anti-Maimunists, although he venerated the Rambam, and regarded the *Yad haChazakah* highly. He was a primary teacher of Rabbe Yonah heChasid of Gerona.

Translators, Grammarians and Biblical Commentators

The Ibn Tibbon Family . . . This period saw the emergence of the Ibn Tibbon family, the well-known translators who translated many important Torah classics from Arabic into Hebrew. Rabbe Yehudah Ibn Tibbon (1120-1190), who was a close life-long friend of Rabbe Zerachiah Ba'al haMa'or, translated Rabbe Bachya's *Chovos haLevavos*, Rabbe Yehudah haLevi's *Sefer haKuzari*, Rav Saadiah Gaon's *Emunos veDe'os*, and other important works. His son, Rabbe Shmuel ibn Tibbon (1160-1230) translated the Rambam's *Moreh Nevuchim*, upon the urging of Rabbe Yehonasan haKohen of Lunel. Rabbe Shmuel corresponded with the Rambam. He also translated the Rambam's *Iggeres Teiman*, *Ma'amar Techiyas haMeisim*, and portions of the *Peirush haMishnah*.

The Kimchi Family . . . Another illustrious Provencal family at this time was the Kimchi family. Rabbe Yosef Kimchi and his sons, Rabbe Moshe and Rabbe David, were well-known Biblical commentators and Hebrew grammarians. Rabbe David Kimchi (Radak, 1160-1235) who studied under his father and his brother, Rabbe Moshe, wrote important grammatical works, *Sefer haMichlol* and *Sefer haSharashim*. He is better known, however, for his important commentary on many parts of *Tanach*, which is known as the commentary of the Radak.

Rabbe Menachem b. Shlomo haMe'iri . . . One of the later Provencal scholars was Rabbe Menachem b. Shlomo of Perpignon, better known as the Me'iri (1249-1315). His teacher, Rabbe Reuven b. Chaim, was a disciple of Rabbe Yitzchak haKohen of Narbonne who wrote a commentary on a large portion of the *Talmud Yerushalmi,* and who was, in turn, a disciple of Ravad of Posquires.

The Me'iri wrote the *Bais haBechirah* commentary on thirty-seven tractates of the Talmud, in which he cites the opinions of all the great Provencal, Sephardic, and Franco-German scholars who preceded him. His masterful commentary, which had lain dormant in manuscript form for many centuries and has only recently been brought to light, is an important bridge, linking all of the early schools of Torah study.

Rabbe Levi b. Gershon (Ralbag) . . . Rabbe Levi b. Gershon (1288-1344) wrote an important commentary on *Tanach,* as well as works on philosophy and astronomy. His *To'aliyos Ralbag* is a popular digest of portions of his Torah commentary.

Rabbe Aharon haKohen of Lunel . . . A great grandson of Rabbe Yitzchak haKohen, Rabbe Aharon haKohen of Lunel (d. 1344), went into exile with his fellow Jews when Philip IV expelled all Jews from France in 1306. Devastated by the expulsion and by the subsequent homelessness and perpetual wandering, Rabbe Aharon nevertheless wrote an important halachic code, *Orchos Chaim,* which was regarded as a popular halachic guide for many years before the advent of the *Shulchan Aruch.* He is believed to have also written the halachic code, *Kol Bo.*

Rabbe Estori haParchi — Kaftor vaPherach . . . Among the Provencal scholars who were expelled by Philip IV in 1306, was Rabbe Estori b. Moshe haParchi (1280-1355) who studied under the Rosh, to whom he refers as "my teacher, Rabbe Asher, *zal.*" Rabbe Estori was only a youth when he was exiled from Narbonne on 10 Av, 1306. After great hardship, Rabbe Estori arrived in Eretz Yisroel where he wrote his encyclopedic work, *Kaftor vaPherach.*

Manifesting vast erudition in Talmudic literature, the author clarifies all halachos which relate to the Land. He cites a wealth of Midrashic sources concerning the special sanctity of Eretz Yisroel and the bountiful love of our Sages for the Holy Land.

The Decline of the Provencal School

After the expulsion of 1306, the French Jewish community was devastated, and even when some remnants of the once proud community were readmitted to France "provisionally" some ten years later by King Philip's successor, Louis X, the community could hardly regain its former glory. The remaining French Jews suffered greatly during the Pastoreaux Crusade of 1320. They were expelled again in 1322, and readmitted in 1359. Their scattered remnants were slaughtered mercilessly during the Black Plague massacres (1348-1349). They were finally expelled again from most of France in 1394 — not to be readmitted again until the late seventeenth century.

The glorious days of the Provencal School — which produced such towering Torah luminaries as Ravad III of Posquires and Rabbe Zerachiah haLevi; Rabbe Yehonasan haKohen and the *Chachmei Lunel*; the Kimchi and Ibn Tibbon families; and later, the Me'iri, Rav Aharon haKohen of Lunel, and Rav Estori haParchi — this glorious era of dynamic Torah growth and vitality, had come to a close after two hundred years of Torah study and Torah dissemination. The Torah, as it were, had to pick up its own wanderer's staff, and like the remnants of its homeless, scattered flock, had to once again seek new pastures, in other climes.

V. THE EARLY FRANCO-GERMAN SCHOOL

The earliest origins of the Franco-German School may be traced to Rabbe Moshe b. Kalonymos and his sons, Rabbe Kalonymos and Rabbe Yekusiel, who were brought by Charlemagne from Lucca, Italy, to establish a Yeshiva in Mainz (Magentza) during the closing decades of the eighth century (787 C.E.). In the tenth century, the earliest scholar known to us is Rabbe Yehudah b. Meir haKohen Leontin, who was the primary teacher of Rabbeinu Gershom Me'or haGolah, who refers to Rabbe Leontin as a "phenomenal Sage."

The "Jewish Pope" . . . This was a generation of great *paytanim* or composers of liturgical poetry, such as Rabbe Meshullam b. Rabbe Kalonymos, and Rabbe Shimon haGadol, whose son, Elchanan, was abducted at an early age and forcibly baptized by agents of the Church. Elchanan rose in the Church hierarchy to become a "Jewish Pope," and was later reunited with his father.

"U'nesaneh Tokef" . . . At this time, Rav Amnon of Mainz wrote his moving *piyyut, "U'nesaneh Tokef,"* which is recited during the *Mussaf* service of Rosh Hashanah and Yom Kippur.

Rabbeinu Gershom Me'or haGolah

The greatest disciple of Rabbeinu Leontin was Rabbeinu Gershom Me'or haGolah (965-1040), who made many important halachic regulations, known as *Takanos Rabbeinu Gershom,* which included, among others, the ban against bigamy. Rabbeinu Gershom wrote a Talmudic commentary, which is included in the *Vilna Shas* on a number of tractates. Others refer to this commentary as Kuntreis Magentza, where Rabbeinu Gershom was *Rosh haYeshiva.* His disciple, Rabbe Meir Sh'liach Tzibbur, wrote the beautiful piyyut, *Akdamos Milin,* which is read before the Torah reading on Shavu'os morning.

Upon Rabbeinu Gershom's death, he was succeeded as *Rosh Yeshiva* in Magentza by his greatest disciple, Rabbe Eliezer haGadol. Three other outstanding disciples of Rabbeinu Gershom were Rabbe Yaakov b. Yakar, Rabbe Yitzchak b. Yehudah, and Rabbe Yitzchak b. Elazar haLevi — the three primary teachers of Rashi.

In the year 1040, Rabbeinu Gershom Me'or haGolah died. In the same year, Rabbe Shlomo Yitzchaki — Rashi, *Rabbon Shel Yisroel* — was born.

The Early "Kuntreisim"

While the great early Torah masters of the Sephardic School, such as the Rif and the Rambam, concentrated primarily upon halachic derivation and codification, the early teachers of Ashkenaz dealt primarily with fundamental elucidation and clarification of the Talmudic text. The Talmud was written in Aramaic, which was the spoken language of the Babylonian Jewish communities. The Babylonian academies, therefore, had little need for commentaries which would elucidate the Talmudic text itself. In the far-flung, independent communities of the Diaspora, however, Aramaic was no longer a spoken tongue.

All the Franco-German academies produced *Kuntreisim* or unstructured notes and glosses upon which the students relied, such as the *Kuntreisei Magentza, Worms,* and *Speyer,* which elucidated the Talmudic text. There was clearly a need now for a structured, cohesive commentary which would clarify, not only the difficult terminology, but the complex Talmudic discussions and halachic concepts of the Talmud, as well.

Rashi: "Rabbon Shel Yisroel"

It was, of course, Rashi, following in the footsteps of Rabbeinu Gershom Me'or haGolah and the Chachmei Magentza, who blazed a path through the Talmud with his *Kuntreisim* — his marginal notes on the entire Babylonian Talmud. It is true, without a doubt, that without Rashi's remarkably lucid commentary, the Talmud would have remained a closed book for all future generations.

Rashi translates difficult words, clarifies difficult concepts, and provides a clear, concise commentary which beautifully elucidates the most complex *sugya,* or integral unit of Talmudic discussion. Manifesting vast erudition and mastery of all Talmudic sources, Rashi often turns to other Talmudic references to throw light upon a difficult text. His explanation is so clear that it often appears to be an extension of the Talmudic text itself. Upon those occasions where Rashi leaves a text without adequate explanation, the serious student is at a loss, until he turns to a similar text elsewhere in the Talmud where Rashi has clarified the matter more fully.

Rashi's commentary is like a Heavenly light which, "uncovered the complexities of the Talmud from obscurity." No other work has played such a dramatic and indispensable role in the preservation, perpetuation, and transmission of the Oral Law for all posterity, as has the *Peirush haKuntres*—Rashi's remarkable Talmud commentary.

The TaNaCh Commentary . . . Rashi's commentary on *Torah, Nvi'im,* and *Kesuvim* combines fundamental comprehension of the Written Law with the deeper insights and Midrashic interpretations of the Oral Law, thereby providing both scholar and layman alike with a far richer comprehension of important Torah concepts, as well as with a far-reaching appreciation of the unity of both the Written and the Oral Laws.

It was Rashi who made the Torah which Moshe transmitted to our people, the living legacy of all Israel, for all generations.

Shortly before Rashi died in 1105, portentous clouds began to hover over the Jewish communities of the Rhine. The First Crusade, in 1096, ushered in an era of terrible massacres and pogroms, known as *"Gezeros Tasnu."* Among the first victims of these terrible massacres were the Ashkenazic *Kehillos* of Worms, Speyer, and Magentza, whose Jewish inhabitants — men, women, and children — offered up their lives as martyrs *al Kiddush HaShem,* rather than violate the sanctity of their covenant with their G-d. Rashi wrote a heart-rending eulogy in memory of his beloved fellow Jews.

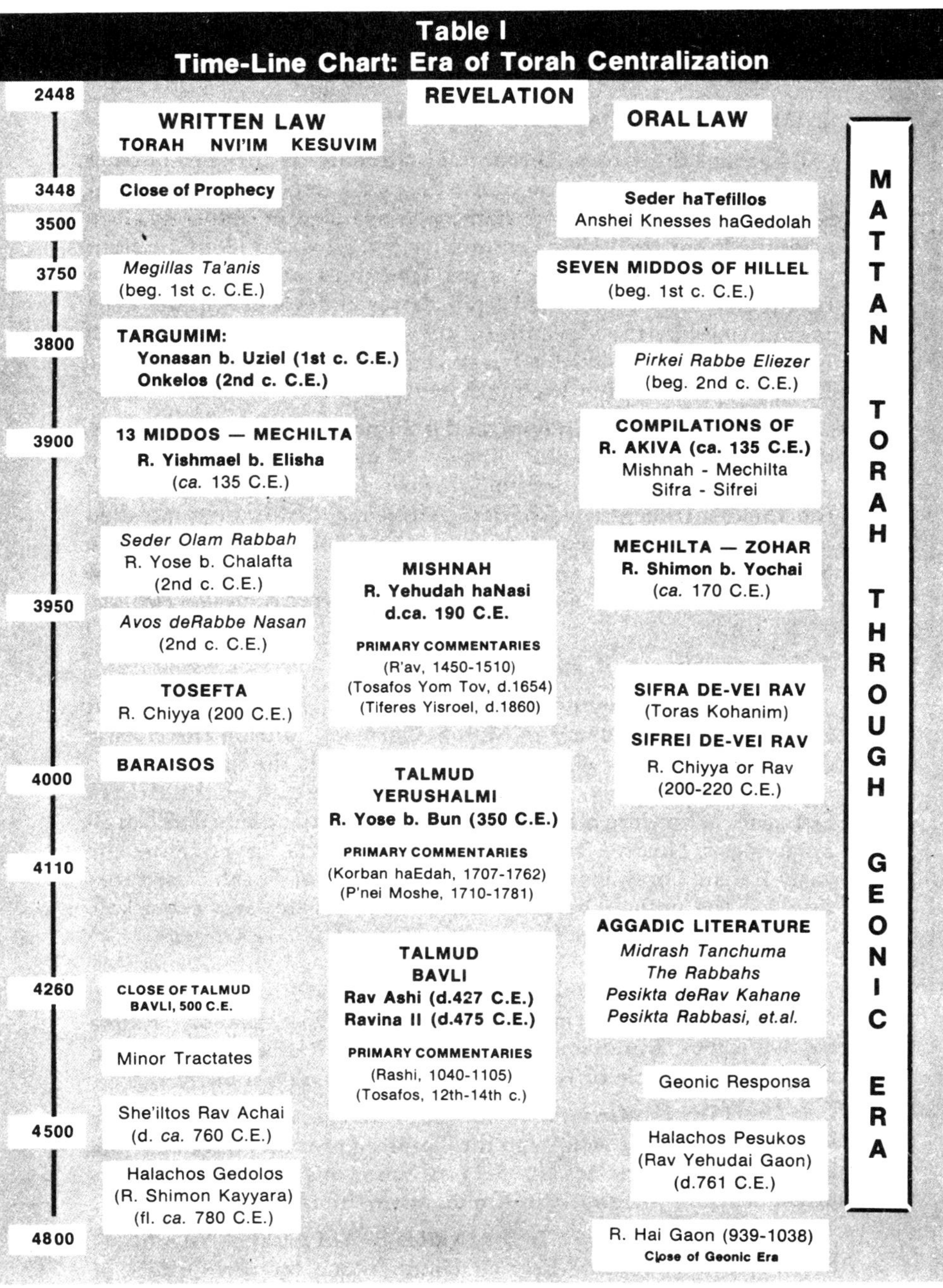

Table I
Time-Line Chart: Era of Torah Centralization
2448
REVELATION
WRITTEN LAW
TORAH NVI'IM KESUVIM
ORAL LAW
3448
Close of Prophecy
3500
Seder haTefillos
Anshei Knesses haGedolah
3750
Megillas Ta'anis (beg. 1st c. C.E.)
SEVEN MIDDOS OF HILLEL (beg. 1st c. C.E.)
3800
TARGUMIM:
Yonasan b. Uziel (1st c. C.E.)
Onkelos (2nd c. C.E.)
Pirkei Rabbe Eliezer (beg. 2nd c. C.E.)
3900
13 MIDDOS — MECHILTA
R. Yishmael b. Elisha (ca. 135 C.E.)
COMPILATIONS OF R. AKIVA (ca. 135 C.E.)
Mishnah - Mechilta
Sifra - Sifrei
Seder Olam Rabbah
R. Yose b. Chalafta (2nd c. C.E.)
MISHNAH
R. Yehudah haNasi
d.ca. 190 C.E.
PRIMARY COMMENTARIES
(R'av, 1450-1510)
(Tosafos Yom Tov, d.1654)
(Tiferes Yisroel, d.1860)
MECHILTA — ZOHAR
R. Shimon b. Yochai (ca. 170 C.E.)
3950
Avos deRabbe Nasan (2nd c. C.E.)
TOSEFTA
R. Chiyya (200 C.E.)
SIFRA DE-VEI RAV
(Toras Kohanim)
SIFREI DE-VEI RAV
R. Chiyya or Rav (200-220 C.E.)
BARAISOS
4000
TALMUD YERUSHALMI
R. Yose b. Bun (350 C.E.)
PRIMARY COMMENTARIES
(Korban haEdah, 1707-1762)
(P'nei Moshe, 1710-1781)
4110
AGGADIC LITERATURE
Midrash Tanchuma
The Rabbahs
Pesikta deRav Kahane
Pesikta Rabbasi, et.al.
4260
CLOSE OF TALMUD BAVLI, 500 C.E.
TALMUD BAVLI
Rav Ashi (d.427 C.E.)
Ravina II (d.475 C.E.)
PRIMARY COMMENTARIES
(Rashi, 1040-1105)
(Tosafos, 12th-14th c.)
Minor Tractates
Geonic Responsa
She'iltos Rav Achai (d. ca. 760 C.E.)
4500
Halachos Pesukos
(Rav Yehudai Gaon) (d.761 C.E.)
Halachos Gedolos
(R. Shimon Kayyara) (fl. ca. 780 C.E.)
4800
R. Hai Gaon (939-1038)
Close of Geonic Era
MATTAN TORAH THROUGH GEONIC ERA

Table II: Time-Line Chart of Torah Transmission and Halachic Development

11th, 12th, 13th Centuries

Franco-German School

1000

R. Gershom Me'or haGolah (965-1040)
R. Yosef Tuv Elem (*Seder Olam Zuta*)

Rashi's Teachers:
R. Eliezer haGadol b. Yitzchak
R. Yaakov b. Yakar (d.1064)
R. Yitzchak b. Yehudah
R. Yitzchak haLevi (d.1070)

1100

R. Shlomo Yitzchaki
Rashi (1040-1105)

R. Meir b. Shmuel of Ramerupt (c.1060-1135)
R. Yehudah b. Nasan (Rivan)

1150

R. Yitzchak b. Asher haLevi (Riva, fl.1150)
R. Shmuel b. Meir (Rashbam, c.1080-1158)
R. Yitzchak b. Meir (Rivam)
R. Shlomo b. Meir
R. Eliezer b. Nasan (Ravan, d.1170)

Rabbeinu Tam (d.1171)
Ri haZaken (d. 1185)

1200

R. Shmuel b. Kalonymos (Chasidei Ashkenaz)
Re'em (*Sefer Yere'im,* 1150-1198)
R. Yitzchak b. Avraham (Ritzva, d.1205)
R. Yehudah of Paris (Sir Leon, 1166-1224)
R. Yehudah heChasid (*Sefer Chasidim,* d.1217)
R. Eliezer b. Yoel haLevi (Raviah, d.1225)
R. Shimshon miShantz (Rash, d.1215)
R. Elazar Ba'al haRokeach (1160-1237)
R. Baruch (*Sefer haTerumah,* d.1237)
R. Yitzchak Or Zarua (1180-1250) A

1250

R. Moshe of Coucy (SeMaG, d.1260)
R. Yechiel of Paris (d.1268)
R. Yitzchak of Corbeil (SeMaK, d.1280)
R. Chizkiah b. Manoach (*Chizkuni*)

1300

R. Eliezer of Touques (*Tosafos Tuch,* d.c.1291)
R. Peretz of Corbeil (Maharaf, d.1298)

Codes

Hilchos
Rav Alfas, NA,S
Rif, (1013-1103)

PRIMARY COMMENTARIES
(Hasagos haRavad, d.1198) SF
(Ba'al haMa'or, d.1186) SF
(Ramban, 1194-1270) S
(Ran, d.c.1380) S
(Nimmukei Yosef, beg. 15th c.) S

Mishneh Torah
Rambam (1135-1204) Eg

PRIMARY COMMENTARIES
Ravad III Ba'al Hasagos (1120-1198) SF
(Maggid Mishneh, 14th c.) S
(Kesef Mishneh, 1488-1575) EY

Hilchos
Rabbeinu Asher
Rosh (1250-1327) S

PRIMARY COMMENTARIES
(Haggahos Ashiri, 14th c.) A
(Pilpula Charifta, 1579-1654) M,P
(Korban Nesanel, 1687-1769) G

Spain, N.Africa, Italy, S.France

1000

R. Hai Gaon (939-1038) Pumbedisa
R. Chanoch b. Moshe (d.c.1025) S
R. Nissim of Kairouan (d.c.1050) NA
R. Chananel b. Chushiel (d.1055) NA
R. Shmuel haNagid (993-1055) S

1100

R. Yitzchak Ibn Ghayyas (Ritzag, 1038-1089) S
R. Yitzchak Albalia (1035-1094) S
R. Yitzchak Al-Bargeloni (1043-1100) S
R. Yitzchak b. Moshe (Baghdad)
R. Nasan b. Yechiel (*Aruch,* 1035-1106) I
R. Bachya Ibn Paquda (*Chovos haLevavos*) S
R. Yosef Ibn Migash (Ri Migash, d.1141) S
R. Yehudah haLevi (*HaKuzari,* d.1141) S

1150

R. Yehudah al-Bargeloni (*HaIttim*) S
Ravad II (*HaEshkol,* d.1158) SF
R. Avraham Ibn Ezra (1090-1164) S
R. Maimon haDayyan b. Yosef (d.1165) S
R. Hillel b. Eliakim (*Peirush Sifra*) Greece
R. Zerachiah haLevi (HaMa'or, d.1186) SF
R. Yitzchak b. Abba Mari (*Ittur,* d.1193) SF

1200

R. Yehonasan haKohen, Lunel (fl.1200) SF
R. Aharon b. Meshullam, Lunel (d.1210) SF
R. Avraham haYarchi (*HaManhig,* d.1215) SF
R. David Kimchi (Radak, 1160-1235), SF
R. Avraham b. haRambam (1186-1237) Eg
R. Meir haLevi Abulafia (Ramah, d.1244) S
R. Yehudah b. Binyamin haRofei (Rivavan)

1250

R. Tzidkiah Anav (*Shibolei haLeket,* fl.1240) I
R. Yishayah diTrani (*Tosafos Rid,* d.1260) I
R. David b. Amram Adani (*Midrash haGadol,* 13th c.)
R. Yonah heChasid (1200-1263) S

1300

R. Moshe b. Nachman
Ramban (1194-1270) S

Table III: Time-Line Chart of Torah Transmission and Halachic Development

14th and 15th Centuries

Ashkenaz

1300

R. Chaim b. Yitzchak Or Zaru'a, A
Maharam Rothenburg (1220-1293) G
R. Mordecai b. Hillel (d.1298) G
R. Meir haKohen *(Haggahos Maimuniyyos)* G
R. Yitzchak of Dueren *(Sha'arei Dura)* G
R. Menachem of Merseburg (ReMaM) G
R. Shimshon of Chinon *(Sefer haKrisus)* F
R. Alexander Suslin haKohen (*Agudah,* d.1349) G
R. Shalom of Austria (Maharash) A

1350

R. Israel of Krems *(Haggahos Ashiri)* Austria, G
R. Shmuel Shlettstadt *(HaMordecai haKattan)* G

1400

R. Meir b. Baruch haLevi (Maharam Sal, d.1404) G
R. Avraham Klausner (*Sefer Minhagim,* d.1407) A
R. Yaakov Moellin (Maharil, d.1427) G
R. Yaakov Weil (Mahariv, d.before 1456) G

1450

R. Yisroel Isserlein (*Terumas haDeshen,* d.1460) G
R. Yitzchak Tyrnau (*Sefer Minhagim,* d.1470) A
R. Yisroel Bruna (1400-1480) G
R. Yaakov Landau (*HaAgur,* d.c.1487) G,I

1500

R. Moshe Mintz (G)

R. Yaakov b. haRosh
(1270-1343)
Arba'ah Turim

Primary Commentaries Surrounding Tur

R. Yosef Caro (1488-1575), *Bais Yosef,* EY
R. Moshe Isserles (1530-1572), *Darkei Moshe,* P
R. Yehoshua Falk (1550-1614), *Derishah u'Perishah,* P
R. Yoel Sirkes (1561-1640) *Bayis Chadash (Bach)* P

Spain, N.Africa, Italy, S.France

1300

R. Aharon haLevi (Re'ah, 1235-1300) S
R. David haNagid Maimuni (d.1306) Eg

R. Shlomo b. Avraham Adres
Rashba (1235-1310) S

R. Menachem Meiri (*Bais haBechirah,* d.1315) SF
R. Shem Tov Ibn Gaon (*Migdal Oz,* fl.1312) S,EY
R. Yom Tov Ishbili (Ritva, c.1250-1330) S
R. David Abudraham (fl.1340) S
R. Aharon haKohen, Lunel (*Orchos Chaim,* d.1334) SF
R. Levi b. Gershon (Ralbag, 1288-1344) S

1350

R. Yerucham b. Meshullam (*Mesharim,* d.1350) S
R. Vidal diTolosa (*Maggid Mishneh,* d.1357) S
R. Nissim of Gerona (Ran, d.c.1380) S

1400

R. Yitzchak b. Sheshes (Rivash, 1326-1407) S
R. Chasdai Crescas (*Or HaShem,* d.1412) S
R. Yitzchak Abohav I *(Menoras haMa'or)* S
R. Yosef Albo *(Sefer haIkkarim)* S
R. Shimon b. Tzemach Duran (Rashbatz, d.1444) NA

1450

R. Yitzchak Canpanton (1360-1463) S
R. Yosef Ibn Chaviv *(Nimmukei Yosef)* S
R. Yitzchak deLeon (haAri haGadol, d.1492) S
R. Yitzchak Arama (*Akedas Yitzchak,* d.1494) S,I
R. Yitzchak Abohav II (1433-1493) S

1500

R. Yehudah Minz (Mahari Minz, 1408-1506) I
R. Don Yitzchak Abrabanel (1437-1508) S
R. Ovadiah miBertinoro (R'av, c.1450-1510) I
R. Yaakov Ibn Chaviv (*Ein Yaakov,* 1445-1516) S,Gr
R. Eliyahu Mizrachi (d.1525) Turkey

LEGEND: A — Austria; Cz — Czechoslovakia; Eg — Egypt; EY — Eretz Yisroel; F — France; G — Germany; Gr — Greece; I — Italy; L — Lithuania; M — Moravia; NA — North Africa; P — Poland; S — Spain; SF — Southern France; T — Turkey.
Note: The central column represents the primary halachic codes.

Table IV: Time-Line Chart of Torah Transmission and Halachic Development

16th—17th Centuries

Poland and Ashkenaz

1500

R. Yaakov Pollack (d.1530) P

1550

R. Shalom Shachna (d.1558) P
R. Shlomo Luria (Maharshal, 1510-1573) P
R. Menachem David Tiktin (Maharam Tiktin)

1600

R. Yehudah Loew (Maharal miPrague, 1512-1609), P,CZ
R. Mordecai Yaffe (*Levush,* 1530-1612) I,P
R. Meir Lublin (Maharam, 1558-1616) P
R. Yeshayah haLevi (Shilah haKadosh, d.1630) P
R. Shmuel Edels (Maharsha, 1555-1631) P
R. Nasan Spiro (*Megaleh Amukos,* 1585-1633) P
R. Ephraim Schor (*Tevu'os Schor,* d.1633) P
R. Meir Schiff (Maharam Schiff, 1605-1641) G
R. Yehoshua Heschel (*Meginnei Shlomo,* d.1648) P

1650

R. Yom Tov Heller (*Tosafos Yom Tov,* 1579-1654) P
R. Menachem Krochmal (*Tzemach Tzedek,* d.1661) P,M

R. Yair Chaim Bacharach (*Chavos Yair,* d.1702) G

R. Yosef Caro
(1488-1575) EY
Shulchan Aruch

R. Moshe Isserles
(Rama, 1530-1572) P
Mapah

Eretz Yisroel, Egypt, Turkey

R. Levi Ibn Chaviv (Ralbach, 1483-1545) EY
1550
R. Yaakov Berav (*semichah,* 1475-1546) EY
R. Meir Katzenellenbogen (Maharam Padua, d.1565)
R. Moshe Cordovero (Ramak, 1522-1570) EY
R. Yitzchak Luria (Ari haKadosh, d.1572) EY
R. David Ibn Avi Zimra (Radvaz, d.1574) EY

R. Moshe DiTrani (Mabit, 1500-1580) EY
R. Avraham Boton (*Lechem Mishneh,* d.1588) Gr
R. Shmuel Medina (Maharashdam, d.1589) Gr
R. Bezalel Ashkenazi (*Shitah,* d.1592) Eg, EY

1600
R. Moshe Alshech (1508-1600) EY
R. Chaim Vital (1542-1620) EY
R. Yosef DiTrani (Maharit, 1568-1639) EY,T

1650
R. Chaim Benveniste (*Knesses haGedolah,* d.1673) T
R. Chizkiah DaSilva (*P'ri Chadash,* d.1695) EY

Primary Commentaries Surrounding the Shulchan Aruch

Orach Chaim	Yoreh De'ah	Choshen Mishpat	Even haEzer
R. David b. Shmuel haLevi, (Taz, 1586-1667): P *Magen David*	R. David b. Shmuel haLevi, (Taz, 1586-1667): P *Turei Zahav*	R. Yehoshua Falk, (Sema, c.1550-1614): P *Sefer Me'iras Einayim*	R. Moshe Lima (1605-1658): L *Chelkas Mechokek*
R. Avraham Abeli Gombiner, (1637-1683): P *Magen Avraham*	R. Shabse b. Meir haKohen, (Shach, 1622-1663): L *Sifsei Kohen*	R. Shabse b. Meir haKohen, (Shach, 1622-1663): L *Sifsei Kohen*	R. Shmuel Phoebus, (1650-1700): P *Bais Shmuel*

1700

R. Moshe Rivkes (d.c.1672) — *Be'er haGolah,* on entire Shulchan Aruch

1700

1

Era of Torah Decentralization: Origins of the Early Schools

,,וזרח השמש ובא השמש״.
[קהלת א, ה]
ללמדך שאין צדיק נפטר מן העולם,
עד שנברא צדיק כמותו.
[קדושין עב:]

"The sun rises and the sun sets,"
[Ecclesiastes 1:5]
To teach you that a tzaddik
does not pass away from the world,
until another tzaddik like him
is born.
[Kiddushin 72b; See Text, p. 32.]

From Rebbe to Talmid: An Unbroken Chain of Torah Masters

ה׳ לא יעזוב עמו באיזו תקופה שתהיה,
שלא יקום חכם שה׳ יתברך משפיע עליו מכחו,
ומעורר אותו ללמד את אחיו,
ולהורות להם את הדרך להרמת והטבת מצבם הרוחני.

G-d will not forsake His people
In any era whatsoever,
That a Torah scholar might not arise
Upon whom the Almighty, blessed is He,
Will bestow an abundance of His power,
And arouse him to teach his brethren,
And to guide them in the path [which will lead]
To an elevation and improvement of their spiritual station.

[Rav Saadiah Gaon, Sefer haGalui;
See Text, at n. 1.]

Regarding the Khazar Kingdom

When we heard about my master, the King, and about his mighty kingdom and his many soldiers, we were astounded by this. Our heads were held high, our spirits were revitalized, and our hands were strengthened. My master's kingdom restored our sense of dignity.

[Letter of Rav Chisdai to
the Jewish Khazar King, Joseph.
See Text, p. 37.]

1

Era of Torah Decentralization: Origins of the Early Schools

The early *Rishonim* ushered in the period of Torah dispersal and decentralization, which began with the death of Rav Hai Gaon and the close of the Geonic era, in the year 4798, or 1038 C.E. It was these towering Torah personalities who made it possible for the process of Torah transmission to continue in an unbroken chain, at the time when the light of the great Babylonian academies of Sura and Pumbedisa had begun to falter and grow dim.

In his *Sefer haGalui,* Rav Saadiah Gaon expresses a thought which runs as an underlying and ever-recurring theme throughout Jewish history.

ה׳ לא יעזוב עמו באיזו תקופה שתהיה, שלא יקום חכם שה׳ יתברך משפיע עליו מכחו ומעורר אותו ללמד את אחיו ולהורות להם את הדרך להרמת והטבת מצבם הרוחני.

> G-d will not forsake His people in any era whatsoever, that a Torah scholar might not arise upon whom the Almighty, blessed is He, will bestow an abundance of His power, and arouse him to teach his brethren, and to guide them in the path [which will lead] to an elevation and improvement of their spiritual station.[1]

(1) Rav Saadiah b. Yosef Gaon (Sura, 928-942 C.E.), *Sefer haGalui, haSha'ar haRevi' i.*

"The Sun Rises and the Sun Sets"

In a similar vein, on the words of King Solomon in Ecclesiastes, וזרח השמש, ובא השמש — *The sun rises, and the sun sets*[2] — the Sages observe that this verse is symbolic of an ever-recurring pattern in Jewish history. Even before the sun has begun to set upon one phase of Torah splendor and dynamic spiritual growth, the sun begins to rise elsewhere upon another phase of Torah dissemination and spiritual rejuvenation.

Thus, citing this verse, the Sages observe,

> כשמת רבי עקיבא נולד רבי, כשמת רבי נולד רב יהודה, כשמת רב יהודה נולד רבא, כשמת רבא נולד רב אשי, ללמדך שאין צדיק נפטר מן העולם עד שנברא צדיק כמותו, שנא׳ (קהלת א, ה), ,,וזרח השמש ובא השמש״, עד שלא כבתה שמשו של עלי, זרחה שמשו של שמואל הרמתי, שנא׳ (שמואל א׳ ג, ג) ,,ונר אלקים טרם יכבה, ושמואל שוכב״, וכו׳. (קידושין עב:)
>
> When Rabbe Akiva died, Rebbe[3] was born; When Rebbe died, Rav Yehudah was born; when Rav Yehudah died, Rava was born; when Rava died,[4] Rav Ashi was born; to teach you that a *tzaddik* does not pass away from the world, until another *tzaddik* like him is born, as it says,[5] *The sun rises, and the sun sets.* Before the sun of Eli was extinguished the sun of Shmuel haRamassi had begun to shine, as it says,[6] *And the lamp of G-d had not yet been extinguished, and Shmuel[7] was lying down.*[8]

In a larger sense this is true, not only of individual Torah leaders, but of the transition between the various *tekufos* or periods of Torah transmission, as well. To an exceedingly great extent, this

(2) Ecclesiastes 1:5.

(3) Rebbe, or Rabbe Yehudah haNasi (Rabbeinu haKadosh), redacted the Mishnah, ca. 190 C.E. See *Legacy of Sinai,* p. 176, n. 98.

(4) According to the Rambam, the correct textual reading is, "Before Rava died, Rav Ashi was born." See annotations of haRav Ransburg, on this Gemara in *Kiddushin* 72b.

(5) Ecclesiastes 1:5.

(6) I Samuel 3:3.

(7) This verse was a prelude to the initial prophetic experience of Shmuel haNavi. See *ibid.,* verses 4-10.

(8) *Kiddushin* 72b.

pattern marked the process of transition between the era of Torah centralization in the great Babylonian academies, and the subsequent era of Torah dispersal and decentralization.

Thus it was that even before the sun of the great Babylonian academies had begun to wane, new Torah beacons began to appear upon the horizon. Independent Torah centers were beginning to emerge in the large communities of Italy, North Africa, Alexandria, Germany, France, Southern France, and Spain.

Origins of Sephardic Jewry

Some early sources indicate that the earliest beginnings of Jewish settlement in Spain may be traced as far back as the destruction of the First Temple by Nebuchadnezzar, in the year 3338 (422 B.C.E.). It is said that as a reward for having aligned his forces with those of Babylon during the siege of Jerusalem, King Aspian of Spain was awarded a share of the bounty in the form of a number of elite captives of royal blood — princes of the House of David — whom he promptly carried off to Spain.[9]

At the time of the Second *Churban* in the year 3828 (68 C.E.),[10] a large number of Jews were once again exiled to Spain by Vespasian, Titus, and later, by Hadrian (135 C.E.).[11] A particularly large Jewish community was established in Cordoba, which contained an ancient synagogue, called *Knesses haMidrash.*

Table V on p. 58 provides an outline of some of the highlights of the North African and Sephardic Schools of Torah Study, as well as the closing decades of the Geonic Era.

In the early centuries after the destruction of the Second Temple, when the Iberian Peninsula was under pagan rule and before the Roman emperors embraced Christianity,[11a] the situation

(9) Solomon Ibn Verga (fl. c. 1492), *Shevet Yehudah* (Jerusalem edition, 1947), p. 33, as cited by M.S. Rabinowitz, *Iggaros haRambam* (Jerusalem: Mosad haRav Kook, 1960), p. 106, n. 17.

(10) To arrive at the equivalent Common Era date, subtract 3760 from any given Jewish date. Thus, we arrive at 68 C.E. as the common era date of the *Churban* of the Second Temple in 3828. See *Legacy of Sinai,* p. 160, n. 16.

(11) *Seder Olam Zuta,* attributed to Rabbeinu Yosef Tov Elem (fl. c. 1070), Chap. 9, parag. 3. See Rabbi M.Y. Weinstock, ed. (Jerusalem, 1957), *ad. loc.,* p. 111, n. 5, in *Seder Zemanim.*

(11a) The Roman Emperor Constantine [307-337 C.E.] adopted Christianity as the official State religion in 313 C.E. (See *Legacy of Sinai,* p. 202.)

of the Jews was favorable. They generally enjoyed many privileges and were active in the economic life of the countries in which they dwelled. It was only after the Roman emperors embraced Christianity, that the situation of the Jews became intolerable. Edict after edict eroded their rights and reduced them to an entirely inferior status. Under later Catholic rulers there were also edicts of forcible baptism and conversion.

The Arabian-Muslim Conquest

It was therefore a great blessing for the Jewish community, not only in a physical sense, but in a spiritual sense, as well, when the Arab Muslim world embarked upon its successful march of conquest of vast segments of the far-flung Byzantine Empire. With the Arabian conquest of Jerusalem in 638 C.E., the situation of the Jews in Eretz Yisroel began to improve appreciably. The Christian prohibitions regarding entry of Jews to Jerusalem were removed. In general, the attitude of the Moslems towards the Jews was far more favorable than that of the Christians, although there were a number of notable exceptions, to be sure.

In 711 C.E. the Arabs invaded the Iberian Peninsula through the Straits of Gibraltar, and Spain came under Muslim rule. By 712, Islam ruled over vast dominions, from south of the Pyrenees to the borders of India, and almost ninety percent of the known Jewish population came under Muslim dominion. This removed the harsh yoke of Christian-Byzantine oppression from large segments of the Jewish population. In the Iberian Peninsula, it ushered in the "Golden Era" of Sephardic Jewry.

The Jews in the western countries of Christian Europe had likewise begun to enjoy a brief respite under the Carolingian Dynasty, during the benevolent reigns of Charlemagne (768-814 C.E.), Louis the Pious (814-840), and Charles the Bald (840-877).

Links With the Babylonian Academies

In the early centuries after the destruction of the Second Temple, the Jewish communities in the Iberian Peninsula relied entirely upon the great Babylonian academies for Torah guidance. While these Jewish communities had begun to breathe more freely and to flourish after the Arabian conquest of Spain in 711 C.E., they nevertheless continued to turn to the great Babylonian academies for Torah guidance.

We do, indeed, find that there was a growing yearning for Torah knowledge in the Spanish Jewish communities during this period. Thus, we find that Rav Paltoi ben Mar Abbaya, *Gaon* of Pumbedisa during the years 841 to 857 C.E., wrote a commentary on the Talmud when he was requested to write "the Talmud and its interpretation" by a Jewish community in Spain.[12] His son, Rav Tzemach ben Paltoi Gaon (Pumbedisa, 871-880) engaged in extensive correspondence with European communities, and particularly with Spain.[13]

Similarly, Rav Natronai bar Hilai Gaon (Sura, 853-858) wrote the entire order of one hundred daily benedictions during the course of his correspondence with a member of the Jewish community of Alisona, Spain. According to an ancient Sephardic tradition, Rav Natronai appeared suddenly in Spain to teach Torah to the Spanish-Jewish community, with whom he had very close ties, and disappeared as suddenly.[14] Rav Amram ben Sheshna Gaon (Sura, 858-876) likewise wrote his famous *Siddur* in response to a query from Spain that he provide information concerning the order of the *tefillos.*[15]

These and other queries from various Spanish communities which were addressed to the great *Geonim* of the Babylonian academies are indicative of a growing thirst for Torah knowledge and a yearning for halachic guidance, which prepared the groundwork for the approaching "Golden Era" of Spanish Jewry.

Rav Chisdai ben Yitzchak Ibn Shaprut

One of the individuals most directly responsible for ushering in the "Golden Age" of Spanish Jewry was Rav Chisdai ben Yitzchak Ibn Shaprut (ca. 915-970 C.E.). One of the leading figures in the Jewish community of Cordoba during the first half of the tenth

(12) See Addendum to *Iggeres Rav Sherira Gaon,* Dr. Benjamin Menachem Lewin, ed. (Haifa, 1921), p. xxiii. See also Simcha Assaf, *Tekufas haGeonim veSafrusah* (Jerusalem: Mosad haRav Kook, 1955), pp. 52 ff.

(13) See Assaf, *op. cit.,* p. 53.

(14) *Otzar haGeonim, Chagigah,* Chap. 28. See also Introduction of Rav Amram b. Sheshna Gaon, to his *Siddur Rav Amram Gaon,* re. the one-hundred benedictions.

(15) Introd. to *Siddur Rav Amram Gaon.*

century, Rav Chisdai was a great statesman, scholar, doctor, and communal leader. As the highly respected court physician and advisor to Caliph Abad Al-Rachman III, Rav Chisdai was a highly influential statesman who used his influence effectively to alleviate the plight of his brethren, not only in Spain, but in far-flung Jewish communities, as well.

Rav Chisdai was fluent in many languages. It was his linguistic abilities, in particular, which made him eminently suitable to serve as the Caliph's translator and intermediary in regard to his relations and contacts with the Christian rulers of Northern Spain. It was not long before the Caliph began to send Rav Chisdai on important missions, as his emissary to foreign lands. In one such mission, Rav Chisdai concluded a highly significant treaty in behalf of the Caliph with some of the Christian rulers of Northern Spain, including the independent kingdom of Navarre.

Rav Chisdai also translated an important medical work by the eminent Greek pharmacologist, Diosciordes, from Latin into Arabic. This elevated his esteem in the eyes of the Caliph even more.

In recognition of Rav Chisdai's skillful statesmanship and his linguistic skills, the Caliph appointed him to the important post of minister for foreign affairs, as well as minister for the treasury. Thereafter, all foreign ministers and foreign emissaries who arrived for audiences with the Caliph, seeking his aid in behalf of their governments, had to first appear before Rav Chisdai and obtain his approval. This, of course, placed Rav Chisdai in a unique position to obtain, in return, important favors and privileges for his co-religionists in foreign lands under Christian control.

The Khazar Kingdom

His great love for his people is manifest in the highly intriguing correspondence which he conducted with Joseph, the Jewish King of the Khazar kingdom, which flourished at that time in the White Steppes of Russia. Not long after the onset of the Geonic era, King Bulan, together with many individuals in the Khazar kingdom, converted to Judaism. This kingdom flourished in the White Steppes of Russia for many centuries. When Rav Chisdai learned about the existence of an independent Jewish kingdom in Russia he wrote the following letter to the Khazar King, Joseph.

> When we heard about my master, the King, and about his mighty kingdom and his many soldiers, we were astounded by this. Our heads were held high, our spirits were revitalized, and our hands were strengthened. My master's kingdom restored our sense of dignity.
>
> Would that the reliability of this report might be further corroborated, for this will add to our own greatness. Blessed be the L-rd, G-d of Israel, who has not removed from us a redeemer, nor did He remove the radiance of a kingdom from the Tribes of Israel.[16]

Rav Chisdai informs the King of the great power and prestige of the Caliph, and of his own important role as foreign minister in the Caliph's court. He used his influential position, he points out further, to always seek out the welfare of his fellow Jews in far-flung lands.

> When the Kings of the earth hear of the greatness and the might [of the Caliph], they send him gifts and make overtures to him with presents and with delicacies. These include the King of the Franks, as well as King Constantine and others. From all these emissaries who bring gifts [for the Caliph], I inquire always concerning the welfare of our fellow Jews, the remnants of the exile.[17]

A Powerful Friend

But Rav Chisdai did much more than merely inquire after their welfare. He used his great influence to help his fellow Jews in distant lands, as the following letters, which were found in the Cairo Genizah,[18] clearly reveal.

(16) Rav Chisdai's Letter to the Jewish Khazar King, Joseph. This letter is included in the Hebrew edition of Rabbe Yehudah haLevi's *Kuzari* (Warsaw: Yitzchak Goldman, 1880).

(17) *Ibid.*

(18) The Genizah was a place where *sefarim* and religious objects, which had holiness and could therefore not be discarded or destroyed, were hidden or buried when they were worn out and could no longer be used. In the Cairo Genizah, which was in the attic of the Ezra Synagogue of Fostat or Old Cairo, many invaluable literary treasures and historical documents were found.

The first letter was written by Rav Chisdai to Queen Helena,[19] wife of the Byzantine King, Constantine VIII. Rav Chisdai informs the Queen that he has performed many kindnesses in behalf of the Christian minority in Cordoba. He goes on to request that the Queen extend her protection to her Jewish subjects, "that they might not be forcibly removed from their religious observances, and . . . in order that their enemies may refrain from persecuting them."[20]

In the Cairo Genizah, too, there are letters addressed to Rav Chisdai from distant communities, asking him to use his influence and to intercede in their behalf. Thus, from Bari, Italy, came a request that Rav Chisdai should try to prevent the implementation of a pending edict which authorized the burning of the Talmud, while in nearby Otoronto they requested that he intercede to prevent pogroms and persecution of the Jewish population. A similar request came from the city of Toulouse, in Southern France.[21]

While we do not have any record of Rav Chisdai's response to these requests, these letters are indicative of Rav Chisdai's extensive contact with Jews all over the world, and of their reliance upon his aid and his intervention in their behalf.

Patron of Jewish Learning

Rav Chisdai was a patron of all forms of Jewish learning and Torah scholarship. Over the years he supported the Babylonian academies of Sura and Pumbedisa generously. He was in contact with the *Geonim,* and was honored by the academy of Pumbedisa with the title of *Reish Kallah.*[22] When the great Torah Sage, Rabbe Moshe b. Chanoch, arrived in Spain, Rav Chisdai helped him establish a great Torah academy, which eventually made the Spanish Jewish community independent of the Babylonian academies.

(19) Queen Helena was the actual ruler of the Byzantine Empire, since King Constantine VIII was completely preoccupied by his intellectual pursuits.

(20) These letters by Rav Chisdai, found in the Cairo Genizah, were published by Yaakov Mann in his "Texts and Studies," Vol. I, pp. 1-30.

(21) *Ibid.*

(22) The term *Reish Kallah* — lit. "Head of the bi-annual study session" (see *Legacy of Sinai,* pp. 206-208) was later conferred upon distinguished scholars and Torah leaders in the *Golah* — in lands far removed from the Babylonian academies.

Thus, it was due, in great measure, to his enthusiastic support that Spain became an outstanding center of Torah study and of all facets of Jewish learning.

It was at Rav Chisdai's request that Rav Dosa, son of Rav Saadiah Gaon, (Sura, 928-942) wrote a biography of his illustrious father. Rav Chisdai similarly encouraged and was the patron of many projects which contributed greatly to all fields of Jewish scholarship. This, in turn, laid the foundation for the "Golden Era" of Torah learning and scholarship in the Spanish-Jewish community, which was to encompass the better part of the ensuing three centuries.

More than two centuries after his death, the Hebrew poet, Rav Yehudah Al-Charizi, wrote the following moving lines concerning Rav Chisdai Ibn Shaprut.

בימים ההם זרחה בספרד שמש תהלה.

> In those days, there shone in Spain a glorious sun, that is, the great prince, Rav Chisdai the Sephardi, son of Yitzchak, for he dispensed unlimited blessing to all who turned to him. . . . This prince revitalized wisdom. He announced that he who is for G-d shall turn to him.[23] Whereupon, every *Gaon* and every Rav in Arabian lands gathered to him, and the scholars of the generation came to him. . . . In his days wisdom became widespread in Israel.[24]

The Early Hebrew Lexicographers

There was a great deal of literary activity in the field of *dikduk*, or Hebrew grammar, in the Sephardic community during this early period — all of which was enthusiastically encouraged, supported, and stimulated by Rav Chisdai. The great Hebrew lexicographer, Menachem ben Yaakov Ibn Saruq (d. 970 C.E.), upon whose Biblical dictionary, *Machberes*, Rashi draws extensively in his commentary on the Torah, was invited to settle in Cordoba as a protege of Rav Chisdai Ibn Shaprut. He later fell into disfavor with Rav Chisdai. His *Machberes* has been regarded as a classic work of Hebrew Biblical lexicography.

(23) See Exodus 32:26 — מי לה׳ אלי — *He who is on the side of the L-rd, let him turn to me.*

(24) Rav Yehudah Al-Charizi (1165-1225), *Tachkemoni, Sha'ar* 18.

Another important tenth century lexicographer was Dunash ben Labrat haLevi of Baghdad (ca. 920-970), a disciple of Rav Saadiah Gaon. He, too, was encouraged to settle in Cordoba by Rav Chisdai who supported him generously, and who encouraged him to continue his research into Hebrew lexicography. In his primary work, *Teshuvos al Menachem ben Saruq,* he makes over two hundred critical comments regarding many of the grammatical principles made by Menachem in his *Machberes.* In a companion volume, *Teshuvos al Rav Saadiah Gaon,* he is likewise critical of some of the grammatical rules set down by his teacher, Rav Saadiah Gaon.

A New Milestone in Hebrew Grammar

In the next generation, Yehudah ben David Ibn Chiyug (fl. 1000) was another illustrious Hebrew lexicographer. Originally from Fez, Morocco, he later moved to Cordoba, where he wrote his *Sefer haPo'alim Ba'alei Osiyos haNach veHemshech* and his *Sefer haPo'alim Ba'alei haKofel,* as well as other important works on Hebrew grammar.

Yehudah Ibn Chiyug attained a milestone in the study of Hebrew grammar. He was the first Hebrew lexicographer to recognize that Hebrew verbs consist of three letter roots. He develops this principle at great length in his *sefarim,* showing that while, in certain grammatical constructions, one or another part of this three-letter root may be dropped, or may be doubled, the *shoresh,* or root itself, nevertheless consists of a three-letter base. This approach is the foundation upon which the study of Hebrew grammar revolves to this day.

Rabbe Avraham Ibn Ezra, who translated some of Yehudah Chiyug's *sefarim* from Arabic into Hebrew, makes reference to him as ראש המדקדקים — "Chief of the lexicographers," and he writes concerning him that "G-d enlightened his eyes to recognize the fundamental principles of Hebrew grammar."[25] In a similar vein, a contemporary grammarian, Shlomo Parchon, writes concerning

(25) Rav Avraham Ibn Ezra, in his introduction to his *Sefer Moznaim,* as cited by Rav Chaim Michal, *Or haChaim* (Jerusalem: Mosad haRav Kook, 1965), No. 986, p. 524.

him, "The Almighty revealed to him that which He did not reveal [even] to Rav Saadiah Gaon, the chief spokesman [of the Sages]."[26]

Yonah Ibn Janach . . . Perhaps the greatest of all the early Hebrew lexicographers was the Cordoban physician, Yonah Ibn Janach (990-1050), author of the *Sefer haRikmah* and the *Sefer haSharashim,* which are regarded as outstanding classics in the field of Hebrew grammar. He also wrote a *Sefer haHashlamah,* which is a supplement to the works of Yehudah Ibn Chiyug, adding, as it does, some fifty verbs and conjugations which the former had overlooked. No slight was intended regarding the stature of Yehudah Chiyug, whom Yonah Ibn Janach refers to with reverence as המורה המעולה והמנהיג המושלם — "the outstanding teacher and the accomplished leader." There were others, however — among them Rav Shmuel haNagid, who had studied under Yehudah Ibn Chiyug — who regarded the *Sefer haHashlamah* as a reflection upon the dignity of Yehudah, and they made their views known publicly.

In his reply to these spurious charges, Yonah Ibn Janach cited a parable to the effect that while he did, in truth, deeply love and respect Yehudah Chiyug, he loved truth even more.[27]

The *sefarim* of Yonah Ibn Janach represented an invaluable contribution to the field of Hebrew lexicography. Outstanding grammarians of subsequent generations, such as Rav Avraham Ibn Ezra and the Radak, used his works extensively.

It should be borne in mind that Hebrew had not been used as a spoken language for many centuries already at this time. These early grammarians, therefore, rendered an invaluable contribution with their incisive research into the roots of Hebrew grammar. It was their work which helped keep the Hebrew language alive and vibrant throughout the centuries of exile.

(26) Shlomo Parchon, as cited by Mordecai Margolios, *Encyclopedia leToledos Gedolei Yisroel* (Jerusalem: J. Chachik, 1969), Vol. II, p. 625.

(27) See the introductory remarks of Rabbe Zerachiah haLevi to his *Sefer haMa'or,* at the beginning of the Rif to tractate *Berachos,* where he cites this parable as an explanation for his critique of the *Hilchos Rav Alfas,* despite the fact that he truly loved and revered the Rif very deeply.

Rav Shlomo Ibn Gabirol

The well-known philosopher-poet, Rav Shlomo ben Yehudah Ibn Gabirol (c. 1020-1057), lived in Saragossa at this time. He was friendly with Yonah Ibn Janach, the grammarian. A three-volume collection of Ibn Gabirol's poems has been published. Perhaps his most beautiful poem is his philosophical poem, *Keser Malchus.* He wrote a number of elegies concerning Rav Hai Gaon, upon the latter's death in 1038. His sefer, *Tikun haMiddos,* which deals with the importance of improving one's character traits, was written in Arabic, and translated into Hebrew by Rav Yehudah Ibn Tibbon.

His primary philosophical work, *Mekor Chaim,* is no longer extant in its original Arabic, but an early Hebrew translation of certain sections of the work is extant, under the name, *Likutim miSefer Mekor Chaim.* Ibn Gabirol does not draw upon the Bible, the Talmud, or the Midrash in this work, and it is probably for this reason that his *Mekor Chaim* was slowly forgotten among Jews. It was translated into Latin, however, and for many years it was believed to have been written by a non-Jew.

Ibn Gabirol led a troubled life, and he died childless at the early age of thirty-seven.

The Arba'ah Shevuyyim

The Ravad relates in his *Sefer haKabbalah* that an event occurred at this time which contributed greatly to the widespread dissemination of Torah scholarship, and to the establishment of independent Torah centers on the European continent and in North Africa. During Rav Sherira Gaon's reign as *Gaon* of Pumbedisa (968-1006), the Ravad writes, the event of the *Arba'ah Shevuyyim,* or the Four Captives, occurred. This event hastened the emergence of these far-flung Jewish communities as self-sufficient Torah centers, which no longer had to turn exclusively to the Babylonian academies for Torah guidance.[28]

(28) *Sefer haKabbalah le-haRavad,* Rabbe Avraham Ibn Daud haLevi (Ravad I, 1110-1180), *s.v. Seder Geonim, HaDor haShevi'i,* in parag. immediately following era of Rav Hai Gaon. Rabbi haLevi, in his *Doros haRishonim,* Vol. IV, pp. 298 and 302, places the date of this narrative at ca. 4720 (960 C.E.), a few years before the beginning of Rav Sherira's accession as *Gaon* of Pumbedisa in 4728.

According to one interpretation of the account in the *Sefer haKabbalah*, the episode of the *Arba'ah Shevuyyim* originated in the Babylonian academies. During the declining decades of the Geonic era, the financial situation of the academies was a precarious one. Whereupon, four outstanding Torah scholars were sent out by the academies on a fund-raising mission, in an effort to augment the dwindling income of the academies.[29] The great Torah scholar and historian, Rav Yitzchak Isaac haLevi, on the other hand, maintains that the origin of these scholars was not Babylon, but rather, Bari, Italy.[30]

The four scholars were captured en route by Demahyn, captain of the fleet of Caliph Eved al-Rachman Alnazzar of Cordoba. The names of the scholars were: Rabbeinu Chushiel ben Elchanan, Rabbeinu Moshe ben Chanoch, and Rabbeinu Shemariah ben

(29) In this regard, Rabbi Yitzchak Isaac haLevi cites the historians Heinrich Graetz (1817-1891) and Abraham Harkavy (1835-1919), both of whom subscribe to this opinion. Rabbi haLevi, however, disagrees with this opinion, and places the origin of these scholars in Bari, Italy, as we shall clarify at length in the text. See *Doros haRishonim*, Vol. IV, pp. 283 ff.

(30) It should be noted here that on the basis of a letter found in the Cairo Genizah, which appears to have been sent by Rabbeinu Chushiel to Rabbeinu Shemariah b. Elchanan of Alexandria, Egypt, the authenticity of some of the narrative aspects of the account of the *Arba'ah Shevuyyim* have come into question. (See Simchah Assaf, *Tekufas haGeonim veSafrusah*, ed. Mordecai Margolios [Jerusalem: Mosad haRav Kook, 1955], p. 53. See also Mordecai Margolios, *Encyclopedia leToledos Gedolei Yisroel, op. cit.*, Vol. II, p. 473, *s.v.* Rabbeinu Chushiel. Cf. Rav Yitzchak Isaac haLevi [1847-1914], *Doros haRishonim* [Frankfort-on-Main, 1901-1918], Vol. IV, p. 299.)

While this letter appears to indicate that Rabbeinu Chushiel arrived in North Africa voluntarily, it does, nevertheless, bear out Rabbi haLevi's contention that these scholars came originally from Italy, rather than from Bavel. In this sense, therefore, it corroborates Rabbi haLevi's approach concerning the significant role of Rabbeinu Chushiel, and later, of his son, Rabbeinu Chananel, in regard to facilitating the convergence of the Babylonian and Eretz Yisroel Schools of Torah Scholarship.

While the story itself is hardly significant to our thesis here, we will continue to make reference to the narrative of the *Arba'ah Shevuyyim*, since this event and these four scholars have been cited by this designation in all Jewish history texts which **deal** with this period, for the past nine centuries.

Elchanan. The Ravad observes that the name of the fourth scholar is unknown to him.[31]

The Ravad relates that Rabbeinu Moshe was traveling with his young son, Chanoch, and with his wife, who was very beautiful. When Rabbeinu Moshe's wife realized that the captain had evil designs concerning her, she cried out to her husband, asking him whether one who drowns at sea will be resurrected at the time of *Techiyas haMeisim* — the Resurrection of the Dead. Rabbeinu Moshe replied in the affirmative, citing the verse in Psalms, *The L-rd said: I will bring [them] back from Bashan; I will bring [them] back from the depths of the sea.* Whereupon, his wife cast herself into the sea, where she was drowned at once.[32]

The captain subsequently sold the four scholars into slavery at various ports along his route, where they were later redeemed by the respective Jewish communities. Rabbeinu Chushiel (d. end 10th c.) was brought to Kairouan, North Africa, where he soon became head of the Kairouan Torah community. Rabbeinu Shemariah (d. 1011 C.E.) was redeemed by the community of Alexandria, Egypt, where he was appointed *Av Bes Din*. Rabbeinu Moshe ben Chanoch (d. end tenth c.), together with his young son, Chanoch (d. 1025 C.E.), was led to Cordoba, Spain, where the Jewish communal leader, Rav Chisdai, helped him establish a great central Yeshiva.

The arrival of these eminent scholars in each of these far-flung communities, served as a bridge, which facilitated the process of Torah transmission from East to West, and which immensely stimulated the development of self-sufficient Torah centers in each of these communities.

(31) It is believed by some historians that the fourth scholar was one Rabbe Nasan haBavli, who was brought to Narbonne, France, where he later established a Yeshiva. Rabbi haLevi, however, disagrees with this opinion. (See *Doros haRishonim,* Vol. IV, p. 302, and n. 48, *ad. loc.*)

(32) *Sefer haKabbalah le-haRavad, loc. cit.,* citing Psalms 68:23. For a similar narrative, which occurred at the time of the *Churban* of the Second Temple, see *Gittin* 57b.

Rabbe Kalonymos: From Lucca to Mayence

Another tradition ascribes the initial dissemination of Torah in the Jewish communities of Western Europe to an earlier event. It is said that in the year 787 C.E., Charlemagne [or Charles the Bald, in the year 876], in an effort to improve the educational standards of his Jewish subjects and to make them independent of the Babylonian academies, invited a great Torah scholar, Rabbe Kalonymos from Lucca, Italy, to settle in Mayence, Germany, where he established a Torah academy. Ten years later, in 797 C.E., Charlemagne requested that the Persian Caliph, Harun-al-Rashid, send him a Torah scholar from Babylon. Whereupon, the Caliph sent Rabbe Machir to settle in Narbonne, Southern France, where he established a Torah academy. These events place the establishment of Torah centers in Germany and France some two centuries before the close of the great Babylonian academies.[33]

Origins of the Italian School of Torah Study

In his *Doros haRishonim,* Rabbi Y.I. haLevi provides us with an entirely different interpretation of the events surrounding the origin and background of the *Arba'ah Shevuyyim,* which will simultaneously shed new light upon the entire course of development of Torah in Spain, North Africa, and Western Europe.[34]

According to Rabbi haLevi, the Four Captives were not on a fund-raising mission for the Babylonian academies. Indeed, they were originally not from Bavel at all, but rather from Bari, Italy,[35]

(33) For more elaborate treatment of this matter, see Chap. 2, nn. 34-35, and Chap. 6, n. 2.

(34) These thoughts concerning the origins of the *Arba'ah Shevuyyim* were already clarified in the concluding chapter of *Legacy of Sinai.* Because of their direct relevancy to the dissemination of Torah in Spain, North Africa, and Western Europe during the era of the *Rishonim,* they are once again cited here, with additional background material.

(35) It should be noted that the text of the *Sefer haKabbalah* does make reference to "*Medinas Bari*" as the point of origin of the boat on which the *Arba'ah Shevuyyim* were traveling.

where they had embarked upon a mission to raise funds for Jewish brides — *hachnassas kallah*.[36]

Rabbi haLevi explains further that more than two hundred years before the close of the Geonic *tekufah*, a great Torah community had already begun to flourish in Italy, with the arrival there of a number of outstanding Torah scholars. These scholars came, not from the Babylonian academies of Sura and Pumbedisa, but from the Yeshivos of Eretz Yisroel. For this reason, in certain instances, their traditions differed from those of the Babylonian academies, particularly in regard to some customs pertaining to the *nusach ha-tefillah* — the text of certain *tefillos*. While it is true that the Torah academies of Eretz Yisroel — like their Babylonian counterparts — had accepted the *Talmud Bavli* as the final definitive halachic authority of all Israel,[37] they nevertheless retained customs and traditions which found their origins in the *Talmud Yerushalmi* and in the *Midrashim*, many of which had originated in Eretz Yisroel.[38] In this connection, Rabbi haLevi cites the following words of Rabbeinu Tam in his *Sefer haYashar*.

> For many [halachic] matters are a tradition in our hands, such as intercalation of the calendar and the arrangement of prayers and benedictions . . . and these matters follow the *Midrashim* and the *Talmud Yerushalmi*.[39]

(36) The term *Hachnasas Kallah*, which is employed by Rabbe Avraham Ibn Daud in his original account of the story of the *Arba'ah Shevuyyim*, may be interpreted either as a fund-raising venture in behalf of the Yeshivos of Sura and Pumbedisa, whose semi-annual sessions were referred to as *Yarchei Kallah* (see *Legacy of Sinai*, pp. 206 ff), or as a fund-raising venture in behalf of impoverished brides and grooms, which has long been regarded as a hallowed tradition in the eyes of Jewish law.

(37) Regarding the unqualified acceptance of the authority of the *Talmud Bavli* by the Yeshivos of Eretz Yisroel, see *Doros haRishonim*, Vol. IV, *"Rabbanan Savorai,"* Chap. 20, pp. 48 ff.

(38) Rabbi Y.I. haLevi, *Doros haRishonim*, Vol. IV, *"Tekufas haGeonim,"* Chap. 36, pp. 287-289.

(39) *Sefer haYashar* of Rabbeinu Tam, Section 619, as cited by *Doros haRishonim*, *op. cit.*, Vol. IV, p. 289.

Of even greater significance, however, is the fact that, unlike the early Sephardic communities which turned with all their halachic questions to the great Babylonian authorities, the Italian Torah scholars, who were still under Christian rule, had little or no contact with the Babylonian academies, which were under Arab rule. They were therefore compelled to rely, instead, upon their own independent analytical research — delving deeply into the original Talmudic sources, clarifying enigmatic texts, elucidating textual inconsistencies, resolving difficulties, and explaining elusive passages, in a determined effort to attain clarity and comprehension of complex halachic problems. It was through extensive and diligent application of this approach to Torah study, rather than through reliance upon Geonic responsa, that the Italian Torah masters arrived at a clarification and determination of definitive halacha.[40]

The Early Ashkenazic School

Drawing upon the tradition which we have already cited above concerning Charlemagne, Rabbi haLevi points out that the great Torah communities of Germany and Northern France, were established as early as the eighth century (787 C.E.), when Charlemagne invited the great Torah scholar, Rabbe Kalonymos of Lucca, Italy, to establish a Torah academy in Mayence, Germany, and to settle there. Rabbe Kalonymos derived many of his customs and traditions, as well as his incisive and analytical approach to Torah study, from the great Italian Torah masters under whom he had studied. Thus, Rabbi haLevi concludes, it is hardly surprising to find that many of the traditions of the Torah communities of France and Germany were based upon an incisive analysis of the Talmudic sources, and upon the traditions of their own teachers and Torah scholars, rather than upon the traditions and halachic rulings of the great Babylonian academies of Sura and Pumbedisa, as manifested in the extensive literature of Geonic responsa and halachic treatises.[41]

(40) *Doros haRishonim*, Vol. IV, p. 294.
(41) *Ibid.*, pp. 288 ff.

In this vein, Rabbi haLevi cites the rationale of Rabbeinu Gershom concerning a halachic decision, in which he overrules the words of the Ba'al Halachos Gedolos, who was, of course, one of the leading exponents of the Babylonian Geonic School of halachic literature. Rabbeinu Gershom points out that since he finds no indication in the Talmud to support the decision of the BaHaG concerning this matter, he therefore feels free to rely upon his own logical deduction and to follow the halachic ruling of his own teacher, Rabbeinu Leon, who was one of the early Ashkenazic Torah masters.[42]

Development of the Sephardic School

During this early period, there existed in Spain and North Africa, too, thriving Torah communities which preceded the arrival of the *Arba'ah Shevuyyim* by many hundreds of years. As noted above, some sources indicate that the earliest beginnings of Jewish settlement in Spain may be traced back as far as the destruction of Jerusalem by Nebuchadnezzar, in 3338.[43] These communities, however, did not possess outstanding Torah scholars and they were entirely dependent upon the Babylonian academies for halachic guidance, as is manifested by the great amount of Geonic responsa which was directed to the leaders of these communities. It was not until the arrival of Rabbeinu Moshe and his son, Rabbeinu Chanoch in Cordova, and Rabbeinu Chushiel, and later, his son, Rabbeinu Chananel in Kairouan, that the Torah communities of Spain and North Africa began to become halachically self-sufficient and independent of their former total reliance upon the Babylonian academies.

According to Rabbi haLevi, the *Arba'ah Shevuyyim*, who, like Rabbe Kalonymos, drew their traditions from the Italian and Eretz Yisroel Schools of Torah scholarship, introduced their analytical approach to Torah study into the already long-established Sephardic Torah communities of Spain and North Africa. Thus, the two great schools of Torah scholarship of both the Babylonian and

(42) Rabbeinu Gershom, as cited in Responsa of Maharam Baruch (Prague, 1895), responsum 264. See *Doros haRishonim*, Vol. IV, p. 294.

(43) Solomon Ibn Verga (fl. 1492), *Shevet Yehudah* (Jerusalem, 1947), p. 33, cited by M.D. Rabinowitz, *Iggaros haRambam* (Jerusalem: Mosad haRav Kook, 1960), p. 106, n. 17.

Eretz Yisroel academies now converged, to take root and to become established as the Sephardic School of Torah Study.[44]

With these thoughts in mind, Rabbi haLevi clarifies a number of otherwise enigmatic passages in the commentaries of Rabbeinu Chananel and other *Rishonim,* which seem to make reference to the existence of not one, but two separate schools of Torah study, which later converged and coexisted side by side.

For example, after having rendered his opinion concerning a difficult halachic question, Rabbeinu Chananel makes the following remark in his commentary on *Eruvin.*

> וראינו לרבותינו הגאונים זצ״ל פירוש זולתי זה הפירוש, אבל זהו קבלה ומסורה בידינו.
>
> We have seen that the *Geonim,* of blessed memory, rendered a different interpretation of this matter, but this is the interpretation which is according to our tradition, and which was transmitted to us.[45]

In a number of other places, too, Rabbeinu Chananel makes a similar observation. Thus, in his commentary on tractate *Shabbos,* Rabbeinu Chananel writes,

> מרבותינו הגאונים אמרו פירוש אחר, ואנן כתבנו מה שקבלנו.
>
> Our teachers, the *Geonim,* clarified this matter differently, but we have clarified it according to the tradition we have received.[46]

The Rosh Hashanah Mussaf Amidah Controversy

To further bear out his conclusions concerning this matter, Rabbi haLevi cites the following halachic dispute regarding the *Mussaf amidah* of the Rosh Hashanah *tefillos.*

(44) *Doros haRishonim,* Vol. IV, p. 295.

(45) Commentary of Rabbeinu Chananel, *Eruvin* 83b (bottom of *daf*).

(46) Commentary of Rabbeinu Chananel, *Shabbos* 123b, *s.v.* אסובי ינוקא. See also Rabbeinu Chananel's commentary on *Shabbos* 8a, *s.v.* אמר אביי זרק כוורת; *Makkos* 5a, *s.v.* מתני׳, אין העדים נעשין זוממין. See also *Doros haRishonim,* Vol. IV, pp. 292 f, for other references.

During the Rosh Hashanah *Mussaf* service, it is customary today for the entire congregation to recite nine benedictions in the *Amidah*.[47] In his repetition of the *Amidah*, the *Shali'ach Tzibbur* — the cantor or the leader of the congregational prayer service — repeats these nine benedictions, with additional supplementary material. While this procedure has been universally followed in all congregations for almost one thousand years now, it was a matter of significant controversy and debate during the era of the early *Rishonim*.

Thus, the Rosh, in his *Hilchos Rabbeinu Asher* on tractate *Rosh Hashanah*,[48] cites the words of the Maharitz Ghayyas,[49] who observes that it was customary in the great academies of Sura and Pumbedisa, as well as in all congregations throughout Bavel, for only the *Shali'ach Tzibbur* to recite all nine benedictions. The congregation itself, on the other hand, recited only seven benedictions.[50]

The Maharitz Ghayyas cites Geonic responsa extensively to this effect, including responsa of both earlier *Geonim* — such as Rav Natronai Gaon[51] and Rav Amram Gaon[52] — and later *Geonim* — such as Rav Sherira Gaon[53] and his son, Rav Hai Gaon,[54] each of whom states clearly and unequivocally that only the cantor recites all nine benedictions, while the members of the congregation recite only seven benedictions during their silent recitation of the *Amidah*. Whereupon, the Ritz Ghayyas concludes with the observation that

(47) In addition to the three opening and three concluding benedictions which are a standard part of every *Amidah*, these nine benedictions also include the three benedictions of *Malchiyos*, *Zichronos*, and *Shoferos*, which are the central theme of the *Rosh Hashanah Mussaf* service.

(48) Rabbeinu Asher b. Yechiel (Rosh, 1250-1327), *Hilchos Rabbeinu Asher*, *Rosh Hashanah* 4:14.

(49) Rabbeinu Yitzchak b. Yehudah Ibn Ghayyas (Ritzag, 1038-1089).

(50) According to this opinion, the congregation recites the same seven-benediction *Amidah* for *Mussaf*, as we recite for *Shacharis*, *Minchah*, and *Ma'ariv*, while only the *Chazzan* recites the longer nine-benediction *Amidah*, which includes *Malchiyos*, *Zichronos*, and *Shoferos*.

(51) *Gaon* of Sura, 853-858 C.E.

(52) *Gaon* of Sura, 858-876 C.E.

(53) *Gaon* of Pumbedisa, 968-1006 C.E.

(54) *Gaon* of Pumbedisa, 1003-1038 C.E.

this custom was prevalent in the academies of both Sura and Pumbedisa, as well as throughout Bavel, during the entire Geonic *tekufah*.

It is intriguing to take note of the fact that, despite his own extensive citations from Geonic responsa to this effect, for his own part, the Ritz Ghayyas does not subscribe to this opinion.

> ואנו קבלנו מחכמים גדולים ובעלי הוראה ואנשי מעשה, שקבלו הם מחכמים שלפניהם, כגון רב שמואל הלוי שקבלו מרב חנוך וזקנים שבדור, הלכה למעשה, שאין מתפללין אלא תשע, וכן מורים ועושים.
>
> But we have a tradition from great Sages, halachic decisors, and righteous individuals, who received this tradition from the Sages who preceded them, such as Rav Shmuel haLevi,[55] who received it from Rav Chanoch[56] and the elders of the generation, that everyone must recite nine benedictions. And so, too, do we teach and practice.[57]

Citing these remarks of the Maharitz Ghayyas, the Ramban observes that while the remarks of the Maharitz are well-founded, it is nevertheless not proper to deviate from the halachic ruling and the custom of the *Geonim* concerning this matter.

> על כן יש לנו לקבל עדותם, שהגאונים קבלו מרבנן סבוראי, ורבנן סבוראי מרבנן אמוראי. ובישיבתן, על כסא של רב אשי הן יושבין, ובבית הכנסת שלו היו מתפללין.
>
> We should therefore accept the testimony [of the *Geonim*], for the *Geonim* received [the Mesorah] from the *Rabbanan Savorai,*[58] and the *Rabbanan Savorai* [received it] from the

(55) This refers to Rabbe Shmuel haNagid (993-1056), author of *Mavo haTalmud,* who was a disciple of Rabbe Chanoch.

(56) Rabbeinu Chanoch ben Rabbeinu Moshe (d. 4785) [1025 C.E.], whose father was one of the *Arba'ah Shevuyyim.*

(57) Rabbeinu Yitzchak b. Yehudah Ibn Ghayyas (1038-1089), as cited by the Rosh in *Rosh Hashanah* 4:14.

(58) As noted at length in *Legacy of Sinai,* Chap. 11, the *Rabbanan Savorai* [475-590 C.E.] succeeded the *Amoraim* of the Babylonian Talmud, and they were the link between the *tekufos* of the Babylonian *Amoraim* and the *Geonim.*

Amoraim.[59] It was in their Yeshivos, on the throne of Rav Ashi[60] that the *Geonim* sat, and it was in Rav Ashi's synagogue that they prayed.[61]

"The Custom of our Ancestors Is Torah!"

Despite this strong argument of the Ramban, the Rosh, for his own part, concurs with the ruling of the Ritz Ghayyas. He concludes with the following words.

וצריכין להתפלל כולן, דאם התפללו שבע יהיו כולן לבטלה, כיון שמחסר מן הברכה. ומנהג אבותינו תורה היא, ואין לשנות.

> It is necessary [for the entire congregation] to recite all [of the nine] benedictions, for if they recited [only] seven, they will all be in vain since they will thereby have deleted a portion of the text of the benediction. The custom of our ancestors is Torah;[62] [i.e. definitive halacha]. It may not be changed.[63]

In a discussion concerning a change in certain customs relating to the order of the blowing of the shofar during the Rosh Hashanah *Mussaf* service, Rabbeinu Zerachiah haLevi concludes with an interesting observation regarding our halacha concerning the recitation of either seven or nine benedictions during the Rosh Hashanah *Mussaf Amidah*.

(59) The Ramban is making reference here to the era of the Babylonian *Amoraim*, which came to a close with the death of Ravina II in the year 475 C.E., while the final redaction of the *Talmud Bavli* took place in 500 C.E., during the period of the earliest *Rabbanan Savorai*. See *Legacy of Sinai*, pp. 231 f, nn. 148-153.

(60) Rav Ashi was the sixth generation Babylonian *Amora* [371-427 C.E.], who presided over the compilation and redaction of the Babylonian Talmud. He is representative of the cumulative Torah wisdom of the *Amoraim* of the Babylonian Talmud.

(61) Rabbeinu Moshe b. Nachman (Ramban, 1194-1270), as cited by the Rosh in his *Hilchos Rabbeinu Asher, Rosh Hashanah* 4:14.

(62) See *Menachos* 20b, *Tosafos*, *s.v.* נפסל.

(63) *Hilchos Rabbeinu Asher* (Rabbeinu Asher b. Yechiel, 1250-1327), *Rosh Hashanah*, Chap. 4, halacha 14.

ואל תתמה על מה שאמרנו שנשתנו המנהגות בדורות האחרונים מדורות הראשונים. כי אני זוכר כי ראיתי בילדותי כל הצבור מתפללין במוספין שבע והש״ץ לבדו היה מתפלל תשע, והיו תולין מנהגן במנהגי ישיבות הגאונים, כי כן מצאו כתוב בספריהם, וכן תמצא בהלכות ה״ר יצחק בן גיאות ז״ל. ועכשו חזרו הכל להיות מתפללין תשע ברכות.

> Nor shall you wonder about what we said concerning a change in the customs between the earlier and later generations. For I recall that in my youth I saw the entire congregation reciting seven benedictions [during the Rosh Hashanah *Mussaf* service], while only the leader of the prayer service recited nine benedictions. In so doing, they relied upon the customs of the Yeshivos of the *Geonim*, for so did they find written in the books [of the *Geonim*], and so too will you find written in the halachos of Rabbeinu Yitzchak Ibn Ghayyas, of blessed memory. Yet now, everyone recites nine benedictions.[64]

What was at the root of this great controversy concerning the Rosh Hashanah *Mussaf* benedictions? Why, indeed, did the Spanish Jewish community change from its original custom of reciting seven benedictions, and begin to recite nine benedictions, instead, when their original custom was rooted, after all, upon the long-established traditions of the great academies of Sura and Pumbedisa, which were, as the Ramban observes, the direct spiritual heirs of the academies of Rav Ashi and all the great Babylonian *Amoraim*?[65]

Why was the Rosh so firm in his ruling that the entire congregation must recite all nine benedictions, saying, מנהג אבותינו תורה היא — "The custom of our ancestors is Torah"[66] — when this custom was, after all, in direct contradiction to the centuries-long tradition of the *Geonim* of Sura and Pumbedisa?

(64) *Sefer haMa'or* of Rabbeinu Zerachiah haLevi (Razah, 1125-1186), in his commentary on the Rif (Rabbeinu Yitzchak b. Yaakov Alfasi, 1013-1103), on *Rosh Hashanah* 34a (p. 11a in the Rif), *s.v.* ונשתנו המנהגות.

(65) *Supra*, n. 61, citing Ramban.

(66) *Supra*, n. 63, citing the Rosh, *Hilchos Asheri, Rosh Hashanah* 4:14.

The Babylonian and Eretz Yisroel Academies

In light of the remarks of Rabbi Yitzchak Isaac haLevi, this entire matter will become quite clear.

As noted above, the ancient Spanish or Sephardic Jewish community, had always relied completely upon the halachic decisions of the *Geonim* of the great Babylonian academies, to whom they turned with all their halachic queries. They therefore recited only seven benedictions during the congregational *Mussaf Amidah* of Rosh Hashanah, while only the cantor recited all nine benedictions, following the long-established tradition of the Babylonian academies. It was not until after Rabbeinu Moshe and his son, Rabbeinu Chanoch arrived in Cordoba, that all this began to change. Coming, as they did, not from the Babylonian academies, but from Bari, Italy, Rabbeinu Moshe and Rabbeinu Chanoch brought with them the traditions of the Italian School of Torah Study, which were based upon their own incisive approach of Talmudic analysis, as well as upon the traditions of the Eretz Yisroel academies.

As noted by Rabbeinu Tam, the Eretz Yisroel School had different traditions, particularly in regard to the arrangement of prayers and benedictions.[67] Hence, Rabbeinu Chanoch, who soon became the head of the Sephardic Torah community, established that all nine benedictions should be recited by the entire congregation, drawing upon the traditions of his own teachers in doing so. Slowly, but steadily, this tradition took precedence in all Sephardic communities, and became firmly entrenched and established as the prevailing custom in all synagogues.

Thus, Rabbeinu Zerachiah haLevi recalls that in his youth (i.e. during the early decades of the twelfth century), the seven-benediction custom prevailed, while in his later years (i.e. a half century later), the nine-benediction custom was prevalent in all Sephardic congregations.[68] As Rabbi haLevi points out, the fact that the Sephardic Jews accepted this new tradition only after many decades of careful deliberation, is indicative of their great reluctance to deviate from their earlier traditions without careful consideration of all halachic implications which this decision entailed.[69]

(67) *Supra*, n. 39, citing Rabbeinu Tam in his *Sefer haYashar*.

(68) *Supra*, n. 64, citing Rabbeinu Zerachiah haLevi.

(69) See *Doros haRishonim*, *op. cit.*, Vol. IV, p. 288, n. 43.

The Rosh, on the other hand, who was one of the leading exponents of the Ashkenazic School, was unequivocal in his opinion concerning this matter. For the Ashkenazic School, which was established in the eighth century by Rabbeinu Kalonymos of Lucca, Italy,[70] had long since traced its traditions to the Italian and Eretz Yisroel academies, as well as to their own incisive process of halachic derivation, which was, after all, a hallmark of the Italian School of Torah Study. Hence, the Rosh was entirely justified in stating unequivocally concerning this matter, מנהג אבותינו תורה היא, ואין לשנות — "The traditions of our ancestors are Torah, and they are not to be changed!"

Convergence of Two Great Schools

Having cited these and numerous other references which point to the existence of the two great schools of Torah study — the Babylonian School and the Eretz Yisroel-Italian School — and their subsequent convergence in the Spanish and North African communities, Rabbi haLevi concludes with the following remarks:

> Therefore, when these great Torah scholars arrived in Spain and Africa, they truly enlightened the earth with their glory, because they brought with them the analytical halachic process which penetrates mountains. This is the very same approach which we find before us in the words of Rashi and the *Tosafists,* that is, the analytical halachic process which was in their possession as a heritage from their ancestors from the very early days — a path which was well-trodden by the great Torah masters who preceded them. It was this approach which the *Arba'ah Shevuyyim* brought with them, and which had until then been lacking in Spain and Africa.
>
> Shortly after this event, we find that in Spain and in Western Europe, something new occurred. These two approaches converged, giving birth to a new approach, which combined the analytical halachic process with the Geonic traditions. When questions arose, these Torah scholars no longer relied solely upon the Geonic decisions, but returned, rather, to the source, clarifying the matter from the intricate deliberations of the Talmud itself. It was then that a new generation arose — that of Rav Shmuel

(70) *Supra,* n. 33; *Infra,* Chap. 2, nn. 34-35; Chap. 6, n. 2.

> haNagid and Rabbeinu Chananel, of Rav Yitzchak Alfasi and the Maharitz Ghayyas. These new [Torah] architects arose and they manifested wondrous Torah wisdom. Whereupon, the citadel of Torah was magnificently rebuilt, and the Torah was developed and clarified in all of its ramifications.[71]

The Guiding Hand of Divine Providence

Rabbi haLevi points out that this entire series of events, which culminated with the story of the *Arba'ah Shevuyyim*, was nothing less than an overt manifestation of the guiding hand of Divine Providence during this crucial transitional period in the process of Torah transmission.

> This was, in truth, one of the wondrous manifestations of Divine Providence, which provided each of these approaches [to Torah study] with its own place, each traveling its own road, until they converged and joined together. It is true that in France and Germany it was yet a while before the Geonic responsa and literature found its rightful place. . . . In the days of the early *Tosafists*, however, the words of the *Geonim* and of the Sephardic Torah scholars began to reach them ever more frequently, while on the other hand, all of the literature of the *Tosafists* was received in the Sephardic communities and was delved into carefully.

> Thus, this combined wealth of halachic literature was mutually clarified during the generations of Rabbeinu Zerachiah Ba'al haMa'or,[72] the Rambam,[73] the Ravad,[74] and all of their contemporaries, and after them, the Ramban,[75] the Rashba,[76] the Rosh,[77] and all the scholars of those subsequent generations. This was truly the developmental approach of Torah scholarship which was ordained

(71) *Doros haRishonim*, Vol. IV, *Tekufas haGeonim*, end Chap. 37, p. 295.

(72) The names cited here by Rabbi Y.I. haLevi span a period of over two hundred years of Torah transmission. Rabbeinu Zerachiah b. Yitzchak haLevi (Razah; Ba'al haMa'or, 1125-1186).

(73) Rabbeinu Moshe b. Maimon (Rambam; Maimonides, 1135-1204).

(74) Rabbeinu Avraham b. David of Posquires (Ravad III, Ba'al haHasagos, ca. 1120-1198).

(75) Rabbeinu Moshe b. Nachman (Ramban; Nachmanides, 1194-1270).

(76) Rabbeinu Shlomo b. Avraham Adres (Rashba, 1235-1310).

(77) Rabbeinu Asher b. Yechiel (haRosh, 1250-1327).

> by the Almighty, and this is a true manifestation of the wondrous guidance of Divine Providence in regard to all that bears upon a clarification of Torah knowledge.[78]

Thus it was that the Almighty, in His inscrutable wisdom, facilitated the transition of Torah from the great Babylonian academies during the era of Torah centralization, to the far-flung communities of the Diaspora, which extended from the communities of France and Germany to those of Spain and North Africa, as they embarked upon a new phase in the process of Torah transmission — the era of Torah decentralization.

The meteoric growth of Torah in these communities during the ensuing era was a truly remarkable phenomenon. Thousands of scholars made an impressive array of multi-faceted contributions to all branches of Torah scholarship and literature in these far-flung Jewish communities all over the world.

This clearly bears out the words of Rav Saadiah Gaon, which were cited at the very outset of this chapter.[79] The Almighty will never forsake His people and permit them to flounder about, without providing them with capable and dedicated Torah leadership. ולא תהיה עדת ה׳ כצאן אשר אין להם רועה — *"That the congregation of G-d might not be like sheep who have no shepherd."*[80]

Instead, in preparation for this most critical period in the history of Torah transmission, the Almighty sent great Torah scholars to distant corners of the exile — much as Yaakov Avinu had done when he sent Yehudah, להורות לפניו גושנה — to establish a Yeshiva and a Torah center in Goshen, as preparation for the Egyptian exile.[81] Like Yehudah, these great Torah scholars established the nuclei of Torah communities, which would develop great Yeshivos and flourishing citadels of Torah. These Yeshivos, in turn, would nurture and produce the great Torah scholars, who would become the future spiritual leaders of Israel in all of the most far-flung corners of the Diaspora.

(78) *Doros haRishonim,* Vol. IV, pp. 295 ff.

(79) See above, n. 1, citing Rabbeinu Saadiah Gaon, in his *Sefer haGalui.*

(80) See Numbers 27:17. These words were uttered by Moshe Rabbeinu when he learned of his own imminent demise, and he requested that the Almighty appoint a leader over Israel — אשר יצא לפניהם ואשר יבא לפניהם — *"who might lead them out and bring them in, that the congregation of the L-rd might not be like sheep who have no shepherd."*

(81) See Rashi, Genesis 46:28.

Table V
Early Sephardic Schools of Torah Scholarship
Post-Geonic Era – Early Rishonim

Tenth Century

NORTH AFRICA – EGYPT

Kairouan, N.A.

R. Chushiel b. Elchanan, d. end tenth c. [one of Arba'ah Shevuyyim]; **R. Chafetz b.Yatzliach,** 10th c., *Sefer haMitzvos; Sefer Chefetz;* **R. Yaakov of Kairouan** [corresponded with R. Sherira Gaon].

Son* and Disciples of R. Chushiel and of R. Hai Gaon

***R. Chananel b. Chushiel,** d.c. 1055 *Commentary on Talmud;* **R. Nissim b. Yaakov of Kairouan,** d.c. 1050, *Commentary on Talmud.*

Alexandria, Egypt

R. Shemariah b. Elchanan [one of Arba'ah Shevuyyim]; *His son and disciple,* **R. Elchanan.**

SPAIN

Early Sephardic School

R. Moshe b. Chanoch [one of Arba'ah Shevuyyim]; **R. Chisdai b. Yitzchak Ibn Shaprut,** c. 915-970 C.E. [Statesman and patron of Torah; communicated with King Joseph of Khazar Kingdom; **Early Hebrew Lexicographers** (see below) **].

Son* and Disciples of R. Moshe

***R. Chanoch b. Moshe,** d. 1025; **R. Yosef ibn Abitur,** ca. 940-1020.

Disciple of R. Chanoch

R. Shmuel haNagid, 993-1055 [Torah scholar, statesman and patron of Torah], *Mavo haTalmud, Hilchasa Gavrasa; His son,* **R. Yehosef haNagid,** d. 9 Teves, 1067

Tenth and Eleventh Centuries

SPAIN

Early Hebrew Lexicographers**

Menachem ibn Saruq, d. 970 C.E.; **Dunash b. Labrat haLevi; Yehudah ibn Chiyug,** fl. 1000; **Yonah ibn Janach,** 990-1050. See Table VIII.

Second Generation of Rabbanim: Five Yitzchaks

R. Yitzchak Alfasi (Rif), 1013-1103; **R. Yitzchak ibn Ghayyas,** 1038-1089; **R. Yitzchak al Bargeloni,** 1043-1100; **R. Yitzchak Albalia,** 1035-1094; **R. Yitzchak of Baghdad.** See Table VIII.

Closing Decades of the Geonic Era [968-1038 C.E.]

SURA

R. Shmuel b. Chofni [father-in-law of R. Hai Gaon], 997-1013, *Wrote many sefarim (not extant)*

R. Dosa b. R. Saadiah Gaon, 1013-1017

R. Yisroel b. R. Shmuel b. Chofni, 1017-1034

R. Azariah haKohen (b. R. Yisroel?), 1034-1038

R. Yitzchak–last Gaon of Sura, 1038-...

PUMBEDISA

R. Sherira Gaon b. R. Chanina Gaon, 968-1006, *Extensive responsa; Iggeres R.S.G.,* 986 [**Arba'ah Shevuyim,** c. 995]

R. Hai Gaon b. R. Sherira Gaon, 1003-1038, *Halachic codes; Extensive responsa: disciples worldwide;* **last major Gaon.**

Close of Geonic Era, 1038. *The Yeshivos remained open 150 years longer, but they no longer served as central Torah academies for the entire Golah.*

2

The Early Sephardic Torah Masters

„כי מבארי תצא תורה,
ודבר ה׳ מאוטורנטו״.
[ספר הישר לרבנו תם, דף צ׳]

"For out of Bari
shall the Law go forth,
And the word of G-d
from Otoronto."
[Sefer haYashar leRabbeinu Tam,
Resp. 46, p. 90, paraphrasing Isaiah 2:3;
See Text, p. 72.]

Early Sephardic Torah Masters: Rabbeinu Chanoch and Rabbeinu Chushiel

מעיד אני על עצמי שמים וארץ,
שאין כמוהו
מספרד עד ישיבת בבל.

I call the heavens and earth to testify
That there is none like Rabbe Chanoch
From Spain until the Babylonian Academies.

[Sefer haKabbalah le-haRavad;
See Text, p. 22.]

ונשמע אצלנו כי יש במקומכם
איש גדול בחכמה,
הר של תורה, בקי בחדרי הלכה,
מר רב חושיאל בן מר רב אלחנן שמו,
ינצרהו יוצרו.

We have heard that there is among you
A man of great wisdom, "a mountain of Torah,"
Who is erudite in the inner sanctums of halacha;
Mar Rav Chushiel ben Mar Rav Elchanan is his name,
May his Creator protect him.

[Letter of Rav Hai Gaon;
re. Rabbeinu Chushiel;
See Text, p. 67.]

2

The Early Sephardic Torah Masters

Rabbeinu Moshe and His Son, Rabbeinu Chanoch

Rabbe Moshe ben Chanoch and his son, Rabbe Chanoch after him, were the two great Torah luminaries who established the central Sephardic Yeshiva which breathed new life into the Spanish Jewish community, and which infused the Sephardic Torah community with a spirit of independence, dynamic growth, and vitality. These great Torah masters were the fountainhead of the Mesorah of the Spanish-Jewish community, and it was their great academy which set the stage for the "Golden Era" of Torah rebirth and spiritual renaissance for Sephardic Jewry.

The Ravad relates that when Rabbeinu Moshe ben Chanoch arrived in Cordoba, he was redeemed by the members of the Jewish community, who were entirely unaware that he was a great Torah scholar. One day, he entered the ancient synagogue, *Knesses haMidrash,* and seated himself unobtrusively in a corner, while the Rabbi, Rav Nasan haDayyan, was teaching Torah to a group of disciples. When Rav Nasan arrived at an intricate Talmudic passage, he was perplexed and found difficulty in clarifying it to his disciples. Whereupon, Rabbe Moshe volunteered a simple interpretation, and he likewise clarified many other questions which had been troubling both the teacher and his disciples. When Rav Nasan recognized the eminent stature of Rabbe Moshe, he quickly announced that he was prepared to abdicate his post as *dayyan* in favor of Rav Moshe, "for he is my teacher, and I am his disciple."[1]

When the great communal leader, Rav Chisdai Ibn Shaprut learned of the eminent stature of Rabbeinu Moshe ben Chanoch, he hastened to lend him his support, and helped him establish a Yeshiva of major importance in Cordoba — a Yeshiva which was destined to revitalize and elevate the standards of Torah study on the Iberian Peninsula for centuries to come.

Rabbeinu Moshe was succeeded by his son, Rabbeinu Chanoch, who, like his father before him, was also an illustrious Torah master. Rav Yosef Ibn Avitur, one of the outstanding *talmidim* of Rabbeinu Moshe, attempted to wrest leadership of the Yeshiva from Rabbe Chanoch immediately upon the death of Rav Chisdai, who was an ardent supporter — first of Rabbe Moshe, and then, of his son, Rabbe Chanoch. Rav Yosef Ibn Avitur, however, was not successful in his attempt to oust Rav Chanoch. In later years he repented concerning his dispute with Rav Chanoch and he told his supporters to discontinue their efforts in his behalf, for he would no longer attempt to assume Rav Chanoch's position as *Rosh haYeshiva* in Cordoba. Whereupon, Rav Yosef Ibn Avitur made the following significant remark concerning Rabbe Chanoch.

> מעיד אני על עצמי שמים וארץ שאין כמוהו מספרד עד ישיבת בבל.
>
> I call the heavens and earth to testify that there is none like him [like Rabbe Chanoch] from Spain until the Babylonian Academies.[2]

Rabbe Chanoch stood at the head of the Cordoban Yeshiva until his death in 1025. Many students flocked to his Yeshiva from far-flung Jewish communities. A portion of the extensive responsa he wrote to Jewish communities near and far, is included in collections of Geonic responsa, such as *Sha'arei Tzedek* and *Teshuvos Geonei Mizrach u-Ma'arav.*

(1) *Sefer haKabbalah le-haRavad, op. cit., s.v.* ובימיו היה ראש ישיבה במתא מחסיא.
(2) *Sefer haKabbalah le-haRavad, op. cit., s.v.* ושלח שליח אחד.

Rabbeinu Shmuel haNagid

Among the illustrious disciples of Rabbe Chanoch was Rav Shmuel ben Yosef haLevi haNagid (993-1055), author of the *Mavo haTalmud,* an introduction to the Talmud, which may be found at the end of tractate *Berachos,* in many editions of the *Shas.* He also wrote an erudite halachic work, *Hilchasa Gavrasa,* in which he drew extensively upon both the *Talmud Bavli* and the *Talmud Yerushalmi,* as well as upon the *She'iltos* of Rav Achai miShabcha (680-760 C.E.), and the halachic decisions of the *Geonim.* While this work is no longer extant, it was highly regarded by leading Talmudists of his day.

The Ravad writes that although Rav Shmuel was a great scholar and a distinguished *talmid chacham,* he was, nevertheless, a poor storekeeper during his early years. His store was adjacent to the residence of Ibn Alarif, who was the scribe and advisor of Emir Chabbus of Granada. When Ibn Alarif was away at the Emir's court, his servant would come from time to time to Rav Shmuel and ask him to send letters for her to her master, Ibn Alarif. When the Emir's scribe returned home, he asked who it was who had written such beautiful letters. He was informed that the Jew, Rav Shmuel haLevi, was the one who had written the letters. Ibn Alarif called upon Rav Shmuel and was amazed by his wisdom. Whereupon, Ibn Alarif engaged Rav Shmuel as his own personal secretary and advisor. He followed Rav Shmuel's advice faithfully in regard to all matters, and was thereupon successful in all his endeavors.

After a while, Ibn Alarif was taken mortally ill. Emir Chabbus came to visit him, and mentioned that with Ibn Alarif gone, he would no longer have anyone to advise him on important matters of State. Whereupon, Ibn Alarif informed the Emir that all the advice he had provided for the Emir was really not his own, at all, but was rather, that of the Jew, Rav Shmuel haNagid.

When Ibn Alarif died shortly thereafter, the Emir appointed Rav Shmuel haNagid as his personal secretary and he became the confidant and advisor of the Emir. It was not long before he was elevated to the post of Vizier.[3]

(3) *Sefer haKabbalah le-haRavad, s.v.* רב שמואל הלוי הנגיד.

Scholar, Statesman, Poet, Benefactor

Like Rav Chisdai Ibn Shaprut in his generation, Rav Shmuel used his highly influential position in the Emir's court and his great wealth to champion the cause of his fellow Jews everywhere, to support Torah scholars, and to further the cause of Torah dissemination.

The Ravad writes in his *Sefer haKabbalah,*

> Rav Shmuel haLevi was appointed to the post of Nagid, or Exilarch, in the year 4787 (1027 C.E.). He performed kindness for Israel in Spain, in Western Lands, in Africa, in Egypt, [in Bavel and in Eretz Yisroel], including the Babylonian academies and the Holy City. All Torah scholars in these lands benefited from his wealth. He bought many holy *sefarim,* and supported all Torah scholars in the aforementioned lands who wanted to devote all their time to Torah study.
>
> He engaged scribes to transcribe the Mishnah and the Talmud, and he gave these as gifts to scholars who were unable to purchase them of their own funds, both in the academies of Spain, as well as in all the aforementioned lands. Each year he supplied all the synagogues of Jerusalem with olive oil. He disseminated Torah extensively. He died at a ripe old age, after he had attained four crowns — the crown of Torah, the crown of greatness, the crown of the Levites, and the crown of a good name and of fine deeds, which surpasses them all.[4] He died in the year 4815 (1055).[5]

"A New Tongue"

The following narrative is indicative of the fine character traits of Rav Shmuel haNagid.

On one occasion, when the Emir was strolling with Rav Shmuel haNagid in Granada, a fanatical Moslem storekeeper emerged from his shop and began cursing Rav Shmuel haNagid. The Emir became very angry, and instructed Rav Shmuel haNagid

(4) See *Avos* 4:13; *Avos deRabbe Nasan* 41:1; *Yoma* 72b. See also *The Torah Ethic,* pp. 337 f.

(5) *Sefer haKabbalah le-haRavad, s.v.* ונסמך רב שמואל הלוי לנגיד.

to cut out the tongue of the Ishmaelite. Instead of following the Emir's instructions, Rav Shmuel sent the storekeeper a fine gift.

When the Emir and Rav Shmuel once again strolled past this store, the same man ran out and began to shower the Nagid with blessings. The Emir expressed amazement that Rav Shmuel had not carried out his instructions. Whereupon, Rav Shmuel replied, "But I have, your majesty. I have 'cut out' his evil tongue and I have replaced it with a good tongue, instead."[6]

Rav Shmuel was greatly revered and beloved by his fellow Jews, who bestowed upon him the title of Nagid, or Exilarch of the Jewish community, a title by which he is known to this day.

The following words, written by the poet, Yosef ben Chisdai, concerning his contemporary, Rav Shmuel haNagid, are indicative of the great reverence in which he was held.

אשר נקרא בהיכל קה פנימה;
שפתיו ישמרו דעת,
ומפיו תבוקש דת האלקים התמימה.

He was called to the inner sanctum of G-d's Temple;
His lips are the guardians of wisdom,
And from his mouth will the perfect law of G-d be sought.[7]

Vizier and Military Leader

Rav Shmuel haNagid was a highly versatile individual. He was a prolific poet and a great statesman. Even after Emir Chabbus' death, he remained Vizier of Granada and was the most influential advisor of Emir Chabbus' son and successor, Emir Vaddis, whose struggle for succession to the throne after his father's death, Rav Shmuel had championed. He was also an accomplished military leader. As Vizier and general of the army, he personally led the Emir's armies to numerous victories, over the course of some eighteen years (1038-1055).

(6) Margolios, *Encyclopedia leToledos Gedolei Yisroel* (Tel Aviv: Joshua Chachik Pub., 1969), Vol. IV, p. 1342.

(7) Rav Yosef b. Chisdai, as cited by Rabbi Yehudah Leib Maimon, in his biography, *Rabbe Moshe ben Maimon* (Jerusalem: Mosad haRav Kook, 1960), p. 11, n. 10; Cf. Malachi 2:7.

When Rav Shmuel haNagid died in 1055, he was succeeded by his son, Rav Yehosef haNagid. While Rav Yehosef shared many of his father's fine traits, his lack of humility caused him to have many enemies at court. It was not very long before he was assassinated, and many Jews of Granada were massacred at that time, as well. This date, 9 Teves, 4827 [1067], was a very tragic date for the Jewish community of Granada.[8]

Rabbeinu Shemariah in Alexandria

The second of the *Arba'ah Shevuyyim*, Rabbeinu Shemariah ben Elchanan, became the leader and the *Av Bes Din* of the Torah community of Alexandria, Egypt. Rav Shemariah studied in the Yeshiva of Pumbedisa. In a letter attributed to Rav Sherira Gaon, he is referred to as *Rosh Shuras Nehardea*, which was a title of great honor in the Yeshiva of Pumbedisa.[9]

Rabbeinu Shemariah's fame as an illustrious Torah scholar spread far and near. He was known as *Av Bes Din shel kol Yisroel* — "the head of the *Bes Din* of all Israel" — a title which vied with the position of central Torah authority of the *Geonim* themselves.[10] His son, Rav Elchanan, was also a great Torah scholar.

The Jewish community in Egypt enjoyed a degree of autonomy under the reign of the Fatima Dynasty. At the head of the Jewish community stood the *Nagid*, whose function was similar to that of the *Resh Galusa*, or the Babylonian Exilarch.

During the later years of Rabbeinu Shemariah, and during the Torah leadership of his son, Rav Elchanan, the Jewish community of Alexandria suffered greatly at the hands of the wicked Caliph Al Chakamim, who issued many cruel and evil decrees. With the Caliph's death in the year 1021, the cruel decrees were abolished, and the Jewish community once again enjoyed a degree of autonomy and an era of comparative peace and tranquility.

(8) *Sefer haKabbalah le-haRavad, s.v.* רב יהוסף הלוי.

(9) Some historians point to the fact that Rav Sherira Gaon referred to Rabbeinu Shemariah as *Rosh Shuras Nehardea*, as an indication that the origin of the *Arba'ah Shevuyyim* was in Bavel. In truth, however, this only indicates that Rav Shemariah studied in Bavel for an extended period of time, as did many individuals from a variety of far-flung countries. See *Legacy of Sinai*, p. 246, n. 39, citing Simchah Assaf, *Tekufas haGeonim veSafrusa*, Mordecai Margolios, ed. (Jerusalem: Mosad haRav Kook, 1955), p. 43.

(10) See Mordecai Margolios, *Encyclopedia, op. cit.*, Vol. IV, p. 1368.

The North African Torah Center

When Rabbeinu Chushiel b. Elchanan, the third of the *Arba'ah Shevuyyim*, arrived in North Africa, he was immediately appointed spiritual leader of the Kairouan Jewish community. The great Torah academy which he subsequently established in Kairouan, transformed the North African Jewish community into an important and vibrant independent Torah center for decades to come.[11]

Rabbeinu Chushiel was revered by the most outstanding Torah scholars of his generation. In a letter to Rabbeinu Yaakov ben Nissim of Kairouan, dated 1006, Rav Hai Gaon writes the following:

> ונשמע אצלנו כי יש במקומכם איש גדול בחכמה, הר של תורה, בקי בחדרי הלכה, מר רב חושיאל בן מר רב אלחנן שמו, ינצרהו יוצרו.
>
> We have heard that there is among you a man of great wisdom, "a mountain of Torah," who is erudite in the inner sanctums of halacha — Mar Rav Chushiel ben Mar Rav Elchanan is his name, may his Creator protect him.[12]

Because of his great stature as an outstanding Talmudist and a most illustrious Torah scholar, Rabbeinu Chushiel was given the honorary title of ראש בי רבנן — "Head of the Torah academy" — by the Babylonian Yeshivos.[13]

True to his origins as a student of the Italian-Eretz Yisroel Torah School, Rabbeinu Chushiel introduced into the North African Yeshivos the study of the *Talmud Yerushalmi*, alongside the Babylonian Talmud.

(11) See Chap. 1, n. 30.

(12) Letter of Rav Hai Gaon, as cited by Margolios, *Encyclopedia leToledos Gedolei Yisroel, op. cit.*, Vol. II, p. 474, *s.v.* בקירואן. These remarks clearly indicate that Rabbeinu Chushiel did not study in the Babylonian Yeshivos, for, had he done so, Rabbeinu Chushiel would have been known far more intimately by Rav Hai Gaon, who would have spoken of him in more familiar terms.

(13) Margolios, *Ibid.*

When Rabbeinu Chushiel passed away, Rav Shmuel haNagid sent a letter of condolence to his son, Rabbeinu Chananel, in which he writes that he had arranged for a eulogy gathering in Granada, in memory of Rabbeinu Chushiel. Paraphrasing a Talmudic eulogy, Rav Shmuel haNagid eulogized Rabbeinu Chushiel with the following words:

אי עניו אי חסיד, אי גדול באפרקיתא, ושם לו ברקת.

> Alas for the humble one; alas for the pious one. Alas for the great Torah giant of Africa, whose fame has spread even unto Tiberias.[14]

Rabbeinu Chananel ben Rabbeinu Chushiel

Rabbeinu Chushiel was the father and teacher of Rabbeinu Chananel (the Rach, d. 1055 C.E.), whose halachic decisions are cited extensively by the *Ba'alei haTosafos,* and by many other *Rishonim.* Rabbeinu Chushiel was also the teacher of Rabbeinu Nissim ben Yaakov of Kairouan (d. 1050 C.E.), whose father, Rabbeinu Yaakov ben Nissim of Kairouan, sent the questions concerning the redaction of the Mishnah to Rabbeinu Sherira Gaon, eliciting the famous *Iggeres Rabbeinu Sherira Gaon* in reply. The Ravad includes Rabbeinu Chananel and Rabbeinu Nissim, as well as Rabbeinu Shmuel haNagid, among the first generation of *Rabbanim,*[15] which may be regarded as the generation of transition between the *tekufos* of the *Geonim* and the early *Rishonim.*

Rabbeinu Chananel and Rabbeinu Nissim were also disciples of Rav Hai Gaon, with whom Rabbeinu Nissim subsequently maintained an extensive correspondence.[16]

Rabbeinu Chananel, who succeeded his father as head of the Kairouan Yeshiva, wrote an incisive commentary on three *sedarim* of the Talmud — *Mo'ed, Nashim,* and *Nezikin* — as well as on a few other tractates, such as *Berachos* and *Chullin.* His commentary on almost the entire *Seder Mo'ed* and part of *Seder Nezikin* is printed in the

(14) See *Megillah* 6a — אמר רבא מי איכא למ"ד רקת לאו טבריא היא.

(15) *Sefer haKabbalah le-haRavad, op. cit., s.v.* ורב חננאל עשיר גדול היה.

(16) Rav Chaim Michal [1792-1846], *Or haChaim* (Jerusalem: Mosad haRav Kook, 1965), Nos. 911 and 1131, pp. 416 and 560.

margin of the *Vilna Shas.* In his commentary on tractate *Avodah Zarah,* Rabbeinu Chananel cites the year 4813 (1053 C.E.) as the year during which the commentary on that particular tractate was being written.[17]

Following in the footsteps of his father before him, the Rach draws extensively in his commentary upon the *Talmud Yerushalmi,* as well as upon interpretations of the Babylonian *Geonim.* In many instances, Rabbeinu Chananel clarifies the correct textual reading in a complex *sugya,* or Talmudic discussion. He also wrote a commentary on the Torah, of which only fragments are still extant.

The Rach is regarded as a towering Torah master, and as one of the pillars of the generation of transition between the *tekufos* of the *Geonim* and the *Rishonim.* Because he also studied under Rav Hai Gaon, his works were instrumental in facilitating the process of Torah transmission from the great eastern Babylonian academies to the far-flung Jewish communities of the West.

Rabbeinu Nissim ben Yaakov of Kairouan

His great colleague, Rabbeinu Nissim, wrote a commentary on Talmud called *HaMafte'ach,* parts of which have been published in the margin of tractates *Berachos, Shabbos,* and *Eruvin,* in the *Vilna Shas,* under the name, Rav Nissim Gaon. He wrote a number of other important *sefarim,* as well, which were highly regarded by his contemporaries and which were used extensively by many *Rishonim,* but which are, unfortunately, no longer extant.

As long as his teacher, Rav Hai Gaon was alive, Rav Nissim turned to him with all his halachic queries. He also maintained extensive correspondence with Rav Shmuel haNagid, to whom Rabbeinu Nissim transmitted much of the Torah knowledge which he had learned from Rav Hai Gaon. Through their extensive correspondence, they established a close bond of friendship. It was not long before Rav Nissim's daughter was betrothed to Rav Yehosef, the son of Rav Shmuel haNagid. Rav Nissim traveled to Granada for his daughter's wedding.

Rabbeinu Nissim died in 1050 and his great colleague, Rabbeinu Chananel, died a few years later (ca. 1055).

(17) See Commentary of Rabbeinu Chananel to *Avodah Zarah* 9a. An emendation to the text renders the date as 4803 (1043 C.E.).

Some decades after the deaths of Rabbeinu Nissim and Rabbeinu Chananel, a fanatical Moslem sect gained power in North Africa. The Jewish community was devastated. Many Jews, including the remaining Torah scholars, were forced to flee to Spain, and Kairouan ceased to function as a great independent Torah center.

Origins of the Italian Jewish Community

At the time of the Second *Churban,* Titus carried off many thousands of Jewish captives to Rome. The Arch of Titus, which still stands in Rome today, was built to commemorate the fall of Jerusalem and the destruction of the Second Temple. The inner walls of the arch depict — in bas-relief — the *Menorah,* the *Shulchan,* and other sacred vessels of the Temple, being carried into captivity by Jewish slaves, under the harsh gaze of triumphant Romans. Together with these sacred vessels, tens of thousands of Jewish captives were sold as Roman slaves. After a while, many of these slaves were redeemed by their fellow Jews who had settled in Italy generations earlier, or they were otherwise set free by their Roman masters.

A similar scene was reenacted some sixty-five years later, when Bar Kochba's stronghold of Betar was destroyed by Hadrian's legions, in 135 C.E. Rivers of Jewish blood were spilled, and so many Jews were sold into slavery that the price of slaves dropped drastically because there was no longer much demand for Jewish slaves.[18] Many of these Jews, too, were redeemed by their coreligionists. Together with those Jews who had settled in Italy generations earlier, these Jews formed the nucleus of a thriving Torah community in Italy.

There was already a flourishing Torah center in Italy, more than two hundred years before the close of the Geonic era in the year 1038. During this early period, there were Talmudic academies in Rome and Lucca, headed by many great Torah scholars, which included members of the Kalonymos family, some of whom later migrated to France and Germany, where they likewise established great Torah centers.

(18) Cf. Deuteronomy 28:68 — והתמכרתם שם לאויביך לעבדים ולשפחות, ואין קונה — *"And you shall be sold there to your enemies as male and female slaves, and no one shall buy you."*

The following remark of the great twelfth century *Tosafist*, Rabbeinu Yaakov ben Meir [Rabbeinu Tam], is indicative of the great reverence and appreciation with which the French *Tosafists* regarded the Torah scholars of Italy. Paraphrasing the words of the Prophet Isaiah, Rabbeinu Tam writes concerning the Torah communities of Bari and Otoronto,

כי מבארי תצא תורה, ודבר ה׳ מאוטורנטו.

From out of Bari shall the Law go forth;
And the word of G-d from Otoronto.[19]

The Scroll of Achima'atz

The Scroll of Achima'atz, also known as *Megillas Achima'atz* or *Megillas Yuchsin*, is an epic poem written by Achima'atz ben Paltiel of Capua, Italy, in 1052. It describes, in Hebrew rhyme, the historical highlights and the genealogy of his own Italian family, during the course of the two centuries preceding the close of the Geonic era (840-1040 C.E.). Since the Achima'atz family consisted of many Italian Torah scholars and leading Jewish personalities, this poem provides us with an insight into the important events in the Italian Jewish community, during the course of the last two centuries of the Geonic era.

As this poem relates, a great Torah scholar, Rav Abu Aharon ben Shmuel haNasi of Bavel, arrived in Lucca, Italy in the early decades of the ninth century. He became acquainted there with Rabbe Moshe ben Kalonymos haZaken, who, together with his son, Rabbe Kalonymos, was later brought from Lucca, Italy to Mainz, Germany by the Carolingian Kings, to establish a Torah academy in Germany.

Rav Abu Aharon transmitted to Rav Moshe ben Kalonymos haZaken Kabbalistic secrets concerning *tefillah*, which remained in the Kalonymos family for many centuries, until the generation of Rabbe Yehudah heChasid (1150-1217), author of the *Sefer Chasidim* and leader of the thirteenth century *Chasidei Ashkenaz*, who was a

(19) *Sefer haYashar leRabbeinu Tam*, Responsum No. 46, p. 90, paraphrasing Isaiah 2:3 — כי מציון תצא תורה, ודבר ה׳ מירושלים.

direct descendant of the Kalonymos family.[20] Rav Abu Aharon moved on to Oria in Southern Italy, where he met, among other important Torah personalities, Reb Achima'atz the Elder.

It was the custom of Reb Achima'atz to make a thrice-annual pilgrimage to Jerusalem, where he studied Torah in the Eretz Yisroel academy, and gave very substantial charitable contributions. Rav Aharon also became acquainted with Rav Shephatiah ben Amitai, and taught his sons Torah. Rav Shephatiah wrote many liturgical poems, such as, ישראל נושע בה׳ תשועת עולמים, which is recited during the *Ne'ilah* service on Yom Kippur, and on the second day of the *Selichos* which precede the onset of Rosh Hashanah.[21]

Rav Shephatiah, who was also a doctor, saved the life of the daughter of Caesar Basil I (867-886 C.E.). In gratitude, the Byzantine Emperor, who was known for his vicious anti-Jewish decrees, granted a reprieve to five cities in Southern Italy, which were therefore excluded from the edict of compulsory conversion which he had decreed upon all Jews of the Byzantine Empire in 868 C.E. Prior to his death, Rav Shephatiah informed those who surrounded his bedside that at this very moment Emperor Basil died, and the Almighty summoned him to appear before Rav Shephatiah in the Heavenly Tribunal to answer the accusations of Rav Shephatiah for his cruel decrees. Shortly after, it was confirmed that at that very moment the cruel Byzantine Emperor had indeed died.

Rav Amitai ben Shephatiah took his father's place as *Rosh haYeshiva.* He also followed in his father's footsteps and composed liturgical poems, which include the famous *piyyut,* ה׳ ה׳ קל רחום וחנון, which is recited during the *Ne'ilah* service on Yom Kippur and on the fifth day of the Ten Days of Penitence.[22]

Accompanying Table VI [p. 73] provides an outline of some of the highlights of the Italian School of Torah Study.

(20) As cited by Rabbe Eliezer b. Kalonymos of Worms (*Ba'al haRoke'ach,* 1160-1237), in his rendition of the Kalonymos family tree, which is included in *Matzref leChachmah* by Joseph Delmedigo, Paris ms, No. 772, p. 60a; *Infra,* Chap. 6, n. 2.

(21) The name Shephatiah is spelled out in acrostic form at the beginning of each stanza. (See *Selichos le-Yom Sheni,* in the Ashkenazic tradition, and *le-Yom Shelishi,* in *Nusach Polin.)*

(22) Here, too, the name Amitai is spelled out in acrostic form at the beginning of each stanza.

Table VI
Early Italian Torah Masters
Post-Geonic Era–Rishonim

Ninth Century

Scroll of Achima'atz–An epic poem describing the historical highlights of two centuries of Torah transmission, 840-1040 C.E., by **Achima'atz b. Paltiel** of Capua, Italy, fl. 1052 C.E.

Rav Abu Aharon b. Shmuel of Bavel [transmitted Kabbalistic secrets to R. Moshe b. Kalonymos haZaken of Lucca, Italy]; **R. Moshe b. Kalonymos,** *and his sons,* **R. Kalonymos and R. Yekusiel,** settled in Mainz, Germany, at request of Carolingian Kings, 787 or 876 C.E. [ancestors of illustrious Kalonymos family, and of twelfth to thirteenth century Chasidei Ashkenaz].

Reb Achima'atz, the Elder [made thrice-annual pilgrimage to Jerusalem]; **R.Shephatiah b. Amitai,** 887 C.E., *wrote piyyutim,* ישראל נושע בהי תשועת עולמים; **R. Amitai b. Shephatiah,** fl. ca. 890 C.E., *Piyyutim,* אזכרה אלקים ואהמיה.

Tenth Century

Ten Italian Martyrs, 925 C.E., including **R. Chasdai, the Elder,** son-in-law of R. Shephatiah b. Amitai; **R. Shabbetai Donnolo,** *Chakmoni (commentary on Sefer Yetzirah).*

R. Yechiel [Rosh Yeshiva in Rome]; **R. Matzliach ibn Al-Bazak** [dayyan of Sicily, disciple of R. Hai Gaon]; **R. Moshe Kalfo of Bari; R. Moshe Paviah;** *Sons and disciples of R. Yechiel:* **R. Daniel, R. Avraham, and R. Nasan** [Roshei Yeshiva in Rome].

Eleventh Century

R. Nasan b.Yechiel of Rome, 1035-1106 [studied under R. Matzliach ibn Al-Bazak, R. Moshe Kalfo of Bari, and R. Moshe haDarshon of Narbonne], *The Aruch (a comprehensive Talmudic lexicon).*

Twelfth Century

R. Yitzchak b. MelchiZedek of Siponto, 1090-1160, *Commentary on Mishnah–Seder Zeraim, Taharos.*

Thirteenth Century

R. Yeshayah b. Mali, the Elder, of Trani, 1180-1260 [corresponded with R. Yitzchak Or Zaru'a], *Tosafos Rid (Talmud novellae), Sefer haMachri'a (incisive halachic analysis), and Sefer Psakim (definitive halacha on entire Shas);* **R. Yehudah b. Binyamin haRofei Anav** (R. Yehudah Ya'aleh, miMishpachas Anavim), 1215-1280, *Shitas Rivavan on Shekalim and Commentary on Rif.*

R. Yeshayah b. Eliyahu, the Younger, of Trani (Ri'az), fl. 1280 [grandson of R. Yeshayah the Elder], *Piskei Halachos (definitive halacha on almost entire Shas); Peirush Rabbe Yeshayah (on Shoftim and on Samuel I and II).*

R. Tzidkiyah b. Avraham haRofei Anav, fl. 1240, *Shibbolei haLeket (halachic anthology); His brother,* **R. Binyamin haRofei Anav,** *revised Sefer Yerei'im of the Re'em;* **R. Yechiel [b. Yekusiel Anav],** *Tanya Rabbasi, [Ma'alos haMiddos].*

The Ten Italian Martyrs

In the year 925 C.E., when the Arabs attacked Southern Italy, *Megillas Achima'atz* relates further, many Jews were put to death in Southern Italy. Included among them were ten great Torah Sages, one of whom was Rabbeinu Chasdai the Elder, son-in-law of Rav Shephatiah. Among his descendants were Reb Paltiel, and after him, his son, Reb Shmuel, both of whom were very wealthy and donated vast sums of money for worthy Torah causes, in Italy, Eretz Yisroel, and Bavel.[23]

The narrative concerning the ten Sages who were put to death in the year 925 is related also by Rav Shabbetai Donnolo, the physician, in the introduction to his sefer, *Chakmoni,* which is a commentary on the kabbalistic *Sefer haYetzirah* — "Book of Creation." Rav Shabbetai Donnolo was twelve years old when he had to flee for his life, during the massacres of 925.[24]

Thus, *Megillas Achima'atz,* together with a few sparce references in some other contemporary sources, provides an insight into the otherwise obscure chapter of the earliest beginnings of the vibrant Torah community which flourished in Italy more than two centuries before the close of the Geonic era.

It is not surprising, therefore, to find that important contributions were made by the Italian Torah community, which have left an indelible imprint upon later generations, and even upon various facets of our own approach to Torah study and Torah fulfillment, in our own generation.

Early Italian Torah Masters

Among the Torah leaders of Italy during the closing decades of the Geonic era was Rabbe Matzliach Ibn Al-Bazak, the *dayyan* of Sicily. Rav Matzliach traveled to Bavel to study Torah under Rav Hai Gaon in Pumbedisa. On his return trip he traveled through Spain, where he transmitted much of what he had learned from Rav Hai Gaon to Rav Shmuel haNagid in Granada.

(23) *Megillas Achima'atz,* written in 1052 by Achima'atz b. Paltiel, a descendant of Rabbe Amitai, the First.

(24) Reference is made to Rav Shabbatai and to his *sefer Chakmoni,* by Rashi, in *Eruvin* 56a, *s.v.* ואין בין תקופה לתקופה.

Other important Italian Torah leaders at this time were Rav Moshe Kalfo of Bari, Italy and Rav Moshe of Paviah. The *Rosh haYeshiva* in Rome at this time was Rabbeinu Yechiel (d. ca. 1070). During Rav Yechiel's tenure as *Rosh haYeshiva*, Rav Hai Gaon made an extensive visit to Rome, and many of the greatest Torah scholars of Europe traveled to Rome to study under Rav Hai Gaon. Among these was Rabbe Yitzchak ben Yehudah of Mainz, who was one of the three primary teachers of Rashi.[25]

Rabbe Yechiel was also among those who studied under Rav Hai Gaon at this time. His sons, Rav Daniel, Rav Avraham, and Rav Nasan, were all great Torah scholars. They succeeded their father as *Roshei Yeshiva* in the Yeshiva of Rome.

Rabbe Nasan ben Yechiel — the "Ba'al haAruch"

Rabbe Nasan ben Yechiel, also known as Rabbe Nasan of Rome, is remembered, in particular, for his *Sefer haAruch*, the earliest extant work of Italian Torah literature, which has been regarded by Torah scholars of all generations as an extremely important contribution to Talmudic literature. The *Aruch*, which Rav Nasan completed in 1101, is an alphabetical Talmudic lexicon, patterned after the *Aruch* of Rav Tzemach ben Paltoi, *Gaon* of Pumbedisa.[26] The *Aruch* of Rav Nasan, however, with thousands of entries, is far more comprehensive than that of his great predecessor, which contained three hundred entries.

The *Aruch* is far more than a dictionary. It clarifies, not only difficult Aramaic terms, but complex Talmudic concepts and passages as well, citing Geonic responsa, *She'iltos* of Rav Achai miShabcha, as well as the commentaries of Rabbeinu Chananel, Rabbeinu Nissim, and Rabbeinu Gershom Me'or haGolah, among others. The *Aruch* of Rav Nasan is cited often by the *Ba'alei haTosafos* and other *Rishonim*, who regarded it as a highly authoritative work and as a valuable source of alternate textual readings, corrigenda, and

(25) See Rashi, *Shabbos* 92a, *s.v.* שכן משא בני קהת, where Rashi cites an explanation which Rabbe Yitzchak b. Yehudah rendered in the name of Rav Hai Gaon.

(26) Rav Zemach b. Paltoi served as *Gaon* of Pumbedisa during the years 4631-4640 (871-880 C.E.). See *Legacy of Sinai*, p. 251.

emendations of the Talmudic and Midrashic texts, selections from which he cites extensively.[27] Comments and explanations of the *Aruch* are often cited alongside the margin of the *Gemara* in the *Vilna Shas*, in order to clarify difficult Talmudic terms and concepts.[28] Rashi also cites the *Aruch* upon occasion.[28a]

The *Aruch* served as the model and forerunner of all subsequent Talmudic lexicons. Attesting to its importance is the fact that numerous supplements and glosses have been written on it, beginning with the *Agur* of Rabbeinu Samuel Ibn Janach (12th c.).

In addition to having studied under his father, Rav Yechiel, Rav Nasan also studied under Rabbe Moshe haDarshon of Narbonne, and under Rav Matzliach ben Elijah Ibn Al-Bazak of Sicily, who studied, in turn, under Rav Hai Gaon. This will account for the numerous references in the *Aruch* to comments and explanations of Rav Hai Gaon, or to "the *Gaon*," as Rav Nasan often refers to this great Torah master. Rav Nasan also studied under Rabbeinu Moshe Kalfo of Bari, and Rabbeinu Moshe of Paviah.

Rav Nasan died in the year 1106, three years after Rabbeinu Yitzchak ben Yaakov Alfasi (Rif, d. 1103), and one year after Rabbeinu Shlomo Yitzchaki (Rashi, d. 1105).

Rabbeinu Yitzchak of Siponto

The first Italian commentator on the Mishnah was Rabbeinu Yitzchak ben Melchizedek of Siponto (ca. 1090-1160), a much younger contemporary of the *Ba'al haAruch*. He wrote a commentary on the two *sedarim* of Mishnah, *Zera'im* and *Taharos*, upon which there is no extant *Talmud Bavli*. His commentary on *Seder Zera'im* is included in the Romm Vilna edition of the Talmud, while excerpts from his commentary on *Seder Taharos* are cited by many other *Rishonim*. His commentary is distinguished for its clarity and its originality.

(27) See, for example, *Kesuvos* 6a, *Tosafos*, *s.v.* האי מסוכרייתא, where *Tosafos* cites the opinion of the *Aruch* regarding a complex and fundamental aspect of the laws of Shabbos.

(28) See, for example, *Chullin* 139b.

(28a) See *Shabbos* 13b, Rashi, *s.v.* האוכל אכל ראשון.

The Tosafos Rid

One of the most illustrious Italian Torah scholars of the early 13th century was Rabbeinu Yeshayah ben Mali of Trani (ca. 1180-1260). Rabbeinu Yeshayah corresponded with his great contemporary, Rabbeinu Yitzchak Or Zaru'a of Vienna (ca. 1180-1250). He was a prolific author. His *Tosafos Rid* on seventeen Talmudic tractates has been published in two volumes, while on tractates *Kesuvos* and *Gittin* his *Tosafos* are printed in the margin of the *Vilna Shas.* In addition, he wrote a work of *Pesakim,* or definitive halacha on the entire Talmud, as well as *Sefer haMachri'a,* which contains an incisive analysis of ninety-two halachos. He also wrote numerous other halachic works which are no longer extant.

Rabbeinu Yeshayah ben Mali is sometimes referred to as Rabbe Yeshayah haZaken — the Elder — to differentiate between him and his grandson, Rabbeinu Yeshayah ben Eliyahu of Trani. Rabbe Yeshayah the Younger (Ri'az, d.c. 1280), was the spiritual successor of his renowned grandfather. In his sefer, *Piskei Halachos,* he renders concise definitive halachic decisions on almost all tractates of the Babylonian Talmud. His halachos are cited extensively by Rabbeinu Yehoshua Boaz miBaruch (d. ca. 1554), in his glosses on the Rif, known as *Shiltei haGibborim.* It is believed that Rabbeinu Yeshayah the Younger (and not his grandfather), also wrote *Peirush Rabbeinu Yeshayah,* the commentary on Judges and Samuel which is included in the *Mikra'os Gedolos Tanach.*

The Anavim Family

Another important thirteenth century Italian scholar was Rabbeinu Yehudah ben Binyamin haRofei Anav (Rivavan, ca. 1215-1280), also known as Rabbeinu Yehudah Ya'aleh.[29] He was a descendant of the distinguished family of Anavim, one of the oldest Italian Jewish families, whose ancestors had been brought to Rome in bondage by Titus at the time of the Second *Churban* in 68 C.E. Rabbe Yehudah wrote a commentary on the Rif on many Talmudic tractates, as well as a commentary on the *Mishnayos* of tractate

(29) Cf. *Shoftim* 1:2 — ויאמר ד׳ יהודה יעלה. Others regard this as an acrostic representing the following words: יהודה ענו למשפחת הענוים. See Margolios, *Encyclopedia, op. cit.,* III:679.

Shekalim, which is included in the *Vilna Shas*, under the title, *Shitas Rivavan*. He corresponded with his great contemporary, Rabbeinu Avigdor ben Elijah haKohen of Vienna, whom the Maharam of Rothenburg addressed as "My teacher, Rabbeinu Avigdor, the *Kohen Gadol*."[30]

Rabbe Tzidkiyah Anav — "Shibolei haLeket"

One of the most outstanding disciples of Rabbe Yehudah Anav was his cousin, Rabbeinu Tzidkiyah ben Avraham haRofei Anav (fl. 1240). Rabbeinu Tzidkiyah was the author of the *Shibolei haLeket*, an extremely important halachic anthology, in which he cites extensively the words of the great French Torah masters, as well as the great Sephardic and Italian Torah masters. More than 230 great Torah scholars are cited by name in this work. In particular, Rabbeinu Tzidkiyah cites extensively the words of Rabbeinu Yeshayah ben Mali *(Tosafos Rid)*, as well as the responsa of Rabbeinu Avigdor haKohen of Vienna. With great humility, Rabbeinu Tzidkiyah writes, "We are like dwarfs riding upon the shoulders of giants . . . From their wisdom have we become wise, that we might be able to say all that we say here."[31] He corresponded extensively with his great contemporary, the Maharam of Rothenburg, who responded with great respect to his halachic questions.

Rabbe Tzidkiyah writes in his *Shibolei haLeket* that he has learned of the tragic burning of 24 wagonloads of the Talmud in Paris, during the week of *Parshas Chukas*, 1244. He writes that he has heard that the great scholars of France beseeched the Almighty that He might inform them whether this was, indeed, a Heavenly decree. The reply, which came in a dream to one of the great Sages, was דא גזירת אורייתא — "This is a Heavenly decree."[32]

His brother, Rabbe Binyamin ben Avraham haRofei Anav, was also a great Torah scholar. He wrote a number of halachic works which were lost, and are no longer extant. He also edited and

(30) See Margolios, *Encyclopedia, op. cit.,* Vol. I, p. 3.

(31) See Margolios, *Encyclopedia, op. cit.,* Vol. IV, p. 1222.

(32) These very words are the *Targum* of the verse זאת חקת התורה (Numbers 19:2). These are the opening words in *Parshas Chukas*, which was read during the week of the Talmud burning. While Rabbe Tzidkiyah cites the date as 1244, it is believed to have been a copyist's error, since the Paris Talmud burning took place in 1242. (See *Shibolei haLeket*, No. 263; Cf. *Later Rishonim*, Chap. 3, p. 93.)

revised the *Sefer Yere'im* of Rabbeinu Eliezer ben Shmuel of Metz (Re'em, 1115-1198). Rav Binyamin wrote a number of *piyyutim* and *selichos*, some of which are included in the text of the Italian *Machzor*. Some of these liturgical poems are of great historical significance, because they deal with a number of events which occurred in his time, and which affected the Jewish community adversely. Some of the events dealt with in his *piyyutim* are: (a) the vicious libelous charges of the rabid anti-Semite, Nicholas Donin [1239]; (b) the Talmud burning in Paris [1242]; (c) the Jewish badge [1257]; (d) desecration of *Sifrei Torah* and Jewish graves in Rome [1267].

Another member of the Anavim family and a disciple of Rav Yehudah Ya'aleh was Rabbe Yechiel, whose father's name is unknown to us. He wrote the sefer, *Tanya Rabbati*, also known as *Minhag Avos Sefer haTanya*, which he completed in Italy in 1314. This *sefer*, which contains *halachos* and *minhagim* which were prevalent in Italy, served as a sort of *Kitzur Shulchan Aruch* — an abridged *Shulchan Aruch* for many subsequent generations of Italian Jews. Rav Yechiel frequently cites Rav Yehudah, whom he refers to as *Chavivi* — "my beloved [teacher]."

Rav Yechiel is thought by some historians to also have been the author of the sefer, *Ma'alos haMiddos*, which was written by Rav Yechiel ben Yekusiel of the Anavim family.[33] The sefer, *Ma'alos haMiddos*, clarifies twenty-four important character traits and their negative counterparts. This popular mussar *sefer* was reprinted many times, in numerous editions.

The Benevolent Carolingian Kings

Some 250 years before the Geonic era came to a close, the important Torah centers of Germany, France, and Southern France, had already begun to emerge. Towards the close of the eighth century, the empire of Charles the Great (Charlemagne, 742-814), embraced all of Central Europe.

The Carolingian Kings, as Charlemagne and his descendants were known, were quick to recognize the value of their Jewish subjects. Due largely to their industriousness, their literacy, their

(33) See Rabbe Chaim Michal, *Or haChaim, op. cit.*, p. 487, No. 1059, who cites the sefer, *Korei haDoros* to this effect.

linguistic abilities, and their contacts with fellow Jews in every corner of the globe, the Jews were excellent merchants and tradesmen. As such, they were indispensable to the commercial growth and economic development of all the towns and villages in which they settled. Because they recognized the Jews as an asset to their kingdom, the Carolingian Kings often favored them and protected them, despite the protests of priests and other rabid anti-Semites.

It was, in fact, in this spirit that Charlemagne's son and successor, Louis the Pious (814-840), introduced the concept of the "Protected Jew." A Jew who received a "letter of protection" from the King, which spelled out his rights in detail, could not be molested or intimidated by anyone.

Moreover, Charlemagne had a great passion and an abiding appreciation for all forms of culture and learning. Hence, according to an ancient tradition, in 787 Charlemagne invited the great Torah scholars, Rabbe Moshe and his son, Rabbe Kalonymos of Lucca, Italy, to settle in Mainz, and to establish an academy there, in order to accommodate his Jewish subjects, so that they might no longer find it necessary to turn to the Babylonian academies for Torah guidance.[34] Some ten years later, Charlemagne requested that Caliph Harun Al-Rashid of Baghdad (764-809) send him an outstanding Torah scholar from the Babylonian academies. The Caliph complied with the Emperor's request, and sent the eminent Babylonian scholar, Rabbe Machir, who established a Torah center in Narbonne, Southern France.[35] The Emperor provided Rabbe Machir with a large tract of land, and granted him rights and privileges which were equal to those of the local bishop.

Both Rabbe Kalonymos and Rabbe Machir, in each of their respective communities, were the predecessors of a long line of scholars who were among the earliest Torah leaders in the rapidly growing Jewish communities of Germany and Northern France, as well as those of the Provence in Southern France.

It was not very long before both Germany and France emerged as important independent Torah centers of great world renown.

(34) Some attribute this tradition to his grandson, Charles the Bald, in 876 C.E. (*Infra*, Chap. 6, n. 2, re. the source of this tradition.)

(35) Rabbe Avraham Zacuto (1442-1515), *Sefer Yuchsin haShalem* (Jerusalem: Vardi, 1963), I, p. 84.

Rabbe Leontin: Colleagues and Disciples

After Rabbe Kalonymos, the earliest Torah scholar of Ashkenaz who is known to us, and who lived during the era of Rabbeinu Sherira Gaon (Pumbedisa, 968-1006), was Rabbe Yehudah ben Meir haKohen Leontin of Mainz, also known as Rabbe Sir Leon.[36] Rabbe Leontin was the primary teacher of Rabbeinu Gershom Me'or haGolah.

Among the colleagues of Rabbe Leontin was Rabbe Meshullam haGadol ben Kalonymos, originally of Lucca, Italy.[37] Rabbeinu Meshullam composed a *piyyut,* אמיץ כח, which is recited during the *Mussaf* service of Yom Kippur.[38]

Another colleague of Rabbe Leontin was Rabbe Shimon haGadol, who composed the song, ברוך ד׳ יום יום, which is included among our Shabbos afternoon *Zemiros.* His grandson, Rabbe Shimon ben Yosef, was the brother of Rashi's mother.[39]

Rav Amnon — "U'Nesaneh Tokef"

During this period, the well-known story regarding Rav Amnon, author of the moving liturgical poem, *"U'Nesaneh Tokef,"* took place.

Rav Amnon was a leader of the Jewish community of Mainz. The ruler of the principality and some of the nobles tried to prevail upon him to convert. He was persistent in his refusal to do so, but they grew ever more adamant. Once, in an unguarded moment, he tried to brush them aside with the casual remark, "I'll think it over

(36) Although very little is known about his early years, it is believed that Rabbe Leontin was a product of the Italian academies. See Margolios, *Encyclopedia leToledos Gedolei Yisroel, op. cit.,* III, p. 668.

(37) This would seem to indicate that Rabbe Kalonymos was brought to Mayence by Charles the Bald in 876, rather than by Charlemagne in 787. The Scroll of Achima'atz, which covers the two-hundred-year period, 840-1040, and which mentions that Rabbe Kalonymos was still in Italy at the beginning of that narrative, also seems to bear out this conclusion. (*Supra,* n. 34.)

(38) See *"Seder haAvodah"* of the Yom Kippur *Mussaf* service, *Nusach Ashkenaz.*

(39) For more information regarding Rabbe Leontin, his colleagues and his disciples, see beginning Chap. 6, nn. 3-7.

for three days." When he returned home, he was deeply grieved and agitated over the words he had uttered so carelessly. He would neither eat nor drink.

At the end of the three days, the ruler sent for him, and demanded his final answer.

"This is my answer," he replied. "Let my tongue which violated the sanctity of my firm belief in G-d, be cut out."

The ruler replied, "I will not cut out your tongue; but rather your feet, which did not bring you to me at the appointed time, will be cut off."

Whereupon, Rabbe Amnon's limbs were cut off and salt was placed upon his wounds. When Rabbe Amnon was returned home in his terrible agony, it was Rosh Hashanah. He asked his loved ones to bring him to the synagogue of Mainz, and he was placed alongside the cantor. Whereupon, Rabbe Amnon began to recite, in a loud, heartrending voice, the words of *"U'Nesaneh Tokef,"* which is one of the most beautiful, soul-stirring poems in the entire Jewish liturgy. As he concluded this magnificent *tefillah,* he passed on. With his very last breath, he had sanctified the Name of his Creator.

Three days later, Rabbe Amnon appeared in a dream to his colleague, Rabbe Kalonymos ben Rav Meshullam haGadol. He taught Rabbe Kalonymos the words of this *piyyut* and asked him to publicize them and to have the *"U'Nesaneh Tokef" tefillah* incorporated in the *tefillos* of Rosh Hashanah and Yom Kippur in all congregations of Israel. The *Rosh Yeshiva,* Rav Kalonymos, complied with the wishes of Rav Amnon.[40]

The Early Torah School of Southern France

While the origins and the traditions of the Torah School of Northern France were the same as those of Ashkenaz and the German cities of the Rhine, those of the Jewish communities of Southern France were entirely different. Whereas the Ashkenazic

(40) This story is related by Rabbe Ephraim b. Yaakov of Bonn (1133-c.1196), one of the greatest Torah scholars of his day. In his original account of this narrative, he relates that when Rav Amnon concluded reciting the words of ונתנה תקף, he disappeared, כי לקח אותו אלקים — *"For he was taken by G-d."* (Cf. Genesis 5:24.)

School traced its roots to Rabbe Kalonymos, who was brought to Mainz from Lucca, Italy, by Charlemagne in 787, the Torah community of Southern France found its origins in the Yeshiva which was established by Rabbe Machir in Narbonne. Brought as he was to Narbonne some ten years later by Charlemagne from Bavel, Rabbe Machir understandably had close ties with the Babylonian academies. He was succeeded by his descendants, Rabbe Todros and his sons, Rabbe Kalonymos haZaken, and Rav Moshe the Parnes, who was regarded as the *Nasi,* or Exilarch of the Jewish community.

Rabbe Moshe haDarshon of Narbonne

Rabbe Moshe haDarshon of Narbonne, contemporary of Rabbe Todros, was *Rosh Yeshiva* in Narbonne during the eleventh century. His Torah commentary is cited often by Rashi.

Among his students was Rabbe Nasan ben Yechiel of Rome (1035-1106), who cites Rabbe Moshe haDarshon frequently in his classic Aramaic lexicon, *HaAruch.* Rabbe Moshe haDarshon's son, Rabbe Yehudah, studied under Rabbeinu Gershom Me'or haGolah, as well as under his own father. Rabbe Yehudah was a teacher of Rav Menachem ben Chelbo, who was, in turn, the uncle and primary teacher of Rav Yosef Kara, author of an important commentary on *TaNaCh,* which is included in many current editions of the *Nvi'im.* The Kara family later moved to Northern France, where Rav Yosef was in close contact with Rashi, and Rashi's grandson, Rashbam, who refers to him as *Chaverenu* — "our colleague."

Rabbe Moshe haDarshon was one of the early leaders of the Provencal School of Torah Study.

Thus, well before the closing decades of the Geonic era brought the magnificent period of Torah centralization to a close, Torah centers had already begun to spring up in Italy, Spain, and North Africa, and even in the comparatively remote communities of Western Europe, in the German cities of the Rhine, in France, and in the cities of the Provence, in Southern France. These distant lands were now prepared to emerge as the new homes of Torah, and to usher in the era of the *Rishonim* and the period of Torah decentralization.

Tracing the Roots of European Anti-Semitism

As we trace the course of Torah transmission during the periods of the *Rishonim* and the *Acharonim,* we will find that during most of the 950 years since the close of the Geonic era until our own day, the Jew was persecuted relentlessly, and driven from land to land. When not actually expelled, he was the victim of insufferable persecution, ruthless pogroms, blood libels, inquisitions, ghettoization, financial exploitation, and human degradation.

While anti-Semitism surely existed sporadically even before the inception and rise of Christianity, it became far more widespread and increasingly virulent with the emergence of Christianity, based as it now was upon a foundation of theological doctrine.

Actually, anti-Semitism finds its earliest roots in the ongoing conflict between Yaakov and Esau concerning the sale of the birthright,[41] and the subsequent bestowal of the coveted blessings of Yitzchak upon Yaakov.[42] While this conflict remained in a semi-dormant state for many centuries, it was overtly renewed as a significant theological doctrine with the emergence of Christianity in the year 3760 (1 C.E.), sixty-eight years before the onset of the Second *Churban,* in 3828 (68 C.E.). Theologically, Christianity has always regarded itself as the rightful heir of the blessings and of the birthright which had, according to early church leaders, been "stolen" from their ancestor Esau, by Yaakov.[43]

It is little wonder, therefore, that with the adoption of Christianity as the official state religion of the Roman Empire by Constantine (307-337 C.E.), the situation of Jews in Eretz Yisroel, Spain, Italy, and all lands of the Roman Empire began to decline steadily.

Table VII [p. 85] provides an outline of major historical events, persecutions, expulsions, and other anti-Semitic incidents during the early medieval period.

(41) See Genesis 25:31-34.

(42) See Genesis, Chap. 27, and in particular, verse 41 — "*And Esau hated Yaakov because of the blessing wherewith his father had blessed him.*" See also Rashi, Genesis 33:4 — אר"ש בן יוחאי, הלכה היא בידוע שעשו שונא ליעקב.

(43) Cf. *Avodah Zarah* 11b, Rashi, *s.v.* אדם שלם; *s.v.* אדם חיגר; *s.v.* אחוה.

960-1555 C.E.: Persecutions and Exiles

Table VII
Major Events: Early Rishonim to Shulchan Aruch

960 C.E.	Arba'ah Shevuyyim narrative occurs
1038 C.E.	**Rav Hai Gaon dies; Close of Geonic Era; Rishonim Era begins**
1066	William of Normandy conquers England; Jewish settlement begins
1096	**First Crusade; Speyer, Worms, Mainz communities destroyed**
1147-1149	**Second Crusade**–2 Shavu'os 1147, Rabbeinu Tam persecuted
1148-1149	Fanatical Almohades conquer Andalusia [Spain]
1171 C.E.	Bloyes blood libel; Fast of 20 Sivan
1182-1198	Jews banished from Paris and environs by Philip II
1189	London Massacre during coronation of Richard the Lion-Hearted
1187-1192	**Third Crusade–March 17, 1190, York Massacres**
1197	22 Kislev, Family of R. Elazar Ba'al haRokeach slain, עקד"ה
13th c.	Reconquista–Gradual Christian reconquest of Andalusia
1202-1204	**Fourth Crusade**
1211	R. Shimshon miShantz and 300 scholars settle in Eretz Yisroel
1215	Pope Innocent III; Fourth Lateran council decrees Jewish badge
1217-1221	**Fifth Crusade; 1228-1229, Sixth Crusade**
1240	Talmud disputation; R. Yechiel of Paris vs. Apostate Nicolas Donin
1242	6 Parshas Chukas, 24 wagonloads of Talmud burned in Paris
1248-1250	**Seventh Crusade; 1270, Eighth Crusade**
1263	July 20, Barcelona disputation; Ramban vs. Apostate Pablo Christiani
1283	**Blood Libels:** Mainz, 1283; Munich, 1286; Oberwessel, 1288
1286	Maharam of Rothenburg imprisoned by Emperor Rudolph I
1290	**English Expulsion,** on Tish'ah be-Av, by Edward I; Readmitted by Cromwell, 1656
1298	**Rindfleisch Massacres;** R. Mordecai b. Hillel and family slain עקד"ה
1306-1315	French Jews expelled by Philip IV
1320	**Pastoureaux Crusade;** Widespread pogroms
1336-1337	**Armleder Massacres.** 110 Jewish communities destroyed.
1348-1349	**Black Death Massacres; European Jewry decimated,** 350 Jewish communities devastated
1391	**June 6, Spanish Pogroms begin;** Jewish communities devastated
1394	**French Expulsion,** by Charles VI; ["Unofficially" readmitted in 1657]
15th c.	**German Expulsions,** from many cities, throughout 15th century
1413-1414	Tortosa disputation. R. Yosef Albo, R. Astruc haLevi
1453	May 29, Mohammed II, the Conqueror, conquers Constantinople **Benevolent Ottoman reign begins**
1480	**Spanish Inquisition begins in September;** Continues over 300 years
1492	January 2, Ferdinand conquers Granada; Reconquista complete
1492	**Spanish Expulsion on Tish'ah be-Av,** by Ferdinand and Isabella; Over 200,000 Jews exiled. [Edict repealed, 1968]. Columbus voyage begins
1496-1497	**Portuguese Expulsion,** by Manuel I
1555	**Rav Yosef Caro completes Shulchan Aruch**

Sowing Seeds of Hatred

When the armies of Gallus, a Roman Caesar under Contantinus II (351-354 C.E.) overran Eretz Yisroel, the last Yeshiva in Sepphoris was completely destroyed.[44] It was at this time that the *Talmud Yerushalmi* came to a close, with the deaths of Rabbe Mana and Rabbe Yose bar Bun (ca. 350 C.E.), the last of the Palestinian *Amoraim*.[45] With the exception only of a brief respite during the reign of Julianus Caesar or Julianus "the Apostate" (361-363 C.E.),[46] — who was anti-Christian, and who was favorably inclined towards the Jews — the situation of the Jews continued to deteriorate during the reign of all subsequent Christian-Roman emperors.

Upon the death of Theodosius I (378-395 C.E.), when the Roman Empire was divided among his sons into the Eastern and Western Roman Empires, Eretz Yisroel came under the dominion of the Eastern emperors. The Jews were burdened by increasingly restrictive laws, and were expelled entirely from major urban centers. In 414 C.E., Bishop Cyril expelled the Jews from Alexandria, Egypt, a city which had been an important Jewish center for 700 years. In 418 C.E., Bishop Severus forcibly baptized all Jews on the island of Minorca.[47]

The Jews were deprived of all social status by increasingly degrading imperial decrees, which, as Theodosius II (408-450 C.E.) explains in his *Novellae* — a judicial code replete with anti-Jewish epithets — were enacted "in order that these dangerous sects [Jews and heretics], which are unmindful of our times, may not spread into life more freely."[48] In 429 C.E., Theodosius II terminated the

(44) See Rabbi Yitzchak Isaac haLevi Rabinowitz (1847-1914), *Doros haRishonim* (Frankfort-on-Maine, 1901-1918), Vol. III, p. 375.

(45) The date rendered here for the closing of the *Talmud Yerushalmi* follows the opinions of Rabbe Yitzchak Isaac haLevi (*Doros haRishonim* III, pp. 373-384), and Rabbi Aharon Heiman, *Toledos Tannaim veAmoraim* (Jerusalem: Kiryah Ne'emanah, 1964), p. 888. For other opinions, see *Legacy of Sinai*, p. 200, n. 87.

(46) It was at this time that Hillel the Second established the permanent Jewish calendar (see *Legacy of Sinai*, p. 201, n. 88).

(47) See Rosemary Radford Ruether, *Faith and Fratricide: The Theological Roots of Anti-Semitism* (New York: Seabury Press, 1974), p. 194.

(48) Novellae III of Emperor Theodosius II, January 31, 438 C.E. (see *Encyclopedia Judaica*, Vol. III, p. 654).

Patriarchate — the *Nesi'us* dynasty which dated back over 450 years, to Hillel haZaken, in the year 32 B.C.E.[49]

Under the Byzantine emperors, who succeeded the East Roman emperors, the enactment of anti-Jewish legislation continued long after the fall of the Western Roman Empire in 476 C.E. The *Corpus Juris Civilis,* known as the Justinian Code, issued by Justinian in 534 C.E., further depressed the status of the Jews by depriving them of their civil and religious rights, while extending their restrictions, and interfering in synagogue affairs.[50] Later emperors decreed forced baptismal conversion upon the Jews. Heraclitus (632 C.E.), Leo III (721 C.E.), Basil I (c.870 C.E.), his son, Leo IV, and Romanus I (932 C.E.), enacted laws ordering all Jews to become Christians.[51] In 1215, the Jew was further degraded when the Fourth Lateran Council ordained that all Jews must wear a distinctive badge on their clothing.

Diabolical Underpinnings of the Holocaust

Moreover, a major portion of the anti-Semitism which ran rampant in subsequent centuries throughout the European continent, may be attributed to the vicious anti-Jewish diatribes of the early Church leaders. Some examples of the virulent anti-Jewish writings of the early Church leaders are: Tertullian's *Adversos Judaeos; Demonstrations Against the Jews,* by Aphrahat, the Syrian; *The Expository Treatise Against the Jews,* attributed to Hyppolytus; *Contra Judaeos,* by the Arian bishop Maximinus; *Adversos Judaeos,* by Augustine; and the hate-filled *Eight Homilies Against the Jews,* which John Chrysostom of the "golden tongue," preached in Antioch (386-388 C.E.).[52]

(49) See *Legacy of Sinai,* p. 147, for names of the fourteen generations of *Nesi'im,* during the four centuries from Hillel haZaken (32 B.C.E.—8 C.E.) until Hillel haSheni (fl. 360 C.E.).

(50) The *Shema* was added secretly to the *Mussaf Kedushah* — an innovation which is retained in our *Mussaf* service to this very day — because Justinian prohibited its recital during the morning services. See Simcha Assaf, *Tekufas haGeonim ve-Safrusah* (Jerusalem: Mosad haRav Kook, 1955), p. 74.

(51) See Ruether, *op. cit.,* pp. 195-198.

(52) See Ruether, *op. cit.,* p. 119, for names of other anti-Semitic diatribes by the early Church leaders.

There can be little doubt that the virulent anti-Semitism and the vicious persecutions, pogroms, blood libels and inquisitions, which prevailed throughout the European continent during the ensuing sixteen centuries — including the diabolical underpinnings of the terrible Holocaust itself — found their roots in the anti-Semitic legislation of this early Christian period, and in the completely dehumanizing anti-Jewish diatribes of these early Church leaders.[53]

It is, of course, true that the Torah Jew was always possessed of a remarkable degree of tenacity and a unique ability to rise above his surroundings and his suffering, to function and develop spiritually despite his handicaps, and even to produce classic works of Torah literature under the most trying circumstances. Nevertheless, it is certainly also true that Jewish communal spiritual life, as well as the literary productivity of the Torah Jew, were affected adversely by adverse conditions.

It is for this reason, for example, that the *Talmud Bavli,* which was compiled under the relatively stable and tranquil conditions which were prevalent in Bavel at that time,[54] is far more clear and lucid than the *Talmud Yerushalmi,* which was compiled under the far more turbulent and unstable circumstances of the Palestinian Jewish community, which was under the oppressive rule of the Christian-Byzantine emperors. It was for this reason, too, that the *Talmud Bavli* was redacted in the flourishing Torah community of

(53) For further clarification and substantiation of this thesis, see Ruether, *op. cit.*; See also Malcolm Hay, *Thy Brother's Blood: The Roots of Christian Anti-Semitism* (New York: Hart Publishing, 1975).

(54) See, for example, the words of *Chazal* regarding Rav Ashi who was the primary architect of the *Talmud Bavli,* which are indicative of the prosperity and tranquility of the Torah community during this era.

מימות רבי עד רב אשי לא מצינו תורה וגדולה במקום אחד.

> From the days of Rabbeinu haKadosh [who compiled the Mishnah], until the days of Rav Ashi, we have not found a combination of Torah greatness and worldly greatness combined within one individual. (*Gittin* 59a.)

Bavel in the year 500 C.E., about 150 years after the intolerable persecutions of the Christian-Byzantine emperors brought the Palestinian Talmud, and with it the era of the Palestinian *Amoraim*, to a premature and hasty close.[55]

A Summation: Five Centuries of Torah Leadership

Despite the seemingly endless trail of pain and suffering which followed in the wake of the Crusades, the inquisitions, the blood libels, the expulsions, and the interminable wandering from land to land in quest of a temporary haven and refuge, the far-flung Jewish communities of the Middle Ages produced some of the most brilliant lights ever to have illuminated the Jewish horizon.

> The Rif,[56] the Ri Migash,[57] Rabbeinu Bachya Ibn Paquda,[58] Rabbe Yehudah haLevi,[59] the first Ravad,[60] the Rambam,[61] the Ravad of Posquires,[62] Rabbe Zerachiah Ba'al haMa'or,[63]

(55) See *Legacy of Sinai*, p. 200, n. 97, for various opinions regarding the date of the final redaction of the *Talmud Yerushalmi*. (*Supra*, n. 45.) To be sure, although the Patriarchate was discontinued by Theodosius II in 429 C.E., an Eretz Yisroel Yeshiva was re-established near the end of the fifth century, at which time some of the Eretz Yisroel Midrashic works, such as *Midrash Rabbah* and *Midrash Tanchuma*, were compiled.

(56) Rif [R. Yitzchak Alfasi], *Hilchos Rav Alfas* (1013-1103). [Ch. 3, n. 14.] Note: The names listed here are not given in strict chronological order. Rather, with but a few exceptions, they follow the order in which these names appear in the book, where these individuals are discussed under their respective Schools of Torah Study.

(57) Ri Migash [R. Yosef b. Meir haLevi], *Talmud novellae* (1077-1141). [Ch. 3, n. 59]

(58) R. Bachya Ibn Paquda, *Chovos haLevavos* (fl. 1080). [Ch. 3, n. 79]

(59) R. Yehudah haLevi, *Kuzari* (1075-1141). [Ch. 3, n. 87]

(60) Ravad I [R. Avraham Ibn Daud haLevi], *Sefer haKabbalah* (1110-1180). [Ch. 3, n. 109]

(61) Rambam [R. Moshe b. Maimon], *Mishneh Torah* (1135-1204). [Ch. 4, n. 2]

(62) Ravad III of Posquires, *Ba'al haHasagos* (1120-1198). [Ch. 5, n. 13]

(63) R. Zerachiah haLevi, *Ba'al haMa'or* (1125-1186). [Ch. 5, n. 52]

Rabbeinu Gershom Me'or haGolah,[64] Rashi,[65] his disciples and grandsons, Rashbam,[66] Rabbeinu Tam,[67] Rabbe Yaakov of Orleans,[68] Ri haZaken,[69] Rabbe Shimshon miShantz,[70] Rabbe Elazar Ba'al haRokeach,[71] Rabbe Yechiel of Paris,[72] Rabbe Moshe of Coucy,[73] the Tosafist School,[74] the Ramban,[75] Rabbeinu Yonah heChasid,[76] the Rashba,[77] Maharam Baruch,[78] the Mordechai,[79] the Rosh,[80] Rabbe Yaakov Ba'al haTurim,[81] Rabbe Aharon haKohen of Lunel,[82] Rabbe Alexander Suslin Ba'al haAgudah,[83] the Maharil,[84] Rabbe Yisroel Bruna,[85] the

(64) R. Gershom Me'or haGolah, *Commentary on Shas* (965-1040). [Ch. 6, n. 7]

(65) Rashi [R. Shlomo Yitzchaki], *Com. on Shas* (1040-1105). [Ch. 6, n. 43]

(66) Rashbam [R. Shmuel b. Meir], *Commentary on Bava Basra* (1080-1158). [See *Masters of the Mesorah: Later Rishonim*, Ch. 1, n. 13]

(67) Rabbeinu Tam [Rabbe Yaakov b. Meir], *Tosafos* (1100-1171). [*Later Rishonim*, Ch. 1, n. 27]

(68) R. Yaakov of Orleans [disciple of Rabbeinu Tam], *Tosafos* (d. 1190). [*Later Rishonim*, Ch. 1, n. 64]

(69) Ri haZaken [R. Yitzchak b. Shmuel of Dampierre], *Tosafos* (d. c. 1190). [*Later Rishonim*, Ch. 1, n. 98]

(70) R. Shimshon b. Avraham of Sens, *Tosafos Shantz* (d. 1215). [*Later Rishonim*, Ch. 2, n. 14]

(71) R. Elazar b. Yehudah of Worms, *Sefer haRokeach* (1160-1237). [*Later Rishonim*, Ch. 2, n. 80]

(72) R. Yechiel b. Yosef of Paris, *Viku'ach* (d. 1268). [*Later Rishonim*, Ch. 3, n. 5]

(73) R. Moshe of Coucy, *SeMaG* (d. 1260). [*Later Rishonim*, Ch. 3, n. 19]

(74) *Ba'alei haTosafos* [French Tosafists], *Tosafos* (1100-1300). [*Ibid.*, Chs. 1-3]

(75) Ramban [R. Moshe b. Nachman], *Torah novellae* (1194-1270). [*Later Rishonim*, Ch. 4, n. 14]

(76) R. Yonah b. Avraham Gerondi, *Sha'arei Teshuvah* (1200-1263). [*Later Rishonim*, Ch. 4, n. 84]

(77) Rashba [R. Shlomo b. Avraham Adres], *Responsa* (1235-1310). [*Later Rishonim*, Ch. 5, n. 1]

(78) R. Meir b. Baruch of Rothenburg, *Responsa* (1220-1293). [*Later Rishonim*, Ch. 3, n. 53]

(79) R. Mordecai b. Hillel, *The Mordecai* (d. 1298). [*Later Rishonim*, Ch. 3, n. 90]

(80) Rosh [R. Asher b. Yechiel], *Hilchos Rabbeinu Asher* (1250-1327). [*Later Rishonim*, Ch. 5, n. 32]

(81) R. Yaakov b. Asher, *Arba'ah Turim* (1270-1343). [*Ibid.*, Ch. 5, n. 86]

(82) R. Aharon haKohen of Lunel, *Orchos Chaim* (fl. 1306). [Ch. 5, n. 111]

(83) R. Alexander Suslin, *Agudah* (d. 1349). [*Later Rishonim*, Ch. 3, n. 92]

(84) Maharil [R. Yaakov Moelin], *Responsa* (1360-1427). [*Ibid.*, Ch. 3, n. 96]

(85) R. Yisroel Bruna, *Responsa* (d.c. 1476). [*Later Rishonim*, Ch. 3, after n. 103]

Ran,[86] the Rivash,[87] Rabbe Chasdai Crescas,[88] Rabbe Don Yitzchak Abrabanel,[89] Rabbe David Ibn Zimra,[90] Rabbeinu Yosef Caro,[91] and the Rama.[92]

These are only some of the thousands of illustrious Torah luminaries who enriched Torah literature for all centuries to come with their multi-faceted contributions to all branches of Torah scholarhip.

Prolific Torah Activity . . .

This remarkably prolific, creative Torah activity is all the more amazing when we realize that many of these individuals suffered persecution personally. As we shall see in subsequent chapters, of the thirty-seven illustrious Torah personalities mentioned here, at least thirty-one experienced personal suffering, tragedy, homelessness, wandering, and exile, as they were driven from land to land.

. . . Amidst a Vale of Tears

In the year 1088, the Rif was compelled to flee from North Africa to Spain.[93] Several years after the death of the Ri Migash in 1141, his son, Meir, had to flee Southern Spain, together with many thousands of his fellow Jews, before the merciless onslaught of the fanatical Almohades.[94] In 1141, Rabbe Yehudah HaLevi died at the hands of an Arab, as he prostrated himself at the Temple site

(86) Ran [R. Nissim b. Reuven of Gerondi], *Rif Commentary* (d. 1380). [*Masters of the Mesorah: Later Rishonim*, Ch. 6, n. 13]

(87) Rivash [R. Yitzchak b. Sheshes Perfet], *Responsa* (1326-1407). [*Later Rishonim*, Ch. 6, n. 39]

(88) R. Chasdai Crescas, *Or HaShem* (1340-1412). [*Ibid.*, Ch. 6, n. 46]

(89) R. Don Yitzchak Abrabanel, *TaNaCh Commentary* (1437-1508), [*Later Rishonim*, Ch. 7, n. 1, and between nn. 8-9]

(90) R. David Ibn Avi Zimra [Radvaz], *Rambam Commentary* (1480-1574), [*Later Rishonim*, Ch. 7, n. 11]

(91) R. Yosef Caro, *Shulchan Aruch* (1488-1575), [*Ibid.*, Ch. 7, nn. 16-50]

(92) Rama [R. Moshe Isserles], *Mapah* (1530-1572), [*Later Rishonim*, Ch. 3, n. 108; Ch. 7, n. 51]

(93) The Rif — see Chap. 3, after n. 13.

(94) The Ri Migash — see Chap. 3, at n. 68.

upon his arrival in Jerusalem.[95] Rabbe Avraham Ibn Daud, the first Ravad, died *al kiddush HaShem* in Toledo, in 1180.[96] The Rambam wrote his Mishnah commentary while he was wandering on the seas in quest of a haven and a refuge — an experience which was to have a detrimental effect on his health for the rest of his life.[97] The Ravad of Posquires was imprisoned on spurious charges by the governor of his principality.[98]

Rabbeinu Gershom Me'or haGolah suffered greatly at the hands of the Church.[99] Rashi, in his declining years, witnessed the ravages of the First Crusade, in 1096.[100] Rabbeinu Tam very nearly lost his life at the hands of the Crusaders during the Second Crusade, in the year 1147.[101] Rabbe Yaakov of Orleans was martyred when a pogrom broke out during the coronation of Richard the Lion-Hearted in London, in 1189.[102] Rabbe Elchanan, the son of the Ri haZaken, was put to death *al yichud HaShem*, in 1184.[103] Because of the terrible excesses of the Crusades, in the year 1211, Rabbe Shimshon of Shantz, together with a group of three hundred Torah scholars, emigrated to Eretz Yisroel, despite the many hardships which this entailed.[104] In 1197, Rabbe Elazar Ba'al haRokeach, and his son, Jacob, were beaten mercilessly, while his wife and two daughters were slain before their eyes.[105] Rabbe Yechiel of Paris, together with Rabbe Moshe of Coucy Ba'al haSeMaG, participated in the debate with Nicolas Donin and other Church officials, which resulted in the burning of twenty-four wagonloads of the Talmud, in 1242.[106] Many other *Ba'alei haTosafos*

(95) Rabbe Yehudah haLevi — see Chap. 3, at n. 102.
(96) Rabbe Avraham Ibn Daud — see Chap. 3, after n. 115.
(97) Rambam — see Chap. 4, at n. 7; nn. 75-76.
(98) Ravad III of Posquires — see Chap. 5, at n. 42.
(99) Rabbeinu Gershom Me'or haGolah — see Chap. 5, at nn. 22-25.
(100) Rashi — see Chap. 5, at nn. 104-109.
(101) Rabbeinu Tam — see *Later Rishonim*, Chap. 1, at n. 40
(102) Rabbe Yaakov of Orleans — see *Later Rishonim*, Chap. 1 bet. nn. 64-65.
(103) Rabbe Elchanan b. Ri haZaken — see *ibid.*, Chap. 1, at n. 131.
(104) Rash miShantz — see *ibid.*, Ch. 2, at n. 82.
(105) Rabbe Elazar Ba'al haRokeach — see *ibid.*, Chap. 2, at nn. 84-88.
(106) Rabbe Yechiel of Paris and SeMaG — see *ibid.*, Chap. 3, at nn. 6-18.

suffered persecution and martyrdom at the hands of their Christian neighbors, and the Crusaders.[107]

The Ramban had to flee to Eretz Yisroel after his great debate with the apostate, Pablo, in Aragon, in the year 1263.[108] Rabbeinu Yonah was devastated and heartbroken when, first the *sefarim* of the Rambam, and then the Talmud, were burned in Paris in 1242.[109] In 1286, the Maharam of Rothenburg was imprisoned by Kaisar Rudolph I of Hapsburg.[110] In 1298, his disciple, Rabbe Mordechai ben Hillel, died as a martyr during the Rindfleisch massacres.[111] Another great disciple, the Rosh, was compelled to flee to Spain in 1303,[112] together with his son, Rabbe Yaakov Ba'al haTurim.[113] The Provencal scholar, Rabbe Aharon haKohen of Lunel, went into exile with thousands of his fellow Jews, after the expulsion of Jews from France in 1306.[114] Rabbe Alexander Suslin, Ba'al haAgudah, died *al kiddush HaShem* in Erfurt, during the Black Death pogroms of 1349.[115] Rabbe Yaakov Moelin (Maharil), the greatest Torah scholar of Ashkenaz in his day, decreed a consecutive three-day fast to save the Jews of Germany from imminent annihilation,

(107) For example, during the terrible massacres of the Jewish community of York, England, in 1190, the *Tosafist*, Rabbe Yom Tov b. Yitzchak of Joygny, (cited in *Yoma* 48a, Tosafos, *s.v.* ומי as Rabbe Yom Tov haKadosh), and Rabbe Eliyahu of York, (cited in Tosafos, *Zevachim* 14b, *s.v.* והרי as Rabbe Eliyahu me'Avrevika [York] haKadosh), died *al kiddush HaShem*, together with hundreds of fellow Jews. (See Ephraim Urbach, *Ba'alei haTosafos* [Jerusalem: Mosad Bialik, 1968], pp. 124 f; 511; See *Later Rishonim*, Chap. 1, nn. 65-70.)

Re. *Gezeros Tasnu* (1096), see *Later Rishonim*, Chap. 3, nn. 7-10; Re. Blois blood libel of 1171, see *Later Rishonim*, Chap. 1, nn. 42-44; Re. French expulsion of 1180-82, see *Later Rishonim*, Chap. 1, at n. 59; Re. Rabbe Petter haKadosh, see *Later Rishonim*, Chap. 1, n. 97; Re. expulsions from France (1182; 1306; 1394), England (1290), Germany (throughout 15th century), see *Later Rishonim*, beginning Chap. 2; Re. Speyer blood libel of 1186, see *Later Rishonim*, Chap. 2, n. 72; Re. Rabbe Uri (1216), see *Later Rishonim*, Chap. 2, n. 75.

(108) Ramban — see *Later Rishonim*, Chap. 4, at nn. 75-78.

(109) Rabbeinu Yonah — see *Later Rishonim*, Chap. 4, at nn. 85-88.

(110) Maharam Baruch — see *Later Rishonim*, Chap. 3, at nn. 72-77.

(111) Rabbeinu Mordecai — see *Later Rishonim*, Chap. 3, at n. 90.

(112) Rosh — see *Later Rishonim*, Chap. 5, at n. 35.

(113) Rabbeinu Yaakov Ba'al haTurim — see *Later Rishonim*, Chap. 5, at n. 86.

(114) Rabbe Aharon haKohen miLunel — see Chap. 5, at n. 111.

(115) Ba'al haAgudah — see *Later Rishonim*, Chap. 3, at n. 93.

in 1421.[116] Rabbe Yisroel Bruna barely escaped being burned at the stake, when an apostate brought a blood libel accusation against him, in 1470.[117]

In Spain, Rabbe Chasdai Crescas, a disciple of the Ran, lost his only son, who died *al kiddush HaShem* during the pogroms of 1391, in Seville.[118] The Rivash was compelled to flee at that time from Spain to Algiers.[119] Rabbe Don Yitzchak Abrabanel led his people into exile during the great Spanish expulsion of 1492.[120] Rabbe David Ibn Zimra (the Radvaz),[121] and Rabbe Yosef Caro, author of the *Shulchan Aruch*,[122] were both only young boys when their families fled from Spain at that time, together with the more than two hundred thousand fellow Jews who were expelled, on Tish'ah Be-Av, 1492.[123]

Despite their terrible personal tragedies, however, these illustrious Torah masters continued to study Torah with phenomenal diligence, to teach their many disciples, to write their great Torah masterpieces, and, through their prolific responsa, to provide Torah guidance for their fellow Jews in all corners of the Diaspora. Despite the suffering, the anguish, and the interminable persecutions which they and their communities experienced first-hand, these spiritual giants instilled within their fellow Jews faith and *bitachon*, *ahavas haTorah* and *yir'as Shamayim*, as they led their people through the vale of tears, during some of the most trying periods in Jewish history.

(116) Maharil — see *Later Rishonim*, Chap. 3, at n. 97.
(117) Rabbe Bruna — see *Later Rishonim*, Chap. 3, after n. 103.
(118) Rabbe Chasdai Crescas — see *Later Rishonim*, Chap. 6, at n. 46.
(119) Rivash — see *Later Rishonim*, Chap. 6, after n. 42.
(120) Rabbe Abrabanel — see *Later Rishonim*, Chap. 7, n. 1; and bet. nn. 8-9.
(121) Radvaz — see *Later Rishonim*, Chap. 7, at n. 11.
(122) Maran Yosef Caro — see *Later Rishonim*, Chap. 7, before n. 16.
(123) Spanish expulsion of 1492 — see *Later Rishonim*, Chap. 7, at n. 1.

3

The Golden Age of Spain: The Rif, Contemporaries and Disciples

„הרים ביום סיני לך רעשו,
כי מלאכי הקל בך פגשו.
ויכתבו תורה בלוחות לבך,
וצבי כתריה לך חבשו.״
[חקוק על קבר הרי״ף,
מחרוזי רבי יהודה הלוי]

"On the day of Sinai,
Mountains surged forth to meet you,
For the Angels of the Almighty
went forth to greet you;
And they inscribed the Torah
on the Tablets of your heart;
Its chosen crowns to you did they impart."
[Euology of Rabbe Yehudah haLevi for the Rif;
See Text, p. 112.]

The Ri Migash: A Tribute

למדו תורה מאין מחיר,
מעל סיני, מעל ארון;
מפי יוסף, מפי בחיר,
זרע משה ואהרן.

הלחות לא נשתברו,
וארון וכרוב לא נקברו;
מימי עיניו יגברו,
וצמא כל צמא ישברו.

Study Torah with no fee,
From Sinai, from the Holy Ark;
From the mouth of Yosef
The chosen descendant
Of Moshe and Aharon.

The Tablets were not broken,
Nor buried were the Cherubim, the Holy Ark.
As from a spring his waters flow,
To quench the thirst
Of all who thirst for Torah.

[Poem by Rabbe Yehudah haLevi
re. the Ri Migash;
See text, at n. 64.]

3

The Golden Age of Spain: Rif, Contemporaries and Disciples

The Five Yitzchaks

We shall now retrace our footsteps and return to the Sephardic School of Torah Study, and to the *Tekufas haZahav* — the Golden Era of Torah scholarship in Spain.

During the second generation of *Rabbanim,* there were five Sephardic Sages by the name of Yitzchak, each of whom was an outstanding Torah scholar.[1] The following were the five Yitzchaks.

(a) Rabbe Yitzchak ben Yehudah Ibn Ghayyas (Ritzag, 1038-1089)

Rabbe Yitzchak Ibn Ghayyas studied under Rav Shmuel haNagid. In his later years, he remained very close to both Rav Shmuel haNagid, and to his son, Yehosef. When Rav Yehosef haNagid was slain by his enemies in 1067, Rabbe Yitzchak took his son, Azariah, into his home, and brought him up as a son. Unfortunately, Azariah died at the early age of twenty.

Rav Yitzchak was appointed Rav of Lucena, Spain, where he stood at the head of a great Yeshiva. He compiled a large halachic

(1) *Sefer haKabbalah, s.v.* והיו שם ה׳ רבנים, ושמות כלם יצחק.

work, *Halachos Kelulos,* which is cited by many *Rishonim,* such as the Ravad, Ramban, Rashba, and the Rosh. Many of his halachos are also cited in later halachic works, such as *Sefer haManhig*[2] and *Orchos Chaim.*[3] The section dealing with the laws of *Shabbos, Mo'adim,* and *Aveilus* (mourning) was published under the name *Sha'arei Simchah.*[4] He also wrote hundreds of *piyyutim* and *selichos* — liturgical and penitential poems — many of which are included in Sephardic *machzorim.*

Included among his numerous *talmidim* were Rav Yosef ben Yaakov Ibn Sahal (d. 1124), who was a *dayyan* in Cordoba; the well-known poet, Rav Moshe Ibn Ezra (ca. 1055-1135); and Rav Yosef Ibn Tzaddik (1070-1149), author of the philosophical work, *Olam Kattan.* Rav Yosef Ibn Tzaddik also served as a *dayyan* in Cordoba, together with Rabbe Maimon, father of the Rambam.

(b) Rabbe Yitzchak b. Baruch Albalia (1035-1094)

Rabbe Yitzchak Albalia also studied under Rav Shmuel haNagid. His ancestor, one Baruch, a *paroches* maker for the Temple in Jerusalem before the *Churban,* was sent to Spain by Titus at the time of the destruction of the Second Temple in 68 C.E., together with many other Jewish captives, almost one thousand years earlier. Rav Yitzchak Albalia was the maternal grandfather of Ravad I, author of the *Sefer haKabbalah.*[5]

Rav Yitzchak Albalia maintained a close relationship with Rav Yehosef haNagid, son of Rav Shmuel haNagid. In 1065, Rav Yitzchak dedicated his work on the intercalation of the Jewish calendar, *Machberes Sod haIbbur,* to Rav Yehosef. On the tragic day of Rav Yehosef haNagid's assassination, 9 Teves 1067, Rav Yitzchak, who was present in the Nagid's home in Granada at the time, was saved miraculously.

Accompanying Table VIII [p. 99] provides an outline of some of the highlights of the Sephardic School of Torah Study during the tenth and eleventh centuries.

(2) *Sefer haManhig* was written by the Provencal scholar, Rav Avraham b. Nasan haYarchi (1155-1215).

(3) *Orchos Chaim* was written by a later Provencal scholar, Rav Aharon haKohen of Lunel (d. 1334).

(4) The *sefer* was published under this name by Rav Yitzchak Dov haLevi Bamberger (1807-1878), with a commentary, *Yitzchak Yeranen,* in 1861.

(5) See *Sefer haKabbalah le-haRavad, s.v.* רבי יצחק בר ברוך.

Table VIII
Sephardic Schools of Torah Scholarship From the Rif to the Rambam

Tenth & Eleventh Centuries

Early Hebrew Lexicographers

Menachem b. Yaakov ibn Saruq, d. 970 C.E., *Machberes;* **Dunash b. Labrat haLevi of Baghdad** [disciple of R. Saadiah Gaon], *Teshuvos al Menachem ben Saruq, Teshuvos al Rav Saadiah Gaon;* **Yehudah b. David ibn Chiyug,** fl. 1000, *Sefer haPoalim;* **Yonah ibn Janach,** 990-1050, *Sefer ha-Rikmah, Sefer haSharashim, Sefer haHashlamah;* **R. Shlomo ibn Gabirol,** c. 1021-1057 [poet, philosopher], *Tikun Middos haNefesh, Keser Malchus.*

Eleventh Century

Second Generation of Rabbanim – 5 Yitzchaks

R. Yitzchak b. Yaakov Alfasi (Rif), 1013-1103 [Fez, N.A.; fled to Spain, 1088], *Hilchos Rav Alfas (halachic compendium on entire Talmud)* [disciple of R. Chananel and R. Nissim].

R. Yitzchak Ibn Ghayyas, 1038-1089, *Sha'arei Simchah;* **R. Yitzchak b. Baruch ibn Albalia,** 1035-1094, *Kupas haRochlim;* **R. Yitzchak b. Reuven of Barcelona,** c. 1043-1100; **R. Yitzchak b. Moshe** [Rosh Yeshiva of Baghdad].

Eleventh and Twelfth Centuries

Disciples* of Rif and their Contemporaries [in Spain]

***R. Yosef b. Meir haLevi ibn Migash (Ri Migash),** 1077-1141; ***R. Ephraim; *R. Yaakov b. haRif; *R. Baruch b. Yitzchak Albalia,** 1077-1126; ***R. Yehudah haLevi,** 1075-1141, *Kuzari;* **R. Bachya ibn Paquda,** ca. 1080, *Chovos haLevavos;* **R. Avraham ibn Ezra,** 1090-1164, *Commentary on Tanach.*

R. Avraham b. David (ibn Daud) haLevi (Ravad I), 1110-1180 [grandson of R. Yitzchak Albalia and disciple of his son, R. Baruch Albalia], *Sefer haKabbalah; HaEmunah haRamah;* **R. Yehudah b. Barzilai of Barcelona,** *Sefer haIttim (halachic compendium);* **Benjamin of Tudela,** fl. 1160-1173, *Sefer Masa'os (travel guide).*

Twelfth Century

Disciples of Ri Migash

R. Maimon b. Yosef, d. ca. 1165, *Novellae, Responsa, Iggeres haNechamah;* **R. Yosef b. Yaakov ibn Tzaddik.** d. 1149, *Olam Kattan;* Almohad Persecutions, 1148-1149.

Rambam: Son and Disciple of Rabbeinu Maimon

R. Moshe b. Maimon (Rambam), 1135-1204, *HaMa'or (Mishnah com.), Sefer haMitzvos, Mishneh Torah (halachic code), Moreh Nevuchim, Iggeres Teiman, Iggeres haShmad.*

Twelfth and Thirteenth Centuries

Son* and Disciples of Rambam, and Contemporary

***R. Avraham b. haRambam,** 1186-1237, *Commentary on Torah, Responsa;* **R. Yosef b. Yehudah ibn Aknin** [or ibn Shimon]. *Contemporary:* **R. Meir b Todros haLevi Abulafia** (1180-1235), *Yad Ramah (commentary on Sanhedrin, Bava Basra).*

Grandson of Rambam

R. David b. Avraham haNagid, 1213-1301, *Midrash Rav Dovid.*

Map I: The Iberian Peninsula: Early Medieval Period

In 1069, Rav Yitzchak was appointed by the King of Seville as the court astronomer, and as *Nasi*, or Prince, over all the Jews of his kingdom. He used his influence in court to intercede effectively in behalf of his fellow Jews.

During the later years of his life, Rav Yitzchak Albalia became involved in a serious dispute with Rav Yitzchak Alfasi (the Rif). On his deathbed, however, he instructed his seventeen-year-old son, Baruch, to go to the Rif in Lucena, to pacify him in his father's name, and to request that he teach him Torah. The Rif wept when Baruch appeared before him and transmitted his father's message. He received Baruch warmly and assured him that he would care for him as for his own son. He taught Baruch the entire Talmud, until Rabbe Baruch became his outstanding disciple, second only to the Ri Migash.[6]

Upon the Rif's death in 1103, Rabbe Baruch became a *dayyan* in Cordoba. He was greatly revered and beloved by his generation. Upon the birth of his son, Yitzchak, his great contemporary, the poet and philosopher Rabbe Yehudah Halevi, wrote the following lines concerning him.

מקור חיים לכל נפש עיפה,
ונוגה לאשר הולך חשכים.
שמו ברוך, והוא כשמו מבורך,
והמתברכים בשמו ברוכים.

Source of life for all who are weary,
And a light for all who walk in darkness.
His name is Baruch; like his name blessed is he.
All who are blessed through him, shall be blessed.[7]

When Rabbe Baruch died suddenly in 1126, at the early age of forty-nine, the entire Sephardic Jewish community greatly mourned the tragic loss. Both Rabbe Yehudah Halevi and Rav Moshe Ibn Ezra wrote moving poetic eulogies concerning him.

His nephew, Rav Avraham Ibn Daud, author of *Sefer haKabbalah*, was numbered among his many *talmidim*.

(6) *Ibid.*; *Infra*, n. 59.
(7) Rabbe Yehudah Halevi, author of the *Kuzari* (1075-1141).

(c) Rabbe Yitzchak ben Reuven Al-Bargeloni (1043-ca.1100)

Rabbe Yitzchak ben Reuven al-Bargeloni was born in Barcelona in 1043. Later he served as *dayyan* in Danya, in Southern Spain.[8] When he was thirty-five years old he translated the sefer, *Mekach u'Memkar* of Rav Hai Gaon, from Arabic to Hebrew.

Rav Yitzchak was an ancestor of the Ramban, who refers to him as אדוננו הזקן — "our master, the elder."[9] Rav Yitzchak wrote a commentary on tractate *Kesuvos*, "which testifies to his wisdom and his understanding."[10] He was the author of many *piyyutim* — liturgical poems. His poem, איזה מקום בינה, which clarifies each of the *Taryag mitzvos* — the 613 Torah commandments — is included in the North African Shevuos *machzor*.[11] His outstanding disciple was Rabbe Yehudah ben Barzilai of Barcelona.[12]

(d) Rabbe Yitzchak ben Moshe

He stood at the head of the Yeshiva of Baghdad. While this was formerly the Yeshiva of the *Geonim* in Bavel, it had declined steadily since the tenure of Rav Hai Gaon (939-1038), the last of the *Geonim*.

(e) Rabbeinu Yitzchak ben Yaakov Alfasi (the Rif, 1013-1103)

The greatest of these five scholars and the most towering luminary during this entire era was Rabbeinu Yitzchak Alfasi (the Rif, 1013-1103). He was born in Qual'at Hammad, Algiers, near Constantine, in the year 1013. After a while, he moved to Fas, or Fez, and he is therefore known as Rav Yitzchak Alfasi. According to

(8) See *Encyclopedia leToledos Gedolei Yisroel*, III:863, that he studied Torah under Rabbe Chanoch in Cordoba. This is an error, however, since he was born in 1043, eighteen years after the death of Rav Chanoch in 1025.

(9) Ramban, in his *Hilchos Nedarim*, as cited by *Or haChaim*, No. 1084, p. 510. Elsewhere, the Ramban refers to him as "*Maran*" — "our teacher." Since Rabbe Yitzchak (d.ca. 1100) lived over one hundred years before the Ramban (1194-1270), these honorary designations would appear to indicate that Rabbe Yitzchak was an ancestor of the Ramban.

(10) *Sefer haKabbalah le-haRavad, s.v. haRevi'i.*

(11) *Or haChaim*, No. 1084, p. 510.

(12) Responsa of Rabbe Shimon ben Tzemach Duran (1361-1444), *Tashbetz* I:15. See nn. 71-75.

the *Sefer haKabbalah,* the Rif studied under Rabbeinu Chananel and Rabbeinu Nissim in the Yeshiva of Kairouan.[13]

Due to libelous charges which were made against him, at the age of seventy-five Rabbe Yitzchak was compelled to flee from North Africa to Spain, where he arrived in the year 1088. He settled first in Cordoba, and then in Lucena, Spain, where he succeeded Rabbe Yitzchak ben Yehudah Ibn Ghayyas (Ritzag, d. 1089), as *Rosh haYeshiva.* The Rif continued to disseminate Torah to many disciples in the Yeshiva of Lucena, until his death in the year 1103.

The Rif was twenty-five years old when Rav Hai Gaon died in 1038. Because of his towering stature, and perhaps because of his nearness to the Geonic *tekufah,* some of the early *Rishonim* refer to the Rif as a *Gaon.* The Rif was a contemporary of both Rabbe Nasan, Ba'al haAruch (1035-1106) of Rome, Italy, and of Rashi (1040-1105) of Troyes, France. Just as Rashi was regarded as the undisputed *Gadol* in Ashkenaz, so, too, was the Rif the undisputed Sephardic *Gadol* of his day.

Among the outstanding *talmidim* of the Rif were Rabbe Yosef ben Meir haLevi Ibn Migash, Rav Ephraim of Qua'alat Hammad, Rabbe Baruch ben Yitzchak Albalia, and Rabbe Yehudah haLevi, author of the *Kuzari.*

Hilchos Rav Alfas — The "Minor Talmud"

His lifework, the *Hilchos Rav Alfas,* has often been referred to as the *Talmud Kattan* — the "Minor Talmud." It has been acclaimed as one of the foremost pillars of halacha, and as one of the most important halachic works of the entire post-Talmudic era, by all of the great *Rishonim* and *Poskim* who followed him. Rav Yosef Caro states that he regards the Rif, the Rambam, and the Rosh, as the three pillars of halacha upon which he will build the edifice of his *Bais Yosef,* and his *Shulchan Aruch.*[14]

The *Hilchos Rav Alfas* is patterned upon the style and wording of the *Gemara.* However, the Rif cites only those portions of the text

(13) *Sefer haKabbalah le-haRavad, s.v.* רבי יצחק ברבי יעקב בן אלפאסי.

(14) Rabbe Yosef Caro (1488-1575), in his introduction to his *Bais Yosef* commentary on *Tur Orach Chaim.*

which he regards as definitive halacha, and omits anything which has no bearing upon the halachic conclusion.[15] If the Rif omits a Talmudic law, it is an indication that he does not regard this as definitive halacha.[16] He also adds brief explanations to elucidate the text, where necessary.

The *Hilchos Rav Alfas* covers three of the six *Sedarim*, or Orders of the *Shas* — *Mo'ed, Nashim*, and *Nezikin* — as well as tractates *Berachos* and *Chullin*. The Rif deals only with those halachos which are relevant to Jewish life during the post-Temple or Exile period, omitting all halachos which deal with *Korbanos* (ritual sacrifices), Temple service, and many other halachos which are limited to the Temple period. For this reason, he omits entirely chapters five through nine in tractate *Pesachim*, and the first seven chapters of *Yoma*, which deal with the laws of the *Korbanos* of those Festivals. On the other hand, the laws of *tum'as Kohen* — defilement of the sanctity of a *Kohen* — *Sefer Torah, tefillin, mezuzah*, and *tzitzis*, which are found primarily in tractate *Menachos* of *Seder Kodshim*, are included under a separate section, called *Halachos Ketanos*, which is printed at the end of tractate *Menachos* in the *Vilna Shas*.

The highly regarded sefer, *Esrim Sha'arei Shevu'os*, which is included after the Rif on tractate *Shevu'os* in the *Vilna Shas*, was written by the Rif's grandson, Rav Yitzchak ben Reuven, and not, as some believed, by the Rif himself, or by Rabbe Yitzchak ben Reuven al-Bargeloni.[17]

The Talmud Yerushalmi vis-a-vis the Talmud Bavli

The following halachic discussion, in which the Rif clarifies the role of the *Talmud Yerushalmi* vis-a-vis the *Talmud Bavli* in regard to

(15) *Teshuvos haRosh*, 84:3, as cited by *Encyclopedia Talmudis*, Rav Shlomo Yosef Zevin, ed. (Jerusalem: 1971), Vol. IX, p. 335, n. 359.

(16) *The Mordecai, Eruvin*, Chap. 1, *siman* 478, in the name of his teacher, Maharam Baruch. (as cited by *Encyclopedia Talmudis*, Vol. IX, p. 335, n. 360.) In regard to final *p'sak halacha*, where *Tosafos* or other great *Rishonim* disagree with the Rif, see *Encyclopedia Talmudis*, pp. 335-336.

(17) *Or haChaim*, No. 1085, p. 510, citing Responsa of Maharam Baruch, *siman* 195, to this effect. In certain instances, this *sefer* contradicts some of the decisions rendered in the *Hilchos Rav Alfas*.

the determination of definitive halacha, is indicative of the decisive nature of the Rif's writings, which placed him in the foremost ranks of the great *Poskim* or halachic decisors.

It is prohibited to create sound on Shabbos by using musical instruments.[18] The *Talmud Yerushalmi* extends this prohibition to include the formulation of sound through any artificial means, such as by knocking on a door, even though this does not result in the formulation of musical sound.[19] According to the conclusion arrived at in the *Talmud Bavli*, however, where it is not *derech shir*, i.e., it does not result in a musical sound, it is permissible.[20] Citing both of these opinions, the Rif concludes,

> וחזינן למקצת רבואתא דסבירא להו כעולא, וסמכי אגמרא דבני מערבא. . . . ואנן לא סבירא לן הכי. דכיון דסוגיין דגמרא דילן להתירא, לא איכפת לן במאי דאסרי בגמרא דבני מערבא, דעל גמרא דילן סמכינן, דבתרא הוא, ואינהו הוי בקיאי בגמרא דבני מערבא טפי מינן, ואי לאו דקים להו דהאי מימרא דבני מערבא לאו דסמכא הוא, לא קא שרו ליה אינהו. (רי״ף, סוף מסכת עירובין)
>
> We have seen that some great scholars[21] hold like Ula,[22] because they rely upon the opinion of the *Talmud Yerushalmi*.[23] [However], we do not hold like this [prohibitive view of the *Talmud Yerushalmi*]. Since the conclusion of our *Talmud [Bavli]* is to permit this practice, we are not concerned by the fact that the *Talmud Yerushalmi* prohibits it. For we rely upon our *Gemara* [the *Talmud Bavli*], since it represents a "later" halachic authority.[24]

(18) See *Shulchan Aruch Orach Chaim* 338:1.

(19) See *Yerushalmi, Beitzah* 5:2 (p. 20b) — אמר רבי אלעזר, כל משמיע קול אסורין בשבת.

(20) See *Eruvin* 104a — א״ל רבה, לא אסרו אלא קול של שיר.

(21) This is a reference to Rabbeinu Chananel, who prohibits this practice, following the conclusion of the *Talmud Yerushalmi*.

(22) Ula, a third generation Palestinian *Amora*, is cited in the *Talmud Bavli* (*Eruvin* 104a), as taking a prohibitive view.

(23) Literally, the Talmud of the West, since Eretz Yisroel is to the west of Bavel [Iraq].

(24) This principle of הלכה כבתראי — "the halacha remains like the later halachic authorities" — is not mentioned anywhere in the Talmud, but is cited often by many of the great *Poskim*. For further clarification of this matter, see *Encyclopedia Talmudis, op. cit.*, Vol. IX, p. 341, *s.v.* הלכה כבתראי.

> They [the redactors of the *Talmud Bavli*] knew the *Talmud Yerushalmi* better than we. If they were not aware that this halacha of the *Talmud Yerushalmi* is not to be relied upon, they would not have concluded that this practice is permissible.[25]

Of course, where there is no indication in the Babylonian Talmud to the contrary, the Rif will cite the *Talmud Yerushalmi* as definitive halacha.[26]

Gathering Halachos and Aggados

At times, the Rif gathers many halachos which pertain to a particular topic, from a number of Talmudic tractates, bringing them together as one integral unit. For example, in *Bava Mezia*, where there is reference to a law concerning *tochachah*, or rendering rebuke to one's neighbor, the Rif cites many halachos pertaining to the mitzvah of rendering rebuke, from a number of Talmudic sources.[27] Similarly, in tractate *Shabbos*, he gathers halachos from various Talmudic sources in regard to the laws of *lashon hara* — evil speech, gossip and slander.[28]

Unlike other halachic codifiers who preceded him, the Rif often cites Aggadic references, which will serve to reinforce a mussar or halachic concept. Thus, in regard to the laws of *kibud av va-em* — honoring one's parents, the Rif cites various Aggadic narratives concerning a number of individuals who went to very great pains to render honor to their parents.[29] In the sixteenth chapter of tractate *Shabbos* he assembles many Aggadic references concerning the importance of rendering honor to the Shabbos.[30]

(25) *Hilchos Rav Alfas*, end tractate *Eruvin*. Cf. *Hilchos Rav Alfas, Shabbos* 130a-b (p. 104 in Rif), *s.v.* לא סמכינן אלא אגמרא דילן.

(26) See, for example, *Hilchos Rav Alfas*, near end of tractate *Rosh Hashanah* (p. 12a in Rif), citing *Talmud Yerushalmi, Rosh Hashanah* 4:10, p. 42a, *s.v.* הלכה כר״ג באילין תקיעתא. This *Yerushalmi* will also have a bearing on the question as to whether the congregation recites seven or nine benedictions in the *Mussaf* Rosh Hashanah service. See above, Chap. 1, nn. 47-66.

(27) *Bava Mezia* 31a, Rif, *ad. loc.* (p. 17a).

(28) *Shabbos* 33a-b; Rif, *ad. loc.* (p. 13b—14a).

(29) See *Kiddushin* 31a-b, Rif, *ad. loc.* (p. 12b).

(30) *Shabbos* 118b, Rif, *ad. loc.* (p. 44a-b).

Because of his undisputed reputation as a phenomenal Torah scholar, halachic questions were sent to the Rif from all over. A few hundred of his responsa are still extant, and have been published in various collections of responsa. Almost all of his responsa were written in Arabic, and have since been translated into Hebrew.

The "Armor Bearers" of the Rif

It goes without saying, of course, that a work of such major significance as the *Hilchos Rav Alfas* would be clarified by a host of commentaries. It is indicative of the great stature of the Rif and a measure of the high esteem in which his *sefer* was held, that some of the greatest Torah Sages of later generations wrote commentaries and critique on the *Hilchos Rav Alfas*. Some of the נושאי כליו — (lit. "armor bearers") — the primary commentaries which surround the text of the Rif in the printed editions are, in chronological order, as follows:

(a) Rabbeinu Shlomo Yitzchaki (Rashi, 1040-1105). This consists of relevant excerpts from Rashi's commentary on the Talmud.[31]

(b) Rav Avraham ben David of Posquires (Ravad III, 1120-1198), *Hasagos haRavad* (on Rif and on Ba'al haMa'or).[32]

(c) Rav Yitzchak ben Abba Mari of Marseilles (Ba'al haIttur, 1122-1193), *Me'ah She'arim*.[33]

(d) Rav Zerachiah haLevi (Ba'al haMa'or, 1125-1186), *HaMa'or haGadol* (on *Nashim, Nezikin*); *HaMa'or haKattan* (on *Berachos, Mo'ed*).[34]

(e) Rav Yehonasan ben David haKohen of Lunel (fl. 1190), Commentary on Rif, *Eruvin*.[35]

(f) Rav Moshe ben Nachman (Ramban, 1194-1270), *Milchamos HaShem* (on critique of *Ba'al haMa'or*); *Sefer haZechus* (on critique of Ravad to *Yevamos, Kesuvos, Gittin*).[36]

(31) Rashi, as a contemporary of the Rif in a distant land, could hardly have seen the *Hilchos haRif*. See page 235, n. 85. Re. Rashi, see Chap. 6, nn. 43-124.

(32) Re. Ravad III, see Chap. 5, nn. 13-51.

(33) Re. Ba'al haIttur, see Chap. 5, after n. 59.

(34) Re. Rabbe Zerachiah haLevi, see Chap. 5, nn. 52-59.

(35) Re. Rabbe Yehonasan haKohen of Lunel, see Chap. 5, nn. 61-62.

(36) Re. Ramban, see *Masters of the Mesorah: Later Rishonim*, Chap. 4, nn. 14-83

(g) Rav Yonah ben Avraham heChasid of Gerona (ca. 1200-1263), Commentary on Rif, *Berachos*.[37]
(h) Rav Asher ben Yechiel (Rosh, 1250-1327), *Likutei u'Piskei haRosh*, on *Halachos Ketanos* of the Rif.[38]
(i) Rav Nissim ben Reuven of Gerona (Ran, d.c. 1380), on fourteen tractates.[39]
(j) Rav Yosef Chaviva (15th c.), *Nimmukei Yosef*, on seven tractates.[40]
(k) Rav Yehoshua Boaz miBaruch (d.c. 1554, author of *Mesoras haShas, Ein Mishpat, Ner Mitzvah, Torah Or*), *Shiltei haGibborim*.[41]

Among the important commentaries on the Rif which were printed separately are the *Sefer haHashlamah* of the Provencal scholar, Rabbe Meshullam ben Moshe of Beziers,[42] and the sefer, *Pekudas haLevi'im* of Rabbe Aharon haLevi of Barcelona.[43] Also, the critical comments on the Rif which were written by the Rif's *talmid*, Rav Ephraim of Qual'at Hammad, Algiers, are cited by many Rishonim, such as Rabbe Avraham ben Yitzchak of Narbonne in his *Sefer haEshkol*, Ravad III of Posquires in his *Temim De'im*, Rabbe Zerachiah haLevi in his *Sefer haMa'or*, and the Ramban in his *Milchamos HaShem*.

A Giant Among Torah Giants

Words can hardly express the profound awe, reverence, and esteem in which the Rif was held by his contemporaries, as well as by the great Torah scholars of subsequent generations. He was regarded as a giant among Torah giants, and as a Torah master who had no peer.

(37) Re. Rabbeinu Yonah, see *Later Rishonim*, Chap. 4, nn. 84-118.

(38) Re. haRosh, see *Later Rishonim*, Chap. 5, nn. 31-85.

(39) Re. haRan, see *Later Rishonim*, Chap. 6, nn. 13-24.

(40) Re. R. Yosef Chaviva, see *Later Rishonim*, Chap. 6, after n. 46.

(41) R. Yehoshua Boaz miBaruch was an early *Acharon*, and is therefore not included within the scope of this work on the *Rishonim*.

(42) R. Meshullam of Beziers (d. 1238), was a grandson of R. Meshullam b. Yaakov of Lunel (d. 1170), one of the primary teachers of Ravad III of Posquires. (See Chap. 5, at n. 12.)

(43) R. Aharon haLevi of Barcelona (Re'ah, d.c. 1305), was a fifth generation descendant of R. Zerachiah haLevi Ba'al haMa'or, and a colleague of the Rashba. (See *Later Rishonim*, Chap. 5, nn. 9-10.)

Maimonides makes a remarkable statement concerning the *Hilchos Rav Alfas.*

> The *Geonim* wrote numerous commentaries [on the Talmud] . . . But the *Halachos* which the great teacher Rabbeinu Yitzchak, *zal,* wrote was preferable to all their works, because it includes all the laws and the halachic decisions which are necessary in our times, that is, during the period of *Galus.* In his halachic decisions he clarified all the errors which may be found in the works of those who preceded him. Nor is it possible to disagree with his decisions in more than a very few instances, *which will be less than ten under all circumstances.*[44]

Maimonides' statement that one cannot find even ten laws — or thirty laws, as he indicates in one of his responsa — upon which to disagree with the decisions of the Rif, is all the more remarkable when one realizes that the *Halachos* of the Rif covers all the laws of the vast *yam haTalmud* — the "sea of Talmud" — which are applicable in our day.

Possessed of "Ru'ach haKodesh"

The Ri haZaken, one of the greatest of the *Ba'alei haTosafos,* provides us with an insight into the formidable, if not almost impossible task which confronted the Rif, with the following remark: "A human being would find it impossible to compose such a work, unless *Ru'ach haKodesh* — the Divine Spirit — had descended upon him."[45]

The Ravad III of Posquires, Rav Avraham Ba'al haHasagos — the Master of Critique — approached the task of writing a critique on the Rif, with great trepidation. Thus, he writes concerning the great master,

(44) Rambam, Introduction to Mishnah, ed. M.D. Rabinowitz (Tel Aviv: Hotza'as Rishonim, 1948), pp. 82 f. Italics mine. In one of his responsa, the Rambam states that he disagreed with the Rif in about thirty instances.

(45) As cited by Rabbe Menachem b. haKadosh R. Aharon b. Zerach [d. 1385], *Tzedah laDerech* (Warsaw: Kelter Pub., 1880), Introduction, p. 6.

הנה ראיתי בהלכות הרב אלפסי דברים נפלאים ממני, ואולי מבלי ראות עיני, כאשר יסתבל בעין השמש מפני חלישות טבעו. ואמת כי היה לי לעצום את עיני ולסגור דלתי פי, וללכת אחריו אל הימין ואל השמאל, מאין נטות.

I have seen things in the halachos of Rav Alfas which are hidden from me. Perhaps this is because of my lack of ability to see, as one who [cannot see] when he looks into the light of the sun. . . . In truth, it would behoove me to close my eyes, and to shut my mouth, and to follow him without deviation, to the right and to the left.[46]

Greatest Halachic Codifier

In his introduction to his *Sefer haMa'or,* Rabbe Zerachiah haLevi likewise speaks of the Rif with great awe and reverence,[47] while Rav Avraham Ibn Daud writes in his *Sefer haKabbalah* concerning the Rif, that "from the days of Rav Hai Gaon, there was none as great in wisdom as he."[48]

The Meiri refers to the Rif as *"Gedolei haPoskim"* — the greatest of the halachic codifiers.

Rabbe Yaakov of Marvege, a thirteenth century *Tosafist,*[49] inquired of Heaven in a dream whether the halacha is like the Rif or like the *Geonim* who disagree with him, in regard to a certain aspect of *Hilchos Tefillin.* The Rif, who regards the *tefillin shel-yad* and *shel-rosh* — the *tefillin* of the arm and of the head — as two parts of the same mitzvah, says that one benediction will suffice while donning *tefillin,* while the *Geonim,* who regard these as two separate mitzvos, require two separate benedictions for the *shel yad* and the *shel rosh.*[50] Whereupon, the following reply came to Rav Yaakov in a dream.

ואת בריתי אקים את יצחק.

(46) R. Avraham b. David of Posquires, in his prefatory remarks to *Hasagos haRavad le-haRif,* beginning *Perek* 3, *Elu Na'aros,* in *Kesuvos* (p. 14b, in Rif).

(47) For these words of Rabbe Zerachiah haLevi concerning the Rif, see Chap. 5, n. 54.

(48) *Sefer haKabbalah, s.v.* ומימות רב האי לא נמצא כמוהו בחכמה.

(49) Rabbe Yaakov of Marvege, *She'elos u'Teshuvos min haShamayim.* Responsum 69 in this work is dated 1203.

(50) See *Shulchan Aruch Orach Chaim* 25:5 and in Rama, where these two opinions are cited.

> *My covenant will I establish with Yitzchak.*[51] *For one have I called him.*[52] I shall regard him as My first-born, *and I have blessed him.*[53] *Even blessed shall he be.*[54]

"Wonder of the World"

On the Rif's tombstone, the following words were inscribed — among many others, too numerous to mention here.

נקבר בקבר הזה ראש הראשים,
ואלוף הקדושים . . .
יחיד העולם ופלאו,
ממזרח שמש עד מבואו,
הר התורה, מקור הבינות,
ושמעו הולך בכל המדינות.

Here lies buried the chief of chiefs,
And the master of the holy ones. . . .
The wonder of the world,
And [among Torah scholars] the only one.
From the rising of the sun,
Until its setting.
A mountain of Torah,[55]
Source of understanding;
His reputation travels
Among all the nations.[56]

"They Inscribed the Torah on the Tablets of your Heart"

The great poet-philosopher, Rabbe Yehudah haLevi, author of the *Kuzari*, who is believed to have studied under the Rif, wrote the following eulogy concerning the great master.

(51) Genesis 17:21.

(52) See Isaiah 51:2 — כי אחד קראתיו ואברכהו.

(53) Genesis 27:33 — גם ברוך יהיה.

(54) Rabbe Yaakov of Marvege, *She'elos u'Teshuvos min haShamayim*, Reuven Margolios, ed. (Jerusalem: Mosad haRav Kook, 1967), Responsum 2, p. 44.

(55) This unusual phrase, "mountain of Torah," was also used by Rav Hai Gaon, in regard to R. Chushiel (see above, Chap. 2, n. 12).

(56) From inscription on tombstone of the Rif, as cited in *Vilna Shas*, preface to *Hilchos Rav Alfas* on tractate *Berachos*. See *Or haChaim*, No. 1078, p. 504, citing the sefer, *Derech Tamim*.

הרים ביום סיני לך רעשו,
כי מלאכי הקל בך פגשו.
ויכתבו תורה בלוחות לבך,
וצבי כתריה לך חבשו.
לא עצרו כח נבונים לעמוד,
לולי תבונות ממך דרשו.

On the day of Sinai mountains surged forth to meet you,
For the Angels of the Almighty went forth to greet you.
And they inscribed the Torah on the tablets of your heart,
Its chosen crowns to you did they impart.
Wise men found not the strength to stand,
Lest wisdom did you teach them to understand.[57]

The poet, Rabbe Moshe Ibn Ezra, also rendered a beautiful poetic eulogy for this great teacher and Torah master, which ends with the following words.

בו נקברו לוחות והארון.

Here lie buried the Tablets [of the Law] and the Holy Ark.[58]

The Rif died in Lucena in 1103, at the age of ninety, two years before the death of Rashi (1105).

Rabbeinu Yosef haLevi — the Ri MiGash

The most eminent disciple of the Rif was Rabbeinu Yosef b. Meir haLevi Ibn Migash (Ri Migash), who was born in Granada, in the year 1077. Already in his early youth he showed signs of having an extraordinary intellect.

Rabbe Yitzchak ben Baruch Albalia was a very close friend of young Yosef's father, Rav Meir, who was also a *talmid chacham.* Rabbe Yitzchak, who recognized Yosef's potential to become a great Torah scholar, urged the father to encourage Yosef to study Torah by day and by night, so that he might realize his great potential.

(57) Eulogy of Rabbe Yehudah HaLevi (1075-1141), as cited in *Vilna Shas,* preface to *Hilchos Rav Alfas* on tractate *Berachos.*

(58) Eulogy of Rabbe Moshe Ibn Ezra (ca. 1055-1135), as cited in *Vilna Shas,* preface to *Hilchos Rav Alfas* on tractate *Berachos.*

In 1089, Yosef went to study Torah in Lucena, where the Rif had only recently assumed the post of *Rosh Yeshiva.* Five years later, when Rav Yitzchak Albalia died, Yosef was joined by his boyhood friend, Baruch b. Rav Yitzchak Albalia.[59] Together they studied under the great master, Rabbe Yitzchak Alfasi, and they both became illustrious Torah scholars.

Rav Yosef studied under the Rif for fourteen years, until the great master's death in 1103. The Rif loved him like a son. Although Rav Yosef was yet only a young man when his great master passed away, the Rif had already previously ordained him and wrote concerning him, "Even in the generation of Moshe, none was found like him."[60]

"Study Torah . . . From the Holy Ark"

In his introduction to his commentary on the Mishnah, the Rambam makes the following intriguing remark concerning the Ri Migash.

> The profound knowledge of that man in Talmud is frightening to one who will penetrate deeply into his words and into the depth of his intellectual comprehension, until one can almost say of him, *"And like him, there was no king before him,"*[61] in his bearing and his manner.[62]

The poet-philosopher, Rabbe Yehudah haLevi, wrote the following words about his illustrious contemporary, the Ri Migash.

למדו תורה מאין מחיר,
מעל סיני, מעל ארון;
מפי יוסף, מפי בחיר,
זרע משה ואהרן.
הלחות לא נשתברו,
וארון וכרוב לא נקברו;
מימי עיניו יגברו,
וצמא כל צמא ישברו.

(59) See above, n. 6.
(60) *Sefer haKabbalah le-haRavad, s.v.* וחמשה אלה הם הדור השני.
(61) Citing II Kings 23:25.
(62) Rambam, Introduction to Mishnah, *op. cit.,* p. 83.

Study Torah with no fee,
From Sinai, from the Holy Ark;
From the mouth of Yosef
The chosen descendant
Of Moshe and Aharon.
The Tablets were not broken,
Nor buried were the Cherubim, the Holy Ark.[63]
As from a spring his waters flow,
To quench the thirst
Of all who thirst for Torah.[64]

Although the Rif had a son who was an ordained Torah scholar, he nevertheless selected his *talmid,* the Ri Migash, to succeed him and to stand at the head of his Yeshiva, a post which the Ri Migash retained for thirty-eight years, until his death in the year 1141.

Rabbe Avraham Ibn Daud, who was a younger contemporary of the Ri Migash, expresses the following sentiments concerning the great master, in his *Sefer haKabbalah.*

> In addition to his great wisdom, his character traits attested to the fact that he was a descendant of Moshe Rabbeinu, for he was far more humble than any man, and the Almighty endowed him with a magnanimous heart, for he was generous in forgiving. May the Almighty repay him for all the kindness which he performed for Israel, Amen.[65]

Among the many disciples of the Ri Migash was Rabbeinu Maimon, father of the Rambam.

The Almohad Invasion

As the Ravad approaches the end of his *Sefer haKabbalah,* he observes sadly that with the death of the Ri Migash in 1141, "the

(63) i.e., as long as Rabbe Yosef is alive, is it as though the Tablets were not broken, and the holy Ark is still with us.

(64) Rabbe Yehudah Halevi, as cited by *Encyclopedia leToledos Gedolei Yisroel,* III:789.

(65) *Sefer haKabbalah, s.v.* ומגדולי תלמידיו של ר״י בר׳ יעקב.

world was desolate of Yeshivos of wisdom."[66] Even though the Ri Migash had a son, Meir, and also a nephew, Meir, who were both great Torah scholars, they could, nevertheless, no longer keep the doors of the Yeshiva open, because of the impending catastrophe and the portentous clouds which hung over the Jewish community. Citing a verse in Isaiah, the Ravad observes further, *"Before the evil, is the tzaddik gathered in,"*[67] [that he might not witness the approaching evil].

Several years after the death of the Ri Migash, Southern Spain came under the rule of the fanatical Almohades. After having devastated the Jewish communities of North Africa, this fanatical Moslem sect came across the sea to Andalusia, laying waste to all the great Jewish communities in Southern Spain. In 1147, they conquered Seville; in 1148, Cordoba fell into their hands. Malaga, Lucena, Majorca and Granada followed shortly after. Every Jewish community in their path was devastated; every synagogue and house of study destroyed.

The decree of forcible conversion and the wave of terrible persecution which followed, made it impossible for Jews to remain in Southern Spain any longer. The two Meirs went into exile at the head of their fellow Jews.[68] Long columns of Jewish refugees streamed northward — fleeing the terrible sword of the Almohades, seeking a haven in Christian Spain.

An Unexpected Haven

Providentially, an unexpected haven opened up for the weary refugees. King Alphonso VII of Castile, had appointed Rabbe Yehudah ben Rav Yosef haNasi Ibn Ezra, a nephew of the poet, Rabbe Moshe Ibn Ezra, as commander of a Castilian military base, Calatrava, which penetrated deeply into Moslem territory. Rabbe Yehudah threw the gates of his military base open to the destitute, homeless refugees. "He loosened the bonds, unfettered the chains; in his home and at his table the wandering refugees found a haven.

(66) *Ibid., s.v.* ולאחר פטירת רב יוסף הלוי ז״ל שמם העולם מן הישיבות.

(67) Isaiah 57:1.

(68) *Sefer haKabbalah, s.v.* ואחר פטירת רב יוסף הלוי ז״ל היו שני חירום.

He fed the hungry, provided drinks for the thirsty, and clothed the ragged," and he led them to Toledo where he helped them become established with dignity.[69]

It is of interest to note that the Ravad sounds an optimistic note when he says that while the great Torah centers of Spain have dwindled, he has heard of a great Torah scholar in France, a Rabbe Yaakov ben Meir of Ramerupt, "May the Almighty grant him life and protect him, that he may be blessed to study and teach and to disseminate Torah in Israel."[70] He is making reference here, of course, to Rabbeinu Tam, and to the great Torah centers of the *Ba'alei haTosafos* which were now flourishing in Northern France and Ashkenaz, despite the terrible persecutions which they themselves were undergoing at this time, at the hands of the Crusaders.

Rabbe Yehudah ben Barzilai haNasi

A scion of a distinguished family whose descendants bore the title, *"Nasi,"* for many generations, Rabbe Yehudah ben Barzilai haNasi al-Bargeloni (late 11th—early 12th c.), was an outstanding Barcelonian Torah scholar. He studied under Rabbe Yitzchak ben Reuven of Barcelona (1043-c.1100),[71] and was the teacher of Rabbe Avraham ben Yitzchak of Narbonne (Ravad II, d. 1158).[72]

Rav Yehudah wrote a comprehensive halachic code on a major portion of the Talmud which, the Meiri observes, "was longer than the earth, and broader than the sea."[73] His work, only parts of which are extant, was divided into several volumes: *Sefer haIttim* — on *Seder Mo'ed* and *Berachos; Yichus She'er Basar* — on *Seder Nashim; Sefer haDin* — on *Seder Nezikin.*

Rav Yehudah, who was erudite in Geonic literature, draws extensively on the words of the *Geonim,* their works and their responsa, and particularly upon *Hilchos Rav Alfas,* whom he cites

(69) *Ibid., s.v.* וכאשר הופקד הנשיא רבי יהודה זה.

(70) *Ibid., s.v.* ושמענו שבארץ צרפת.

(71) Rabbe Shimon ben Tzemach Duran (1361-1444), *Tashbetz* I:15, as cited by *Or haChaim* No. 976, p. 449. See above, n. 12.

(72) *Or haChaim,* No. 133, p. 52, citing *Tashbetz* III:238.

(73) Rabbe Menachem b. Shlomo Meiri (1249-1315), Introd. to *Avos,* p. 67, paraphrasing Job 11:9.

frequently, and whom he refers to as "the *Gaon*, Rav Yitzchak." Many sections of this comprehensive code have been preserved in the writings of later scholars, who frequently cite excerpts from this work, in either full or abridged form. Many Geonic responsa have been preserved for us through his *sefarim*. The halachos of Rabbe Yehudah ben Barzilai are cited by the *Ba'alei haTosafos*,[74] and by many other *Rishonim*.[75] To a large extent, the sefer *haEshkol* of Rav Avraham ben Yitzchak of Narbonne, consists of a digest of the *Sefer haIttim* of his teacher, Rabbe Yehudah bar Barzilai, with additional material of his own.

Rav Yosef Ibn Tzaddik — "Olam Kattan"

As noted above, one of the outstanding disciples of Rabbe Yitzchak b. Yehudah Ibn Ghayyas was Rabbe Yosef b. Yaakov Ibn Tzaddik. Born in Southern Spain (c. 1070), Rav Yosef served as *dayyan* in Cordoba together with Rav Maimon, the father of the Rambam, from 1138 until his death in 1149.

Besides having been a *dayyan* and a great *talmid chacham*, Rav Yosef was also a Torah philosopher. He wrote the philosophical work, *Olam Kattan*, which deals with important principles of Torah faith, and the relationship of man to his universe. The following words, which he writes near the beginning of his *sefer*, explain why he called the sefer, *Olam Kattan* — "A Miniature World."

> על כן יקרא האדם עולם קטן, לפי שיש בו דמות מכל מה שבעולם. גופו כמעלת העולם הגשמי, ונפשו החכמה כמעלת העולם הרוחני.
>
> Therefore is man called *olam kattan* — a miniature world, for he contains within himself a replica of all that exists in the world. His body contains the essence of the material universe, while his intellectual soul contains the essence of the spiritual universe.[76]

In a letter to the translator of the *Moreh Nevuchim*, Rabbe Shmuel b. Yehudah Ibn Tibbon, the Rambam writes the following concerning Rav Yosef Ibn Tzaddik.

(74) See *Berachos* 17b, Tosafos, *s.v.* תרי; *Eruvin* 104a, Tosafos, *s.v.* הכי גריס.

(75) See *Hilchos Rabbeinu Asher, Shabbos*, Chap. 3, Sec. 1; *Chidushei haRamban, Yevamos* 117a.

(76) Rabbe Yosef Ibn Tzaddik (ca. 1070-1149), *Olam Kattan*, p. 2.

ואמנם, ספר עולם קטן לא ראיתיו, אבל אני ידעתי את האיש ואת שיחו, והכרתי ערך מעלתו וערך ספרו.

> I have never seen the sefer, *Olam Kattan*. However, I know the man and his manner of speech, and I recognize his stature and the stature of his *sefer*.[77]

Rav Yosef Ibn Tzaddik died in Cordoba in 1149, shortly after the Almohades began their fanatical persecution of the Jews in Southern Spain.[78]

Rabbeinu Bachya Ibn Paquda — The Chovos HaLevavos

As noted above, this era, which was known as the "Golden Age" of Spanish Jewry, was a period of prolific Jewish literary activity, not only in the area of halacha, but in other areas, as well. One of the major contributions to Jewish philosophical thought which emerged during this period was the *Chovos haLevavos* — "Duties of the Heart" — by Rabbeinu Bachya Ibn Paquda, of Saragossa. Originally written in Arabic (ca. 1080), and translated by Rabbe Yehudah Ibn Tibbon (ca. 1120-1190), the *Chovos haLevavos* has gained a reputation as one of the foremost works of Torah hashkafah, and its popularity among Torah scholars as an important mussar treatise has endured throughout the centuries.

As the name of this work implies — "Duties of the Heart" — Rabbeinu Bachya places emphasis upon the conceptual mitzvos — the commandments which deal with all aspects of Torah thought and hashkafah, as being at least equal in importance to the *mitzvos ma'asiyos* — the functional mitzvos which deal with those commandments which entail fulfillment through some physical means.

ואנחנו חייבים לעבוד אותו בעבור זה עבודה גלויה ועבודה צפונה.

(77) Rabbeinu Moshe b. Maimon, in his letter to R. Shmuel ibn Tibbon (ca. 1160-1230).

(78) See *Sefer haKabbalah le-haRavad, loc. cit.* For further information concerning R. Yosef ibn Tzaddik and the significance of his sefer, *Olam Kattan,* see R. Yehudah Leib Maimon, *R. Moshe ben Maimon* (Jerusalem: Mosad haRav Kook, 1960), p. 12, n. 14.

> It is our duty, therefore, to serve Him both in a revealed and in a hidden manner. The revealed approach is through the duties of the limbs — such as through prayer, fasting, charity, studying Torah and teaching it, making a sukkah, lulav, tzitzis, mezuzah, and a fence [upon our roofs],[79] and all similar mitzvos which are performed through the individual's actions. But the hidden service is through the duties of the heart — such as acceptance of His Unity in our hearts; belief in G-d and in His Torah; acceptance of His service; fear of the Creator; subjecting ourselves to His will; being ashamed [of our errant behavior] before Him; to love Him; to trust in Him; and to entrust our souls to Him.[80]

In its ten sections, the *Chovos haLevavos* deals with many of the most important aspects of Torah faith and Torah thought, such as belief in the existence and in the Unity of the Creator; attaining an awareness of the magnificence of His creation; serving the Creator; *bitachon* — placing trust in Him; repentance; love of G-d. Rabbe Bachya deals with these and many other fundamental Torah concepts comprehensively, clearly, logically, and methodically.

. . . on the Creation concept

For example, in regard to recognition of the existence of the Creator, Rabbeinu Bachya observes that the world is wondrously made.

> כי אנחנו רואים אותו בהרגשותינו ושכלנו, כבית הבנוי אשר זומן בו כל הצריך לו. . . והאדם כבעל הבית המשתמש בכל אשר בו.
>
> For we recognize with our senses and our intellect that the world is like a house which was constructed together with everything that it needs. . . while man is like the owner of the house, who may make use of all that it contains. . . . As King David said,[81] *"You have given [man] dominion over the works of Your hands; You have placed everything beneath his feet."*[82]

(79) See Deuteronomy 22:8.

(80) Rabbeinu Bachya, *Chovos haLevavos* (Warsaw: Y. Goldman, 1875), Introd., p. 15.

(81) Psalms 8:7.

(82) *Chovos haLevavos, op. cit., "Sha'ar haYichud,"* Part 1, Chap. 6, pp. 53 f.

Now, Rabbeinu Bachya goes on to explain, should someone venture to say that a simple water wheel, which is used to irrigate crops in a field or garden, came about by itself, without the purposeful design of a human being, we would greet such an opinion with total incredulity and derision. Or, for that matter, if someone should say that meaningful words were formed on paper by the accidental spilling out of a bottle of ink, we would likewise regard such a remark with derision and disdain.

> Now since this is entirely inconceivable in our eyes [concerning a self-made water wheel, or an authorless manuscript] . . . how is it possible to say concerning a work which is infinitely more intricate [i.e. the entire universe] . . . that it may have come about without the purposeful design of an intelligent and omnipotent Creator.[83]

. . . on the Bitachon concept

In his chapter on *bitachon*, Rabbeinu Bachya provides us with a deeper insight into the meaning of this fundamental, albeit somewhat elusive Torah concept.

He begins by pointing out that while it is proper that the individual shall make efforts to earn his livelihood, he should never regard these efforts as the source of his livelihood, but rather, he should regard the Almighty alone as the source of his livelihood.

> ואל יחשוב כי טרפו מועמד על סיבה ידוע, ושאם תמנע הסיבה ההיא ממנו, לא יבוא בסיבה אחרת. אבל יבטח על האלקים בטרפו . . .

> The individual shall not believe that his sustenance is contingent upon any particular factor, so that if that factor should be withheld from him his sustenance will not be forthcoming from another source. Rather, he shall rely upon the Almighty for his sustenance, and he should know that all methods [of providing an individual's sustenance] are equal in His eyes. The Almighty will provide the individual's sustenance through any means, at any time, and in

(83) *Chovos haLevavos, "Sha'ar haYichud,"* Part 1, Chap. 6, p. 58.

any way that He may desire. As it says,[84] *For there is no restraint upon the L-rd to save, by many or by few.* And it says,[85] *For it is He who gives you power to acquire wealth.*[86]

Poet and Philosopher — Rabbe Yehudah HaLevi

One of the individuals who is most frequently thought of as having personified the enduring literary productivity of the *Tekufas haZahav* — the "Golden Age" — was the beloved poet-philosopher, Rabbe Yehudah haLevi (1075-1141). Rabbe Yehudah haLevi, who is believed to have been a disciple of the Rif and who was a contemporary and friend of the illustrious Rabbeinu Yosef Ibn Migash, endeared himself to the Jewish people with his extremely beautiful and soul-stirring poetry, in which he often expresses a profound yearning for Eretz Yisroel.

ציון הלא תשאלי — Ode to Zion

ציון הלא תשאלי לשלום אסיריך;
דורשי שלומך, והם יתר עדריך. . . .

O' Zion, will you not inquire
After the welfare of your exiles?[87]
They who constantly seek your welfare;
They are the remnants of your flock. . . .

אבחר לנפשי להשתפך במקום
אשר רוח אלקים שפוכה על בחיריך.

I will seek to pour forth my soul
At that very place
Where the Divine Spirit was poured forth
Upon your chosen ones.

את בית מלוכה ואת כסא ה';
ואיך ישבו עבדים עלי כסאות גביריך.

(84) I Samuel 14:6.
(85) Deuteronomy 8:18.
(86) *Chovos haLevavos, "Sha'ar haBitachon,"* end Chap. 3, p. 223.
(87) Lit., "your captives" — i.e., your people who are in exile and in captivity.

You are the house of royalty,[88]
You are the throne of G-d.
How do slaves now sit
Upon the thrones of your princes?

מי יתנני משוטט במקומות
אשר נגלו אלקים לחוזיך וציריך.

O' that I might wander in those places,
Where the glory of G-d was revealed,
To your Prophets and to your envoys.

מי יעשה לי כנפים וארחיק נדוד,
אניד לבתרי לבבי בין בתריך.

O' who will make me wings
That I might travel afar;
That I might bring my broken heart
To wend its way among your ruins.

אפול לאפי עלי ארצך;
וארצה אבניך מאד, ואחונן את עפריך.

I will prostrate myself upon your earth;
I will hold your stones very dear,[89]
I will cherish your very dust.[90]

With his beautiful poetry, Rabbe Yehudah haLevi helped keep the dream of a return to Zion alive within the hearts of our people throughout the centuries of exile.

The "Sefer haKuzari"

Rabbe Yehudah haLevi's monumental contribution to Jewish literature was his *Sefer haKuzari,* which is a beautifully written exposition of Jewish philosophical thought, based upon the historical episode concerning the eighth century Khazar King, Bulan, who embraced Judaism, and who subsequently influenced his subjects to do likewise. Rabbe Yehudah haLevi describes the episode which led King Bulan to embrace Judaism.

(88) See Jeremiah 3:17, בעת ההיא יקראו לירושלים כסא ד'.

(89) See Psalms 102:15, כי רצו עבדיך את אבניה, ואת עפרה יחננו.

(90) This beautiful poem by Rabbe Yehudah haLevi is included among the *Kinos* which are recited during the Tish'ah Be-Av service.

The King, who was very zealous in the performance of his pagan idol-worship, had an ever-recurring dream. In his dream, he is informed repeatedly that although his intent is acceptable, his actions are not. He embarks, therefore, upon a serious quest for the proper approach, in regard to man's service of his Creator. He calls first upon a philosopher and then upon both Christian and Mohammedan scholars to expound upon their beliefs, but he quickly rejects their views. Whereupon, he turns, albeit reluctantly, to the despised Jewish faith, and calls in a Rabbi — Rav Yitzchak Sangari — who is referred to throughout this work as the *Chaver.* A dialogue ensues between them concerning all the fundamental principles of Torah faith.

Although this narrative occurred some four hundred years before his own day, Rabbe Yehudah haLevi skillfully describes the soul-searching quest of the King for a meaningful faith, by reconstructing for the reader the ensuing dialogue between the King and the *Chaver.* Rabbe Yehudah haLevi places an impressive array of philosophical questions into the mouth of the King, and the *Chaver* replies to each of these questions with wisdom and with understanding.

The Historical Imperative of Torah Faith

When the King asks the *Chaver* to clarify the fundamental principles of Judaism, the *Chaver* begins by remarking that he believes in the G-d of Abraham, Isaac, and Jacob, who led the Jewish people out of Egypt with wondrous miracles, who split the sea before them, who provided them with water and manna in the desert, and who gave them the Torah at Mt. Sinai. This provokes the ire of the King, who felt that the *Chaver* should rather have spoken of his belief in G-d, "who created the world, who established it and guides it, and who created you and sustains you."[91]

Whereupon, the Rabbi replies that he speaks, not in terms of philosophical conjecture, but rather in those terms which point most forcefully to the chain of historical tradition, and to that historical imperative which is the cornerstone of Torah faith. He

(91) Rabbe Yehudah haLevi (1075-1141), *Sefer haKuzari* (Warsaw: Y. Goldman, 1880), I:11-12.

points out that the Almighty did not reveal Himself at Sinai as the Creator of heaven and earth, but rather, as the G-d who delivered the Israelites from Egyptian bondage, because this was an event with which the people were familiar from their own recent experiences.[92] This provided them, therefore, with a rational imperative for Torah faith.[93]

This exposition of the *Chaver* — so eloquently expressed in his subsequent dialogues with the King — regarding the historical experiences of the Jewish people, which were, in turn, transmitted to all future generations through an unbroken chain of Torah transmission — this "Mesorah" approach to Torah faith — has been accepted as the fundamental approach to authentic Jewish thought by outstanding Jewish scholars throughout the generations, from Ramban through Rabbi Samson Raphael Hirsch.[94]

The *Kuzari* is a treasure-trove of Torah hashkafah and authentic Jewish values regarding every aspect of life and thought.

. . . on love, and fear, and joy

תורתנו נחלקת בין היראה, והאהבה, והשמחה. וכללו של דבר, תתקרב אל אלקיך בכל אחת מהנה. . . .

The great principle is this: Our Torah is divided between fear, love, and joy. You should approach your G-d through each of these. Nor is your contriteness on a Fast-day more acceptable to G-d than your joy on Sabbaths and Festivals, if you will rejoice with sincere intent and with a full heart.[95]

. . . on tefillah

ויהיה פרי יומו ולילו השלש עתות של תפלה, ופרי השבוע יום השבת.

(92) The Ramban makes a similar observation in his comment on the First Commandment (Exodus 20:2), "And this is the meaning of אשר הוצאתיך — that they knew and were witness to all this."

(93) *Kuzari* I:13-25.

(94) For more elaborate clarification of this thought, see *Anvil of Sinai*, Ch. 4, "The Mesorah Approach," pp. 75 ff.

(95) *Kuzari* II:50.

> The thrice-daily *tefillah* intervals — [*Shacharis, Minchah,* and *Ma'ariv*] — should be regarded as the climax of the individual's day, and the climax of the week should be the Shabbos.[96]

. . . on communal prayer

> אבל היתרון לקהל מכמה פנים . . .
>
> Communal prayer has numerous advantages. . . . One individual will supplement the omissions of the other. . . . And all of the people will attain the blessings. . . . For the individual is to the community, as one limb is to the body.[97]

. . . on the Bais HaMikdash

> כאשר ימצא פגע את ליבנו, אשר הוא בית מקדשנו — אבדנו; וכאשר ירפא — נרפא גם אנחנו.
>
> If our "heart" — that is, our Temple — is destroyed, we are lost; when it is intact, we are saved, as well.[98]

Much as he does in his poetry, so too, in his *Kuzari,* does Rabbe Yehudah haLevi express a profound yearning for Eretz Yisroel, for only there, he submits, can the Jew attain spiritual perfection and complete fulfillment as man-Israel. In his concluding essay, the *Chaver* informs the King of his decision to spend the remaining years of his life in the Holy Land. With the King's blessing that the Almighty might grant him success in this hazardous journey, the dialogue comes to a close.[99]

An Exposition of Fundamental Torah Concepts

The *Kuzari* has gained universal recognition as an outstanding contribution to Jewish philosophy, and it has left an enduring impact upon Jewish life and intellectual thought throughout the centuries. The Vilna Gaon is cited as having remarked,

(96) *Kuzari* III:5.
(97) *Kuzari* III:19.
(98) *Kuzari* II:32.
(99) *Kuzari* V:22-end.

ספר הכוזר הוא קדוש וטהור,
עיקר אמונת ישראל ותורה תלויין בו.

The *Sefer haKuzari* is pure and holy. The fundamental principles of Torah and of Jewish faith are embodied within it.[100]

In a popular allegorical play on a Biblical verse, the expression, פן תעזוב את הלוי — *Do not forsake the Levite,*[101] is often applied to Rabbe Yehudah haLevi as a token of reverence and appreciation for his *Sefer haKuzari*. So strong was Rabbe Yehudah haLevi's love for Zion that, in his later years, he did, in fact, leave family and friends behind, as he embarked upon the long, perilous journey to fulfill his lifelong dream to settle in the Holy Land. It is said that no sooner had he arrived in Jerusalem to pour out his heart at the Wailing Wall, than he died a martyr's death at the hands of an Arab.[102]

Rabbe Yehudah haLevi left a legacy of faith and hope, and his words have served as an inspiration for his people in all generations.

Rabbe Avraham Ibn Ezra — Prolific Scholar and Poet

An illustrious contemporary and intimate friend of Rabbe Yehudah haLevi was the eminent Biblical scholar, poet, and Hebrew grammarian, Rabbe Avraham ben Meir Ibn Ezra (1088-1164).[103] He was a brilliant and exceedingly prolific scholar. In an extensive biographical introduction to the *Sefer Mechokekei Yehudah*, an elaborate commentary on the Ibn Ezra Torah commentary, the author cites by name more than sixty-seven *sefarim* which were written by Rabbe Avraham Ibn Ezra.[104]

His primary contribution was his commentary on Torah and on many of the books of *Nvi'im* and *Kesuvim*. Numerous commentaries have been written to elucidate the sometimes elusive words of

(100) Rabbeinu Eliyahu b. Shlomo Zalman of Vilna (Vilna Gaon, 1720-1797), *Tosafos Ma'asei Rav*.

(101) Deuteronomy 12:19.

(102) Rabbe Gedaliah b. Yosef Ibn Yachya (1515-1587), *Shalsheles haKabbalah* (Jerusalem: HaDoros haRishonim, 1962), p. 92.

(103) *Shalsheles haKabbalah, op. cit.*, states that he married the only daughter of Rabbe Yehudah haLevi (*ibid.*, p. 93).

(104) Rav Yehudah Leib b. Yitzchak Krinski, *Mechokekei Yehudah* (New York: Reinman Pub.), Introd., Vol. I, pp. 25-33.

the Ibn Ezra. His commentary on the Torah, in particular, comes under a great deal of critical analysis and discussion by the Ramban, in the Ramban's masterful Torah commentary. The Ramban writes concerning him,

> ועם רב אברהם בן עזרא תהיה לנו תוכחת מגולה ואהבה נסתרה.
>
> And with Rav Avraham ben Ezra we will have open rebuke and hidden love.[105]

In his *Iggeres haMussar,* the Rambam instructs his son, Avraham, to study the Torah commentary of the Ibn Ezra, "for it is extremely helpful for anyone who studies it in depth, and who has fine intellectual perception and understanding."[106]

Rabbe Avraham Ibn Ezra traveled extensively all over Europe. In Northern France, he met Rabbeinu Tam, with whom he later exchanged correspondence in which they both addressed one another warmly and with great respect.[107]

The World Travelers

It was at this time that Benjamin of Tudela embarked upon his famous voyage throughout many of the major countries of the world. His travels, over a period of thirteen years, took him through many parts of Europe and Asia. He traveled to the Provence in Southern France, to Italy, Greece, Cyprus, Persia, Syria, the Holy Land, Yemen, Egypt, and back to Spain. Reb Binyamin, who was a scholarly Torah Jew, provides a wealth of information concerning the Jewish communities he visited — their economic structure, their Yeshivos, and their Torah scholars. Much of the information provided in his *Sefer Masa'os* is unavailable from any other source. While no dates are given in the *Sefer haMasa'os,* his travels appear to have taken place during the thirteen-year period from 1160 to 1173.

(105) Rabbe Moshe b. Nachman (1194-1270), Introduction to his Torah commentary. Cf. Proverbs 27:5.

(106) Rambam's *"Iggeres haMussar," Rabbeinu Moshe ben Maimon: Iggarosav veToledos Chayyav,* M. Bar-Joseph, ed. (Tel Aviv: Mordecai Inst., 1970), p. 136.

(107) Rabbe Avraham Ibn Ezra is cited in the following *Tosafos: Rosh Hashanah* 13a, *Tosafos, s.v.* דאקירבו; *Ta'anis* 20b, *Tosafos, s.v.* בהכינתו; *Kiddushin* 37b, *Tosafos, s.v.* ממחרת.

Another world traveler at this time was Rav Pesachiah of Regensburg. He describes his itinerary in his *Sefer Sivuv*, or, "Traveling About." Over the course of fifteen years, he traveled from Prague to Poland to Kiev. From there he traveled to Asia Minor. He traveled across the length and breadth of Eretz Yisroel, where he visited graves and holy places. He, too, places particular emphasis upon the conditions of the Jewish communities to which he traveled. His travels took place shortly after those of Reb Binyamin, approximately during the years 1170 to 1175.

Rav Pesachiah was a brother of the *Tosafist*, Rabbe Yitzchak ben Yaakov of Bohemia, better known as Rabbe Yitzchak haLavan.[108]

Ravad I — The "Sefer haKabbalah"

Rabbe Avraham ben David Ibn Daud haLevi (Ravad I, 1110-1180), was a grandson of Rabbe Yitzchak Albalia (1035-1094).[109] He studied under his uncle, Rabbe Baruch b. Yitzchak Albalia (1077-1126), who was a disciple of the Rif, and a close friend and colleague of the Ri Migash. Rabbe Avraham Ibn Daud wrote the concise historical work, *Sefer haKabbalah*, which has been cited often in this work.

This small, but important historical work, which traces the course of Torah transmission from Creation until his own day, is cited as an invaluable historical source by all Jewish historians of subsequent generations. As the author explains at the very outset of this work, he wrote it to provide the reader with an awareness of the unbroken chain of Torah tradition, and to thereby strengthen and reinforce belief in the Mesorah.

Strengthening the Mesorah

זה ספר הקבלה כתבנוהו להודיע לתלמידים כי כל דברי רבותינו ז״ל חכמי המשנה והתלמוד, כולם מקובלים חכם גדול וצדיק מפי חכם גדול וצדיק, ראש ישיבה וסיעתו מפי ראש ישיבה וסיעתו, מאנשי כנסת הגדולה, שקבלו מהנביאים, זכר כלם לברכה.

ולעולם חכמי התלמוד, וכל שכן חכמי המשנה, אפילו דבר קטן לא אמרו מלבם, חוץ מן התקנות שתקנו בהסכמת כולם כדי לעשות סייג לתורה.

(108) Re. R. Yitzchak haLavan, see *Masters of the Mesorah: Later Rishonim*, Ch. 1, n. 95.

(109) Re. R. Yitzchak Albalia, see above, at n. 5.

> We have written this *Sefer haKabbalah* in order to make it known to the students that all the words of our teachers, of blessed memory, the Sages of the Mishnah and the Talmud, were received by one great and righteous Sage from the mouth of another great and righteous Sage, by one *Rosh Yeshiva* and his entourage, from another *Rosh Yeshiva* and his entourage, from the *Anshei Knesses haGedolah*, who received [the Oral Law] from the Prophets, may all their memories be blessed.
>
> The Sages of the Talmud, and certainly the Sages of the Mishnah, never said even a small [halachic] matter by themselves, [which was not derived through the guidelines of Torah transmission and halachic derivation],[110] other than the Rabbinic ordinances which they ordained with a general consensus of all the Sages, in order to provide a fence[111] around the Torah.[112]

In addition to his great stature as an outstanding Torah scholar and historian, Rav Avraham Ibn Daud was also a doctor, and a Torah philosopher. In his philosophical work, *HaEmunah haRamah*, he places emphasis upon the concept of *bechirah* or free will, as a fundamental Torah doctrine. He also wrote *Divrei Malchei Yisroel baBayis haSheni* — a history of the Jewish kings during the Second Temple era. In each of his works, he attempts to discredit the Karaitic sect, which was, at that time, an insidious threat to authentic Judaism.

Martyred "Al Kiddush HaShem"

As contemporary sources relate, at the end of his days Rabbe Avraham Ibn Daud sanctified the Name of G-d when he steadfastly refused to renounce his faith upon the pain of death. He was put to death *al Kiddush HaShem* in the year 1080 in Toledo, when he was seventy years old.[113]

(110) For more information re. the process of halachic derivation, see *Anvil of Sinai*, pp. 214-224.

(111) See *Avos* 1:1 — עשו סיג לתורה.

(112) Rabbe Avraham Ibn Daud, Introduction to *Sefer haKabbalah*.

(113) *Or haChaim*, No. 78, p. 21, citing the contemporary source, *Midrash haChachmah*, by Rabbe Yehudah b. Shlomo haKohen.

It is of interest to note that in his *Sefer haKabbalah,* Rabbe Avraham observes that the tragedy of his generation was, in a sense, more severe, even, than that of the period of the *Churban.* For, concerning that era, Jeremiah said,[114] *"Such as are for death, for death; such as are for the sword, for the sword; such as are for famine, for famine; such as are for captivity, for captivity."* Yet, no mention is made there of forcible conversion. While, in his generation, the Ravad laments, the terrifying sword of the Almohades is poised to eradicate the faith of the Jewish people through forcible conversion.[115]

Little did the Ravad know at that time that it would not be long before he himself would be confronted with this terrible challenge. When he was indeed confronted with this supreme test, this great Torah scholar and philosopher, who had given so much to his people, offered up his life *al kiddush HaShem* — in sanctification of the Name of his Creator.

A Sapling Planted in Spain

While we conclude our history of the "Golden Era" of Spain on this tragic note, the ever-recurring theme of וזרח השמש ובא השמש — *"The sun rises and the sun sets,"*[116] was soon to be re-enacted once again. A small sapling was planted in Spain at this time which was to grow and be nurtured in other climes, until it would become a mighty cedar — an endless source of spiritual vitality for our people throughout all ensuing generations.

The story of this spiritual giant, Rabbeinu Moshe ben Maimon, who was compelled to flee with his family from his Spanish homeland when he had but turned thirteen, will be related in the following chapter.

(114) Jeremiah 15:2.
(115) *Sefer haKabbalah, s.v.* ולאחר פטירת רב יוסף הלוי ז"ל.
(116) Ecclesiastes 1:5; *Supra,* Chap. 1, nn. 1-8.

4

Rambam: Prince of Torah

,,ממשה ועד משה,
לא קם כמשה״.
[חקוק על קבר הרמב״ם]

"From Moshe unto Moshe,
There arose none
Like Moshe."
[Inscription on Rambam's monument;
See Text, p. 162.]

Transmitting the Mesorah: From the Rambam to the Chachmei Lunel

חיזקו ונתחזק ביד עמנו וביד ערי אלקנו.
השתדלו להיות אנשי חיל כי הדבר תלוי בכם,
ועליכם להיות החלוצים.
אל תישענו ואל תסמכו על מלחמתי.
אני היום לא אוכל עוד לצאת בראש המחנה,
שכבר זקנתי, ושיבה זרקה בי.

הבורא יתברך יסייע על ידכם
להרים תורת משה וישראל;
וישים אתכם לשם ולתהילה בקרב הארץ, אמן.

Be strong and let us strengthen ourselves for the sake of our people and for the cities of our G-d. Try to be men of valor, for this matter depends upon you, and it is for you to be the vanguard. Do not rely upon my battle. I can today no longer go out at the head of the camp for I have already grown old, and old age has come upon me. . . .

May the Almighty help you in your efforts to elevate the dignity of Toras Moshe and of Israel, and may He cause your names to become a blessing in the land.

[Letter of Rambam to Chachmei Lunel;
See Text, at n. 120.]

4

Rambam: Prince of Torah

The Trials and Tribulations of Rabbe Maimon

The Almohad invasion of 1147 swept across the Iberian Peninsula like an ominous cloud which brought death, destruction, and relentless religious persecution to the hitherto thriving Jewish communities of Andalusia. Many thousands of Jewish families fled for their lives before the fanatical Almohades, who offered only a choice of death or conversion to Islam.

Among the families who lived in Cordoba during these troubled times was the Maimon family. Rav Maimon ben Rav Yosef, scion of a distinguished Torah family, was a great Torah scholar. He was a friend and colleague of Rav Yosef Ibn Tzaddik, and, like him, a disciple of the Ri Migash. Together with Rav Yosef, Rav Maimon served as a *dayyan* in Cordoba.

When the Almohad invasion made life unbearable for the Jews of Cordoba, Rav Maimon did as so many of his fellow Jews had done before him, and as so many have done since. In the year 1148, he picked up the wanderer's staff, and led his family into exile. Leaving friends and fortune behind, they fled from Cordoba, and wandered about from city to city in Christian Spain, seeking a peaceful haven.

After a number of years of wandering on the Iberian Peninsula, Rav Maimon set out for Morocco. The Jews of Morocco were also undergoing persecution at that time, although not quite as severe as that of the Jews in Cordoba. When Rav Maimon arrived, he found that many Jews were losing hope entirely, some even falling prey to the enticement of conversion to Islam, because they were afraid that the Almighty had forsaken His people. Whereupon, Rav Maimon wrote an *Iggeres Nechamah* — a letter of consolation — to instill within the hearts of the Jews of Morocco faith and hope in the coming of *Mashiach*. Rav Maimon also wrote a commentary on Torah, as well as on various aspects of halacha, some of which are cited by his son, the Rambam.[1]

It was not very long before the persecution intensified in Morocco, and the Maimon family was forced to flee once again, in 1165, first to Eretz Yisroel, and then to Egypt. It is believed by some that Rav Maimon decided to spend his declining years in Jerusalem, while the family, which found the condition of Jews in Eretz Yisroel too precarious, moved on to Egypt.

Rambam — Prince of Torah

On Shabbos, Erev Pesach, one hour and twenty minutes after noon, in the year 4895 (1135), the great light of Israel, Rabbeinu Moshe b. Maimon, was born. He was descended from a long line of Torah scholars, who traced their ancestry back to Rabbeinu haKadosh and to the House of David.[2]

The Rambam studied under his father, Rabbeinu Maimon, who was a disciple of the Ri Migash. Upon occasion, the Rambam, too, refers to the Ri Migash as his teacher.[3]

There is an interesting tradition which relates that when the Rambam was a child, he was brought by his father before the venerable Ri Migash, as he lay upon his deathbed. Young Moshe kissed the hand of the great Sage. The Ri Migash, who had already upon previous occasions become acquainted with the unusual qualities of the boy, kissed the Rambam and blessed him. It is said that in

(1) Rambam, Introduction to Mishnah, *"Sefer haMa'or: Otzar haHakdamos,"* M.D. Rabinowitz, ed. (Tel Aviv: Hotza'as Rishonim, 1948), p. 83. For other sources where the Rambam cites his father, see Rabbi Y.L. Maimon, *Rabbe Moshe ben Maimon* (Jerusalem: Mosad haRav Kook, 1969), p. 14, n. 11.

(2) *Or haChaim*, No. 1122, p. 533; Rabbi Y.L. Maimon, *op. cit.*, pp. 13 f.

(3) Rambam, *Mishneh Torah, Hilchos She'elah u'Pikadon*, 5:6.

later life, Maimonides remarked that all the Torah wisdom which he possessed was derived from the blessings which he had received at that moment from the venerable Sage.[4]

Words are entirely inadequate to describe the remarkable impact which the Rambam exerted upon Jewish life and thought, from his own time until this very day.

A Prolific Pen

Already during his early youth, the Rambam embarked upon his prolific writing career. In his introduction to the Mishnah, which he started writing when he was twenty-three years old, he writes that he had already completed a commentary on three entire *Sedarim* of the Talmud — *Mo'ed, Nashim,* and *Nezikin* — as well as on tractate *Chullin.*[5] He also wrote a *sefer* on the halachic conclusions of the *Talmud Yerushalmi* — *Hilchos Yerushalmi* — wherein he set out to accomplish for the *Yerushalmi* much the same as the Rif had accomplished for the *Talmud Bavli.*[6] Unfortunately, both of these *sefarim* are no longer extant, except for a commentary which is attributed to the Rambam on *Rosh Hashanah,* and a few small fragments on other tractates, which have only recently come to light.

"Sefer HaMaor" — The Mishnah Commentary

At the age of twenty-three, while his family was wandering from land to land in exile, seeking desperately for a haven, the Rambam embarked upon his first enduring major literary effort, the *Sefer haMaor,* a comprehensive commentary on the Mishnah. Writing under the most trying conditions, he completed this monumental work seven years later, at the age of thirty. כי מה שהשתדלתי בו אינו מעט — "My efforts in regard to this commentary," the Rambam writes in an illuminating autobiographical note, "were not few."[7]

(4) Rabbi Y.L. Maimon, *op. cit.,* p. 16, n. 14.

(5) Rambam, Introduction to Mishnah, *op. cit.,* p. 83. The Rambam writes that he did not yet complete his commentary on four tractates, which he hopes to complete in the near future.

(6) Rambam, Mishnah commentary, *Tammid* 5:1; See also Rabbi Y.L. Maimon, *op. cit.,* p. 301.

(7) See Rambam, *Mishnah commentary,* end tractate *Uktzin; Infra,* n. 77.

In addition to the commentary itself, the Rambam includes his own definitive halachic conclusions concerning all the Tannaitic disputes throughout the vast range and scope of the entire Mishnah. The *Sefer haMa'or* also includes a number of comprehensive introductory essays to various sections of the Mishnah. At one point in his Mishnah commentary, the Rambam makes the following intriguing statement.

כי יקר בעיני ללמד עיקר מעיקרי הדת והאמונה, יותר מכל אשר אלמדהו.

> It is more precious in my eyes to teach one of the fundamental principles of Torah faith, than anything else that I might teach.[8]

It was surely with this thought in mind that the Rambam availed himself of the opportunity to include important facets of Torah thought and hashkafah in various places throughout his writings. It is in this vein, for example, that in his Mishnah commentary, the Rambam makes an important observation on the last Mishnah of tractate *Makkos.*

רבי חנניא בן עקשיא אומר: רצה הקב"ה לזכות את ישראל לפיכך הרבה להם תורה ומצות.

> Rabbe Chanania ben Akashiah says: The Holy One, blessed be He, wanted to make Israel worthy, therefore did He provide them with an abundance of Torah and mitzvos.

Whereupon, the Rambam comments,

> It is among the fundamental principles of Torah faith that if an individual should fulfill any one of the 613 Torah commandments properly and correctly, without any extraneous thoughts whatsoever, but if he performs it, rather, only for the sake of the mitzvah itself, out of love [for the Creator] . . . he will thereby be worthy of attaining eternal life. Therefore did Rabbe Chanania [ben Akashiah] say, that since there are so many mitzvos, it is impossible that an individual should not perform [at least] one of them perfectly and completely during his lifetime. And when he does so, his soul will thereby be infused with eternal life.[9]

(8) Rambam, Mishnah commentary, *Berachos,* Chap. 9, end of last Mishnah.
(9) Rambam, Mishnah commentary, last mishnah in tractate *Makkos.*

The Introductions of the Rambam

Throughout his introductions to various sections of his Mishnah commentary, the Rambam clarifies many important facets of Torah hashkafah. Some of these introductions are so thoroughly permeated with a wide variety of important Torah concepts and are so highly significant, that they may be regarded as important *sefarim* in their own right. The introductions of the Rambam have, in fact, been published separately, as a self-contained volume.[10]

Thus, in his introduction to the Mishnah, at the beginning of the Order of *Zera'im,* the Rambam renders a concise history of Torah transmission, as well as many important thoughts concerning the transmission process. This introduction also contains a wealth of information concerning various facets of the concept of prophecy and prophetic revelation.

In his introduction to *Perek Chelek,* the tenth *perek* of *Sanhedrin,*[11] the Rambam formulates and clarifies the Thirteen Fundamental Principles of Torah Faith.[12]

In his introduction to *Pirkei Avos,* known as *Shemonah Perakim le-haRambam,* the Rambam provides the reader with an insight into the far-reaching significance of character development, as well as with methods of improving one's character flaws. And in his introductions to the Orders of *Kodshim* and *Taharos,* he provides a masterful summary and overview of the difficult halachos contained in each of those *sedarim.*

Rabbe Menachem ben Zerach speaks in glowing terms concerning these introductions of the Rambam.

מי שלא ראה הקדמותיו בסדרים, לא ראה מאורות מימיו.

> He who never saw these introductions [of the Rambam] to the Orders of the Mishnah, never saw light during his lifetime.[13]

(10) See M.D. Rabinowitz, "*Otzar haHakdamos,*" in *Rambam leAm* (Tel Aviv: Hotza'as Rishonim, 1948).

(11) In the Mishnah and in the *Talmud Yerushalmi* it is the tenth *perek* of *Sanhedrin,* while in the *Talmud Bavli* it is the eleventh and last *perek.*

(12) For a concise list of the Thirteen Ikkarim, see text at n. 66.

(13) Rabbe Menachem b. haKadosh Aharon b. Zerach (c. 1310-1385), *Tzedah laDerech* (Warsaw: Kelter, 1880), Introduction, p. 6.

The "Sefer haMitzvos"

The Rambam wrote his *Sefer haMitzvos* as an introduction and guideline for his much larger work, the *Yad haChazakah.* The *Sefer haMitzvos,* originally written in Arabic, has since been translated more than once into Hebrew. It is regarded as an extremely important work in its own right, and numerous comprehensive commentaries have been written on it.[14]

This *sefer* is based upon the following words of *Chazal,* which teach us that there are *Taryag Mitzvos* — 613 primary Torah commandments.

> דרש רבי שמלאי: שש מאות ושלש עשרה מצות נאמרו לו למשה; שלש מאות ושׂשים וחמש לאוין, כמנין ימות החמה, ומאתים וארבעים ושמונה עשה, כנגד איבריו של אדם.
>
> א״ר המנונא: מאי קרא? ,,תורה צוה לנו משה מורשה״. ,,תורה״ בגימטריא שית מאה וחד סרי. ,,אנכי״ ,,ולא יהיה לך״ מפי הגבורה שמענום. (מכות כג.־כד.)
>
> Rabbe Simlai expounded: 613 mitzvos were given to Moshe; 365 negative Torah commandments, corresponding to the days of the solar year; and 248 positive Torah commandments, corresponding to the [248] organs of the human body.[15]

(14) Some of the primary commentaries surrounding the *Sefer haMitzvos* are:
- (a) Comprehensive critical commentary of the Ramban (Rabbe Moshe b. Nachman), 1195-1270.
- (b) *Megillas Esther,* Rabbe Yitzchak de Leon II b. Eliezer Ibn Tzur, fl. c. 1546, Italy.
- (c) *Lev Same'ach,* Rabbe Avraham Alegre, 1560-1652, Constantinople.
- (d) *Marganissa Tava,* Rabbe Aryeh Leib Zital Horowitz, fl. c. 1760, Minsk.

(15) This implies that man must serve his Creator, with all the limbs of his body, every day of the year. (See Rashi, *Makkos* 23b, *s.v.* רמ״ח and *s.v.* שס״ה. The Rambam, in his introduction to *Sefer haMitzvos,* cites the *Midrash Tanchuma, Parshas Ki Seitsei,* to this effect.) Elsewhere, an analogy to the 365 negative commandments is drawn to the 365 sinews and tendons of the human organism, with a similar implication. (See *Mi sheberach* prayer for one who is ill.)

> Rav Hamnuna said: From which verse [may we derive this]? It says,[16] *Moshe commanded us Torah as a legacy.* The numerical value of the word Torah is 611. The first two commandments, *"I am the L-rd, your G-d,"* and *"You shall have no other god,"*[17] we heard from the Almighty.[18]

With these thoughts of *Chazal* in mind, the Rambam proceeds to enumerate and to clarify each of the 613 positive and negative Torah commandments. Before he does so, however, he sets down fourteen principles which will serve as guidelines, to determine which mitzvos should be included among the 613 Torah commandments and which mitzvos should not be included among them. On the basis of these guidelines he refutes the approach of others who preceded him — particularly the BaHaG[19] — and finds fault with their enumeration of the *Taryag Mitzvos.* In a brilliant exposition of scholarly erudition, the Ramban, on the other hand, undertakes to defend the words of the BaHaG, while finding numerous objections to some of the general guidelines of the Rambam, as well as to his enumeration of some of the individual mitzvos.

The "Yad haChazakah," or "Mishneh Torah"

In the year 1171, when the Rambam was thirty-six years old, he began working upon his magnum opus, *Mishneh Torah,* which is also called *Yad haChazakah,* because the numerical equivalent of the word, *Yad* is 14, for the fourteen primary books into which the Rambam's code is divided. It is also so named, after the last verse in Deuteronomy, ולכל היד החזקה . . . אשר עשה משה — *And for all the mighty hand [Yad haChazakah] . . . which Moshe wrought before the eyes of all Israel.*[20]

(16) Deuteronomy 33:4.

(17) Exodus 20:2-3; Deuteronomy 5:6-7.

(18) *Makkos* 23b-24a; *Midrash Tanchuma, Parshas Ki Seitsei.* See also Introd. of Rambam to *Sefer haMitzvos.*

These words of *Chazal* follow a tradition of the Sages that after having heard the first two commandments from the Almighty, the Jews were afraid lest they might die, and they asked Moshe to be their intercessor for the remaining eight commandments. (See Deuteronomy 5:20-24.)

(19) BaHaG is an acronym for *Ba'al Halachos Gedolos.* The *Halachos Gedolos,* by Rabbe Shimon Kayyara, is one of the earliest extant *sefarim* from the Geonic period (ca. 780 C.E.).

(20) Deuteronomy 34:12.

At the end of his introduction to *Mishneh Torah,* the Rambam includes a comprehensive listing of all the halachos contained in this Code. He includes in this introduction, too, a complete listing of the *Taryag mitzvos.* This is actually an abridged version of his *Sefer haMitzvos,* which he used as his basic guideline for his *Yad haChazakah.*

The Fourteen Sefarim of the Yad haChazakah

The fourteen *sefarim* of the Rambam's *Yad haChazakah,* and some of the halachos they contain, are as follows:[21]

(1) מדע — Wisdom
(a) Fundamental Torah principles; (b) Ethical values; (c) Torah study; (d) Idolatry; (e) Repentance
(2) אהבה — Love [of G-d]
(a) Reading the *Shema;* (b) Prayer; (c) *Tefillin; Mezuzah; Sefer Torah;* (d) *Tzitzis;* (e) Benedictions; (f) Circumcision
(3) זמנים — Holidays
(a) Shabbos; (b) *Eruvin;* (c) All Torah Festivals; (d) Fast-days; (e) New Moon; (f) *Shekalim;* (g) Rabbinic Festivals: Purim; Chanukah
(4) נשים — Women
(a) Marriage; (b) Divorce; (c) Levirate marriage; (d) *Chalitzah;* (e) Seduction and compulsion; (f) *Sotah*
(5) קדושה — Sanctity
(a) Illicit sexual relations; (b) Prohibited foods [kashrus]; (c) Kosher slaughtering
(6) הפלאה — Verbal pronouncement
(a) Swearing; (b) Vows; (c) Nazarite and other vows
(7) זרעים — Planting
(a) Hybridization; (b) Tithes for the poor; (c) All tithes; First fruit, etc.; (d) Sabbatical and Jubilee Years

(21) In most editions, the *Mishneh Torah* is divided into five volumes, as follows:
Vol. I — (1) ספר מדע; (2) אהבה; (3) זמנים
Vol. II — (4) ספר נשים; (5) קדושה
Vol. III — (6) ספר הפלאה; (7) זרעים
Vol. IV — (8) ספר עבודה; (9) קרבנות; (10) טהרה
Vol. V — (11) ספר נזיקין; (12) קנין; (13) משפטים; (14) שופטים

(8) עבודה — Temple service
(a) Temple and its sanctity; (b) Temple vessels and priestly service; (c) Temple entry; (d) *Korban* prerequisites; (e) *Korbanos* — ritual sacrifices; (f) Daily and Festival sacrifices; (g) Yom Kippur Temple service; (h) Unfit *Korbanos;* (i) Sacreligious use of sacred objects

(9) קרבנות — Ritual service
(a) *Korban Pesach;* (b) Festival *Korbanos;* (c) First-born; (d) Sin-offerings; (e) *Mechusrei kaparah*

(10) טהרה — Purity
(a) Laws of purity and impurity; (b) Red heifer; (c) Leprosy; (d) Ritual bath purification *[mikvah]*

(11) נזיקין — Damages
(a) Torts and damages; (b) Theft; (c) Inflicting wounds; (d) Murder

(12) קנין — Acquisitions
(a) Buying and selling; (b) Gifts; (c) Partnerships; (d) Servitude

(13) משפטים — Civil law
(a) Rentals; (b) Borrowing; Deposits; (c) Borrowing and lending; (d) Claims and counterclaims; (e) Inheritance

(14) שופטים — Judges
(a) The Sanhedrin; (b) Witnesses; (c) Rebelliousness; (d) Mourning; (e) Laws of Kings; *Mashiach*

Ten Years of Toil

The Rambam worked ten years on his *Mishneh Torah,* completing it in 1181, at the age of forty-six. The Rambam writes to the *Chachmei Lunel,*

> How abundantly have I toiled by day and by night, over a period of ten years consecutively, in compiling this work. Great individuals like yourselves will appreciate what I have done, for I have gathered and compiled matters which were widely scattered and dispersed, and I have joined them together.[22]

(22) From a letter of the Rambam to Rabbe Yehonasan haKohen of Lunel, in Southern France. (See *Rabbeinu Moshe ben Maimon: Iggarosav veToledos Chayyav,* M. Bar-Joseph, ed. [Tel Aviv: Mordecai Inst., 1970], p. 162.)

There was an intriguing tradition in the Rambam's family that during the night after the Rambam completed his *Mishneh Torah*, on 8 Kislev, 4941 (1181),[23] his father, Rav Maimon, appeared to him in a dream, together with another Sage. His father said, "This is Moshe Rabbeinu." The Rambam was astounded. Moshe Rabbeinu said, "I have come to see what you have done." When he looked through the *Mishneh Torah* of the Rambam, he said, יישר כחך — "Well done!"[24]

A Monumental Halachic Edifice

The *Mishneh Torah* is an unparalleled masterpiece of comprehensive halachic erudition, which covers virtually every facet of Jewish life and thought. In its 81 sections and its 982 chapters, the Rambam's code includes not only the laws which are relevant to the *galus*-Jew, but also *Hilchasa li-Meshicha* — those laws which will be applicable only upon the advent of *Mashiach*, and the final return to Zion. Unlike the work of his great predecessor, the Rif, which follows the arrangement and sequence of the Talmud, Maimonides introduced an elaborate, highly systematic sequence of halachic classification, which makes it remarkably simple for the student to find any particular halacha.

And yet, the *Mishneh Torah* is far more than a comprehensive halachic compendium. Citing numerous verses from Torah, *Nvi'im*, and *Kesuvim*, as well as a vast array of ethical-Aggadic citations of *Chazal*, the Rambam provides the reader with a wealth of ethical-mussar concepts, while at the same time, he clarifies all the fundamental tenets of Torah hashkafah and Torah faith.

The *Mishneh Torah* is a monumental edifice, which elucidates the broad outline, as well as the intricacies of all facets of Torah

(23) See Rambam, *Mishneh Torah*, *Hilchos Shemittah veYovel* 10:4, where he cites the date 4936 (1176) as the year when that particular section of the *Yad* was being written. Cf. *Hilchos Kiddush haChodesh* 12:2, where the date 4938 (1178) is given.

(24) *Seder haDoros* of Rav Yechiel Halpern (Warsaw: Y. Goldman, 1882), Vol. I, Part I, p. 206, citing an ancient manuscript attributed to Rav Dovid haNagid, grandson of the Rambam.

law, while it reaches beyond the letter of the law, into the very heart and spirit of the myriad halachos of the Torah, thereby making the Torah a true *Toras chaim* — a living, vibrant Torah. It infuses the halachos of the Torah with a deeper dimension of life and vitality, placing emphasis always upon fundamental *emunah*-values, as well as upon the underlying moral and ethical values of the Torah.

A Lesson in Torah Hashkafah . . .

Thus, for example, when the Rambam concludes his discussion of the laws of *Me'ilah,* which concern the sacreligious use of vessels and property which were consecrated to the Temple service, he sees this as an opportunity to clarify the over-all concept of *chukim* — the enigmatic Torah statutes which elude man's finite comprehension.

> It is proper for an individual to delve deeply into the laws of the holy Torah and to understand them thoroughly, according to his ability. A law whose reason he does not comprehend and for which he finds no purpose shall not be taken lightly in his eyes. He shall not audaciously ascend into G-dly matters, lest the Almighty be angry with him.[25]
>
> He shall not fabricate untruths concerning the Almighty, nor shall he treat the *chukim* as secular matters. The Torah writes, *And you shall observe all My statutes and all My judgments, and you shall fulfill them.*[26] Whereupon, the Sages remark, "This teaches us to equate the observance and the fulfillment of the statutes *[chukim]* with that of the judgments *[mishpatim].*[27] *"Fulfillment,"* understandably, refers to the individual performance of the *chukim;* while *"observance,"* means that he shall take heed, and shall not consider the *chukim* less significant than the *mishpatim.* . . .

(25) Lit., this last phrase reads, "He shall not break through to ascend unto the Almighty, lest He break forth upon him." (See Exodus 19:21-22.)

(26) Leviticus 19:37.

(27) *Toras Kohanim,* Leviticus 18:5.

All the *korbanos* — the ritual sacrifices — are included in the category of *chukim*. The Sages said that because of the ritual sacrifices the world exists.[28]

Through the fulfillment of the *chukim* and the *mishpatim*, the righteous become worthy of achieving eternal life. The Torah gives precedence to its instructions concerning the *chukim* [stipulating them before the *mishpatim*], as is written,[29] *And you shall keep My statutes [chukim] and My ordinances [mishpatim], which man shall fulfill, so that through them he might live.*[30]

. . . in morality

At the conclusion of his הלכות איסורי ביאה — laws concerning illicit sexual relations — the Rambam provides a concise guide to the Torah concept of morality.

> The individual shall control his evil inclination, [particularly] in regard to sexual temptation. He shall conduct himself with great sanctity, with pure thought and with proper intellect, in order to guard himself against this temptation. And he shall refrain from secluding himself with a female, for this provokes temptation greatly. . . . The individual shall distance himself from frivolity, from drunkenness, and from sensual discussions, since these are highly provocative, and they are stepping-stones to illicit sexual behavior. Nor shall he remain unmarried, since marriage is conducive to great sanctity.
>
> Above all, the Sages said, the individual shall occupy himself and his thoughts with Torah study, and he shall broaden his intellectual comprehension.[31] For illicit sexual thoughts will only emerge in a heart devoid of [Torah] wisdom.[32]

(28) *Avos* 1:2, *Al sh'loshah devarim ha-olam omed;* See also *Ta'anis* 27b, *Ilmalei ma'amados lo niskayemu shamayim va-aretz.* For further comments concerning the *Korbanos,* see Ramban, Leviticus 1:9, *s.v. Ve-yoser ra'ui; Sefer haChinuch, mitzvah* 95; See also *Meshech Chachmah* of Rabbe Meir Simcha haKohen of Dvinsk (1843-1926), beginning of *Vayikra.*

(29) Leviticus 18:5.

(30) Rambam, *Mishneh Torah, Hilchos Me'ilah* 8:8. For further development of this topic, see *Anvil of Sinai,* pp. 170-174.

(31) See *Kiddushin* 30b, *s.v.* אם פגע בך.

(32) Rambam, *Mishneh Torah, Hilchos Isurei Bi'ah* 22:20-21.

. . . and in ethical values

At the conclusion of his *Hilchos Megillah* — the laws of Purim — the Rambam places great emphasis upon the importance of charity and kindness, while he compares the relative merits of the three mitzvos of Purim to one another: (a) *Matanos la-evyonim* — gifts to the poor; (b) *Se'udas Purim* — the Purim meal; (c) *Mishlo'ach manos ish le-re'eyhu* — sending gifts to one's friend.[33]

> It is preferable for an individual to give an abundance of gifts to the poor, than it is for him to make a bountiful *Se'udas Purim* for himself, or to send presents to his friends. For there is no greater or more glorious [fulfillment of the mitzvah to rejoice on Purim] than by bringing joy to the hearts of the poor, the orphan, the widow, and the stranger. For he who brings joy to the hearts of these unfortunate individuals, is likened to the Almighty, concerning whom it says that,[34] *He revives the spirit of the humble, and He revives the spirit of the downtrodden.*[35]

A Comprehensive Life-Guide

Thus, in addition to its definitive rendition of a myriad halachos on every conceivable topic, the Rambam's *Mishneh Torah* is permeated with fundamental *emunah*-values and ethical-mussar concepts, covering virtually every facet of the life of a Torah Jew. It is, essentially, a life-guide for the Jew throughout all generations. The vast scope of the topics covered by the Rambam's code is as diversified, as vibrant, and as comprehensive as life itself.

When the great *Semichah-Sanhedrin* renewal controversy erupted in 1538,[36] its central focus revolved around interpretation

(33) According to the halacha, one must give charity to at least two poor people on Purim, and he must send two gifts of food to at least one friend. These mitzvos, of course, are in addition to the mitzvah of the *Megillah* reading in the evening and in the morning, and the mitzvah of *Se'udas Purim* — the festive Purim meal. (See *Mishneh Torah, Hilchos Megillah* 2:15-16.)

(34) Isaiah 57:15.

(35) Rambam, *Mishneh Torah, Hilchos Megillah* 2:17.

(36) See *Masters of the Mesorah: Later Rishonim*, Chap. 7, n. 14, re. the *semichah* controversy.

of the Rambam's text concerning this matter.[37] The Rambam's code contains laws concerning the Sabbatical year, which are so relevant in Israel today, laws concerning construction of the *Bais HaMikdash,* laws of ritual sacrifices [*korbanos*] and laws of purity and impurity. The rules for the deportment of a king, of a Torah Sage, of a penitent individual [*ba'al teshuvah*] — among many others — are outlined in detail in this comprehensive code.

. . . on penitence

> How magnificent is the role of *teshuvah*! Yesterday this individual was set apart from the L-rd, G-d of Israel, as it says,[38] *For your sins have made a separation between you and your G-d.* But today he is attached to the *Shechinah,* as it says,[39] *And you who cleave to the L-rd, your G-d, are alive each one of you this day.* He cries [to the Almighty] and is answered at once, as it says,[40] *And it shall come to pass, that before they call I will answer.* And when he performs mitzvos, they will be received with joy and satisfaction, as it says,[41] *For G-d has already accepted your deeds.*[42]

. . . on the role of the King in Israel

> The king shall be concerned for the dignity of the lowliest individual. And when he speaks to the people as a communal group, he shall speak softly. As it says,[43] *Listen to me, my brothers and my People.* He shall always conduct himself with very great humility [as Moshe Rabbeinu did]. . . . He shall bear their burdens, their troubles, their anger and their complaints, as a nurse carries the infant.[44] The Torah refers to the king as a shepherd,[45] *[and He chose His servant David*

(37) See Rambam, *Mishneh Torah, Hilchos Sanhedrin* 4:11, and see Radvaz commentary, *ad. loc.*

(38) Isaiah 59:2.

(39) Deuteronomy 4:4.

(40) Isaiah 65:24.

(41) Ecclesiastes 9:7.

(42) Rambam, *Mishneh Torah, Hilchos Teshuvah* 7:7.

(43) I Chronicles 28:2 — שמעוני אחי ועמי.

(44) Numbers 11:12 — כאשר ישא האומן את היונק. See *Sanhedrin* 8a, *s.v.* עד כמה and see *Torah Ethic,* pp. 105-106.

(45) Psalms 78:71 — לרעות ביעקב עמו.

> *. . .] to be the shepherd of His People, Jacob.* The bearing of a shepherd is clarified by the Prophets:[46] *Like a shepherd shall He feed His flock. He shall gather the lambs with His arm, and carry them in His bosom.*[47]

. . . on the ethical deportment of a talmid chacham

> Just as the Torah Sage can be recognized by his wisdom and by his knowledge, and he is thereby set apart from all other individuals, so, too, should he be recognizable through his deportment, his eating and drinking, his sexual behavior . . . his speech, his walking, his dress, his personal habits, and his business dealings. His behavior in all of these areas should be exemplary.[48]

After the Rambam clarifies each of these matters at length separately, he concludes with the following words.

> The individual who behaves in this exemplary fashion in regard to each of these areas, concerning him does the Prophet [Isaiah] say,[49] *You are My servant; Israel, through whom I will be glorified.*[50]

A Vast Repository of Torah Wisdom

As the Rambam notes in his introduction to his *Mishneh Torah,* he draws upon the accumulated wealth of Torah literature of all earlier generations — the Mishnah, the Jerusalem and Babylonian Talmuds, the Tosefta, both Mechiltas, the Sifra and Sifrei, as well as all other Tannaitic, Amoraitic, Geonic, and post-Geonic sources, placing particular emphasis upon the *Hilchos Rav Alfas.* Unlike some of his other *sefarim,* such as his Mishnah commentary and his *Moreh Nevuchim* which were written in Arabic, the Rambam wrote his *Mishneh Torah* in very clear, precise Hebrew. For centuries, great Torah scholars have pored diligently over every word in the Rambam's text, deriving important halachic distinctions from his choice of words, as well as from his inclusion or omission of certain key phrases and halachos.

(46) Isaiah 40:11 — כרועה עדרו ירעה, בזרועו יקבץ טלאים, ובחיקו ישא.
(47) Rambam, *Mishneh Torah, Hilchos Melachim* 2:6.
(48) Rambam, *Mishneh Torah, Hilchos De'os* 5:1.
(49) Isaiah 49:3.
(50) Rambam *Mishneh Torah, Hilchos De'os* 5:12.

Although his words are so profound that scholars have written many hundreds of volumes in their attempts to elucidate some of his complex halachic decisions,[51] the lucidity of style, the clarity of organization, and the simple beauty of the Hebrew employed by the Rambam, make the *Mishneh Torah* an eminently readable book. Like the work of Rav Alfas before him, the *Yad haChazakah* has become one of the major fountainheads of halacha for all ensuing generations.[52]

Even the Rambam's greatest critic, Rabbe Avraham ben David of Posquires, begrudgingly acknowledged that "he performed a great task in having gathered the words of the *Talmud [Bavli],* the *Yerushalmi,* and the *Tosefta.*"[53]

The vast breadth and scope of this work are truly breathtaking. It is little wonder that it has occupied such a central place in Jewish thought and halacha, from the day it was written, until today.

The following are some of the primary commentaries which surround the text of the *Mishneh Torah.*

(a) *Glosses of Ravad III,* Rabbeinu Avraham b. David of Posquires, c. 1120-1198.[54]
(b) *Maggid Mishneh,* Rabbeinu Vidal Yom Tov di Tolosa of Spain, 14th c. (contemporary of Rabbeinu Nissim of Gerondi).[55]
(c) *Migdal Oz,* Rabbeinu Shem Tov ben Avraham Ibn Gaon of Spain, b.c. 1287.[56]
(d) *Haggahos Maimuniyos,* Rabbeinu Meir haKohen of Rothenburg, 13th c. (disciple of Maharam of Rothenburg).[57]

(51) For a list of 342 published commentaries on the Rambam, see Rabbi Y. Rubinstein, *Otzar Meforshei Mishneh Torah,* end Vol. V, *Mishneh Torah* (New York: Shulsinger Brothers, 1947).

(52) *Supra,* Chap. 3, n. 14, re. comment of Rav Yosef Caro in his introduction to his *Bais Yosef* commentary on *Tur, Orach Chaim; See Later Rishonim,* Chap. 5, n. 41.

(53) *Hasagos haRavad* to *Mishneh Torah, Hilchos Kelayim* 6:2.

(54) Re. Ravad III of Posquires, see Chap. 5, nn. 16-27.

(55) Re. Rabbe Vidal Yom Tov of Tolossa, see *Later Rishonim,* Chap. 6, nn. 25-33.

(56) Re. Rabbe Shem Tov Ibn Gaon, see *Later Rishonim,* Chap. 5, between nn. 27-28.

(57) Re. Rabbe Meir HaKohen of Rothenburg, see *Later Rishonim,* Chap. 3, between nn. 90-91.

(e) *Kessef Mishneh*, Rabbeinu Yosef Caro, 1488-1575 (author of *Bais Yosef*, and *Shulchan Aruch*).[58]
(f) *Radvaz*, Rabbeinu David Ibn Avi Zimra, 1480-1574.[59]
(g) *Lechem Mishneh*, Rabbeinu Avraham diBoton of Salonika, 1560-1606.[60]
(h) *Mishneh laMelech*, Rabbeinu Yehudah Rosanes of Constantinople, 1657-1727.

The "Moreh Nevuchim"

The Rambam's writings, as well as his sphere of influence, were hardly limited to the area of halacha alone. His *Moreh Nevuchim* clearly established him as a philosopher of towering stature. Written in Arabic, the Rambam's *Moreh* was translated into Hebrew by Rabbe Shmuel ben Yehudah Ibn Tibbon of Southern France (c. 1160-1230), at the request of Rabbe Yehonasan haKohen of Lunel.

Rabbe Shmuel corresponded with the Rambam concerning various aspects of the translation. When, in the course of the correspondence, he indicated that he would like to visit the Rambam in Egypt to discuss certain aspects of the translation personally, the Rambam advised him not to make the hazardous journey, although he would truly take great delight in seeing him.

In an unusual autobiographical note, the Rambam describes his obligations as the Sultan's doctor, which occupy, at the very least, his entire morning each day, unless a member of the Sultan's court is taken ill, in which event he must remain there the entire day. When he returns home, his office is filled with patients — both Jewish and Gentile — to whom he dispenses prescriptions throughout the remaining hours of the day, and often into the evening hours, as well, leaving him terribly weak and barely able to speak. This exceedingly difficult schedule, together with his obligations towards the Jewish community which occupy him entirely on Shabbos, leave him with virtually no free time or energy at all, which he might devote to such a distinguished visitor.

(58) Re. Rabbe Yosef Caro, see *Later Acharonim*, Chap. 7, at nn. 16-49.

(59) Re. Rabbe Dovid ibn Avi Zimra, see *Later Rishonim*, Chap. 7, at n. 11.

(60) Rabbe Avraham di Boton of Salonika and Rabbe Yehudah Rosanes were both early *Acharonim*. The time-frame of their activity is therefore beyond the scope of this work.

While the Rambam rules out the advisability of a personal visit by Rabbe Shmuel to Egypt, he indicates his readiness to reply to all of Rabbe Shmuel's questions concerning the *Moreh Nevuchim*, and he encourages him to diligently pursue and complete his translation.[61]

Vindication of the Rambam's "Moreh"

It is true that for a while a great controversy raged around the *Moreh Nevuchim*, which draws, to an extent, upon Aristotelian philosophy. Many Torah scholars felt that this type of philosophical speculation has no place in Torah thought, and presents a threat to a student's pursuit and attainment of unadulterated Torah values.[62] The Ramban, however, in two famous letters which he sent to the *Chachmei Tzorfas* — the Torah scholars of Northern France — in an effort to bring an end to this great Maimonidean controversy, vindicated the role of the *Moreh Nevuchim* and the Rambam's purpose in writing it — "not for those who have been taught reliance upon Torah tradition from infancy," but rather, "to bring back the dwellers in the far ends of the earth to the fortress of Torah, who, if not for his words and the teachings of his books by which they live, would long ago have faltered."[63]

When the Maimonidean controversy erupted once again during the lifetime of the Rashba, that great Barcelonian scholar came to the defense of the *Moreh Nevuchim* against its detractors, saying that the Rambam's sefarim are "more precious than gold and great treasure."[64]

It is of interest to note that, during the last generation, the great Torah Sage, Rav Yosef Rosen (the Rogachover Gaon, 1858-1936), has shown that all the philosophical concepts of the *Moreh Nevuchim* find their origin in Talmudic and Midrashic sources.[65]

(61) Rambam's letter to R. Shmuel ibn Tibbon of 8 Tishrei, 4960 (1200), cited in *Iggarosav* (Bar-Joseph ed., *op. cit.*, pp. 122 f); *Infra*, Chap. 5, nn. 83-86.

(62) For further information concerning this Maimonidean controversy, see *Later Rishonim*, Chap. 4, nn. 84-89. For citations from the *Moreh Nevuchim*, see *infra*, pp. 156-157, nn. 84 and 89.

(63) *Iggeres haRamban* to *Chachmei Tzorfas* (the French *Tosafists*), as cited by Rabbi Charles B. Chavel in his *Ramban: His Life and Teachings* (New York: Feldheim, 1960), p. 37.

(64) See *Later Rishonim*, Chap. 5, n. 8.

(65) See Rabbi Chavel, *Ramban* (Eng. biog.), p. 41.

The Thirteen Principles of Torah Faith

The Thirteen Articles of Faith which the Rambam set forth in his introduction to *Perek Chelek* in *Sanhedrin*, have become a byword in Judaism and are universally regarded as the definitive formulation of the fundamental concepts of Torah faith.[66] The *Ani Ma'amin*, which is a concise rendition of the Thirteen Principles of Maimonides, has become a clarion call to Torah faith for the Jew throughout the centuries. In every generation since his time, Jews have submitted to martyrdom and have sanctified the Name of G-d, with the Rambam's *Ani Ma'amin* on their lips.

In summary form, the Thirteen Fundamental Principles of the Rambam are as follows:

Our Knowledge of the Creator

1. Existence of an omnipotent Creator
2. Oneness of the Creator
3. Non-corporeality of the Creator
4. Eternity of the Creator [and Creation ex-nihilo]
5. G-d alone must be worshipped

Prophecy and Divine Origin of Torah

6. Truth of Prophecy and of the Prophets
7. Moshe — Greatest of all Prophets
8. Divine Origin of Written and Oral Laws
9. Immutability of Torah

Divine Providence: Reward and Retribution

10. G-d knows all deeds and thoughts of man
11. Reward and Retribution, and *Olam HaBa*
12. Coming of *Mashiach*
13. *Techiyas haMeisim* — Resurrection

Iggeres haShmad and Iggeres Teiman

In his *Iggeres haShmad* and in his *Iggeres Teiman*, the Rambam displays the warm, tender concern for his fellow Jews, which has been the hallmark of the leader of Israel in every generation.

(66) For a comprehensive discussion of the Thirteen *Ikkarim*, see *Torah Faith: The Thirteen Principles* (N.Y.: Hashkafah Publications, 1986).

In the *Iggeres haShmad,* the Rambam emphatically points out that a Jew who accepts another faith under duress is still a Jew, but he must, under all circumstances, flee before the tyrannical oppression, abandon his homeland, and go into exile in quest of a haven where he might serve his G-d freely and openly, as a G-d fearing Jew.[67]

His *Iggeres Teiman* — the famous letter to the downtrodden, persecuted Jews of Yemen, and his efforts in their behalf, left such an indelible imprint upon those previously forlorn and forsaken Jews — elevating their spirits and strengthening their faith — that they included the name of the Rambam thereafter in their recitation of the *Kaddish,* saying, "May the great Name of the Almighty be exalted . . . in your days and in your lifetime and in the lifetime of our teacher, Rabbeinu Moshe ben Maimon."[68]

At the conclusion of his *Iggeres Teiman* the Rambam writes that he had, at first, grave misgivings about sending this letter to the Yemenite Jewish congregations and to their spiritual leaders for fear that it might fall into the wrong hands, thereby placing both himself and the recipients in great peril. But he then decided that because of the great need for these words of encouragement for the Jews of Teiman, and because of the great mitzvah involved in strengthening the faith of his downtrodden brethren, he would send the letter to them, and he would rely upon the dictum of *Chazal* that, "mitzvah messengers will not come to harm."[69]

נאה דורש ונאה מקיים

The Rambam, of course, was נאה דורש ונאה מקיים — he fulfilled meticulously all that he taught.[70] Thus, we find, for example, that the Rambam tells us that it was his custom to follow the custom of the *Chasidim haRishonim* — the Early Pietists, in regard to *erev Tishah B'Av.*

(67) See Rambam's *Iggeres haShmad,* near end — ולא יעמוד בשום פנים במקום השמד.

(68) See *Iggeres* of the Ramban to *Chachmei Tzorfas,* as cited by *Or haChaim, op. cit.,* no. 1122, p. 535.

(69) Rambam, end of *Iggeres Teiman,* citing *Pesachim* 8a — שלוחי מצוה אינן ניזוקין.

(70) See *Chagigah* 14b, where this phrase is used in regard to Rabbon Yochanan ben Zakkai.

ומימינו לא אכלנו ערב ט׳ באב תבשיל אפילו של עדשים, אא״כ היה בשבת.

> We have never eaten on *erev* Tishah B'Av any cooked food, even lentils, unless it fell on Shabbos.[71]

Man of Impeccable Integrity . . .

In his *Iggeres haMussar,* which he wrote as an ethical bequest to his son, the Rambam explains the secret of his remarkable success in life.

> At such time as I shall bequeath unto you that which the Creator bequeathed unto me, I will bequeath unto you the trait of impeccable integrity, because of which the Creator endowed me with all my success. . . .
>
> Integrity has gained for me access to places into which my forebears did not lead me, [and through it] I have inherited that which my ancestors did not bequeath unto me. It has given me mastery over greater and better men than myself. I have become successful, and I have been able to help others, as well as myself. Therefore, take heed [concerning the trait of integrity], even in regard to matters concerning which the Torah did not instruct us.[72]

. . . and of great Humility

In his Ethical Bequest, the Rambam also speaks highly of the trait of humility.

תתנהגו בענוה, כי הוא סלם לעלות המעלות הרמות.

> Conduct yourselves with humility, for it is a ladder whereby we may ascend to the loftiest heights.[73]

"Follow in My Footsteps"

In his personal correspondence, we see how the Rambam implemented this principle in his daily life. In a letter to his beloved disciple, Rav Yosef ben Yehudah Ibn Aknin, he speaks of certain individuals who belittled the significance of his *Mishneh Torah,* and who often took pains to disparage the Rambam himself, as well. The response of the Rambam is fascinating.

(71) Rambam, *Mishneh Torah, Hilchos Ta'anis* 5:9.
(72) "Ethical Bequest of the Rambam," as cited in *Torah Ethic,* p. 362.
(73) "Ethical Bequest of the Rambam," *Torah Ethic,* p. 371.

> They make it appear that if any of them would attempt to write a better and larger work, he could do so readily. And if they should find it expedient to say that I am not a religious Jew or to question my religious observance, they will say so.
>
> Yet all this, I swear to you, my son, does not bother me, nor does it provoke me to anger. And even if I would see it with my own eyes, or hear it with my own ears, or if they should speak this way in front of me, I would not be concerned. On the contrary, I would humble myself before them, and reply pleasantly and softly, or keep my silence. . . .
>
> Nor will I attempt to vindicate myself, for the honor of my soul and the integrity of my middos are more precious to me than that I should prevail with words over these foolish individuals. . . . I never boastfully claim that I have never erred. On the contrary, when it becomes clear to me that something I have selected or that I have written is incorrect, I retract, in regard to any matter at all, whether it be in regard to my book, my character traits, or my natural habits.[74]

And then the Rambam urges his *talmid* not to become involved in any arguments, or in any exchange of harsh words. He concludes with the following words.

> In general, I beg of you, if you are my disciple, that you shall follow in my footsteps and in my traits. That is best for you. If certain individuals should curse you, curse them not. Be among those who are humiliated rather than among those who humiliate.[75] Do not cast your words about. Think of the Almighty first.[76]

(74) Letter of Rambam to his disciple, Rav Yosef b. Yehudah Ibn Aknin, *Iggaros u'Teshuvos haRambam* (Jerusalem: haAchim Levin-Epstein), p. 49. For a somewhat diferent version of this *Iggeres,* see the Bar-Joseph edition, *Iggarosav, op. cit.,* p. 102.

(75) See *Gittin* 36b; *Yoma* 23a. Cf. Rambam, *Mishneh Torah, Hilchos De'os* 2:3.

(76) Letter of Rambam to Rav Yosef Ibn Aknin, *Iggaros u'Teshuvos haRambam* (Jerusalem: haAchim Levin-Epstein), p. 51. Cf. Bar-Joseph ed., *Iggarosav, op. cit.,* p. 106.

A Life of Hardship and Suffering

It is entirely remarkable that one individual should have found it possible to write such a vast array of Torah literature. It is almost incredible, however, that the Rambam could have done so at all, driven as he was from land to land, hounded by the relentless persecution which engulfed Sephardic Jewry in his day. At the conclusion of his commentary on the Mishnah, the Rambam writes that this work was written while he was experiencing "that which the Almighty decreed upon us concerning exile and wandering among the nations, from one end of the heavens to another," some of these commentaries having been written while he "was traveling on the road, and others, aboard boats in the Dead Sea."[77]

In a letter written to the *Chachmei Lunel* during the last years of his life, the Rambam observes that this wandering in exile had a detrimental effect upon his health. It brought upon him serious illnesses, from which he suffered all the years of his life.[78]

In another letter, the Rambam describes some of the severe trials and tribulations which he suffered during his lifetime. He indicates in this letter to a friend of his youth that in the intervening years since he saw him last, he suffered severe illness, very substantial monetary loss, and was also the target of libelous charges which very nearly cost him his life.

More severe, however, than all these trials, he writes, was the loss of his beloved younger brother, *"ha-tzaddik Rabbe Dovid,"* who drowned at sea when his boat capsized and sank, together with his entire fortune, and the fortunes of others which had been entrusted to him. The Rambam was a silent partner in Rav Dovid's enterprises, and in this way Rav Dovid supported the Rambam entirely so that he would be able to devote his full time to Torah study. The Rambam was devastated by this loss, for his love for his brother knew no bounds. In this letter, the Rambam observes that eight years have already gone by since that tragic day, but he has found no consolation.[79]

(77) Rambam, upon conclusion of his Mishnah commentary to tractate *Uktzin*, last tractate in *Shas*. See above, n. 7.

(78) Rambam's letter to *Chachmei Lunel*. See *Rabbeinu Moshe b. Maimon: Iggarosav veToledos Chayyav*, Bar-Josef, ed., *op. cit.*, p. 193.

(79) Rambam, in a letter to Rav Yefes b. Eliyahu haDayyan, *Iggarosav, op. cit.*, p. 165. See n. 2, *ad. loc.*

In a letter to his disciple, Rav Yosef Ibn Aknin, the Rambam speaks of a daughter who had passed away,[80] and in yet another letter, he writes that his son, Avraham, had been taken critically ill, and all hope was given up for his recovery, until, with the help of G-d, his condition suddenly began to improve, and he was on the road to recovery.[81]

Words of Faith and Hope

All these tribulations and tragic circumstances notwithstanding, the words which came forth from the Rambam's pen were not words of despair or hopelessness, but rather vibrant, dynamic words of Torah wisdom, which brought faith and hope to his downtrodden people everywhere.

. . . on recognizing G-d's existence

> יסוד היסודות ועמוד החכמות,[82] לידע שיש שם מצוי ראשון, והוא ממציא כל נמצא.
>
> The foundation of all foundations and the pillar of all wisdom is to know that there exists a Primary Being, who infuses all that exists with existence.[83]

. . . on attaining nearness to G-d

> השתדל בכל יכלתך לרבות העתים ההם אשר אתה בהם עם ה׳, או שאתה משתדל להגיע אליו.
>
> Try with all your might to increase those moments when you are with G-d, or when you are striving to attain nearness to Him.[84]

(80) End of Rambam's letter to Rav Yosef Ibn Aknin, as cited in *Iggarosav, op. cit.*, p. 109. Some regard this as a reference to the daughter of his brother, Rav Dovid. See *Iggarosav,* ad. loc., n. 30.

(81) End of Rambam's letter to Rav Chisdai haLevi. See *Iggarosav,* p. 148.

(82) These four words, יסוד היסודות ועמוד החכמות, which are the opening words in the Rambam's *Mishneh Torah,* begin with the four Hebrew letters which spell out the Tetragrammaton — the ineffable Name of G-d, as a token of reverence to the Creator.

(83) Rambam, *Mishneh Torah, Hilchos Yesodei haTorah* 1:1.

(84) Rambam, *Moreh Nevuchim* 3:51.

. . . on attaining perfection

אין האדם שלם אלא כשהיה כולל הדעות והמעשה.

An individual has not attained perfection until he has acquired both profound understanding [of Torah hashkafah] and practical implementation.[85]

. . . on pursuing the "middle path"

Observing that the Sages were opposed to ascetic behavior and to the inculcation of character extremes, the Rambam writes,

> If an individual will constantly measure his deeds and aspire to pursue the middle path, he will attain the highest possible stature for a human being, and he will thereby come closer to G-d and be blessed with His goodness. This is the perfect approach to one's service of G-d.[85a]

. . . on truth and righteousness

דעו, כי האמת והצדק הם תכשיטי הנפש.

Know that truth and righteousness are ornaments of the soul.[86]

. . . on dealing with a haughty individual

האלקים יצילך ממי שהוא גדול וחשוב אצל עצמו.

May the Almighty protect you from one who is great and important in his own eyes.[87]

. . . on measuring one's words

ראוי לו לאדם שיחמול על דבורו יותר מחמלתו על ממונו.

An individual should be more concerned about his choice of words than about his wealth.[88]

(85) Rambam, Introduction to Mishnah commentary.

(85a) *Shemonah Perakim le-haRambam,* end Ch. 4. Cf. *Mishneh Torah, Hil. De'os* 1:4. For exceptions to this rule, see *Shemonah Perakim* and *Mishneh Torah, ad. loc.*

(86) Rambam, *Iggeres haMussar.* See *Torah Ethic,* pp. 362-363.

(87) Rambam, in letter to his disciple, Rabbe Yosef Ibn Aknin.

(88) Rambam, in his essay, *"Kiddush HaShem,"* or *"Iggeres haShmad"*

. . . on the purpose of Creation

תכלית העולם וכל אשר בו, איש חכם וטוב.

The purpose of the world and all that it contains, is a wise and good individual.[89]

. . . on the written word

That which one inscribes with his hand and writes in a book, it is proper that he shall [first] review it a thousand times.[90]

. . . on performing kindness

אל תחדלו להיטב לכל אשר יוכלו.

Do not refrain from performing kindness to whomever you can.[91]

. . . on strengthening Torah faith

המלכים עובדי אלילים ניסו ללחוץ עלינו כדי לערער אמונתנו בתורתו, אולם נותן התורה הלא אלקים הוא, ומי יכול לעמוד כנגדו!

The idolatrous kings have attempted to oppress us, in order to undermine our faith in His Torah. However, the Giver of Torah is G-d, and who can oppose Him![92]

"Among All the Exiles, There Was None Like Him"

The name of the Rambam appears to have cast a spell over our people — a spell of awe and reverence, love and gratitude, which grows ever stronger with the passing of the centuries.

In his letter to the *Chachmei Tzorfas* — the French *Tosafists* — which he wrote in order to bring an end to the Maimonidean controversy, the great 13th century Torah master, Rabbe Moshe ben Nachman (Ramban, 1194-1270), refers to the Rambam as,

(89) Rambam, *Moreh Nevuchim* 3:51.

(90) Rambam, in his essay, *"Kiddush HaShem" ["Iggeres haShmad"].*

(91) Rambam, *"Iggeres haMussar."* See *Torah Ethic,* pp. 368-369.

(92) Rambam, *Iggeres Teiman,* Bar Joseph ed. (Tel Aviv: Mordecai Institute 1970), p. 54.

האיש הקדוש ההוא, בכל גלות צרפת וספרד לא קם כמוהו.

". . . That saintly individual, among all the exiles of France and Spain, there arose none like him."[93]

A contemporary of the Ramban, Rabbe Hillel of Verona, who witnessed the burning of the Rambam's *sefarim* in Paris in 1242, wrote the following remarks concerning the Rambam.

הלא תחשוב כי רבנו משה היה כמעט משנה בדורו אל משה רבנו, וצדקת כל הדור היה תלוי בו.

Be aware that Rabbeinu Moshe [ben Maimon] was almost second in his generation to Moshe Rabbeinu, and the righteousness of the entire generation depended upon him.[94]

Rabbeinu Shlomo min haHar, the teacher of Rabbeinu Yonah heChasid, who stood at the forefront of the anti-Maimunists, explained that his quarrel was only with the advisability of studying the *Moreh Nevuchim*, but that he never questioned the greatness of the Rambam.

חי ה', אשר לשמו נכנסתי לדברים האלה, כי מעולם לא יצא מפינו שום שמץ וגנות ברב ותורתו, כי חביבים וערבים עלינו דבריו מאד.

I swear by the Name of the Almighty, for whose sake I entered into this controversy, that I never uttered any disparaging remark against the Rav [the Rambam] and his Torah, for his words are exceedingly sweet and beloved to us.[95]

Rabbe Yehudah Alpachar of Toledo, another militant anti-Maimunist, writes,

ובכל זאת מצוה עלינו לחוס על כבוד של רבנו משה ז"ל, ולהודות כי היה בדורו כאיש חמודות . . . ומפיו תורה יבקשו, כי מלאך ה' צבאות הוא, ואחריו לא קם כמוהו.

(93) As cited by Meir Uryan, *HaMoreh laDoros* (Jerusalem: Mosad haRav Kook, 1968), p. 105; R. Chaim Dov Chavel, *Ramban* (Heb. biog.), p. 128.

(94) Letter of R. Hillel of Verona, at the time of the Talmud burning in Paris, 1242, as cited by Meir Uryan, *HaMoreh laDoros, op. cit.*, p. 107. See *Later Rishonim*, Chap. 4, nn. 86-87.

(95) R. Chaim Dov Chavel, *Rabbe Moshe ben Nachman* (Heb. biog.), *op. cit.*, p. 122, citing *Yeshurun*, Vol. VIII, p. 101. *Infra*, Chap. 5, n. 69.

> Nevertheless, it is a mitzvah for us to be deeply concerned for the honor of Rabbeinu Moshe [ben Maimon] *zal,* and to admit that he was in his generation like [Daniel], the "delightful man."[96] . . . "From his mouth will Torah be sought, for he is an angel of G-d,"[97] and after him none arose like him.[98]

The Vilna Gaon, it is said, was once asked where reference can be found in the Torah to the Rambam. He replied by citing the verse, למען רבות מופתי בארץ מצרים — *That My wonders may increase in the land of Egypt.*[99] The first letters of each of these words, the Gaon pointed out, spell out the name, "RaMBaM."

"Greater Than a Prophet"

The great Sephardic Torah scholar and statesman, Rabbe Don Yitzchak Abrabanel, wrote a sefer, *Rosh Amanah,* in which he clarifies thoroughly every aspect of the Rambam's "Thirteen Principles of Torah Faith." In his introduction to this *sefer,* he expresses his great awe and reverence for the Rambam, whom he describes allegorically as "a new creation" of G-d, who had spiritual dominion over all Israel. And he concludes with the following words.

כי ראיתי אלקים פנים אל פנים דבר אל משה — עדיף מנביא.

> For I have seen [as though] G-d had spoken with Moshe [Maimonides] *"face to face."*[100] He is greater, even, than a prophet.[101]

Like Ezra, Hillel haZaken, Rabbe Akiva, Rabbeinu haKadosh, and Rav Ashi before him, so too did Maimonides represent the glory of Torah. Like each of these, he too was everything all at once

(96) See Daniel 9:23; 10:11; 10:19.

(97) See Malachi 2:7.

(98) Rabbi Chaim Dov Chavel, *loc. cit.,* citing *Iggeres Kena'os* (Leipzig), p. 2b; Cf. Deut. 34:10.

(99) Exodus 11:9.

(100) Cf. Exodus 33:11; Numbers 12:8; Deuteronomy 34:10.

(101) Rabbe Don Yitzchak Abrabanel (1437-1508), *Rosh Amanah* (Tel Aviv: Sifreisi, 1958), Introduction, p. 9. Cf. *Bava Basra* 12a — *Chacham adif miNavi.*

— venerated Torah Sage, beloved and devoted communal leader, Talmudist, philosopher, doctor, and statesman. This was Maimonides, scion of the House of David, prince of Torah, the living embodiment of the legacy of Sinai, a legacy which came to him through an unbroken chain of Torah transmission, from father to son, from *Rebbe* to *talmid*, and which traced its source to the great Babylonian academies, and thence to Sinai.

"From Moshe Unto Moshe, None Arose Like Moshe"

When the Rambam died on the 20th of Teves, 4965 (1204), the Jewish community of Jerusalem expressed its grief by reading the Torah portion concerning the terrible *tochacha*[102] — the admonishment in *Parshas Bechukosai* — during the synagogue service. The Torah reading was followed by the *Haftorah*, taken from the first chapter in Joshua, which begins with the words,[103] משה עבדי מת — *My servant, Moshe, died.*[104]

According to some sources,[105] the *Haftorah* reading was then concluded with the following words in Samuel.

> גלה כבוד מישראל, כי נלקח ארון האלקים.
>
> *The glory has departed from Israel,*
> *For the Ark of the L-rd has been removed.*[106]

It is related that when the Rambam's *aron*, or coffin, was being carried from Egypt to Eretz Yisroel, a band of some thirty armed robbers tried to steal the coffin. They drove off the Jewish escort, and attempted to lift the *aron* and cast it into the sea. Try as they might, however, the *aron* would not budge from its place; it was rooted to the spot. They decided that it contained the body of a holy

(102) See Leviticus 26:14-46.

(103) Joshua 1:1.

(104) See Rabbe Yosef Abudraham [fl. 1340, disciple of Rabbeinu Yaakov Ba'al haTurim], in his *Sefer Abudraham* (New York: Saphograph Pub.), under *Seder haParshiyos ve-haHaftoros*, p. 163.

(105) Rav Avraham Zacuto (1425-1515), *Sefer Yuchsin haShalem* (Jerusalem: 1963), *Ma'amar Chamishi, Doros Acharonim*, p. 220; *Or haChaim*, *op. cit.*, No. 1122, p. 538.

(106) I Samuel 4:22.

man. Whereupon, the thieves told the Jews to continue their journey, and they joined the procession as it escorted the Rambam to his final resting place.[107]

The following words were engraved upon his tombstone.

אדם ולא אדם, ואם אדם היית,
ממלאכי רום אמך הרתה.
או, אומרה לקל, באין אשה ואיש,
מלאך בעולם תחתון בראת.

A man, yet not a man, but if in truth a man you were,
Then from the Angels on high did your mother conceive.
O', will I cry out to the L-rd: "With neither woman nor man,
An Angel in the lower spheres hast Thou created."[108]

In his final resting place in Tiberias, the following words may be seen to this very day above the grave of Maimonides.

ממשה ועד משה, לא קם כמשה.

"From Moshe unto Moshe, there arose none like Moshe."

Rav Avraham haNagid ben haRambam

The Rambam was succeeded as *Nagid* or Exilarch over the Jewish community in Egypt by his only son, Rabbe Avraham, who was born in 1186, when the Rambam was fifty-one years old. In a letter to his disciple, Rav Yosef ben Yehudah, the Rambam expresses his high regard for his son.

> The Almighty has endowed my son, Avraham, with the grace and the blessings of him by whose name he is called [Avraham Avinu] . . . . May He strengthen him and grant him long life, for he is an exceedingly modest and humble individual, with excellent character traits. He has a fine

(107) *Sefer haYuchsin, loc. cit.*

(108) See Rav Yehudah Leib Maimon, *Rabbe Moshe ben Maimon* (Jerusalem: Mosad haRav Kook, 1960), p. 182.

> intellect and a pleasant personality. [With G-d's help, he will undoubtedly attain a name among the great ones.][109]

Rav Avraham was an outstanding Torah scholar and a dedicated communal leader. Like his father before him, he was a doctor in the court of the Sultan, and he stood at the head of the Cairo hospital. He presided over the Jewish community, exercising his authority judiciously, but always with great integrity, compassion, and humility. Because of his great piety, he was known as Rav Avraham heChasid.

In regard to a dispute between one of the *dayyanim* of Alexandria and the *Nasi* of Damascus, which was brought to him for adjudication, Rav Avraham writes to the *dayyan* in Alexandria as follows.

> Heaven forbid that a great man like yourself should suspect that I might exercise false flattery in judgment, whether to small or to great.[110]

And in a related letter to the *Nasi* of Damascus concerning this matter, Rav Avraham writes,

> What can he say about me? That I have been overly harsh with the community, where it was not for the sake of Heaven? That I have perverted justice? That I have taken bribery? That I have sought unjust gain? . . .
>
> The path and the custom which I pursue is that of my father, of blessed memory — the path of kindness and respect.[111]

(109) Rambam, in a letter to his disciple, Rav Yosef b. Yehudah (*Iggarosav, op. cit.*, p. 109). In most editions the name is given as Rav Yosef b. Yehudah Ibn Aknin (1150-1220). Some scholars, however, maintain that Ibn Aknin was not the Rambam's disciple. Instead, these scholars believe, Rav Yosef ben Yehudah Ibn Shimon was the *talmid* for whom the Rambam wrote his *Moreh Nevuchim*, and to whom this letter was addressed. [Words in brackets in our text are included in *Iggaros u'Teshuvos haRambam*, Jerusalem, HaAchim Levin-Epstein edition, but are not included in Bar-Joseph edition.]

(110) Letter of Rav Avraham ben haRambam to the *dayyan* in Alexandria. (See Margolios, *Encyclopedia leToledos Gedolei Yisroel, op. cit.*, Vol. I, p. 77.)

(111) Letter of Rav Avraham ben haRambam to the *Nasi* of Damascus. (See Margolios, *loc. cit.*)

"Sefer haMaspik leOvdei HaShem"

Rav Avraham wrote *Sefer haMaspik leOvdei Hashem*, an encyclopedic work of Torah thought, mussar, and halacha, written in Arabic, one section of which has recently been published, in Hebrew translation. The following is an example of the lofty mussar concepts which are dealt with in this work.

> ההסתפקות היא מן המידות התרומיות, ופירושה שיהא האדם שמח בחלקו מקנייני העולם הזה ולא יהא בהול ולהוט להוסיף עליהם.
>
> Contentment with one's lot is one of the finest of all middos. This means that the individual should rejoice in his portion of material acquisitions in this world and he shall not be in a state of frenzy and eagerness to increase them. This will be indicative of the absence of covetousness and of a minimal desire for the pleasures of this world — traits which lead an individual to numerous transgressions, and which are detrimental to the attainment of spiritual perfection.[112]

It is of interest to note that the author refers the reader, at times, to his father's writings, for the attainment of greater clarity and deeper comprehension of the thought under discussion. On such occasions, the translator includes large passages from the Rambam's writings, as designated by Rav Avraham in his text.[113]

Rav Avraham also wrote a commentary on the Torah, of which only the sections on *Bereshis* and *Shemos* have been published, and three works, *Birkas Avraham*, *Ma'asei Nissim*, and *Milchamos HaShem*, in which he defends his father's *sefarim* against those who criticize them. The *Birkas Avraham* also contains some of the many hundreds of responsa which Rav Avraham sent to Jews in distant communities.[114]

(112) Rav Avraham b. haRambam, "*HaMaspik leOvdei HaShem*" (Jerusalem: Keren Hotza'as Sifrei Rabbanei Bavel), 1973, p. 109.

(113) See, for example, *HaMaspik, op. cit.*, p. 147, where Rav Avraham refers the reader to certain sections of the *Shemonah Perakim le-haRambam* — the Rambam's introduction to *Pirkei Avos*. Whereupon, the translator includes in the text the first five chapters of the *Shemonah Perakim*, in their entirety. See also *HaMaspik*, p. 167, where a large segment of the Rambam's commentary on *Avos* 1:17 is included in the text, for the same reason.

(114) A number of the responsa of Rav Avraham b. haRambam have been included as an appendix to the Shulsinger Brothers edition of *Mishneh Torah* (New York: 1947).

Rav Dovid ben Avraham haNagid

When Rav Avraham died in Fostat, Egypt, on 18 Kislev, 1237, at the early age of fifty-one, he was mourned deeply by the entire Jewish community. He was succeeded in his post of *Nagid* by his son, Rabbe Dovid.

The Rambam's grandson, Rabbe Dovid ben Avraham, was born in Cairo in 1213. Rav Dovid was twenty-five years old when he assumed his father's post of *Nagid* in 1238.[115] In the year 1285, during Rav Dovid's forty-seventh year as *Nagid,* libelous charges were brought against him, and he was deposed from his high post. He went into exile, and settled in Acre, Israel.

While he was in Acre, a *Mekubal,* Rabbe Shlomo Petit of Acre, began to renew the controversy against the Rambam's *Moreh Nevuchim.* He went to great lengths to gain support for a ban against the *Moreh.* This upset Rav Dovid greatly, and he fought to restore the dignity of his grandfather, Maimonides. Rav Yeshayah ben Chizkiah, the Jewish Exilarch of Damascus, Rav Shmuel haKohen, *Rosh Yeshiva* of Baghdad, and others, came to Rav Dovid's support, and issued a ban against anyone who would offend the memory of the Rambam.

Rav Dovid also turned to the Rashba, Rabbe Shlomo ben Avraham Adres of Barcelona, the greatest Spanish scholar of his time, to come to his aid. The Rashba supported him, and finally succeeded in restoring peace between Rav Dovid and his antagonists.[116]

After five years in Acre, Rav Dovid was restored to his post as *Nagid* in Egypt. Upon his return, he was greeted with great honor, and he accomplished much for his fellow Jews. In his declining years, he appointed his son, Avraham, to share his duties as *Nagid.* Rav Dovid died in Cairo in 1301, and was buried near the grave of his grandfather, in Tiberias. His passing was mourned greatly by Jewish communities near and far.

(115) According to some opinions, he was born in 1223. This would make him only fifteen years old when he became *Nagid.*

(116) See *Later Rishonim,* Chap. 5, after n. 8.

Rav Dovid wrote a highly regarded *sefer* of sermons, on the weekly Torah reading. The selections on *Bereshis* and *Shemos* were translated from Arabic to Hebrew, and published under the name, *Midrash Rav Dovid haNagid.* A second work on *Pirkei Avos,* was likewise translated into Hebrew, and published as *Midrash Dovid.*

Rav Dovid's son, Rav Avraham, assumed the post of *Nagid* after his father's death. The high post of *Nagid* remained as a legacy in the Rambam's family for five generations.

Admirers and Critics of the Rambam's "Mishneh Torah"

To be sure, the Rambam's monumental *Yad haChazakah,* despite — or perhaps more accurately, because of its great popularity, did not long remain without its critics. The primary point of contention and critique — a point which the Rambam himself later regretted — was the fact that the Rambam had not cited the sources for his myriads of halachos.

It is of interest to note that some of the Rambam's greatest critics, as well as some of his greatest admirers, came from the Provencal School of Southern France. The illustrious master of the Provencal School, Rabbe Avraham ben David of Posquires, known as Ravad III Ba'al haHasagos, an older contemporary of the Rambam and one of the most towering Torah luminaries during the entire era of the *Rishonim,* wrote the masterful comprehensive critique on the entire *Mishneh Torah,* known as *Hasagos haRavad.*

On the other hand, the Ravad's great disciple, Rabbe Yehonasan haKohen of Lunel, the leader of the *Chachmei Lunel,* maintained an extensive correspondence with the Rambam. The *Chachmei Lunel* expressed their profound reverence for the Rambam, and their deepest admiration for his *Mishneh Torah,* as well as for his Mishnah commentary and his *Moreh Nevuchim,* which they took great pains to have translated from Arabic to Hebrew, by Rabbe Shmuel Ibn Tibbon.

It is appropriate, therefore, to conclude this chapter with the following excerpts of letters which the Rambam sent to Rabbe Yehonasan haKohen and to the *Chachmei Lunel.*

In his letter to Rabbe Yehonasan haKohen, we see the great humility of the Rambam. After having stated that he worked diligently for ten years consecutively, "by day and by night," to compile his *Mishneh Torah*,[117] the Rambam observes further,

> אספתי הלכות שהיו מפוזרות בין גבעות והרים . . . אולם משגיעות מי יכול להנצל.
>
> I gathered halachos which were scattered among hills and mountains; I arranged them, and I wove them together in an orderly fashion. But who can be spared from errors;[118] and forgetfulness is prevalent to all, especially among the elderly. It is therefore fitting for you to examine that which I have written. Say not, "Who am I that I might have the audacity to question the words of the Rav." That is incorrect. I myself request this [of you]. I welcome this.
>
> On the contrary, any scholar who might make me aware of an error is performing a great kindness for me. This is a kindness for me . . . to remove the stumbling blocks from the students.[119]

"Rely No Longer Upon My Battle"

In a letter to the *Chachmei Lunel*, written in his later years, the Rambam describes in detail the terrible decline of Torah in all countries of the East. He then informs them that he can no longer take command on the battlefield of Torah. He enjoins them, rather, to carry on and to hold the banner of Torah proudly aloft.

> חזקו ונתחזק בעד עמנו ובעד ערי אלקינו.
>
> Be strong and let us strengthen ourselves for the sake of our people and for the cities of our G-d. Try to be men of valor, for this matter depends upon you, and it is for you to be the vanguard. Do not rely upon my battle. I can today no longer go out at the head of the camp for I have already grown old, and old age has come upon me. Nor is this only because I have many years, but rather primarily because of serious illnesses which have sapped my strength and weakened me, from the day I fled from my homeland, until today.

(117) See above, n. 22.
(118) Cf. Psalms 19:13, שגיאות מי יבין — *"Who can discern errors?"*
(119) See *Iggarosav*, Bar-Joseph edition, *op. cit.*, pp. 162 f.

> May the Almighty help you in your efforts to elevate the dignity of *Toras Moshe* and of Israel, and may He cause your names to become a blessing in the land.[120]

The Rambam concludes his letter to Rabbe Yehonasan haKohen with the following beautiful blessing.

> May the Omnipresent help you and us to study His Torah, and to acknowledge His Unity, forever and ever. And in your days and in our days, may this verse of Jeremiah[121] be fulfilled.
>
> *For this is the covenant which I shall establish with the House of Israel after those days, says the L-rd. I will place My Torah among them, and upon their hearts will I inscribe it. And I will be their G-d, and they shall be My People.*[122]

Among many others, the scholars of the Provencal School of Southern France, did indeed carry aloft the torch of Torah which had fallen from the Rambam's hands, as they continued to delve deeply into the study of Torah, to write many classic Torah masterpieces, and to disseminate Torah to many thousands of disciples, during the course of the twelfth and thirteenth centuries. The ensuing chapter will provide the reader with some of the highlights of the Provencal School of Torah Study in Southern France.

(120) This letter, written by the Rambam to the *Chachmei Lunel* (ca. 1202), is believed to have been one of the last letters written by the Rambam, before his death in 1204. (See *Iggarosav*, Bar-Joseph edition, *op. cit.*, p. 193; See also p. 191, n. 1, *ad. loc.*)

(121) Jeremiah 31:32.

(122) *Iggarosav, op. cit.*, p. 163.

5
The Provencal School: Ravad III, Teachers and Disciples

„אמנם ה׳, כי מלאו חלחלה מתני,
וקולמוסי וקנדרוסי ינועו בין הידים,
כאשר ינוד הקנה במים,
כאשר ידעתי מעלת האיש ההוא בחכמה,
וגדולתו ביראת אלקים״.
[הקדמת הרמב״ן לספר הזכות,
אודות השגות הראב״ד]

"But in truth, O' G-d,
I am filled with trembling,
And my quill and my parchment
tremble in my hands
as a reed trembles in the water.
For I am aware of this individual's
great stature in [Torah] wisdom,
And his greatness in regard to the fear of G-d."
[Introduction of Ramban to Sefer haZechus,
regarding Ravad of Posquires;
See Text, p. 177.]

The Sad Odyssey of Rabbe Aharon haKohen of Lunel During the French Expulsion of 1306

נדדתי ממעוני אל ארץ מאפליה,
ארץ עיפתה וציה,;
היה מלוני צלמות ולא סדרים,
יושבי על מדין בחדרים.

I wandered from my home to a land of darkness;
A land of weariness and desolation.
My shelter was in death's shadow,
With no regimens of study;
Sitting fearfully within,
In fear of the enemy without.

[Rabbe Aharon haKohen of Lunel,
In his introduction to Orchos Chaim;
See Text, at n. 114.]

5

The Provencal School: Ravad III, Teachers and Disciples

The Three Primary Architects of the Provencal School

In the early decades of the twelfth century, a vibrant Torah community had begun to flourish in the cities of the Provence, in Southern France. At the forefront of this dynamic activity and this dramatic upsurge in Torah study stood three outstanding Torah scholars who laid the foundations of the Provencal School, which was to exert a major influence in the field of Torah scholarship during the ensuing two centuries. These three Torah scholars, Rabbe Avraham ben Yitzchak, *Av Bes Din* of Narbonne, Rabbe Moshe ben Yosef ben Mervon haLevi, and Rabbe Meshullam ben Yaakov of Lunel, were the primary teachers of the Ravad of Posquires and of Rabbe Zerachiah haLevi, as well as of an entire generation of outstanding Torah scholars.

Ravad II — Ba'al haEshkol

Rabbe Avraham ben Yitzchak, also known as Rabi Abad or Ravad II (1110-1179), who was the *Av Bes Din* — president of the *Bes Din* of Narbonne — was one of the great Torah masters of Southern France during the first half of the twelfth century. He studied under Rav Yitzchak ben Mervon haLevi, in the Yeshiva of Narbonne. He then traveled to Spain where he studied under the great Sephardic Torah master, Rabbe Yehudah ben Barzilai of Barcelona

(d. beg. 12th c.).[1] Upon his return to Narbonne, Rabbe Avraham was appointed to the prestigious post of *Av Bes Din* by the president of the community, Reb Todros ben Moshe haParnes.

Rabbe Avraham of Narbonne wrote the halachic work, *Sefer haEshkol,* in which he abridged the longer halachic work, *Sefer haIttim,* of his teacher, Rabbe Yehudah ben Barzilai, while adding much additional material of his own, as well. He was highly revered by his contemporaries. A younger contemporary, Rabbe Yitzchak ben Aba Mari of Marseilles (1122-1193), known as the *Ba'al haIttur* (after his work, *Ittur Soferim* or *Sefer haIttur*), refers to him as החסיד הקדוש — "the holy pious one." It has been said by some early *Kabbalists* that Eliyahu haNavi appeared to Rabbe Avraham, and revealed to him the secrets of the *Kabbalah.*[2] Others, however, attribute this early transmission of the secrets of the *Kabbalah* by Eliyahu haNavi to Rav Avraham's son-in-law, Ravad of Posquires.

Rabbe Avraham of Narbonne became the father-in-law of his disciple, the Ravad of Posquires, who married his daughter, Sarah. At the end of the Ravad's commentary to tractate *Kinim,* Rabbe Avraham expresses his gratitude to the Almighty and his joy in that he was privileged to have become the father-in-law of the Ravad, whom he refers to simply as, *Maran* — "our master." He compares himself to Chovav ben Re'uel, or Yisro, father-in-law of Moshe Rabbeinu.[3]

Rabbe Avraham Ba'al haEshkol was an ancestor of the Me'iri, who refers to him as זקננו הנבחר — "our choice ancestor." The Me'iri renders the date of his death as 20 Marcheshvon 4919 (1158).[4] Others, however, place his death some twenty years later, in 1179.

(1) See Chap. 2, n. 10.

(2) See *Or haChaim,* No. 133, p. 52, citing *Sefer haEmunos, Sha'ar* 4, Chap. 6.

(3) See closing remarks of Rabbe Avraham b. Yitzchak at the end of Ravad's commentary to tractate *Kinim,* in *Talmud Bavli.* Chovav b. Re'uel is another name for Yisro. (See Rashi, Exodus 18:1.)

(4) Rabbe Menachem b. Shlomo haMe'iri (1249-1315), in his introduction to his *Bais haBechirah* commentary on *Pirkei Avos* (Jerusalem, 1944), p. 69.

Rabbe Moshe b. Yosef b. Mervon haLevi

The second of these three great Provencal scholars who flourished during the early decades of the twelfth century, Rabbe Moshe ben Yosef ben Mervon haLevi (d. 1165), was *Rosh Yeshiva* of the Yeshiva of Narbonne. Unlike the Ba'al haEshkol, Rav Moshe studied only under Provencal scholars. His approach to Torah study, therefore, was steeped in the traditions of Southern France. He was recognized as a master Talmudist, an individual of great scholarship and erudition, and as one of the primary architects of the Provencal School of Torah Study. The Ravad speaks of him with great reverence, and refers to him as רבי המובהק — "my primary teacher."[5] At the conclusion of one halachic discourse, the Ravad cites an opinion rendered by "our teacher, Rabbe Moshe ben Yosef . . . which I did not understand for many years, but now . . . I see a support for his words."[6]

Rav Moshe ben Yosef was also the teacher of Rav Zerachiah haLevi, who likewise cites his words with great reverence. He also exerted great influence upon the Ramban, who quotes him extensively.

Rabbe Meshullam of Lunel — Scholar and Patron of Torah

The third great Provencal scholar of this early period was Rabbe Meshullam ben Yaakov of Lunel (d. 1170). Besides having been an illustrious Torah scholar, he was also independently wealthy and a great philanthropist, who supported Torah scholars and was a patron of every type of Torah learning. His role in the development of the Provence as a bastion of Torah scholarship is reminiscent of the activities of Rav Chisdai Ibn Shaprut and of Rav Shmuel haNagid, both of whom stood at the forefront of the development of the Spanish center of Torah scholarship, in their respective generations.

Rabbe Meshullam was eager to build bridges of communication between the Sephardic and the Provencal Schools of Torah Study. To this end, he urged and prevailed upon Rav Yehudah Ibn Tibbon to undertake the translation of the *Chovos haLevavos* of Rabbe Bachya Ibn Paquda from Arabic into Hebrew. Rav Yehudah Ibn Tibbon speaks of Rabbe Meshullam in glowing terms.

(5) See *Or haChaim*, No. 79, p. 24.
(6) *Temim De'im le-haRavad* (Jerusalem, 1974), Responsa 111, p. 47.

המנורה הטהורה, נר מצוה ותורה אור, הרב הגדול החסיד והקדוש רבנא משולם נר״ו בן החכם הישיש רבי יעקב ז״ל.

> The pure candelabrum, lamp of the mitzvos and light of Torah, the great saintly and holy teacher, Rabbe Meshullam, son of the venerable sage, Rabbe Yaakov *zal* . . . He yearned for books of wisdom which were written by great Torah sages, and according to his means, he gathered, disseminated, and transcribed them.[7]

The Ravad, who studied under Rabbe Meshullam, cites his opinion often, and refers to him as "our teacher, the light of Israel."[8]

Rabbe Aharon b. Meshullam and the Rosh of Lunel

Rabbe Meshullam had five sons. They were all great Torah scholars, and they were also very wealthy. His two sons who are most well-known are Rabbe Aharon ben Meshullam (d. 1210) and Rabbe Asher ben Meshullam (d. before 1210), also known as *haRosh miLunel.* Both Rav Aharon and Rav Asher were colleagues of the Ravad, and they were both outstanding Torah scholars.

Rav Meir ben Todros haLevi wrote to Rav Aharon to enlist his support in his efforts to curtail the study of the *Moreh Nevuchim.* In his reply, Rav Aharon came out very strongly in defense of the Rambam.

כי אמנם מימות רבינא ורב אשי לא קם עוד בישראל כמשה.

> From the days of Ravina and Rav Ashi, there has arisen none in Israel like Moshe. . . . For we have not heard nor have our ancestors told us of another work which was composed after the redaction of the Talmud, which is like the *Mishneh Torah.*[9]

(7) Rabbe Yehudah Ibn Tibbon, Introduction to his translation of the *Chovos haLevavos*.

(8) *Sifran shel Rishonim,* ed. Simcha Assaf (Jerusalem, 1935), p. 195. This volume includes the *Issur Mah-shehu* of the Ravad, Responsa of Rabbe Avraham of Narbonne and of Rabbe Yosef Ibn Plat, and other primary sources.

(9) Letter of Rabbe Aharon b. Meshullam to Rabbe Meir b. Todros haLevi Abulafia (haRamah, 1170-1244), as cited by Margolios, *Encyclopedia leToledos Gedolei Yisroel, op. cit.,* Vol. I, p. 120.

His brother, Rabbe Asher ben Meshullam (the Rosh of Lunel), was exceedingly pious. Reb Binyamin of Tudela, the famous twelfth century traveler, who visited Lunel in 1165, refers to Rabbe Asher as a *Parush* — extremely pious — "who separated himself from worldly matters and who was absorbed in Torah study by day and by night, fasting, and abstaining from meat entirely. He is a great Talmudic Sage."[10]

He was in frequent correspondence with the French *Tosafists* and is cited by the Ri haZaken in *Tosafos* on the tractate *Bava Kamma.*[11] His *Hilchos Yom Tov* are included in the sefer, *Temim De'im le-haRavad.*

Rabbe Meshullam of Beziers and the "Sefer haHashlamah"

Rabbe Meshullam also had a son-in-law, Rabbe Moshe ben Yehudah of Lunel, who was a prominent Torah scholar. He was a colleague of the Ravad of Posquires and of Rabbe Zerachiah haLevi. Rav Moshe had four sons, the best known of whom was Rabbe Meshullam ben Moshe (c. 1175-1250), who was named after his illustrious grandfather.

Rav Meshullam later moved to Beziers, and is therefore known as Rabbe Meshullam of Badresh or Beziers. He wrote the *Sefer haHashlamah,* which he regarded as a "completion" of, or as complementary to the *Hilchos Rav Alfas.* In the *Sefer haHashlamah,* Rav Meshullam of Beziers includes halachos omitted by the Rif, and also defends the Rif from the critique of Rabbe Zerachiah Ba'al haMa'or, although, at times, to be sure, Rav Meshullam disagrees with the Rif, and agrees with the *Ba'al haMa'or.*

The *Sefer haHashlamah* is cited often by many *Rishonim.* Rabbe Menachem haMeiri refers to Rabbe Meshullam of Beziers as, הרב הגדול, אבי כל יושב אהל — The great Rav, father of all who dwell in the tent [of Torah].[12]

(10) Benjamin of Tudela, the 12th century traveler, in his *Sefer haMasa'os.*

(11) *Bava Kamma* 64a; *Tosafos, s.v.* יאמר.

(12) Rabbe Menachem b. Shlomo haMe'iri, Introd. to *Avos, op. cit,* p. 66. The phrase cited is drawn from Genesis 25:27, where Yaakov Avinu is referred to as יושב אהלים — *a dweller of tents* (see Rashi that this refers to the Torah tents of Shem and Ever).

Rabbe Meir haKohen of Narbonne

Rabbe Meir ben Shimon haKohen of Narbonne was the son of Rabbe Meshullam of Beziers' sister, as well as his disciple. Rabbe Meir also studied under his own father, as well as under Rabbe Nasan ben Meir of Trinquetaille, who was also one of the primary teachers of the Ramban. Rabbe Meir was a life-long friend of the Ramban, with whom he subsequently maintained an extensive correspondence.

Rabbe Meir wrote *Sefer haMeoros* which includes laws of *berachos* and all halachos of *Seder Mo'ed*, as well as many other halachos. The author frequently cites the Sages of Southern France, and in particular, the *Sefer haHashlamah* of his uncle, Rabbe Meshullam of Beziers. Rabbe Meir also wrote *Milchemes Mitzvah* which contains refutations to the arguments of Christian priests, which were rendered during the course of a debate in 1245.

In his later years, Rabbe Meir moved to Toledo, Spain, where he died in 1263.

The Ravad Ba'al haHasagos: Master of Critique

Born in Narbonne, France, in 1120, Rabbeinu Avraham ben David of Posquires (Ravad III, Ba'al haHasagos), was the recognized leader of the Torah sages of Southern France during the closing decades of the twelfth century. The three great Provencal scholars cited above were the primary teachers of the Ravad. The Ravad was also in correspondence with Rabbe Yosef Ibn Plat, who was an illustrious Torah scholar. Rav Avraham of Narbonne addresses Rav Yosef Ibn Plat as, "Light of Israel . . . I have come to draw [Torah] waters from your fount of salvation. Blessed is the Creator who privileged you to teach laws and statutes in Israel."[13]

The Ravad was revered, not only by his own generation — a generation of outstanding Torah scholars — but also by the Torah scholars of succeeding generations. He wrote a commentary on the entire Talmud, most of which is, unfortunately, no longer extant, except for his commentaries on the tractates *Ediyos* and *Kinim*, which

(13) Assaf, *Sifran Shel Rishonim*, *op. cit.*, p. 200. Cf. *Temim De'im le-haRavad*, p. 5., *s.v.* גם מפי הרב יוסף בן פלאתי ז״ל נעזרתי.

are included in the *Vilna Shas,* and his commentary on *Bava Kamma,* which has recently been published. Fragments of his novellae on many other tractates of *Shas,* however, are cited in the works of other *Rishonim,* particularly in the *Shitah Mekubbetzes* of Rav Bezalel Ashkenazi, which frequently cites the words of the Ravad.

The Ravad also wrote an extensive and comprehensive commentary on the *Sifra,* which has been printed a number of times.

The Ravad is remembered primarily for his critical glosses on the works of the Rif and the Rambam, which earned for him the title, *Ba'al haHasagos* — the master of critique. In his glosses on the Rif, he defends the Rif against the critique of Rabbeinu Zerachiah haLevi (1125-1186), the Ba'al haMa'or, although, to be sure, he often adds his own critical comments on the words of Rav Alfas, always manifesting the greatest awe and reverence for the words of the great master.[14] The Ramban, who, in his *Sefer haZechus,* defends the Rif against the critique of the Ravad, writes in his introduction that he does so with the greatest trepidation, lest he appear to be offending the dignity of the Ravad.

ואמנם ה', כי מלאו חלחלה מתני . . .

> In truth, Almighty, I am filled with trembling, and my pen and my parchment tremble in my hands as a reed trembles in water, because I am aware of this individual's great stature in [regard to Torah] wisdom, and his greatness in regard to the fear of G-d.[15]

Hasagos haRavad — Critical Glosses on "Mishneh Torah"

The critique of the Ravad on the Rambam is so thorough and comprehensive that where the Ravad does not voice his disagreement, it is assumed by the later commentaries that he is in accord with the Rambam's ruling, thereby giving the opinion of the Rambam added weight halachically. Although the Ravad is openly critical of the Rambam's attempt to have the *Yad haChazakah* become

(14) Rav Avraham b. David of Posquires, in his prefatory remarks to *Hasagos haRavad le-haRif,* beg. Chap. 3 of *Kesuvos* (p. 23 in Rif).

(15) See introduction of Ramban to his *Sefer haZechus* on Rif, beginning tractate *Yevamos.*

recognized as the final word in definitive halacha,[16] he nevertheless does concede that "he did a great thing in having gathered the words of the Babylonian Talmud and the Yerushalmi and the Tosefta."[17]

While the Ravad, in his *Hasagos,* does primarily attempt to refute and contradict many of the halachos of the Rambam, there are, on the other hand, a number of instances where he subscribes enthusiastically to the Rambam's point of view. In this vein, he makes remarks such as סברא יפה היא — "this is a nice thought";[18] יפה אמר—"well said";[19] אמת הוא זה—"this is true";[20] יפה עשה שפסק כשמואל—"he did well to rule like Shmuel";[21] סברא היא זו, והיא יפה בעיני — "this is [his own] logical deduction, and it pleases me";[22] ולשון שלו ערב יותר — "his choice of words is sweeter [than that of the Tosefta]."[23]

In certain instances, the Ravad states that he prefers the opinion of the Rambam to that of Rav Alfas,[24] whom he refers to reverently as *haRav.* In at least two places, the Ravad refers to the Rambam as "the Sage."[25]

The Rambam, on the other hand, refers in his correspondence to the Ravad as הרב המפורסם מפושקיירא — "the famous Rav of Posquires."[26] It is related that the Rambam once remarked, regarding the Ravad,

מעולם לא נצחני אלא בעל מלאכה אחת.

(16) See *Hasagos haRavad* on Rambam's introduction to *Mishneh Torah, s.v. Savar.*

(17) *Hasagos haRavad* on Rambam, *Mishneh Torah, Hilchos K'laiyim* 6:2.

(18) *Hasagos haRavad* on Rambam, *Mishneh Torah, Hilchos Shechenim* 9:9.

(19) *Ibid., Hilchos Gezelah vaAvedah* 13:15.

(20) *Ibid., Hilchos Terumos u'Ma'asaros* 3:3.

(21) *Ibid., Hilchos Sukkah* 5:22.

(22) *Ibid., Hilchos Ma'achalos Asuros* 10:20.

(23) *Ibid., Hilchos Parah Adumah* 8:8.

(24) *Hasagos haRavad* on Rambam, *Mishneh Torah, Hilchos Yom Tov* 1:14; *Hilchos Ishus* 18:28; *Hilchos Zechiyah u'Mattanah* 10:20.

(25) *Hasagos haRavad* on Rambam, *Mishneh Torah, Hilchos Mechirah* 22:15; *Hilchos Gezelah vaAvedah* 2:4.

(26) Letter of the Rambam to Rabbe Shmuel Ibn Tibbon, of 8 Tishrei 4960 (1200), in *Rabbeinu Moshe ben Maimon, Iggarosav veToledos Chayyav,* M. Bar-Joseph, ed. (Tel Aviv, 1970), p. 122.

> In all my life I have never been vanquished except by a man of a single occupation.[27]

This expression, "of a single occupation," is a reference to the fact that the Ravad was single-minded in his commitment to Torah study, without the distraction of any secular studies whatsoever.

The Ravad was an ancestor of the Me'iri, who refers to him as זקננו הגדול — "our great ancestor."[28] Throughout his *Bais haBechirah*, the Me'iri refers to the Ravad as גדולי המפרשים — "the greatest of the commentators."[29]

"Ba'alei HaNefesh le-haRavad"

A number of the Ravad's responsa are included in the sefer, *Temim De'im le-haRavad.*[30] He also wrote the sefer, *Ba'alei haNefesh*, which is a masterful halachic work dealing with the laws of *niddah-tevilah*. This *sefer*, as well as other works of the Ravad, are cited by *Tosafos* and by many other *Rishonim.*[31] In his introduction to *Ba'alei haNefesh* — which clarifies all facets of the laws of Jewish family purity — the Ravad explains why he called the *sefer* by this somewhat unusual name — "Masters of the Soul."

> נקראו הצדיקים בעלי הנפש, כי הם בעלים בנפשותם, ואדונים בתאוותם. ועל כן קראתי הספר הזה ,,בעלי הנפש".

> The righteous are called "masters of the soul," because they are masters of their souls, and masters over their passions. Therefore have I called this sefer, *Ba'alei haNefesh*.[32]

(27) Rabbe Shimon ben Zemach Duran (1361-1444), *Sefer Tashbatz* (Amsterdam, 1738), p. 72.

(28) Me'iri, Introduction to *Avos*, S. Wachsman, ed. (Jerusalem/N.Y., 1944), p. 69.

(29) See Preface to Me'iri on tractates *Gittin* and *Yevamos*.

(30) The sefer, *Temim De'im le-haRavad* (Jerusalem, 1974), also includes the writings of other *Rishonim*, e.g. *Sefer haTzavah* of Rabbe Zerachiah haLevi, with *Hasagos haRamban*, and *Hilchos Yom Tov* of Rabbe Asher b. Meshullam.

(31) *Tosafos* mentions the Ravad in the following places: *Temurah* 12b, *Tosafos, s.v. Yosef; Ta'anis* 25a, *Tosafos, s.v. Ha; Avodah Zarah* 38a, *Tosafos, s.v. Ela mi-deRabbanan; Yoma* 18b, *Tosafos, s.v. Yichudi.*

(32) Ravad, at outset of his Introduction to *Ba'alei haNefesh*.

In a similar vein, he observes that abstinence from sin is the path to holiness.

הפורש מן העברות פרישה גמורה, נקרא טהור וקדוש.

> He who separates himself from sin totally [including his thoughts], is called "pure" and "holy."[33]

It is of interest to note that the Ravad himself was referred to as אחד קדוש — "a holy one," by the great *Rishonim* of later generations.[34]

Ru'ach haKodesh of the Ravad

The Ravad was known, not only as an illustrious Talmudist, but also as an outstanding *chasid,* whose piety and sanctity were legendary.

In his discussion concerning one of the laws of the four species of the Sukkos festival, the Ravad makes the following remark, which speaks for itself concerning the exceptional stature of its author.

כבר הופיע רוח הקודש בבית מדרשנו מכמה שנים.

> The Divine Presence has already appeared in our house of study, many years ago.[35]

Elsewhere, he concludes his annotation on the Rambam with the words,

כך נגלה לי מסוד ה׳ ליראיו.

> So has it been revealed to me through the process of,[36] *"The secrets of G-d [are revealed] to those who fear Him."*[37]

(33) *Ba'alei haNefesh le-haRavad,* beginning *Sha'ar heKedushah,* p. 79.

(34) See Introduction to *Hilchos Niddah* of the Ramban, and the Introduction of the Rashba to his *Toras haBayis, Bais haNashim.*

(35) *Hasagos haRavad* on Rambam, *Mishneh Torah, Hilchos Lulav* 8:5.

(36) Psalms 25:14. This verse is making reference to a process akin to Divine Revelation, or *Ru'ach haKodesh.*

(37) *Hasagos haRavad* on Rambam, *Mishneh Torah, Hilchos Bais haBechirah* 6:14. See also *Hasagos haRavad* on *Hilchos Tum'as Mishkav u'Moshav* 7:6.

In his prefatory remarks to his commentary on tractate *Ediyos*, the Ravad makes a similar observation.

> That which may be found in this work to be good and worthy, know that this is in the category of סוד — "secret revelation" — as it says,[38] *The secrets of G-d [are revealed] to those who fear Him, and His covenant, to make [it] known to them.*[39]

In his *Ba'alei haNefesh*, he concludes a halacha with the words, כך הראוני מן השמים — "So has it been revealed to me by Heaven."[40]

It is in this vein, too, that it is said that because of the Ravad's exceedingly great piety, Eliyahu haNavi appeared to him, and he taught him the secrets of the *Kabbalah*.[41] The Ravad's two sons, Rav David and Rav Yitzchak *Sagei Nahor*, were both great *Ba'alei Kabbalah* — masters of the esoteric study of *Kabbalah*.

The Ravad was very wealthy, and he personally supported many of the students who came to his Yeshiva in Posquires from far and near to study Torah.[42] His great wealth, however, also caused him great anguish. The ruler of the city of Posquires had designs on his wealth. He therefore had the Ravad imprisoned on false charges. It was only through the intercession of Rogers II, the ruler of the entire province of Carcassonne, which included Posquires, that the Ravad was released.

The Me'iri observes that, as a token of reverence, the *Kohanim* in Narbonne insisted that the Ravad be called up to the Torah first, although he was not a *Kohen*.

> ומפי רבותי שמעתי על גדולי המפרשים שהיו הכהנים שבנרבונא נוהגים להם כבוד, ומפצירים בם לקרות בפניהם ראשון, אף על פי שאף הם היו חכמים גדולים.

(38) Psalms 25:14.

(39) Ravad, Introduction to commentary on *Ediyos*. Cf. *Midrash haGadol* on Genesis, ed. S. Schechter (Cambridge, 1902), p. 754.

(40) *Ba'alei haNefesh le-haRavad*, end *Sha'ar haMayim*, p. 78.

(41) *Or haChaim*, No. 79, p. 25, citing *Orchos Chaim*, *Hilchos Rosh Hashanah*, *siman* 26.

(42) *Or haChaim*, No. 79, p. 25, citing *Sefer haMaso'os* of the well-known twelfth century traveler, Binyamin of Tudela (near beginning of *sefer*).

> I have heard from the mouths of my teachers concerning the greatest of the commentators,[43] that the *Kohanim* of Narbonne treated him reverently, and that they entreated him to be the first to read in the Torah [before the *Kohanim*], even though they were great Sages themselves.[44]

"Unique in his Generation"

So greatly revered was the Ravad by the Torah leaders of his generation, that when he died in the year 1198 they announced, *Batlah Kedushah* — "The sanctity of *Kohanim* is suspended" — as had been announced at the time of the death of Rabbeinu haKadosh[45] — and *Kohanim* were permitted to participate in his burial[46] — a signal honor which is rendered only to a חד בדורו — an individual who is unique in his generation, as the Rambam observes in his *Mishneh Torah.*

> נשיא שמת הכל מטמאים לו, אפילו כהנים. עשאוהו כמת מצוה לכל, מפני שהכל חייבין בכבודו.
>
> If a *Nasi* — a prince [or a recognized leader of all Israel] — dies, everyone may become impure because of him, even *Kohanim.* The Sages regard him, insofar as all are concerned, as a מת מצוה — a deceased who has no relatives,[47] since everyone is duty-bound to render him honor.[48]

The Ravad had two sons, Rav David and Rav Yitzchak, both of whom were his disciples. Little is known about the older son of the Ravad, although it is known that he was a great Torah scholar. His

(43) גדולי המפרשים — This is the designation which the Me'iri always uses in regard to the Ravad. (See above, n. 29.)

(44) Rabbeinu Menachem haMe'iri (1249-1315), *Bais haBechirah* on *Gittin* 59b (Jerusalem: Zichron Yaakov, 1979), p. 275.

(45) See *Kesuvos* 103b.

(46) R. Avraham Zacuto (1442-1515), *Sefer Yuchsin haShalem* (Jerusalem: Vardi, 1963), V, p. 220b; *Shevet Yehudah* of Solomon ibn Verga, p. 158. See Margolios, *Encyclopedia, op. cit.,* Vol. I, p. 45. Cf. *Later Rishonim,* Chap. 1, nn. 47 and 60 for a similar remark regarding Rabbeinu Tam.

(47) If a person dies without any relatives who might make arrangements for his burial, it is regarded as an exceedingly great mitzvah for everyone — even a *Kohen Gadol,* if necessary — to participate and assist in his burial.

(48) Rambam, *Mishneh Torah, Hilchos Aveil* 3:10.

younger brother, Rav Yitzchak, refers to him as, "My teacher, my brother, the sage Rav David, of blessed memory."[49]

The younger brother, Rav Yitzchak *Sagei Nahor* — a euphemism for "the blind" — was regarded as one of the most important of the early *Kabbalists*. He is, in fact, often designated as *Avi haMekubalim* — the father of the *Mekubalim*, by later Kabbalistic authorities.[50] The Ravad transmitted his Kabbalistic wisdom to his sons, and they, in turn, transmitted these esoteric insights to a select group of disciples, among whom were Rabbe Ezra and Rabbe Azriel, two outstanding *Kabbalists* of the next generation. Rav Yitzchak wrote a commentary on the *Sefer Yetzirah*. His importance as a leader of the early *Kabbalists* may be seen in a letter which he wrote to two of the greatest *Rishonim* of the twelfth century, the Ramban and Rabbeinu Yonah of Gerondi, in which he instructs them in the proper methods of studying and writing Kabbalistic concepts.[51]

Rabbeinu Zerachiah haLevi, Ba'al HaMa'or

Among the outstanding contemporaries of the Ravad was Rabbeinu Zerachiah ben Yitzchak haLevi (Razah), who studied under Rabbeinu Moshe ben Yosef in Narbonne, Rabbeinu Avraham ben Yitzchak Av Bes Din of Narbonne, and Rabbeinu Meshullam ben Yaakov of Lunel, the three outstanding scholars of the Provence, in Southern France, who were also the teachers of the Ravad Ba'al haHasagos. Like the Ravad of Posquires, Rabbe Zerachiah, too, refers to Rabbeinu Moshe ben Yosef as הרב המובהק שלנו — "our primary Torah teacher . . . of whose waters we drank, and in whose shadow we sat, and in whose tents we dwelt."[52]

Rabbeinu Zerachiah was born into the Yitzhari family, a highly respected family in Gerona, Italy. When he was yet very young, his family moved to the Provence in Southern France, where he soon gained a reputation as an outstanding Torah scholar in this community which was famed far and wide for its illustrious Torah scholars.

(49) As cited by G. Scholem, *Te'udah Chadashah leToledos Reishis haKabbalah* (Tel Aviv: Sefer Bialik, 1934), p. 144.

(50) See Rabbeinu Bachya b. Asher (d. 1340), in his Torah commentary, *Midrash Rabbeinu Bachya*, on *Parshas VaYeshev*.

(51) Scholem, *Te'udah Chadashah*, *op. cit.*, p. 143.

(52) See *Or haChaim*, No. 826, p. 367, citing Rabbe Zerachiah haLevi, in *Gittin*, *Perek haMeivi*.

Rabbeinu Zerachiah's primary work was his *Sefer haMa'or,* in which he is critical of many of the halachic rulings of the Rif. The *Sefer haMa'or* was written in two parts, *HaMa'or haGadol* on the Orders of *Nashim* and *Nezikin,* and *HaMa'or haKattan* on the Order of *Mo'ed,* and on tractates *Berachos* and *Chullin.*

"Old Wine in New Vessels"

Rabbeinu Zerachiah wrote his *Sefer haMa'or* when he was only nineteen years old, as he writes in his introduction:

> *Say not that he is young and his years are few,*
> *Since he is lacking one from twenty years of age, . . .*
> *And perhaps he was therefore not careful*
> *Regarding laws of greater or lesser severity . . .*
> *For sometimes old wine is found in new vessels.*[53]

In his introduction, too, he is profusely apologetic for being critical of the work of the great master.

> I need not elaborate concerning the Rif's greatness and his wisdom, for it is clear to all who can see, as is the sun at midday. His merits in having compiled his *Hilchos Rav Alfas* will extend over his own generation and all future generations. For there is no work which was written on the Talmud which is as excellent as this, since the completion of the Talmud.[54]

Nevertheless, he concludes, he is motivated to write his critique, by his great quest for truth.

In a brief Aramaic poem which the Ba'al haMa'or's father wrote as a preface to his son's work, he expresses his profound gratitude to the Almighty who answered his prayers and blessed him with a son "who uproots [Torah] mountains, with excellent words, which are like precious stones and emeralds."[55]

(53) Rabbe Zerachiah haLevi, introduction to*Sefer haMa'or,* at beginning of Rif to tractate *Berachos,* in the *Vilna Shas, s.v. Bi-Mekomos.*

(54) *Ibid.*

(55) See Preface of Rav Yitzchak b. Zerachiah, father of Ba'al haMa'or, to *HaMa'or haKattan* commentary on *Berachos,* in *Vilna Shas,* preceding the Rif.

The *Sefer haMa'or* elicited an immediate strong response from Rabbe Zerachiah's great contemporary, the Ravad, and later, from the Ramban, both of whom hastened to the defense of the Rif. The Ramban refers to Rabbeinu Zerachiah with great reverence in his introduction to the second part of his *Milchamos HaShem* commentary, on *HaMa'or haKattan.*[56] The *Sefer haMa'or,* together with the Glosses of the Ravad and the *Milchamos HaShem* of the Ramban, accompany the text of the Rif in all printed editions. The provocative and stimulating arguments of these great Torah masters are intriguing, and they have continued to fascinate Talmud students in all generations.

"A Light for the Righteous Shone in the Darkness"

Rabbeinu Zerachiah also wrote *Sefer haTzava,* which deals with thirteen principles of Talmudic methodology. In this *sefer,* which is included in the sefer *Temim De'im le-haRavad,* Rabbeinu Zerachiah includes a number of additional critical comments on the Rif. Here, too, the Ramban hastens to the defense of the Rif, with his critical comments on the *Sefer haTzava.* The Ramban's comments, too, are included in the *Temim De'im le-haRavad.* Rabbeinu Zerachiah also wrote critical comments on the sefer *Ba'alei haNefesh* of the Ravad.

One of the *Ba'alei haTosafos,* Rabbe Yaakov of Marvege, directed a number of halachic questions to Heaven — *She'elos u'Teshuvos min haShamayim* — and the replies were given to him in his dreams at night. In one such exchange, he asked whether the halacha is like Rashi or like Rabbe Zerachiah haLevi in regard to the interpretation of three complex halachos in tractate *Rosh Hashanah.* In his dream that evening, a cryptic reply was rendered, citing the following verse in Psalms. זרח בחושך אור לישרים[57] — *A light for the righteous shone in the darkness.*[58]

This reply was regarded as an indication that in regard to these three halachos the interpretation of the Ba'al haMa'or is preferable,

(56) See introduction of Ramban to *Milchamos HaShem,* on the Rif, tractate *Berachos,* in the *Vilna Shas, s.v. Techilas.*

(57) Psalms 112:4.

(58) Rabbe Yaakov of Marvege, *She'elos u'Teshuvos min haShamayim — Questions and Responsa from Heaven,* ed. Reuven Margolios (Jerusalem: Mosad haRav Kook, 1957), Responsum 61, p. 77.

since the verse cited is reminiscent of his name, Rabbe Zerachiah.[59]

Rabbeinu Zerachiah died in 1186, twelve years before the death of his great colleague, the Ravad. Both Rabbeinu Zerachiah haLevi (1125-1186), and the Ravad of Posquires (1120-1198), were contemporaries of Rabbeinu Tam (1100-1171), the great leader of the French *Tosafists.*

Rabbe Yitzchak ben Abba Mari, Ba'al HaIttur

Another great Provencal scholar at this time was Rabbeinu Yitzchak ben Abba Mari of Marseilles (ca. 1122-1193). A disciple of his father, Rabbeinu Yitzchak wrote a work on the laws of *shechitah* when he was only seventeen years of age. He maintained extensive correspondence with his great contemporaries, the Ravad of Posquires, and the illustrious *Tosafist,* Rabbeinu Yaakov Tam, both of whom were related to him.

Rabbeinu Yitzchak's primary work is the *Ittur Soferim* or *Sefer haIttur,* a comprehensive halachic code which is cited extensively by later halachic authorities. Rabbe Yitzchak toiled laboriously over the preparation of this *sefer,* during the course of many years. As a result, the *Sefer haIttur* is regarded as an important and authoritative halachic code.

The Chida, in his sefer, *Shem haGedolim,* cites a unique tradition among the elders of Jerusalem to the effect that the *Sefer haIttur* is regarded as being בבחינת סוד עלמא דאתכסיא — in the realm of "hidden" Torah wisdom. As a result, he observes, any commentary written on the *Sefer haIttur* will either be lost or will remain incomplete.[60]

Rabbe Yitzchak also wrote annotations on the Rif, under the title, *Me'ah Shearim,* which are included alongside the Rif in the *Vilna Shas.*

Accompanying Tables IX and X [pp. 187-188] provide the names of some of the early and later Masters of the Provencal School.

(59) See *Or haChaim,* No. 826, p. 367. Margolios, however, renders a different interpretation in *She'elos u'Teshuvos min haShamayim, loc. cit.,* n. 4, which would make the reply entirely ambiguous. The verse cited, however, appears to clearly favor the approach of the Razah to these halachos.

(60) See R. Yosef Chaim David Azulai (Chida, 1724-1806), *Shem haGedolim, Ma'areches Sefarim,* under עטור (Warsaw: Goldman, 1876), p. 77, n. 32. See *Later Rishonim,* Chap. 5, n. 30, for a similar remark re. the *sefarim* of Rabbeinu Yerucham.

Table IX
The Provencal School
Early Torah Masters of Southern France

Ninth & Tenth Centuries

Rabbe Machir [came from Bavel at request of Charlemagne, ca 800 C.E.; established Yeshiva in Narbonne]; *Descendants of R. Machir:* **R. Todros, and sons, R. Kalonymos the Great, and R. Moshe the Parnes; R. Todros b. Moshe haParnes.**

Eleventh Century

R. Moshe haDarshon of Narbonne; *his son,* and disciples:* **R. Yehudah b. R. Moshe haDarshon; R. Nasan b. R. Yechiel of Rome, Ba'al haAruch,** 1035-1106; Disciple of R. Yehudah b. R. Moshe haDarshon: **R. Menachem b. Chelbo Kara** [uncle and teacher of R. Yosef Kara, who wrote commentary on Tanach].

Twelfth Century

R. Yitzchak b. Mervon haLevi [Rosh Yeshiva of Narbonne].

Three Architects of Provencal School

R. Avraham b. Yitzchak, Av Bes Din of Narbonne **(Ravad II),** 1110-1179, *Sefer haEshkol (halachic code);* **R. Moshe b. Yosef b. Mervon haLevi** [Rosh Yeshiva of Narbonne], d. 1165; **R. Meshullam b. Yaakov of Lunel,** d. 1170.

Ravad III and Razah: Disciples of Ravad II, R. Moshe haLevi, and R. Meshullam of Lunel

R. Avraham b. David of Posquires (**Ravad III,** Ba'al haHasagos), 1120-1198 [son-in-law of Ravad II], *Commentary on Rif (refutes critique of Ba'al haMa'or), Hasagos haRavad (critical comments on Yad haChazakah of Rambam), Ba'alei haNefesh (Hilchos Niddah); Temim De 'im (responsa); Commentary on Sifra, and on tractates Ediyos, Kinim and Tammid.*

R. Zerachiah haLevi (Razah, Ba'al haMa'or), 1125-1186, *Sefer haMa'or (critique on Rif, HaMa'or haGadol on Nashim and Nezikin, HaMa'or haKattan on Mo'ed, Berachos, and Chullin); Sefer haTzavah (Talmudic methodology).*

Contemporaries: Five sons* of R. Meshullam, including ***R. Asher b. Meshullam** (Rosh of Lunel), d. before 1210; ***R. Aharon b. Meshullam,** d. 1210.

R. Yitzchak b. Abba Mari of Marseilles (Ba'al haIttur), 1122-1193, *Ittur Soferim, or Sefer haIttur (comprehensive halachic code), Me'ah She'arim (glosses on the Rif).*

End Twelfth Century

Disciples of Ravad III of Posquires

R. Meir b. Yitzchak of Trinquetaille, *Sefer haEzer (defends Rif from critique of Ba'al haMa'or, ascribed to either R. Meir, or his son, R. Nasan).*

R. Yehonasan b. Dovid haKohen of Lunel, *Commentary on the Rif, Eruvin,* [maintained extensive correspondence with Rambam, dated 1199, and with R. Shimshon of Sens; made aliyah to Eretz Yisroel with 300 Rabbanim in 1211]; **Chachmei Lunel** [corresponded with Rambam].

Table X
The Provencal School
Later Torah Masters of Southern France

Twelfth to Thirteenth Centuries

Disciples of Ravad III of Posquires (cont'd)

R. Avraham b. Nasan haYarchi, 1155-1215, *Sefer haManhig (halachos and minhagim);* **R. Yitzchak haKohen of Narbonne,** *wrote commentary on three sedarim of Talmud Yerushalmi; Disciple of R. Yitzchak haKohen:* **R. Reuven b. Chaim** [Rebbe of the Me'iri].

Grammarians and Translators

Kimchi Family–Grammarians: R. Yosef Kimchi; *His sons,* **R. Moshe Kimchi: R. David Kimchi (Radak),** 1160-1235, *Sefer haMichlol and Sefer haSharashim (Heb. grammar), Commentary on Tanach.*

Ibn Tibbon Family–Translators: R. Yehudah b. Shaul Ibn Tibbon, 1120-c.1190 ["father of translators"], *Translated: Chovos haLevavos, Kuzari, Emunos veDe'os, Sefer haRikmah; his son,* **R. Shmuel b. Yehudah ibn Tibbon,** 1160-c. 1230, *Translated: Moreh Nevuchim, Iggeres Teiman, Ma'amar Techiyas haMeisim, Shemonah Perakim le-haRambam; his son,* **R. Moshe ibn Tibbon,** d. ca. 1283, *Translated Sefer haMitzvos of the Rambam.*

Thirteenth Century

R. Nasan b. Meir of Trinquetaille [studied under the French Tosafist Ritzva; teacher of Ramban].

R. Meshullam b. Moshe of Beziers, 1175-1250, [grandson of R. Meshullam of Lunel], *Sefer haHashlamah (supplement to Hilchos haRif); his nephew and disciple,* **R. Meir haKohen of Narbonne,** d. 1263 [colleague of Ramban], *Sefer haMe'oros, (Hilchos Berachos u'Mo'adim), Milchemes Mitzvah (disputation).*

R. Shlomo b. Avraham min haHar, fl. 1232 [teacher of R. Yonah of Gerondi; *opposed study of Moreh Nevuchim and of Sefer haMada].*

Fourteenth Century

R. Menachem b. Shlomo leBais Meir (Me'iri), 1249-1315 [disciple of R. Reuven b. Chaim], *Bais ha Bechirah (commentary on 3 Orders of the Talmud); Commentaries on Mishlei, Tehillim; Chibur haTeshuvah.*

R. Avraham min haHar [contemporary of Me'iri and Rashba], *Commentaries on three Orders of Talmud, wrote commentary on Kiddushin, wrongly ascribed to Ri haZaken.*

French Expulsion, 1306. R. Aharon haKohen of Lunel, 1344 [was among Megurashei Tzorfas, 1306], *Orchos Chaim, Kol Bo (popular halachic codes);* **R. Levi b. Gershon (Ralbag),** 1288-1344 [Biblical exegete; astronomer, philosopher], *Commentary on Nvi'im, Kesuvim; To'aliyos Ralbag on Torah; invented Jacob Staff (astronomical instrument);* **French Expulsion, 1394** [until 17th century].

Rabbeinu Yehonasan haKohen and the Chachmei Lunel

One of the greatest disciples of the Ravad, and a leader of the *Chachmei Lunel* — the Sages of Lunel in the next generation, was Rabbe Yehonasan ben David haKohen of Lunel. Rav Yehonasan wrote a comprehensive commentary on the Rif throughout *Shas*. Only his commentary on tractate *Eruvin*, however, is printed alongside the Rif in the *Vilna Shas*, while his commentary on tractate *Chullin* was printed separately, under the name *Avodas haLevi'im* [Frankfort, 1871]. His commentary on many other tractates is still in manuscript form, in a number of libraries containing rare Hebrew manuscripts.

Rav Yehonasan haKohen venerated the Rambam greatly. He corresponded with the Rambam directly concerning numerous halachic matters. Addressing the Rambam with great reverence, Rav Yehonasan presented twenty-four difficult questions concerning some of the halachic rulings in the Rambam's *Mishneh Torah*. The Rambam replied to each of these questions, while indicating that he was overjoyed that the Sages of Lunel were studying the *Mishneh Torah* diligently. It is said that Rabbe Yehonasan haKohen wrote a *sefer* in which he defended the Rambam against all of the critical comments of his own teacher, the Ravad of Posquires.[61]

Rav Yehonasan urged the Rambam to send him a copy of the *Moreh Nevuchim*. When the Rambam sent him a copy of the *Moreh* in Arabic, Rabbe Yehonasan prevailed upon Rav Shmuel Ibn Tibbon to translate it into Hebrew.

According to one source, Rav Yehonasan was among the three hundred *Tosafists* and great Torah scholars from France and England who settled in Eretz Yisroel in the year 1211, where he died not long after.[62]

Rabbe Meir of Trinquetaille

As a youth, Rabbe Meir ben Yitzchak was brought to the Provence from Karkashuna by his father, so that he might study under the Ravad of Posquires. He later settled in Trinquetaille, and he remained in Southern France his entire life. Rabbe Meir became

(61) Rabbe Yitzchak diLatish, in his sefer *Sha'ar Tzion*, as cited by Margolios, *Encylopedia leToledos Gedolei Yisroel*, *op. cit.*, Vol. III, p. 699.

(62) *Ibid.*, citing the sefer, *Shevet Yehudah*.

an illustrious Torah scholar and one of the outstanding disciples of the Ravad. Regarding a disagreement he had with the Ravad concerning the validity of a certain *Get,* or bill of divorce, Rabbe Meir writes,

> אל יכפרני אדוני בשעת הדין ואל יקל בכבודי, שאם הוא יחיד ברבנים אני אחריו יחיד בתלמידים.
>
> My master shall not deny my words concerning [this] judgment, nor shall he take liberties with my dignity. For if he is indeed unique among Torah masters, I am unique among disciples. So long as I agree with [the ruling of] our teacher, let he who wishes to disagree, do so. But if I disagree with him, regardless of who else may agree with him, the halachic dispute may very well remain intact.[63]

It goes without saying, of course, that only a scholar of the highest caliber would venture to express such sentiments to the Ravad of Posquires.

The Me'iri, who refers to Rabbe Meir as אחד מגדולי משפחתינו — "one of the great scholars of our family," regards him as having had a *talmid-chaver,* or "disciple-colleague" relationship with the Ravad of Posquires.[64] Elsewhere, the Me'iri includes Rabbe Meir together with Rabbe Zerachiah haLevi, in regard to the circle of Torah scholars who were closely associated with the Ravad.[65]

Rabbe Nasan of Trinquetaille — "Sefer HaEzer"

Rabbe Meir's son, Rabbe Nasan of Trinquetaille, travelled to Northern France, where he studied under the great disciple of the Ri haZaken, Rabbe Yitzchak ben Avraham (Ritzva). The Me'iri refers to him as "the great Rav, Rabbe Nasan of Trinquetaille." Rabbe Nasan later became one of the primary teachers of the Ramban.[66]

(63) Me'iri, Introduction to *Avos*, S. Wachsman ed. (Jerusalem/NY, 1944), p. 67, citing letter of Rabbe Meir to Ravad III.

(64) *Ibid.*

(65) *Ibid.*, p. 69.

(66) See Rabbi Chaim Dov Chavel, *Rabbeinu Moshe ben Nachman,* Heb. biog. (Jerusalem: Mosad haRav Kook, 1967), pp. 44-46; see *Later Rishonim,* Chap. 4, at n. 17.

The *Sefer haEzer*, which was written to defend the Rif against the critique of Rabbe Zerachiah Ba'al haMa'or, was written either by Rabbe Meir of Trinquetaille, or by his son, Rabbe Nasan.

Rabbe Avraham b. Nasan haYarchi: Sefer haManhig

Another important disciple of Ravad III of Posquires and of the early *Chachmei Lunel* was Rabbe Avraham ben Nasan haYarchi (i.e. "of Lunel," 1155-1215), author of *Sefer haManhig*. Born in Avignon, Rav Avraham haYarchi subsequently traveled through many countries. He studied under the Ri haZaken in Northern France. He then traveled to Britain, and later to Toledo, Spain, where he finally settled and apparently became a member of the Rabbinical court, together with Rabbe Meir ben Todros haLevi Abulafia of Toledo (haRamah, 1170-1244).

During the course of his travels, he observed the wide diversity of customs which were prevalent in the various communities which he visited. Whereupon, he wrote his *Sefer Manhig Olam*, better known as *Sefer haManhig*, in which he describes the customs and *minhagim* of Southern and Northern France, of England, Germany, and Spain. Drawing upon Talmudic, Midrashic, and Geonic sources, as well as upon the works of many French and Spanish *Rishonim*, the *Sefer haManhig* establishes the halachic basis of each of the *minhagim* of all of the various communities. The *Sefer haManhig* was highly regarded and is cited often by many *Poskim*.[67]

Rabbe Shlomo Min haHar and the Maimonidean Controversy

Born in Barcelona, Spain, Rabbe Shlomo b. Avraham min haHar moved to Montpelier in Southern France during the early decades of the thirteenth century. He was recognized as a Torah scholar of great stature by his contemporaries, such as Rabbe Meir haLevi Abulafia (the Ramah), Rabbeinu Moshe ben Nachman (Ramban), and later, by Rabbe Shlomo Adres (Rashba), all of whom speak of him with great reverence. Among his disciples were Rabbeinu Yonah heChasid of Gerona, and Rav David ben Shaul.

Rabbe Shlomo of Montpelier vehemently opposed the study of philosophy, and, as a result, he was strongly opposed to the study of

(67) See Rivash, Responsum 40, as cited by *Or haChaim*, No. 197, p. 101.

the Rambam's *Moreh Nevuchim* and the *Sefer haMada*, the first *sefer* of the Rambam's *Mishneh Torah*. In truth, however, Rav Shlomo regarded both the Rambam and the *Mishneh Torah* itself very highly, as we have already noted above.[68] Together with his two devoted disciples, he stood at the forefront of the anti-Maimunists.[69]

While the *Chachmei Lunel* and a majority of the Torah scholars of Southern France were strong advocates of the Rambam, in 1232 Rav Shlomo enlisted the support of some of the great *Tosafists* of Northern France in his attempts to prohibit the study of the *Moreh*, which he regarded as a threat to the transmission of unadulterated Torah values. The Maimonidean controversy raged in the Jewish community for many years, provoking bans and counterbans from each of the sides in the controversy. The Maimonidean controversy reached its climax when some of the anti-Maimunists elicited the support of the Dominican Monks in their efforts to have the *Moreh Nevuchim* banned. This resulted in the tragic episodes of the burning, first of the Rambam's *sefarim*, and then of the Talmud itself, by the Dominican Monks in Montpelier in 1234, and then again in Paris in 1242.[70]

Rabbe David Kimchi — the Radak

An extremely important commentary on a large portion of Tanach was written at this time by Rabbeinu David ben Yosef Kimchi (Radak, ca. 1160-1235), of Narbonne, in Southern France. The Radak studied under his brother, Rabbe Moshe Kimchi, who, like his father, Rabbe Yosef Kimchi before him, was also a well-known grammarian and Biblical exegete. Among the Radak's important grammatical contributions are his *Sefer haMichlol* and his *Sefer haSharashim*.

The Radak is better known, however, for his comprehensive commentary on Tanach, which covers Genesis, all of the early and

(68) See Chap. 4, at nn. 95-98.

(69) Re. Rabbeinu Yonah's repentance for having joined the anti-Maimunists and for having been opposed to the *Moreh Nevuchim*, see *Later Rishonim*, Chap. 4, n. 88.

(70) Re. the tragic impact of the Talmud burning on the European Jewish communities, see *Later Rishonim*, Chap. 3, nn. 8-17 (pp. 91-95).

later Prophets, Chronicles, and Psalms. His commentary, which places great emphasis upon basic *p'shat,* or the plain meaning of Scripture, includes many Rabbinic and Midrashic interpretations. It is regarded as a classic work of Biblical exegesis, and is included among the standard commentaries in many printed editions of the Books of the Prophets. The following are excerpts from his commentary on Isaiah.

. . . on the eternal Torah covenant

ואני זאת בריתי אותם אמר ה׳, רוחי אשר עליך ודברי אשר שמתי בפיך לא ימושו מפיך ומפי זרעך ומפי זרע זרעך, אמר ה׳, מעתה ועד עולם.

"As for Me, this is My covenant with them,"[71] *says the L-rd. "My spirit which is upon you, and My words that I have placed in your mouth, shall not be removed from your mouth, and from the mouths of your children, and from the mouths of your children's children," says the L-rd, "from now until eternity."*[72]

Citing a verse in Jeremiah, the Radak observes that this refers to an eternal Torah covenant, which will never again be violated by Israel through their transgressions.

"This is the covenant that I will form with the House of Israel after those days,"[73] *says the L-rd. "I will place My Torah in their midst, and I will inscribe it upon their hearts, and I will be their G-d, and they will be My people."*[74]

Thus, too, the Radak concludes, does Isaiah say here, "*My spirit which is upon you,* that is, the spirit of purity that I shall place among them that they shall sin no more[75] . . . I shall never again remove this spirit from them, from their children, or from their children's children, forever and ever."[76]

(71) First, the Radak cites his father, Rav Yosef Kimchi, who interprets בריתי, *My covenant,* literally, as the Torah covenant of Sinai.

(72) Isaiah 59:21.

(73) After their return from exile (see *Metzudas Dovid* commentary on Jeremiah 31:32).

(74) Jeremiah 31:30-32.

(75) See Ezekiel 36:27.

(76) Radak, Isaiah 59:21.

. . . on the Final Redemption

כי כאשר השמים החדשים והארץ החדשה אשר אני עושה עומדים לפני, נאום ה׳, כן יעמוד זרעכם ושמכם.

"For as the new heavens and the new earth[77] *which I am making, stand before Me," says the L-rd, "so shall your seed and your name remain."*[78]

Those Jews who will be living at the time of the Redemption shall not say that their children will yet once again be exiled from their land and that their name will be lost in the Diaspora. This will not be. Rather, those benefits which they will enjoy at that time will remain with their children forever, as long as the heavens are upon the earth. The name of Israel will never be destroyed, and they will never again be exiled from their land.[79]

The significance which the Jewish community attached to the commentaries of the Radak may be seen in the following popular expression which was often applied to the writings of the Radak. In a play on his family name, Kimchi, the following words of *Pirkei Avos* have often been applied to the Radak.

אם אין קמח אין תורה.

Where there is no bread [no *kemach*], there is no Torah.[80]

In his later years, the Radak became involved in the anti-Maimonidean controversy regarding the study of philosophy in general, and the *Moreh Nevuchim* and the *Sefer haMada* of the Rambam's *Mishneh Torah,* in particular. The Radak came out in favor of the study of philosophy and of the *Moreh,* but only for one who is G-d fearing, and whose primary intellectual foundation and approach to wisdom is based upon Torah study.

(77) The heavens and the earth, which are as new today as at the time of Creation (Radak).

(78) Isaiah 66:22.

(79) Radak, Isaiah 66:22.

(80) *Avos* 3:17.

The Ibn Tibbon Family: The Translators

Born in Granada, Spain, in the year 1120, Rabbe Yehudah ben Shaul Ibn Tibbon fled with his family to Lunel in Southern France, to escape the intense persecution of the Jews by the Almohades. He was a great Torah scholar, as well as a respected physician. In Lunel, he met Rav Zerachiah haLevi, and they became devoted life-long friends. In his ethical bequest to his son, Shmuel, Rav Yehudah writes that Rabbe Zerachiah did not write any poem or engage in correspondence with anyone, including his own brother, Rabbe Berachiah, without showing it to Rabbe Yehudah first, although, he writes, היה יחיד בדורו, והיה חכם ממני — "He was unique in his generation, and he was a greater scholar than I."[81]

Upon the urging of Rabbe Meshullam ben Yaakov of Lunel, Rav Yehudah Ibn Tibbon, who was fluent in both Hebrew and Arabic, embarked upon his first translation — translating the first chapter, the *"Sha'ar haYichud"* of the *Chovos haLevavos* of Rabbeinu Bachya Ibn Paquda, from Arabic into Hebrew. This was the beginning of his long, fruitful career as a translator, which spanned almost thirty years. The Ravad subsequently persuaded Rabbe Yehudah to translate the remaining nine chapters of the *Chovos haLevavos,* although they had already been translated previously by Rav David Kimchi (the Radak).

During the ensuing three decades, Rabbe Yehudah translated the *Mivchar Peninim* and the *Sefer haMussar* of Rav Shlomo Ibn Gabirol (1021-1057), the *Sefer haKuzari* of Rabbe Yehudah haLevi (1075-1141), the *Sefer haRikma* of Yonah Ibn Janach (990-1050), and the sefer, *Emunos veDe'os* of Rav Saadiah Gaon (882-942).

Rabbe Yehudah Ibn Tibbon explains that he found it necessary, at times, to coin new Hebrew terms, because Hebrew was a Biblical language and not a living, spoken language, as Arabic was at that time.[82] Rabbe Yehudah Ibn Tibbon died in Lunel in c. 1190.

(81) Ethical Bequest of Rav Yehudah Ibn Tibbon to his son, Shmuel.

(82) Rabbe Yehudah Ibn Tibbon, in his introduction to *Chovos haLevavos,* near end, *s.v. Ve-al ya'ashimeni.*

Rabbe Shmuel Ibn Tibbon: Following in his Father's Footsteps

Rabbe Yehudah transmitted this legacy of translating classic works of great Jewish authors and Torah philosophers from Arabic into Hebrew, to his son, Rav Shmuel Ibn Tibbon.

Rav Shmuel was born in Lunel, in the year 1160. He studied under his father, and under Rabbe Zerachiah haLevi. In his ethical bequest, Rav Yehudah Ibn Tibbon instructs his son, Shmuel, to maintain the close bond of love and friendship which existed between Rabbe Zerachiah's family and his own.

> ולבן הרב זרחיה ז״ל רבך תזכור אהבת אביו בי ובך, ותאהב אותו כאח ותכבדהו כחבר גדול, כי כן היה מכבדך ואוהבך ומשבח אותך אביו זצ״ל.
>
> In regard to the son of your teacher, Rabbe Zerachiah of blessed memory, you shall always remember his father's love for me and for yourself. You shall love him as a brother and you shall render him honor as towards a great colleague. For thus did his father, of blessed memory, honor you and love you, and praise you.[83]

Rabbe Shmuel Ibn Tibbon, who, under his father's tutelage had acquired great fluency in Arabic, was urged by Rabbe Yehonasan haKohen, the leader of the *Chachmei Lunel* — the Sages of Lunel, to translate the Rambam's *Moreh Nevuchim* into Hebrew. Rav Shmuel was reluctant to do so at first, because of the many difficult terms and philosophical concepts which this *sefer* contains. He finally agreed to undertake the translation, in the hope that the Rambam himself might guide him in this difficult task.

Corresponding With the Rambam

Whereupon, he did engage in correspondence with the Rambam, and the Rambam provided him with answers concerning numerous difficulties which he had with the text of the *Moreh Nevuchim,* as well as with general guidelines concerning the art of translation itself. Regarding the latter, the Rambam observes that

(83) Ethical Bequest of Rav Yehudah Ibn Tibbon, *loc. cit.*

while translation must, of course, always be accurate and faithful to the author's original text, it should, nevertheless, not be an entirely literal translation. It should flow freely from the translator's pen, with the accurate transmission of the author's thoughts always uppermost in his mind. A too literal translation, the Rambam observes, will give rise to mistakes and inaccuracies, and to an inaccurate rendition of the meaning of the original text.

The Rambam was overjoyed that Rav Shmuel was undertaking to translate the *Moreh*. He speaks in glowing terms of reports he had heard from reliable sources concerning the eminent stature of Rav Shmuel's father, Rabbe Yehudah Ibn Tibbon. He also speaks highly of the favorable impression conveyed by Rav Shmuel's letters, and by his perceptive questions concerning the text of the *Moreh Nevuchim*, which show a fine, scholarly grasp of the difficult subject matter and the philosophical terms and concepts which the *sefer* deals with. The Rambam expresses his profound joy that such a fine scholar has undertaken this translation, and he extends his warmest blessings that he may be successful in his work.

הקל יתברך יאיר עיניך במאור תורתו,
עד אשר תהיה מאוהביו, כצאת השמש בגבורתו.

> May the Almighty enlighten your eyes with the light of His Torah, that you might be among[84] *those who love Him, who will be as the sun when it goes forth in its might.*[85]

In reply to Rav Shmuel's suggestion that he might take a journey to visit the Rambam, the Rambam writes that he would be delighted to meet him, but that his schedule as the Sultan's physician is so demanding and his other responsibilities as a doctor and as the spiritual advisor of the Jewish community are so time consuming, that he would have virtually no time to spend with Rav Shmuel at all.[86]

(84) Judges 5:31.

(85) Letter of the Rambam to Rav Shmuel Ibn Tibbon, of 8 Tishrei 4960 (1200), in *Rabbeinu Moshe ben Maimon, Iggarosav ve-Toledos Chayyav*, M. Bar-Joseph, ed. (Tel Aviv: Mordecai Inst., 1970), pp. 122 ff.

(86) *Ibid.*; See above, Chap. 4, n. 61.

Besides the translation of the *Moreh Nevuchim*, which he completed in the year 1204 — the year of the Rambam's death — Rav Shmuel Ibn Tibbon translated also the *Iggeres Teiman* and the *Ma'amar Techiyas haMeisim* of the Rambam, as well as some sections of his *Peirush haMishnah*. Rav Shmuel later settled in Marseilles, where he died in ca. 1230.

Rav Shmuel's son, Rav Moshe Ibn Tibbon, was a Torah scholar, philosopher, and translator. He earned his livelihood as a doctor. In May, 1246, it was prohibited for Jewish doctors in the Provence to attend non-Jewish patients. Whereupon, Rav Moshe followed in his family's footsteps, and began to translate many works on philosophy and medicine from Arabic into Hebrew. He translated the *Sefer haMitzvos* of the Rambam, although it had already been translated previously, and he also translated some of the Rambam's works on medicine. He wrote a number of *sefarim*, some of which are still extant in various libraries, in manuscript form. From the dates given in his *sefarim*, it would appear that he died in approximately the year 1283.

The Jewish community is deeply indebted to the Ibn Tibbon family, whose arduous labors as translators saved many of the classical works of Torah philosophy from oblivion by making them accessible to all future generations.

Rabbe Menachem ben Shlomo: The Me'iri

During the ensuing decades many other important contributions were made by Provencal scholars to the ever-expanding field of Torah and halachic literature. One of the more prominent among these was the *Bais haBechirah* of Rabbeinu Menachem ben Shlomo leBais Meir, better known as the Me'iri.

Rabbeinu Menachem was born in 1249 in Southern France, where he studied under the great Torah masters of Narbonne. His teacher, Rabbeinu Reuven ben Chaim, studied under Rabbeinu Yitzchak haKohen of Narbonne, who wrote a commentary on three *sedarim* of the *Yerushalmi*, and who was, in turn, a disciple of Rabbe Avraham ben David of Posquires (Ravad III). In his illuminating introduction to *Pirkei Avos*, in which he traces the Mesorah process from Sinai to his own day, and which therefore serves as an extremely important historical source, the Me'iri makes the following remarks concerning his teacher, Rabbeinu Reuven.

> He knew the entire Talmud thoroughly and was well-versed in many other branches of wisdom. He arrived at many novel Talmudic deductions, which he derived with his intellect. The profundity of his intellect,[87] *"skipped upon the mountaintops, and leaped above the hills."*[88]

The Bais HaBechirah

The *Bais haBechirah,* which was the Me'iri's major work, is a masterful treatise on three Orders of the Talmud — a total of thirty-seven tractates — in which the Me'iri skillfully combines definitive halacha with a remarkably lucid commentary, which clarifies many difficult passages of the Talmud. The Me'iri quotes a large variety of earlier authorities in his *Bais haBechirah,* to whom, instead of referring by name, he assigns intriguing descriptive titles. Thus, he refers to the Rif as *Gedolei haPoskim* — the greatest of the halachic decisors; to Rashi, as *Gedolei haRabbanim* — the greatest of the Rabbis; to the Ravad, as *Gedolei haMeforshim* — the greatest of the commentators; to Maimonides, as *Gedolei haMechabrim* — the greatest of the codifiers; to the Ramban, as *Gedolei haDoros* — the great leader of earlier generations; and to his contemporary, the Rashba, as *Gedolei haDor* — the great leader of the generation.[89]

In addition to his *Bais haBechirah,* Rabbeinu Menachem wrote many other important works, including his *Chibur haTeshuvah,* as well as commentaries on *Tehillim* and on *Mishlei,* and another, more exhaustive commentary on the Talmud, most of which, unfortunately, is no longer extant.

Infusing the Halacha with Vitality

The Me'iri's writings are replete with references to fundamental hashkafah concepts and with eloquent expressions of ethical Torah values. Throughout his Talmud commentary, his commentaries on *Mishlei* and on *Tehillim,* and his *Chibur haTeshuvah,* the Me'iri infuses the halacha with life and vitality. Like the

(87) *Shir haShirim* 2:8.

(88) Me'iri, end of Introduction to *Avos,* ed. R. Shmuel Waxman (New York, 1944), p. 69.

(89) See Preface to Me'iri on *Yevamos,* by R. Chanoch Albeck (New York, 1947), pp. vi ff, for a comprehensive list of titles used by the Me'iri.

Rambam before him, the Me'iri looks beyond the letter of the halacha itself, to capture and transmit the spirit of the halacha, as well. As the name Me'iri implies, he illuminates the halacha with the radiance of understanding, enriches it with perceptive Torah thoughts, and clarifies it with illuminating insights.

. . . on tzedakah

כל הרודף אחר הצדקה, יהא בטוח שהקב״ה ממציא לו מעות לעשות צדקה, וכן ממציא לו בני אדם המהוגנין, שצדקתו עומדת לעד בהטבתו להם. וכן יהא בטוח ששכרו מזומן לו אף בעולם הזה, בו ובממונו ובבנים עוסקי תורה ובעלי עושר וכבוד.

He who pursues [the mitzvah of giving] *tzedakah* may be assured that the Almighty will provide him with the financial means to perform *tzedakah*. So, too, will the Almighty provide him with worthy individuals, whereby his righteousness will be everlasting when he performs kindness for them. He may be assured, too, that his reward will be prepared for him even in this world, in regard to himself and his wealth, and that he shall have children who will study Torah, and who will be wealthy and respected individuals.[90]

. . . on the performance of chesed

לעולם יהא אדם רדוף בכל כחו, ליתן לב לעזור למי שאפסו עוזריו.

An individual shall take heed to pursue [this] with all his might, to give thought to helping one who has no one to help him.[91]

. . . on the mitzvah of rebuke

החכם מצד הוכיחו שאר בני אדם, כמה נבלים מקנאים בו ומחפשים מומיו, כשהוא מוכיח דרך כעס וקנטור; אבל כשהוא בעל מוסר, ומוכיח דרך חבה ואהבה הם נזהרים בכבודו הרבה.

(90) Me'iri, *Bava Basra* 9b.
(91) Me'iri, *Kesuvos* 50a.

When a Sage rebukes others, how numerous are those fools who will regard him with disdain, and who will seek out his faults, if he censures in a spirit of contentiousness and harsh criticism. But if he is a mussar-oriented individual, and he censures in a spirit of love and friendship, people will take heed to render him honor.[92]

. . . on refined ethical traits

„כל המכבד את התורה, גופו מכובד על הבריות". מכבד את התורה, שמעטר אותה בנועם מדותיו. שזה הוא וודאי כבוד התורה, בהיות לומדיה מסולסל ונקי ובעל מדות נכבדות. ואז הוא מכובד על הבריות, כמאמר הכתוב, „סלסלה ותרוממך".

"Whoever renders honor to Torah, will be honored by others."[93] How does one render honor to Torah? By adorning it with his refined character traits. For this is certainly an honor for Torah, that those who study it shall be refined and pure, and be possessed of fine character traits. Then will he be honored by others. As is written.[94] *Exalt her [the Torah], and she will elevate you.*[95]

. . . on Prophecy

הנבואה ורוח הקודש לא יכללו רק האמת, והאמת אינו אלא אחד.

Prophecy and Divine Revelation will only embrace truth, and there is but one truth.[96]

. . . on Torah study

לעולם יהא אדם זריז ללמוד תורה, מפני שכל חייו תלויים בו.

An individual should always be zealous in regard to Torah study, for his entire life is contingent upon it.[97]

(92) Me'iri, *Avos* 2:2.
(93) *Avos* 4:8.
(94) Proverbs 4:8.
(95) Me'iri, *Avos* 4:8.
(96) Me'iri, Introd. to *Mishlei* commentary.
(97) Me'iri, *Sanhedrin* 7a.

. . . on mitzvah performance

לעולם לא יהא אדם מתרשל לקיום מצוה, אלא יעשנה בזריזות בדרך חבה.

An individual shall never be lax in the performance of a mitzvah. Rather, he shall perform it with alacrity and with love.[98]

. . . on interpersonal relations

לעולם ישתדל אדם להיותו אהוב אצל הבריות, שכל האהוב למטה כלל מסור עליו שהוא אהוב למעלה.

An individual should always try to be beloved by his fellow human beings. For there is a general rule: Whoever is beloved below, is beloved Above [by the Almighty].[99]

. . . on tefillah

אע״פ שרוב תפלה אי אפשר שלא ליענות בה, מ״מ כשהיא יוצאה מעמקי הלב עד שהדמעה גוברת עליו, מקובלת ביותר.

Even though it is hardly likely that any prayer will go unanswered, nevertheless, if it emanates from the depths of one's heart until he is overwhelmed by tears, he will be answered more readily.[100]

. . . on life and Torah

אין סוד נכבד בעולם שלא נכתב בתורה, אם בפשטות ואם ברמיזות.

There is no worthy secret about the universe which is not included in the Torah, either directly or in a hidden manner.[101]

The works of the Me'iri had been lying dormant in manuscript form for almost six centuries, and have only recently been brought to light by scholars of our own generation, to whom we owe a great debt of gratitude. The Me'iri died in Perpignon, in 1315.

(98) Me'iri, *Pesachim* 112a.
(99) Me'iri, *Bava Basra* 10b.
(100) Me'iri, *Bava Mezia* 59a.
(101) Me'iri, Introd. to *Mishlei* commentary.

Rabbe Avraham min haHar

Rabbe Avraham b. Yitzchak of Montpelier (min haHar), was a contemporary of the Me'iri and of the Rashba. He was highly regarded by the Me'iri, who recognized him as an outstanding Torah scholar. Rabbe Avraham min haHar wrote a commentary on three *sedarim* of the Talmud. His commentaries on tractates *Yevamos, Nedarim,* and *Nazir,* were published in 1962 by Rabbi Yehudah Blau, from long-dormant manuscripts, written by the author himself.

In his introduction to the commentary on *Yevamos,* Rabbi Blau maintains that the *Tosafos Ri haZaken,* printed in the margin of the *Vilna Shas* on tracate *Kiddushin,* which has long been ascribed to the great twelfth century *Tosafist,* Rabbe Yitzchak b. Shmuel of Dampierre (d. 1185), was actually written by Rabbe Avraham of Montpelier. He bases this contention upon a comparative analysis between the *Tosafos Ri haZaken* and excerpts from the works of Rabbe Avraham min haHar.

Rabbe Levi b. Gershon: The Ralbag

Rabbe Levi ben Gershon (Ralbag, or Gersonides, 1288-1344), lived in Southern France. He was a Torah scholar, astronomer, mathematician, and philosopher. His primary philosophical work, *Milchamos HaShem,* was criticized by a number of later scholars, such as the Rivash (1326-1407), Rav Chasdai Crescas (1340-1412), Rav Yitzchak Arama (1420-1494), and Rav Don Yitzchak Abrabanel (1437-1508), among others, who maintained that it is prohibited to accept some of his views.

His commentary on many of the Books of *Nvi'im* and *Kesuvim* is included in the *Mikra'os Gedolos Tanach.* Of particular interest is his *To'aliyos Ralbag,* which is a digest of the more practical and relevant aspects of his Torah commentary, as the following excerpts from this *sefer* will show.

. . . on expressing gratitude

ויקד האיש וישתחו לה׳; ויאמר, ברוך ה׳ אלקי אדוני אברהם.

. . . And the man [Eliezer] bowed and prostrated himself before the L-rd. And he said, "Blessed is the L-rd, G-d of my master, Abraham."[102]

(102) Genesis 24:26-27.

ראוי לאדם כשיכונו מחשבותיו ויצליחו ענייניו, שיודה לה׳ יתברך אשר הכל מאתו. כי בזה תועלת להתיישר אהבת ה׳ יתברך ולהתקרב אליו כפי היכולת.

When the individual's aspirations materialize and his endeavors prove to be successful, it is proper that he should express his gratitude to the Almighty, from whom everything is derived. For in this way the individual's love for the Almighty will be reinforced, and he will be drawn near to Him, to the extent that it is possible for him to do so.[103]

. . . on tefillah

ויאמר, אלקי אבי אברהם ואלקי אבי יצחק. . . הצילני נא מיד אחי מיד עשו.

And he said, "G-d of my father Abraham and G-d of my father Yitzchak . . . Deliver me, I pray Thee, from the hand of my brother, from the hand of Esau. For I fear him, lest he come and smite me, the mother with the children."[104]

אין ראוי שימנע האדם מהתפלל אל ה׳ יתברך, ואפילו בעת הסכנה העצומה. כאז״ל, „אפילו חרב חדה מונח על צוארו של אדם, אל ימנע עצמו מן הרחמים.״

It is not proper that the individual shall refrain from praying to the Almighty even when danger is exceedingly great. As *Chazal* said,[105] "Even if a sharp sword is placed upon an individual's throat, he shall not refrain from [praying for] mercy."[106]

. . . on Torah dissemination

יורו משפטיך ליעקב, ותורתך לישראל.

They will teach Thy judgments to Jacob, and Thy Torah to Israel.[107]

(103) Rabbe Levi b. Gershon, *To'aliyos Ralbag* (Tel Aviv: Netzach, 1951), *ad. loc.*, p. 19, no. 81.
(104) Genesis 32:10-12.
(105) *Berachos* 10a.
(106) *To'aliyos Ralbag* on Genesis 32:10, p. 31, n. 148.
(107) Deuteronomy 33:10.

ראוי לכל מי שיש לו חלק משלימות האנושי, שישלים בו זולתו, כי זה הוא דרך ה׳ יתברך.

> It is proper that any individual who has attained a degree of human perfection, shall help others attain perfection, for this is the way of the Almighty. . . . After an individual knows the Torah, it is his responsibility to teach it to Israel.[108]

Because of its great usefulness, the *To'aliyos Ralbag* has been published separately a number of times. The Ralbag also wrote the sefer, *Sha'arei Tzedek,* a commentary on the Thirteen Hermeneutic Principles of Halachic Derivation, as set forth in the *Baraisa of Rabbe Yishmael.* He wrote extensively on mathematics and astronomy, and he invented the Jacob Staff, which was used as an important navigational tool.

Rabbe Aharon haKohen of Lunel: Orchos Chaim

Rabbe Aharon haKohen of Lunel (d. 1344) was a descendant of great Torah scholars. His great grandfather, Rabbe Yitzchak haKohen, studied under the Ravad of Posquires, and compiled a commentary on almost three complete *sedarim* of the Talmud Yerushalmi. He was also the teacher of Rabbe Reuven ben Chaim, who was, in turn, the teacher of the Me'iri.[109] In his *Orchos Chaim,* Rav Aharon cites his grandfather, Rabbe David ben Yitzchak haKohen, who wrote a *sefer* on *Hilchos Tereifos* — Laws of Kashrus.

Rav Aharon haKohen was among the *Megurashei Tzorfas* — the Jews expelled from France in 1306. Together with thousands of his fellow Jews, Rav Aharon haKohen went into exile when Philip IV expelled all Jews from France in August, 1306, confiscating everything they owned while he did so. Rav Aharon was already an accomplished Torah scholar at that time. As a result of his terrible tribulations, however, he writes in the introduction to his sefer, *Orchos Chaim,* אבדה עצה מכהן — "wise counsel was hidden from the *Kohen.*"[110] When asked halachic questions, he frequently found it difficult to answer correctly.[111]

(108) *To'aliyos Ralbag, ad. loc.,* p. 76, no. 362.

(109) Me'iri, Introd. to *Avos,* p. 69. See above, n. 88.

(110) Cf. Isaiah 29:14, ואבדה חכמת חכמיו — *The wisdom of their wise men will be lost.*

(111) Rabbe Aharon haKohen of Lunel, Introduction to his sefer, *Orchos Chaim.*

Rav Aharon therefore decided to write his sefer, *Orchos Chaim*, which would include all halachos which are relevant in our time, so that he and others might use it as a halachic guideline. In his great humility, he writes that he has done nothing original, but that he is only like a scribe, transcribing the words of others.[112] While he does gather his halachos from many other *sefarim* which he mentions by name, such as the Rambam's *Mishneh Torah*, the *Sefer Mitzvos Kattan (SeMaK)* of Rabbe Yitzchak of Corbeil, and the Responsa of the Rashba, Rav Aharon arranged these halachos and selected them carefully. For a number of years his *Orchos Chaim* was regarded as a popular halachic guide and as a *Shulchan Aruch*. The *Orchos Chaim* is cited by many later *Poskim*, and Rabbe Yosef Caro cites this *sefer* hundreds of times in his *Bais Yosef*.

The sefer, *Kol Bo*, a popular halachic work, is drawn, to a large extent, upon the words of the *Orchos Chaim*. While the author of the *Kol Bo* is not definitely known, it is thought by some to have been written by Rav Aharon in his younger years. It may have been the first draft of his *Orchos Chaim*, which he later expanded upon greatly.

The French Expulsion of 1306

It should be borne in mind that the sad oddysey of Rabbe Aharon haKohen of Lunel was shared by the many thousands of his fellow Jews who were expelled from France in 1306. Rav Aharon vividly describes the awesome magnitude of the problem — homelessness, weariness, anxiety and trepidation — with the specter of death lurking behind every door and every bend in the road. This was his lot, and the lot of his fellow Jews.

> נדדתי ממעוני אל ארץ מאפליה, ארץ עיפתה וציה, היה מלוני צלמות ולא סדרים, יושבי על מדין בחדרים.
>
> I wandered from my home to a land of darkness; a land of weariness and desolation. My shelter was in death's shadow, with no regimens of study; sitting fearfully within,[113] in fear of the enemy without.[114]

(112) *Ibid.*

(113) See Judges 5:10 — ישבי על מדין, and see commentaries of Radak and Ralbag, *ad. loc.*, that they could not travel on the roads, for fear of the enemy.

(114) Rabbe Aharon haKohen of Lunel, in his introduction to his sefer, *Orchos Chaim*.

Rabbe Estori haParchi — Kaftor VaPherach

Among the Provencal scholars who were expelled by Philip IV in 1306, was Rabbe Estori b. Moshe haParchi (1280-1355) who studied under the Rosh, to whom he refers as "my teacher, Rabbe Asher, *zal.*"[115] Rabbe Estori was only a youth when he was exiled from Narbonne, on 10 Av, 1306.[116] After great hardship, Rabbe Estori arrived in Eretz Yisroel where he began writing his encyclopedic work, *Kaftor vaPherach,* which he completed in 1322.

Manifesting vast erudition in Talmudic and Midrashic literature, the author clarifies all halachos which relate to the Land. He cites a wealth of Midrashic sources concerning the special sanctity of Eretz Yisroel and the bountiful love of our Sages for the Holy Land. Rabbe Estori spent many years traveling across the length and breadth of the Land, so that he might be able to determine its boundaries, its history, and its topography, all of which are included in this remarkable work. Despite the hardships it entailed, he regarded this journey as a labor of love.

> בחסד עליון עברתי עיירותיה, מדינותיה וכרכיה, רובם דרכתי . . . וזה החיפוש חביב אצלי מחיפוש מקומות הכוכבים ברקיע.
>
> By the grace of G-d, I traveled across its cities, provinces, and villages.[117] . . . This quest is more beloved to me than a quest of the places of the stars in the heavens.[118]

This is in sharp contrast to the author's description of the hardships entailed in his journey many years earlier, when he went into exile during the French Expulsion of 1306.

> מבית הספר הוציאוני, כתנתי הפשיטוני, כלי גולה הלבישוני . . .
>
> Out of my Yeshiva did they lead me, from my homeland did they banish me. . . . From nation to nation did I wander.[119]

He found no surcease to his travail, he observes, until he came to the Holy Land.

> I found no peace until the King of Peace brought me into His chambers, from captivity — into the Holy Land.[120]

(115) *Kaftor vaPherach,* Chap. 16. See *Later Rishonim,* Chap. 5, n. 85.
(116) *Kaftor vaPherach,* Chap. 51.
(117) *Kaftor vaPherach,* Introduction.
(118) *Kaftor vaPherach,* Chap. 11.
(119) *Kaftor vaPherach,* Introduction.
(120) *Kaftor vaPherach,* Introduction.

Rabbe Estori's journey into exile from Narbonne, together with many thousands of his fellow Jews, marked the end of the once glorious era of the Provencal School, and of the thriving Torah community of Southern France. Like Rabbe Aharon haKohen of Lunel and many others, Rabbe Estori haParchi was privileged to continue his work in other climes, and despite the hardships entailed in his exile, succeeded in making an enduring contribution to Torah literature.

The Decline of the Provencal School

The French Jewish community was devastated, and even when some remnants of the once proud community were readmitted to France "provisionally" some ten years later by King Philip's successor, Louis X, the community could hardly regain its former glory. The remaining French Jews suffered greatly during the Pastoreaux Crusade of 1320. They were expelled again in 1322, and readmitted in 1359. Their scattered remnants were slaughtered mercilessly during the Black Plague massacres (1348-1349). They were finally expelled again from most of France in 1394 — not to be readmitted again until the late seventeenth century.

The glorious days of the Provencal School — which produced such towering Torah luminaries as Ravad III of Posquires and Rabbe Zerachiah haLevi; Rabbe Yehonasan haKohen and the Chachmei Lunel; the Kimchi and Ibn Tibbon families; and later, the Me'iri, Rabbe Aharon haKohen of Lunel, and Rabbe Estori haParchi — this glorious era of dynamic Torah growth and vitality had come to a close after two hundred years of Torah study and Torah dissemination. The Torah, as it were, had to pick up its own wanderer's staff, and like the remnants of its homeless, scattered flock, had to once again seek new pastures, in other climes.

In the following chapter we will again turn back to the late tenth and the early eleventh centuries, and trace the establishment and development of the Jewish communities of the Rhine and of Northern France. We will witness the remarkable vitality and growth of the Franco-German School of Torah Study — the School of Rashi, his disciples and grandsons, the founders of the great Torah academies of the *Ba'alei haTosafos* — whose prolific writings and incisive commentaries on the Talmud, laid the groundwork for our own approach to Torah study, until this very day.

6

Early Franco-German School: Rashi: Teacher of All Israel

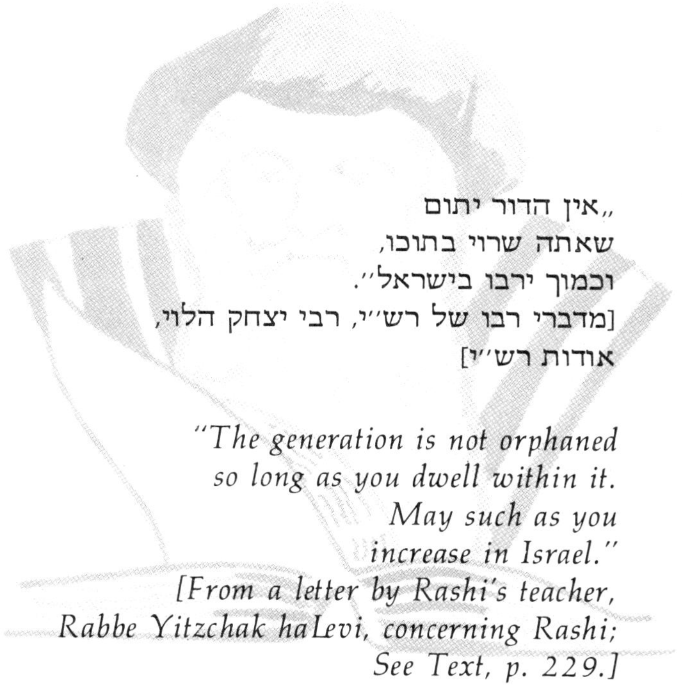

„אין הדור יתום
שאתה שרוי בתוכו,
וכמוך ירבו בישראל״.
[מדברי רבו של רש״י, רבי יצחק הלוי,
אודות רש״י]

"The generation is not orphaned
so long as you dwell within it.
May such as you
increase in Israel."
[From a letter by Rashi's teacher,
Rabbe Yitzchak haLevi, concerning Rashi;
See Text, p. 229.]

Rashi's Lamentation for the Martyrs of the First Crusade, 1096

תורה התמימה, אלפים קדומה.
חלי נא פני קל, בעד יונה תמה . . .

בקשי עלבון חסידיך, ושפיכת דם למודיך,
מיד בני זנונים, מכריתי תלמידיך.

אשר קרעו יריעותיך, ורמסו אותיותיך.
ושצף קצף, החריבו משכנותיך.

שאלי מאת הנורא, להתעיל מחץ ומוסרה;
מבין מכעיסיו, יקבץ עם מפזרה.

O' perfect Torah;
Preceding [Creation] by two thousand years.
Offer supplication to G-d,
For [Israel] the perfect dove. . . .

Seek [to avenge] the humiliation of your pious ones,
And the spilled blood of your scholars,
At the hands of the children of harlotry,
Those who have destroyed your disciples.

They have torn your parchment,
They have trampled your script.
And in great fury,
Have they destroyed your dwelling places.

Beseech the awesome One
To eliminate the crushing blows and the fetters.
From among those who arouse His anger,
Shall He gather the scattered nation.

[Poetic eulogy by Rashi,
re. the persecutions of the First Crusade, 1096;
See Text, at n. 109.]

6

Early Franco-German School: Rashi: Teacher of All Israel

Beginnings of the Mainz Community: The Kalonymos Family

As we have already noted above, even before the Geonic era came to a close, yet another important Torah center had begun to emerge in the cities of the Rhineland and of Northern France. Towards the close of the eighth century, the empire of Charles the Great (Charlemagne, 742-814), embraced all of Central Europe. King of the Franks from 768 to 814, in the year 800 C.E. Charlemagne was also crowned Emperor of the Holy Roman Empire.

According to an ancient tradition which we cited above, Charlemagne, who had a deep interest in learning and culture, invited Rabbe Moshe ben Kalonymos ben Yehudah of Lucca, Italy,[1] and his sons, Rabbe Kalonymos and Rabbe Yekusiel, to establish a Yeshiva in Mainz, in 787 C.E. This, he hoped, would contribute to the development of a self-contained Torah center in Europe, so that the Jews of his empire would no longer have to look to either Eretz Yisroel or Bavel for Torah guidance. This tradition is verified by Rabbe Elazar ben Yehudah ben Kalonymos of Worms (1160-1237), author of *Sefer haRoke'ach*, who traces the history of the

(1) Rabbe Moshe wrote the *piyyut*, אימת נוראותיך. This *piyyut*, written as an alphabetical acrostic, is recited on the morning of the last day of Pesach, during the *Chazaras haShatz* of *Tefillas Shacharis*.

Kalonymos family, of which he was a descendant, from the eighth century until his own day.[2]

The Kalonymos family was a highly illustrious one, which provided the German-Jewish community with many Torah scholars, *paytanim* — composers of liturgical poems — and communal leaders. The leaders of the twelfth century *Chasidei Ashkenaz*, Rabbe Shmuel heChasid and his son, Rabbe Yehudah heChasid (1150-1217), author of *Sefer Chasidim*, were descendants of this family, as were Rabbe Yehudah b. Kalonymos b. Meir of Speyer (13th century), author of the comprehensive Talmudic biographical encyclopedia, *Yichusei Tannaim veAmoraim*, and Rabbe Elazar b. Yehudah of Worms (Ba'al haRokeach, 1160-1237).

Prominent members of the Kalonymos family had an abiding and far-reaching impact on all branches of Torah scholarship and communal development in Ashkenaz during the course of more than five centuries (from the late eighth century through the thirteenth century). In 1096, Rabbe Moshe ben Meshullam haParnes, leader of the Mainz community, was martyred together with his entire community during the *Gezeros Tasnu* — the terrible pogroms which accompanied the First Crusade.

It was not very long after the Kalonymos family arrived in Germany near the close of the eighth century, that the Jewish communities of Germany and nearby Northern France began to emerge as independent Torah centers.

Rabbe Yehudah ben Meir haKohen Leontin

The greatest Torah Sage in Germany in the tenth century was Rabbe Yehudah b. Meir haKohen, also known as Rabbe Sir Leon or Rabbe Leontin. Little is known about Rabbe Leontin's background, but he is believed to have emigrated to Germany from Italy. He was the primary teacher of Rabbeinu Gershom Me'or haGolah, who regarded him as a phenomenal Torah Sage. In one of his responsa, Rabbeinu Gershom writes that he would rely upon

(2) This elaborate rendition of the Kalonymos family tree by Rabbe Elazar b. Yehudah of Worms *(Ba'al haRoke'ach*, 1160-1237), was published by Joseph Delmedigo in his *Matzref leChachmah* (from Paris Ms No. 772, p. 60a). It is not clear whether the king in question was Charlemagne (and the date 787 C.E.), or his grandson, Charles the Bald (and the date of this episode, 876 C.E.). See above, Chap. 2, n. 34.

the halachic rulings of his teacher, Rabbe Leontin, even when they might contradict decisions rendered by the *Geonim* because "Rabbe Leon, *zatzal*, who was my primary teacher of Talmud, was a phenomenal Sage. . . . He was outstanding in his generation, and one should not deviate from his words."[3]

Rabbe Meshullam b. Kalonymos . . . Among the great contemporaries of Rabbe Yehudah Leontin was Rabbe Meshullam ben Kalonymos, author of the *piyyut*, *Amitz Ko'ach*, which is recited as the Ashkenazic *Seder haAvodah* of Yom Kippur. Rabbe Meshullam, who was the son of Rabbe Kalonymos of Lucca who settled in Mainz at the bidding of Charlemagne, was in correspondence with Rav Sherira Gaon and Rav Hai Gaon.

It was at this time that Rabbe Amnon of Mainz composed the moving liturgical poem, *U'nesaneh Tokef*, which is recited during the Mussaf services of Rosh Hashanah and Yom Kippur. Three days after his death, Rabbe Amnon appeared in a dream to his colleague, Rabbe Kalonymos ben Rabbe Meshullam haGadol, and asked him to include this *piyyut* as an integral part of the Mussaf services of the High Holy Days.[4]

Rabbe Shimon haGadol . . . An older colleague of Rabbeinu Gershom Me'or haGolah was the great *tzaddik* and *paytan*, Rabbe Shimon b. Yitzchak, also known as Rabbe Shimon haGadol. Rabbe Shimon was in correspondence with Rabbe Meshullam b. Kalonymos.

Rabbe Shimon haGadol was one of the greatest *paytanim* of Ashkenaz. He wrote the song, *Baruch HaShem Yom Yom*, which is included in our Shabbos morning *zemiros*. Many of his liturgical poems are included in our *machzorim*, and are recited during Yom Tov services. It was said of him that he was a descendant of the House of David, and that he was מלומד בניסים — "accustomed to perform miracles." Because of his greatness in Torah learning and in piety, he was known as Rabbe Shimon haGadol. His *piyyutim* reflect the suffering and persecution of the Jewish community of

(3) Responsa of Maharam of Rothenburg (Prague, 1895), Responsum 264. See *Or haChaim*, p. 307, no. 677, and p. 462, no. 1001.

(4) See above, Chap. 2, n. 40

his generation. A collection of his *piyyutim* has been published under the name *Piyyutei Rabbe Shimon ben Yitzchak.*[5]

The Jewish Pope

An intriguing narrative is related concerning Rabbe Shimon haGadol. It is said that one of his two sons, Elchanan, was abducted and forcibly baptized by agents of the Church, and brought up as a priest. He rose rapidly in the Church hierarchy, until he became the Pope. At this time, harsh edicts were promulgated against the Jews, and Rabbe Shimon haGadol was sent at the head of a Jewish delegation to Rome, to intercede in their behalf. When he appeared before the Pope, the son recognized his father, whom he had not seen for many years. Father and son were joyously reunited. The son secretly abdicated his high post, but not before he had rescinded the harsh decrees against the Jewish community. To commemorate this event, Rabbe Shimon haGadol included his son's name in one of his *piyyutim.*[6]

Rabbe Shimon haGadol had a grandson of the same name, who was also known as Rabbe Shimon haGadol. This grandson, Rabbe Shimon haGadol II, was the brother of Rashi's mother. His words are cited occasionally by Rashi.[7]

The first Rabbe Shimon haGadol brought up his cousin, Eliezer, who was orphaned at a young age. Eliezer studied under Rabbe Shimon haGadol, and also under Rabbeinu Gershom Me'or haGolah. Rabbe Eliezer haGadol, as he was later known, was an ancestor of Rabbe Shmuel and Rabbe Yehudah heChasid, leaders of the thirteenth century *Chasidei Ashkenaz.* When Rabbeinu Gershom died, Rabbe Eliezer haGadol assumed his post as *Rosh Yeshiva* of Mainz.

Accompanying Table XI [p. 215] provides an outline of the origins of the Franco-German School of Torah Study.

(5) A.M. Haberman, ed. (Berlin/Jerusalem, 1938).

(6) This story is cited in many sources. See *Bais haMidrash,* Lelinick, V:148; VI:137. See also J. Prinz, *Popes from the Ghetto* (1966), pp. 17-20.

(7) See *Shabbos* 85b, Rashi, *s.v.* בנוטה שורה, where Rashi writes, "I found support for my explanation in the writings of Rabbe Shimon, the Elder, my mother's brother, in the name of Rabbeinu Gershom, father of the exiles." See also *Eruvin* 42b, *s.v.* וזהו לשון דודי ר׳ שמעון — "These are the words of my uncle, Rabbe Shimon."

Table XI
Post-Geonic Era – Early Rishonim
Franco-German School of Torah Scholarship

Origins – Eighth to Ninth Centuries

Italian Origins

Rabbe Moshe b. Kalonymos b. Yehudah of Lucca, Italy, *and his sons,* **R. Kalonymos and R. Yekusiel** *[established Yeshiva in Mainz, Germany,* at bidding of Charlemagne, in 787 C.E., or Charles the Bald, in 876 C.E.].

Tenth Century

Ashkenazic Origins

R. Yehudah b. Meir haKohen Leontin (R. Sir Leon) [teacher of R Gershom Me'or haGolah]; **R. Meshullam b. R. Kalonymos** of Lucca, Italy, *Piyyut, Amitz Ko'ach* [corresponded with R. Sherira Gaon and R. Hai Gaon]; **R. Amnon,** *U'nesaneh Tokef*

R. Shimon b. Yitzchak (R. Shimon haGadol), *Piyyutim; Shabbos Zemiros, "Baruch HaShem Yom Yom"; his son,* **Elchanan** [abducted, became the "Jewish Pope," subsequently reunited with his father]; **R. Shimon haGadol II** [grandson of R. Shimon haGadol I], Rashi's uncle, brother of Rashi's mother.

Eleventh Century

R. Gershom: Disciple of R. Yehudah b. Meir haKohen Leontin and of R. Hai Gaon

R. Gershom b. Yehudah Me'or haGolah, 965-1040 [Mainz], *commentary on Talmud, Responsa, and Takanos; Contemporaries:* **R. Shimon b. Yitzchak haGadol I,** *Piyyutim;* **R. Yosef Tuv Elem I** [colleague of R. Eliyahu haZaken, brother-in-law of R. Hai Gaon], *Ascribed with authorship of Seder Olam Zuta;* **R. Machir** [brother of R. Gershom Me'or haGolah], *Alpha Beisa (Talmudic lexicon).*

Disciples of R. Gershom Me'or haGolah

R. Eliezer haGadol [Mainz]; **R. Yaakov b. Yakar** [Worms]; **R. Yitzchak b. Yehuda** [Mainz]; **R. Yitzchak haLevi** [Worms], d.ca. 1070; **Chachmei Lutir.**

R. Meir b. Isaac Nehorai [Sh'liach Tzibbur of Worms], *Akdamos Millin (Shavu'os piyyut);* **R. Eliyahu haZaken,** *Piyyutim;* **R. Shimon haGadol II** [Rashi's uncle].

End Eleventh Century

Rashi: Disciple of R. Yaakov b. Yakar, R. Yitzchak b. Yehudah, and R. Yitzchak haLevi

Rashi (R. Shlomo b. Yitzchak) [Troyes], 1040-1105, *Primary commentary on Torah, Nvi 'im, Kesuvim, and on entire Talmud; "Sifrei Devei Rashi" (a collection of Rashi's halachic decisions, including: Sefer haPardes, Sefer haSedarim, Issur veHetter, Sefer haOrah, Machzor Vitri, Siddur Rashi, Teshuvos Rashi).*

First Crusade, 1096-1099, Gezeros Tasnu, Jewish communities of Speyer, Worms, Mainz, destroyed "al Kiddush HaShem."

Twelfth Century

Sons-in-Law of Rashi

R. Yehudah b. Nasan (Rivan), *Completed Rashi's commentary on Makkos, Commentary on Talmud;* **R. Meir b. Shmuel of Ramerupt,** ca. 1060-1135, *Tosafos.*

Disciples and Grandsons* of Rashi

R. Simchah b. Shmuel of Vitri, *Machzor Vitri;* **R. Shemaiah,** *Rashi's scribe; Sefer haPesakim; Commentary on Middos;* **R. Yitzchak b. Asher haLevi (Riva)** [Speyer]; ***R. Shmuel b. Meir (Rashbam),** c. 1080-1158; ***R. Yitzchak b. Meir (Rivam).**

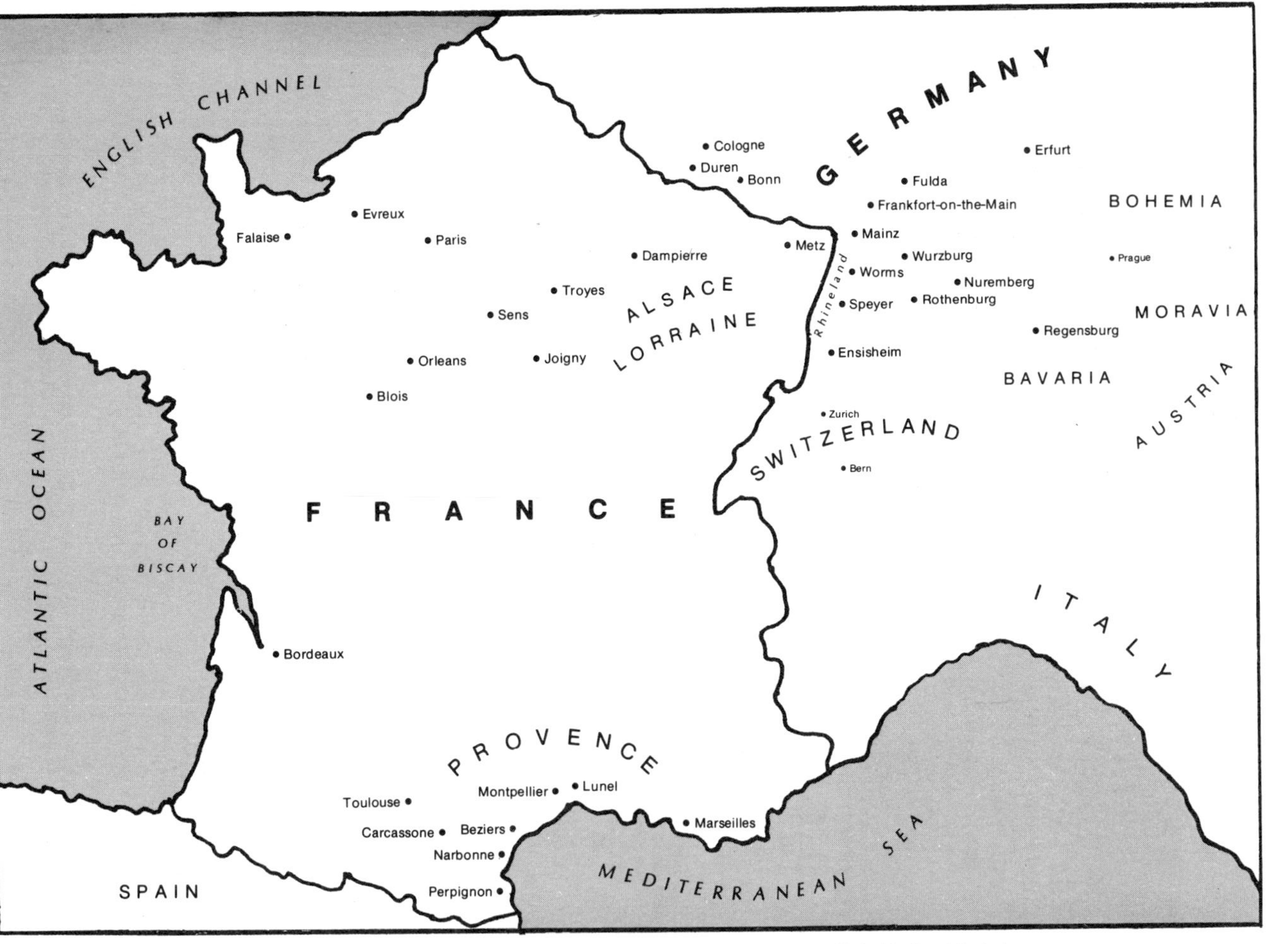

Map II: France, Southern France, and Germany: Early Medieval Period

Rabbeinu Gershom — "Light of the Exile"

Born in 965, Rabbeinu Gershom was the most eminent Torah master of the Franco-German School during the tenth century. Besides having studied under Rabbe Leontin, who was his primary teacher, Rabbeinu Gershom also studied under Rav Hai Gaon, who was *Gaon* of Pumbedisa at this time (939-1038).[8]

After the death of his illustrious teacher, Rabbe Leontin, Rabbeinu Gershom took his place as head of the Yeshiva in Mainz. Students flocked to the Yeshiva, not only from Germany and from Northern France, but from Southern France and from Spain, as well.[9] Indeed, he exerted such a profound influence upon his generation — and upon succeeding generations, as well — that he was known as *Me'or haGolah* — the "Light of the Exile" — a title by which he is referred to by both Rashi and the *Ba'alei haTosafos*, who frequently quote his halachic decisions.[10] Rashi writes concerning him,

> וכל שכן רבנו גרשום, זכר צדיק וקדוש לברכה, שהאיר עיני גולה, וכולנו מפיו חיין, וכל בני גלות אשכנז וכתים תלמידי תלמידיו הן.
>
> And surely Rabbeinu Gershom, may the memory of the saintly and holy one be blessed. He enlightened the eyes of the exile, and by his words do we all live. All exiles of Ashkenaz are disciples of his disciples.[11]

Rabbeinu Gershom had a brother, Rav Machir, who wrote a Biblical Talmudic lexicon, *Alpha Baisa*, which is, unfortunately, no longer extant.

"Akdamos Millin": A Magnificent Piyyut

Among the disciples of Rabbein Gershom was Rabbe Meir ben Isaac Nehorai Shliach Tzibbur of Worms, author of the beautiful

(8) *Or haChaim*, p. 307, no. 677, citing Responsa of Maharshal, no. 29.

(9) *Sefer haYashar* of Rabbeinu Tam, Responsum no. 620, in a letter to Rabbe Meshullam.

(10) See *Menachos* 65b, *Tosafos*, *s.v.* Rabbe Yehudah b. Basyra, where *Tosafos* uses the expression מאיר עיני הגולה. See also *Sefer haYashar* of Rabbeinu Tam, *loc. cit.*

(11) Responsa of Rashi, *Teshuvos Chachmei Tzorfas veLutir* (Vienna: J. Miller ed., 1881), Responsum 21, p. 11.

piyyut, Akdamos Millin. Akdamos, which is recited before the Torah reading on the first day of Shavuos, is a magnificent expression of the eternal covenant of love between G-d, Israel, and Torah.

The nations ask Israel,

מנן ומאן הוא רחימך, שפירא בריותא,
ארום בגיניה ספית מדור אריותא?

From where and who is your beloved, O' beautiful one,
That for His sake you would perish in a lion's den?

Whereupon, Israel replies,

רבותכון מה חשיבא, קבל ההיא שבחתא.
רבותא דיעבד לי, כד מטיא ישועתא.

Of what value is your greatness as compared to that great glory,
Which He will perform for me at the time of Redemption.

במיתי לי נהורא, ותחפי לכון בהתא;
יקריה כד יתגלי, בתוקפא ובגבורתא.

When He will bring me light, and cover you with shame,
When His glory will be revealed, with might and with grandeur.

Akdamos concludes with the following declaration of Israel's joyous acceptance of G-d's dominion and of His gift of Torah.

מרומם הוא אלקין, בקדמא ובתריתא,
צבי ואתרעי בן, ומסר לן אוריתא.

Exalted is G-d; first is He and Eternal.
He desired and selected us, and gave us His Torah.[12]

Rashi cites Rabbe Meir Shliach Tzibbur a few times in his commentary on *Tanach.*[13] Rabbe Meir Nehorai's son died *al Kiddush HaShem* during the *Gezeros Tasnu* — the terrible excesses of the First Crusade, in 1096.

Other illustrious *talmidim* of Rabbeinu Gershom were the great scholar and *paytan,* Rabbe Eliyahu haZaken, brother-in-law of Rav

(12) Excerpts from the liturgical poem, *Akdamos Millin.*
(13) Hoshea 6:9; Amos 3:12; Psalms 73:12.

Hai Gaon; Rabbe Shimon haGadol II, Rashi's uncle; as well as Rashi's teachers: Rabbe Yaakov ben Yakar, Rabbe Yitzchak ben Yehudah, and Rabbe Yitzchak ben Elazar haLevi.

Rabbeinu Gershom wrote a commentary on the entire Talmud, only small portions of which are extant. This commentary is also known as *Kuntreis Magentza*—Glosses of the Yeshiva of Magentza, which was the Yeshiva headed by Rabbeinu Gershom.[14] Rabbeinu Gershom wrote a copy of the *Mesores haGedolah* on the Torah, as well as copies of the Mishnah and Talmud, to be sure that they would be free of textual errors. He also wrote *Hilchos Terefos* and responsa, which are cited often by many *Rishonim.*

Takanos of Rabbeinu Gershom Me'or haGolah

Rabbeinu Gershom also made many extremely important *takanos*—halachic regulations, which left an indelible imprint upon Jewish life, until our own day. Some of the significant *takanos* of Rabbeinu Gershom, as cited in the *Sefer Kol Bo,* in the responsa of Maharam of Rothenberg, and in other early sources, are as follows:

(a) a *cherem* or ban against bigamy.[15]

(b) a ban against divorcing one's wife against her will.[16]

(c) a ban against bringing a fellow Jew into litigation before a non-Jewish court, except in circumstances where a very great loss will be entailed by a failure to do so.[17]

(d) if an individual lends the community space for use as a synagogue, he may not prohibit its use to any single Jew unless he prohibits it to all.[17]

(e) a ban on an individual who strikes a fellow Jew.[17]

(f) a ban against opening someone's private mail.[18]

(14) See Eliezer Meir Lipschutz, *Rashi* (Jerusalem: Mosad haRav Kook, 1966), p. 59.

(15) Cited in responsa of Maharam of Rothenburg (Prague, 1895), no. 866; *Shulchan Aruch Even haEzer* 1:10.

(16) Responsa of Maharam of Rothenburg (Prague, 1895), no. 1121; *Shulchan Aruch Even haEzer* 119:6, in the annotations of the Rama.

(17) See end of *Sefer Kol Bo, siman* 116.

(18) *Ibid.* It was customary to write on the envelope, ח״ל בחדר״ג — *Cherem lifto'ach, be-cherem deRabbeinu Gershom* — "It is a *cherem,* or ban to open [this letter], according to the *cherem* of Rabbeinu Gershom."

(g) to announce a lost article in the synagogue, and to place a *cherem*-ban upon one who finds it but does not return it.[19]

(h) if one is the tenth for a *minyan* and the services have already begun, there is a ban upon him if he should walk out before completion of the services.[20]

(i) an individual who is called to a *din Torah* — litigation by a *Bes Din* — should be called to the *Bes Din* of a nearby city, and not be required to travel to a *Bes Din* of a more distant city, even if the Rabbi there is greater.[21]

(j) a prohibition against reminding a forcibly baptized Jew, who had since repented and returned to Judaism, of his transgressions.[22]

"Requite Those Who afflict Us"

This last *takanah* of Rabbeinu Gershom, in particular, is a reflection of the terrible trials and tribulations of the German-Jewish communities of his day. In the year 1012, Friederich II issued an edict of forcible conversion or expulsion regarding the Jewish community of Mainz. With such terribly harsh edicts hanging over their heads, and with virtually nowhere to turn, a few Jews underwent forcible conversion, while inwardly they fully intended to return to Judaism as soon as their dire circumstances would be alleviated. This *takanah* was enacted to save the dignity and self-esteem of these Jews.

Rabbeinu Gershom also wrote moving liturgical *piyyutim* which likewise reflect the suffering of the Jewish community. In one of his most famous *piyyutim*, זכור ברית, he writes,

ברית אבות ואמהות והשבטים,
רחמיך וחסדיך ברבות עתים,
קה זכור למכים ונמרטים,
ועליך כל היום נשחטים.

(19) *Ibid.*

(20) *Ibid.*

(21) *Ibid.*

(22) Responsa of Rashi, *Teshuvos Chachmei Tzorfas veLutir* (Vienna: J. Miller ed., 1881); responsum 21, p. 11; *The Mordecai* on *Bava Kamma*, halacha 210.

The covenant of the Avos, the Imahos, and the Shevatim,
And Thy oft-repeated kindness and mercifulness,
Remember, O' L-rd, for those who are tortured and stricken,
And who are slaughtered for Thy sake all the day.[23]

דורש דמים דון דיננו;
השב שבעתים אל חיק מענינו.
חנם נמכרנו ולא בכסף פדנו;
זקוף בית מקדשך השמם לעינינו.

O' Thou who avenges blood, avenge our cause,[24]
Requite sevenfold those who afflict us.
We have been sold for naught; without ransom redeem us.
Raise up Thy desolate Temple before our eyes.[25]

A collection of some of Rabbeinu Gershom's *selichos* has been published, as have some of his responsa.[26]

Rabbeinu Gershom died in the year 1040, two years after the death of Rav Hai Gaon in the year 1038.

Rabbeinu Yosef Tov Elem

A very great French contemporary of Rabbeinu Gershom was Rabbeinu Yosef Tov Elem whose words are cited by Rashi,[27] by *Tosafos,*[28] and by other *Rishonim.*[29] He was a colleague of Rabbe Eliyahu haZaken, brother-in-law of Rav Hai Gaon. Rabbe Yosef

(23) Cf. Psalms 44:23, כי עליך הרגנו כל היום — *Because for Thy sake have we been slaughtered all the day.*

(24) Cf. Psalms 9:13, כי דרש דמים אותם זכר — *For He who avenges blood will remember them.*

(25) *Piyyut* by Rabbeinu Gershom Me'or haGolah, recited during the *erev Rosh Hashanah Selichos* service.

(26) His liturgical poems were collected by A.M. Haberman (Jerusalem, 1944). His responsa were collected by S. Eidelberg.

(27) See Rashi, *Chullin* 114b, top, *s.v.* ורואה אני את דברי ר׳ יוסף טוב עלם ז״ל. See also *Kesuvos* 14a, *s.v.* תרי.

(28) *Tosafos, Pesachim* 30a, *s.v.* אמר רבא; *Tosafos, Chullin* 97a, *s.v.* אמר רבא, near bottom; *Tosafos, Avodah Zarah* 57b, *s.v.* לאפוקי, near top; *Tosafos, Gittin* 85b, *s.v.* ולא.

(29) See *Hilchos Rabbeinu Asher, Kiddushin,* Chap. 1, halacha 16.

Tov Elem is believed to have been the author of the important historical source, *Seder Olam Zuta*.[30]

Rashi's Teachers

Upon Rabbeinu Gershom's death (ca. 1040), he was succeeded as *Rosh haYeshiva* in Mainz by his greatest disciple, Rabbe Eliezer haGadol ben Yitzchak. Rabbe Eliezer was orphaned at an early age, and was brought up by the great colleague of Rabbeinu Gershom, Rabbe Shimon haGadol, who also taught him Torah. He also studied under Rabbe Yehudah haKohen, author of *Sefer haDinim*, who was among the earliest students of Rabbeinu Gershom.

Rabbe Eliezer haGadol was an ancestor of Rabbe Shmuel ben Kalonymos of Regensburg and his son, Rabbe Yehudah heChasid (*Sefer Chasidim*, 1150-1217), who were the leaders of the twelfth century *Chasidei Ashkenaz.*

In addition to Rabbe Eliezer haGadol, three other outstanding disciples of Rabbeinu Gershom were Rabbeinu Yaakov ben Yakar, Rabbe Yitzchak ben Yehudah, and Rabbe Yitzchak ben Elazar haLevi. They were the three primary teachers of Rashi.

Rabbe Yaakov ben Yakar

Rabbeinu Yaakov ben Yakar was among the earliest *talmidim* of Rabbeinu Gershom, and a colleague of Rabbe Eliezer haGadol. After his great teacher, Rabbeinu Gershom passed away, Rabbe Yaakov established a Yeshiva in Worms, where Rashi was his most illustrious disciple.

Rashi's reverence for his teacher, Rabbe Yaakov ben Yakar, knew no bounds. In one instance, where Rashi disagrees with his teacher, Rabbe Yitzchak ben Yehudah, concerning a certain halacha, Rashi bemoans the fact that, לא זכיתי לשאול את פי רבינו יעקב בדבר זה — "I did not have an opportunity to ask our teacher, Rabbe Yaakov, concerning this matter," before he passed away.[31]

(30) See Introd. to *Seder Olam Zuta haShalem*, Rabbe Moshe Yair Weinstock, ed. (Jerusalem: Toras Chesed, 1957), pp. 7 f. In *Avodah Zarah* 57b, *Tosafos, s.v.* לאפוקי writes, "And also in the *Seder Tannaim veAmoraim*, handwritten by the great Rav Yosef Tuv Elem" . . .

(31) Rashi, *Beitzah* 24b, *s.v.* ולערב.

A Personification of Humility

Elsewhere, Rashi makes the following remark concerning Rabbe Yaakov ben Yakar:

> ידעתי מדתו, בחר לו גדולה מכלן, והנהיג עצמו כאסקופה הנדרסת ושם עצמו שיירי שיירים. ולא מלאו לבו לעטרה הראויה לו, לחדש דבר בדורו.
>
> I well know his character. He chose the path of true greatness, for in his humility, he was as a threshold which is trodden underfoot, and he made himself as an insignificant remnant. Nor did he aspire to don the crown which was fitting for him, by attempting to innovate anything in his generation.[32]

On one occasion, Rabbe Yaakov ben Yakar and Rabbe Eliezer haGadol purchased a bull in partnership. After the ritual slaughter, a question arose concerning the animal's *kashrus.* Rabbe Eliezer haGadol, following a tradition from his teachers, ruled that the animal was not kosher, while Rabbe Yaakov ben Yakar had a tradition that it was kosher. The animal was divided in half, and Rabbe Eliezer haGadol promptly discarded his half, having ruled that the animal was *treif.* When the second half was brought to Rabbe Yaakov's home, he laughed and said, "How can I eat from this animal, half of which has been discarded in a dung-heap?" Whereupon, he discarded his half as well.[33]

On another occasion, when a non-Jew brought barrels of wine to Worms, Rabbe Yaakov ben Yakar began to hide himself unobtrusively, so that he might not be asked to rule on the kashrus of the wine. Rashi and a friend pursued him, however, and asked him the halacha. He finally ruled that the wine was permissible.[34]

When the communal leaders would appear before the king or other officials on important communal business, Rabbe Yaakov stayed home and removed his shoes, as a sign of contriteness and a

(32) *Machzor Vitri,* p. 358. See Rabbi Eliezer M. Lipschutz, *Rashi* (Jerusalem: Mosad haRav Kook, 1966), p. 22, n. 33.

(33) *Sefer haPardes,* p. 219. See Lipschutz, *op. cit.,* p. 23.

(34) See Lipschutz, *op. cit.,* p. 23, n. 24, citing *Nachlas Shadal,* 40.

prelude to prayer.[35] He said, "I am poor. They will [approach the king] with money [and with bribes], while I will pray for mercy. Hence, they will go with their methods, and I with mine."[36]

Rabbe Yitzchak ben Yehudah

Another of Rashi's primary teachers, Rabbe Yitzchak ben Yehudah, was one of the *Geonei Lutir* — the Sages of Lorraine. In addition to having studied under Rabbeinu Gershom, who was his primary teacher, Rabbe Yitzchak ben Yehudah also studied under Rav Hai Gaon when Rav Hai visited the Italian Jewish community in Rome. The thirteenth century halachic codifier, Rabbe Mordecai ben Hillel, writes in his halachos on tractate *Shabbos*,

> על מה שנהגו העולם שכל ימי השבוע מתעוררין בבקר לבית הכנסת להתפלל או ללמוד ובשבת ישנים יותר בשחרית, זהו טעמו של דבר. שבכל ימי השבוע נאמר בתמיד של שחר, בבקר בבקר, ובתמיד של שחר דשבת לא נאמר בבקר, אלא, וביום השבת, ולשון זה משמע איחור (כדמשמע ביומא לג:). וטעם זה שמע רבי יצחק ברבי יהודה בעיר רומא מפי רב האי גאון. (מרדכי שבת הלכה שצ"ח)

> It is customary for Jews to rise early each day to *daven* and learn Torah in the synagogue, while on Shabbos they sleep a little longer. The reason for this is that in regard to the daily sacrifice — the *Korban Tamid* — the Torah specifies, בבקר בבקר — *"in the morning,"*[37] whereas in regard to the regular Shabbos sacrifice, the *Korban Tamid* of Shabbos — it does not specify בבקר — "in the morning," but it says, rather, וביום השבת — *"on the Sabbath day."*[38] This reason was heard by Rabbe Yitzchak ben Yehudah in Rome, from Rav Hai Gaon.[39]

(35) See Mishnah, *Ta'anis* 12b.

(36) *Or haChaim*, p. 492, no. 1064, citing *Sefer Chasidim*, Sect. 128.

(37) Exodus 29:39; Numbers 28:4. The Torah does not use the repetitious phrase, בבקר.בבקר in regard to the *Korban Tammid* — the daily sacrifice — as it does in regard to the burning of the incense (Exodus 30:7) or the kindling of the wood upon the *Mizbe'ach* (Leviticus 6:5). The words בבקר בבקר used twice here, apparently refer to the two verses cited above (Exodus 29:39; Numbers 28:4). Cf. Ezekiel 46:13,15.

(38) For further clarification, see the *Bigdei Yesha* commentary on *The Mordecai, ad. loc.*

(39) *The Mordecai*, by Rabbe Mordecai b. Hillel (1240-1298), in tractate *Shabbos*, halacha 398.

Rashi cites Rabbe Yitzchak ben Yehudah often and regards his words highly. Upon the death of Rabbe Eliezer haGadol, Rabbe Yitzchak ben Yehudah assumed his post as *Rosh haYeshiva* in Mainz.

In the year 1096, both Rabbe Yitzchak's son, Rav Yehudah, and his grandson, Rav Yitzchak, died as martyrs at the hands of the Crusaders in Mainz, during the terrible excesses of the First Crusade.

Rabbe Yitzchak haLevi

Often referred to by Rashi as Rabbeinu haLevi, or Rabbeinu haKadosh, Rabbe Yitzchak ben Elazar haLevi studied under Rabbeinu Gershom and also under Rabbe Eliezer haGadol. After the death of Rabbe Yaakov ben Yakar, Rabbe Yitzchak haLevi succeeded him as *Rosh haYeshiva* in Worms. He was exceedingly humble and a great *tzaddik*. He fasted two days consecutively for Yom Kippur, much as we observe two days in the *Golah* for each of the three major festivals.[40]

Rabbe Yitzchak haLevi had three sons, Rav Yaakov, Rav Eliezer, and Rav Shmuel. They are cited in halachic literature as *Rabboseinu haLevi'im.*[41]

Rabbe Yitzchak haLevi was succeeded as *Rosh haYeshiva* in Worms by Rabbe Kalonymos b. Shabse of Rome. Rashi writes that he heard that Rabbe Kalonymos was a venerable Sage who was בקי בכל הש״ס — "well-versed in the entire *Shas.*"[42] Rabbe Kalonymos died as a martyr in Worms, during the *Gezeros Tasnu* — the wild pogroms which accompanied the First Crusade in 1096.

(40) Margolios, *Encyclopedia leToledos Gedolei Yisroel, op. cit.*, 3:933. See Rama in *Shulchan Aruch Orach Chaim* 624:5, and *Mishnah Berurah*, nn. 16-17, *ad. loc.*, and see Rav Avraham Danzig [1748-1820], *Chayyei Adam* 145:43, who writes that "We have never heard of anyone doing such a thing" in regard to Yom Kippur. Cf. *Masters of the Mesorah: Later Acharonim*, p. 56, n. 121, re. Ri haZaken.

(41) See Or haChaim, p. 508, no. 1081, citing *Sefer haPardes*, Sect. 289.

(42) See Rashi, *Beitzah* 24b, *s.v.* ולערב.

Rashi — Teacher of All Israel

The ever-recurring theme in Jewish history of וזרח השמש ובא השמש — *"The sun rises and the sun sets"*[43] — upon which the Sages comment, "A *tzaddik* is not removed from this world until another is born to replace him,"[44] now occurred once again.

Thus it was that in the year 4800 (1040) — the very same year during which the sun had set upon the life of Rabbeinu Gershom Me'or haGolah — a boy was born in the city of Troyes, in the province of Champagne, France, who was to bring the light and radiance of Torah into every Jewish home, in every corner of the *Galus.* His name was Shlomo b. Yitzchak, and he was to become known to Jews everywhere simply as Rashi — *Rabbon shel Yisroel*[45] — the revered and beloved teacher of all Israel.

A Heavenly Blessing

The following well-known story which is related concerning the birth of Rashi, provides us with an insight into the unique place which Rashi occupies in Jewish history.

Rashi's father, Rabbe Yitzchak, owned a precious diamond which the priests of his city were anxious to obtain as an adornment for a religious statuette in their church. Although they offered Rabbe Yitzchak vast sums of money, he adamantly refused to permit his diamond to be used for such a purpose. The priests lured Rabbe Yitzchak onto a boat, and, when they were far from the safety of shore, attempted to coerce him into parting with the diamond. In desperation, Rabbe Yitzchak cast the diamond into the sea, where it might never be used to desecrate the name of G-d.

When he returned to shore, a *Bas Kol* — a Heavenly Voice — called out in his *Bais haMidrash:* "You have cast away a precious diamond, lest the Name of the Creator might become desecrated through you. You shall therefore be blessed with a son who will

(43) Ecclesiastes 1:5.

(44) *Kiddushin* 72b.

(45) The acronym Rashi, which stands for Rabbe Shlomo Yitzchaki, also spells out the words *Rabbon Shel Yisroel.*

enlighten the eyes of Israel with Torah, and through whom the Name of the Almighty will become exalted."[46]

The Wall Bent Inward

Another narrative is related concerning the birth of Rashi. On one occasion, when Rashi's mother was expecting, she was walking to *shule* through one of the very narrow streets of Worms, Germany. Suddenly, a large carriage of a nobleman came thundering down the street. There was no room for Rashi's mother to stand, and it appeared certain that she would be trampled to death. Petrified, she pressed hard against the wall as the wagon rolled by. Miraculously, the wall bent inward, and she and her unborn child emerged unscathed.

For many centuries thereafter, until very recently, visitors to the city of Worms were taken to this narrow street, where the indentation in the wall which was still clearly visible was pointed out to them, as a perennial reminder of this great miracle. Shortly after this occurrence, it is said, Rashi's father moved to the city of Troyes in France, where Rashi was born, lest his wife be accused of sorcery by the non-Jewish inhabitants of Worms.[47]

Eliyahu HaNavi

In yet another narrative, it is related that shortly before Rashi was born, his father had a dream, in which he was informed that Eliyahu haNavi would attend the *bris.* When a stranger of venerable appearance did appear at the *bris,* the father made him the *sandik* — the individual who holds the child on his knees during the circumcision. Upon the completion of the *bris,* the *sandik* recited the benediction, אשר קדש ידיד מבטן — "He who sanctified the beloved from the womb."[48] Whereupon, the *sandik* then discussed the

(46) Rabbe Gedaliah b. Yosef Ibn Yachya (1515-1587), *Shalsheles haKabbalah* (Jerusalem: 1962), p. 111.

(47) See *Avodah Zarah* 75a, Rashi, *s.v.* ולא פליגי. Rashi writes as follows, לשון אבא מורי מנוחתו כבוד, והוא נראה בעיני — "These are the words of my father, my teacher, may he rest with honor, and they find favor in my eyes."

(48) According to Rashi, this is a reference to the Patriarch, Yitzchak, while according to Rabbeinu Tam, this benediction is making reference to each of the three Patriarchs. (See *Shabbos* 137b, Rashi, *s.v.* אשר קידש, and *Tosafos, s.v.* ידיד מבטן.)

weekly *Haftorah* reading, which began, most appropriately, with the words, וה׳ נתן חכמה לשלמה כאשר דבר לו — *And the L-rd gave Solomon wisdom, as He had promised him.*[49] The venerable stranger concluded his discourse by reciting the 127th Psalm, שיר המעלות לשלמה — *A Song of ascent of Solomon.*

Upon conclusion of the *Birkas haMazon* — Grace after Meals — the *sandik* — the venerable stranger — left the synagogue and disappeared.

Beloved by his Teachers

Rashi was a descendant of the fourth generation *Tanna,* Rabbe Yochanan haSandelar, who, in turn, traced his lineage to the House of David.[50]

As a young man, Rashi studied in the Yeshiva of Worms under Rabbeinu Yaakov ben Yakar, to whom he frequently refers with great reverence as *Mori haZaken* — "my venerable teacher."[51]

The profound humility of his great teacher made an indelible imprint upon Rashi, which was to remain with him throughout his entire lifetime.

When Rabbeinu Yaakov ben Yakar passed away, Rashi continued to study in Worms under Rabbeinu Yitzchak haLevi (d. 1070), to whom he refers frequently as Rabbeinu haLevi.[52] Rashi then traveled to the Yeshiva of Mainz, which had been established by Rabbeinu Gershom, where he studied under Rabbe Yitzchak ben Yehudah, to whom Rashi refers as *Mori tzedek.*[53]

(49) I Kings 5:26. This *Haftorah* reading, which deals with the construction of the *Bais HaMikdash,* always accompanies *Parshas Terumah* (Exodus, Chapters 25-27), which deals with the construction of the *Mishkan* — the Desert Tabernacle. This was the *Parshas haShavu'a* — the Weekly Portion — during the week of Rashi's *bris.*

(50) *Shem haGedolim* of the Chida (Rabbe Chaim Yosef Dovid Azulai, 1724-1806), *Ma'areches Gedolim,* p. 74, citing *Seder haDoros,* p. 169.

(51) See *Sukkah* 35b, Rashi, *s.v. Tanni; Gittin* 59b, Rashi, *s.v. Nisparda.*

(52) *Shabbos* 59b, Rashi, *s.v. Trei; Ibid,* 119a, Rashi, *s.v. Saineih;* See *Or haChaim,* no. 1080, pp. 507 f.

(53) *Yoma* 16b, Rashi, *s.v. Rubba,* end; see *Or haChaim,* no. 1076, p. 502.

Rashi's teachers recognized his greatness. Rabbe Yitzchak haLevi once wrote concerning him, "I am deeply aware that he is thoroughly familiar with all areas of Torah knowledge."[54] On another occasion, Rabbe Yitzchak haLevi wrote to Rashi,

> אין הדור יתום שאתה שרוי בתוכו, וכמוך ירבו בישראל.
>
> The generation is not orphaned so long as you dwell within it. May such as you increase in Israel.[55]

The sefer *Chofes Matmonim* writes,

> ורבו אוהבו ר׳ יצחק הלוי שואל לכל עובר ושב שלותו וחניתו, ושש על טובתו.
>
> "His teacher, Rabbe Yitzchak haLevi, who loved him, asked every traveler concerning his welfare, and he rejoiced in his happiness."[56]

Rashi kept in frequent contact with his teachers, through both visits and correspondence. At the conclusion of one of his letters to Rashi, his teacher, Rabbe Yitzchak ben Yehudah requested that Rashi pray in his behalf.[57]

Humility and Determination

Rashi's humility was exemplary. His writings are permeated with expressions of humility. He is not reluctant to write לא ידעתי — "I don't know;"[58] nor is he reluctant to admit that he was wrong.

> אני הייתי נוהג בו היתר עד עתה, וטועה הייתי.
>
> I was accustomed to regard this as permissible until now, but I was mistaken.[59]

Elsewhere Rashi writes,

(54) *Teshuvos Chachmei Tzorfas veLutir, op. cit.*, responsum 69, p. 42.

(55) Rabbi Eliezer M. Lipschutz, *Rashi* (Jerusalem: Mosad haRav Kook, 1966), p. 24, n. 35, citing the sefer, *Chofes Matmonim*.

(56) Lipschutz, *loc. cit.*, citing *Chofes Matmonim*, 10, n. 34.

(57) Lipschutz, *loc. cit.*, citing *Chofes Matmonim*, 14, n. 31.

(58) See Genesis 28:5; Leviticus 13:4. See also *Gilyon haShas* in *Berachos* 25b, on Rashi, *s.v.* מאן שמעת ליה, where Rabbe Akiva Eger (1761-1837) cites 44 other places in *Shas* where Rashi writes לא ידעתי — "I don't know," or a similar expression.

(59) *Pardes*, No. 239, as cited by Lipschutz, *op. cit.*, p. 28, n. 8.

אני כבר נשאלתי על זאת זה כמה שנים, והשיבותי ושגיתי בה. אבל עתה יישר כחו של אחי ויוסיף אומץ, שלמדתי מפלפולו, וכן נראין הדברים, וחוזרני בי מבראשונה.

> I have already been asked concerning this matter many years ago, and I replied, but I was mistaken. But now, thanks to my dear friend, may his strength increase, I have become enlightened by his Talmudic discourse. And so does it now appear to me [that he is correct]. I have therefore changed my mind concerning my previous opinion.[60]

Despite his great humility, however, and his exceedingly great reverence for his teachers, Rashi strongly defended his own halachic decisions, even when they differed from the opinions of his teachers. Thus, we find that in regard to a halachic question concerning a small amount of milk which fell into a large pot of meat, Rashi ruled that it is בטל בששים — the milk is nullified if there are sixty parts of meat against it, and the mixture is then kosher. On the other hand, Rashi's teacher, Rabbe Yitzchak haLevi, ruled that אפילו באלף לא בטיל — even if there are a thousand parts of meat against it, the few drops of milk are never nullified, and the mixture is not kosher in any event. Whereupon, Rashi argued this point — respectfully, to be sure, but with great determination, nevertheless — until his teacher agreed with Rashi's opinion. והודה לדברי — "And he [finally] agreed with me."[61]

Elsewhere, where Rashi disagrees with his teacher, Rabbe Yitzchak haLevi, regarding another halachic matter, he informs us that he discussed this point at great length with his teacher, but was not successful in changing his mind regarding this matter.[62] Nevertheless, Rashi writes, that while in the interim he follows his teacher's halachic ruling concerning this matter, he hopes to pursue the matter further and to convince his teacher to change his mind concerning this halachic ruling, much as he did concerning the question cited above.[63]

(60) *Melo Chofnayim*, 36, as cited by Lipschutz, *op. cit.*, p. 28, n. 9; *Machzor Vitri*, p. 444.

(61) See *Teshuvos Chachmei Tzorfas veLutir, op. cit.*, responsum 11, p. 6a. See editor's note 8, *ad. loc.*, citing *Pardes*, no. 242; *Teshuvos Chachmei Tzorfas veLutir*, responsum 84, p. 46, n. 43.

(62) Rashi, *Beitzah* 24b, *s.v.* ולערב.

(63) *Teshuvos Chachmei Tzorfas veLutir, op. cit.*, responsum 11, p. 6a.

The Master Commentator

Rashi's first great work was his commentary on the entire Babylonian Talmud, known as the *Kunteres* or *Glosses*, which he first began to write while he was still studying at the Yeshiva, and which he continued to revise, edit, and improve upon, completing three separate revisions during his lifetime.

Since the close of the Babylonian Talmud (500 C.E.), until our own day, there has never been another work of Torah scholarship which has played as unique and as dramatic a role in the preservation of the Oral Law and in the perpetuation of the transmission process, as Rashi's commentary on the Talmud. We may safely say that without Rashi's commentary, the *Talmud Bavli* might have become entirely incomprehensible to us, and irretrievably lost in a maze of profound intricacies and obscure halachic terminology.

Rabbe Menachem, author of the *Tzedah laDerech* and a disciple of Rabbe Yehudah b. haRosh, makes this point quite succinctly.

> *Ruach HaKodesh* — Divine inspiration — descended upon Rabbeinu Shlomo. He was a master of Talmud, and he wrote a commentary upon the *Talmud Bavli*, in clear, concise language, the likes of which had never previously existed. Were it not for him, the approach to the *Talmud Bavli* would have been forgotten in Israel.[64]

The Rivash likewise writes:

> המאור הגדול רבנו שלמה זצ״ל גלה עמוקות התלמוד מני חשך. לא עממוהו כל סתום. ובזולת פירושו היה כדברי הספר החתום.
>
> The great light, Rabbe Shlomo, *zatzal*, uncovered the complexities of the Talmud from obscurity. No complexity was hidden from him. Without Rashi's commentary, the Talmud would have been like the words of a sealed book.[65]

(64) Rabbeinu Menachem b. haKadosh Aharon b. Zerach, *Introd. to Tzedah laDerech*, *op. cit.*, p. 6.

(65) Rabbe Yitzchak b. Sheshes (1326-1407), *She'elos u'Teshuvos haRivash* (Jerusalem, 1968), resp. 394, p. 240a. Cf. Ephraim Urbach, *Ba'alei haTosafos* (Jerusalem: Mosad Bialik, 1968), p. 19.

An Indispensable Guide to Talmud

Rashi's remarkably lucid commentary is recognized as a virtually indispensable tool in achieving comprehension of the Talmudic text. Its style is so simple and so perfectly clear that it is considered a basic prerequisite for all beginners in Talmud study. At the same time, Rashi's explanations of difficult Talmudic passages are painstakingly pored over by the most advanced Talmud students, for they are aware that in Rashi's words they will invariably find the clue which will elucidate the most complex Talmudic passages.

It would be entirely inconceivable today to publish a text of the Talmud without Rashi's commentary, for Gemara and Rashi have become almost synonymous and practically inseparable. Perhaps never before in history has a commentary played so vital a role in regard to the basic comprehension and, indeed, the very preservation and perpetuation of the text which it was its purpose to clarify.

A Torah Commentary for All Generations

Rashi's commentary on *Chumash* has similarly gained acclaim as a masterpiece by Torah scholars of all generations. In his lucid, concise style, Rashi presents the literal interpretation of Scriptures side by side with the Midrashic interpretations of the Sages. He thereby weaves the Written and Oral Laws into one beautiful fabric, showing that they are, indeed, inseparable. It is a token of the unique acceptance of Rashi's commentary, that the *Shulchan Aruch* stipulates that one may fulfill his halachic requirement to review the weekly Torah portion, by substituting Rashi for *Targum Onkelos*.[66]

Many great Torah scholars have written important works which revolve entirely around Rashi's commentary on the Torah. Some examples are: *The Mizrachi;*[67] *Gur Aryeh;*[68] *Levush haOrah;*[69]

(66) *Shulchan Aruch Orach Chaim* 285:2.

(67) *Mizrachi*, by Rabbe Eliyahu Mizrachi of Constantinople (Re'em, c.1450-1525).

(68) *Gur Aryeh*, by Rabbe Yehudah Loew b. Bezalel (Maharal of Prague, 1512-1609).

(69) *Levush haOrah*, by Rabbe Mordecai b. Avraham Yaffe (Ba'al haLevushim, 1530-1612).

Sifsei Chachamim.[70] These four *sefarim* have been printed individually, as well as in one combined volume.[71] Two other early *sefarim* which clarify all aspects of Rashi's grammatical observations are *Be'er Rechovos*[72] and *Mira Dachya.*[73] These *sefarim* have been published in one volume under the name *Dikdukei Rashi.*[74]

There is a tradition that Rashi fasted 613 days — corresponding to the 613 Torah commandments — before writing his Torah commentary, and that, when he completed it, Moshe Rabbeinu congratulated him for his excellent commentary.[75] It is related further that Rashi's illustrious grandson, Rabbeinu Tam, remarked that while it might have been possible for him to have written a commentary on the Talmud similar to that of his grandfather, Rashi, he could under no circumstances have emulated Rashi's commentary on the Torah.[76]

The Ramban, who frequently analyzes Rashi's commentary in his own masterful commentary on the Torah, makes the following remarks about the great master in his introduction.

ואשים למאור פני נרות המנורה הטהורה,
פרושי רבנו שלמה, עטרת צבי וצפירת תפארה.
מכתר בנימוסו, במקרא, במשנה, ובגמרא,
לו משפט הבכורה.

בדבריו אהגה, באהבתם אשגה,
ועמהם יהיה לנו משא ומתן, דרישה וחקירה,
בפשטיו ומדרשיו וכל אגדה בצורה,
אשר בפרושיו זכורה.

(70) *Sifsei Chachamim,* by Rabbe Shabsi Meshores (d. 1719).

(71) *Arba'ah Peirushim al Rashi* (Warsaw, 1861). Either the *Sifsei Chachamim* or the condensed version, *Ikkar Sifsei Chachamim,* accompany Rashi's commentary in many editions of the *Chumash.*

(72) *Be'er Rechovos,* by Rabbe Yitzchak Isaac b. haKadosh Yeshayah Reiss Auerbach of Pirda, published by his son, Aharon, in 1762.

(73) *Mira Dachya,* by Rabbe Mordecai b. Yechiel Michel of Slavich (fl. 1613).

(74) *Dikdukei Rashi* (Warsaw, 1878).

(75) Rabbe Chaim Yosef David Azulai (Chida, 1724-1806), *Shem haGedolim* (Warsaw: Y. Goldman, 1876) I, p. 116, *s.v.* ושמעתי מפה קדוש, citing also *Ma'amar haIttim* of הרמ״ע.

(76) *Ibid.*

I shall place as an illumination before me,
The lights of the pure candelabrum,[77]
The commentary of Rabbeinu Shlomo [Rashi].
A crown of glory, and a diadem of beauty;[78]
Adorned with his fine traits;[79]
With Scripture, with Mishnah, and with Gemara,
His is the right of the first-born.[80]

In his words will I meditate,[81]
By their love shall I be enraptured.[82]
And with them shall we have discussions,
Investigations and examinations.
Regarding his plain explanations,
His Midrashic interpretations,
And every difficult Aggadic reference,
Which are cited in his commentary.[83]

"Parshan Dassa"

Because of the remarkable lucidity of his commentary, Rashi is often referred to as *Parshan Dassa* — master interpreter of the Law. Rashi's commentary includes *Nvi'im* and *Kesuvim*, as well as Torah itself. In addition to his commentaries, Rashi wrote numerous responsa. Many of his halachic decisions were recorded in separate works, such as *Machzor Vitri, Sefer haPardes, Sefer haOrah,* and *Siddur Rashi,* by his great disciples, foremost among whom were Rabbeinu Shemaiah, and Rabbeinu Simchah of Vitri. A collection of Rashi's responsa, which have been gathered from a variety of sources, has been published under the name *Teshuvos Rashi.*

(77) Exodus 31:8.

(78) Isaiah 28:5.

(79) See *Megillah* 12b, מרדכי מוכתר בנימוסו היה; See also Rabbe Nasan b. Yechiel of Rome (1035-1106), *Sefer haAruch* (Tel Aviv: Bais Rafael), p. 358, *s.v.* נמס, that this refers to Mordecai's total Torah deportment.

(80) Deuteronomy 21:17.

(81) See Psalms 1:2, ובתורתו יהגה יומם ולילה — *And in His Torah does he meditate by day and by night.*

(82) See Proverbs 5:19, באהבתה תשגה תמיד — *By its love [i.e., By your love of Torah] shall you be enraptured always.*

(83) Rabbe Moshe b. Nachman (Ramban, 1194-1270), Introd. to his Torah commentary.

The commentary on *Bereshis Rabbah* which is ascribed to Rashi, is believed not to have been written by Rashi, although it may be based, in part, on Rashi's writings.[84] The commentary of Rashi on the Rif, and that which is included in the *Ein Yaakov* of Rabbe Yosef Ibn Chaviv, are abbreviated versions of Rashi's commentary on the Talmud.[85]

An Indelible Imprint

During the course of his many years of prolific literary activity, Rashi wrote incisive comments on every conceivable topic. Because of his unique role as master-commentator on Torah and on Talmud, Rashi's comments have been studied diligently by great Torah scholars, as well as by simple, pious Jews of all walks of life, throughout the centuries. As such, Rashi's writings have exerted a decisive influence upon Jewish life and thought; they have molded the character and personality of the Torah Jew, and they have left an indelible imprint upon the Jewish *neshamah* — the "soul" of the Jewish people. Frequently, Rashi's comments are drawn from *Chazal*, but it is in Rashi's careful selection of these comments, that we see a reflection and an extension of his own remarkable personality and character traits.[86]

. . . on humility

טוב להתחבר את ענוים ולהיות אתם שפל רוח, מהיות מחלק שלל את גאים.

It is better to join together with the humble and to be humble along with them, than to divide spoils with the haughty.[87]

. . . on Torah study

שיהיו דברי תורה חדשים עליך כאלו היום נתנו.

(84) See Lipschutz, op. cit., p. 194, n. 91, citing an article by Rabbi Avraham Epstein in *HaChoker*.

(85) See Lipschutz, *op. cit.*, p. 155, n. 40.

(86) For an excellent anthology of hundreds of beautiful citations from Rashi's commentaries, see R. Moshe Chesed (d. 1989), *Peninei Rashi laTorah* (Jerusalem: Hotza'as Reuven, 1989). See also R. Shaul Kleiman, *Yalkut Rashi* (Kansas City, 1942).

(87) Rashi, Proverbs 16:19.

The words of Torah shall be ever new in your eyes, as though they had been given this very day.[88]

. . . on readiness to perform mitzvos

"הנני"—כך היא ענייתם של חסידים, לשון ענוה הוא, ולשון זימון.

"Here I am" — Such is the response of the pious. [It is] an expression of humility; an expression of readiness.[89]

. . . on greatness and humility

כל מה שהוא גדול ביותר, צריך להכניע ולהשפיל עצמו.

The greater the individual, the more he must humble and lower himself.[90]

. . . on Bitachon

„ובוטח בה' אשריו" — כשהוא מפלס דרכיו ורואה בה מצוה שיש בה סכנה או חסרון כיס, ובוטח בהקב"ה ועושה הטוב, „אשריו" — הן אשוריו שלו.

"He who places his trust in the L-rd, happy is he." When the individual embarks upon his path and he sees a mitzvah which entails danger or financial loss, if he trusts in the Almighty and does that which is right, *"happy is he."* This is his [guaranteed path for] happiness.[91]

. . . on the rewards of Torah study

„לב יודע מרת נפשו" — טרחו ויגיעו שעמל בתורה; לפיכך „בשמחתו לא יתערב זר" — כשיקבל שכרו לעתיד.

"The heart knows the bitterness of its own soul" — its toil and its weariness as the individual strives to study Torah; therefore, *no stranger will share in his joy* — when he receives his reward in the Hereafter.[92]

(88) Rashi, Exodus 19:1. Rashi makes a similar observation in a number of places. See Deuteronomy 6:6; Deut. 11:13; Deut. 26:16; Deut. 27:9.

(89) Rashi, Genesis 22:1.

(90) Rashi, *Berachos* 34b, *s.v. Kohen Gadol.*

(91) Rashi, Proverbs 16:20.

(92) Rashi, Proverbs 14:10.

. . . on Exile and Redemption

דבר אחר — ישראל שהם מרי נפש בגלות, והם נהרגים על קדושת ה׳; בשמחתם לא יתערב זר לעתיד.

Another explanation: *"The heart knows the bitterness of its own soul"* — [this refers to the people of] Israel, whose souls are embittered by the Exile, and they are slaughtered in sanctification of G-d's Name; no stranger will share in their joy in the future.[92]

. . . on the modesty of the Jewish home

„מה טובו אוהליך יעקב״ — על שראה פתחיהן שאינן מכוונין זה אצל זה.

"How goodly are your tents, O' Jacob" — because he saw that the doors of their tents were not placed one opposite another.[93]

. . . on Israel's tenacious adherence to mitzvos

„הן עם כלביא יקום, וכארי יתנשא״ — כשהן עומדין משנתם שחרית, הן מתגברין כלביא וכארי, לחטוף את המצות — ללבוש טלית, לקרוא את שמע, ולהניח תפילין.

Behold a people that rises up as a lioness, and as a lion does he arise. When they arise from their sleep in the morning they strengthen themselves as a lioness and as a lion, to hasten to perform mitzvos — to don a *tallis,* to recite the *Shema,* and to put on *tefillin.*[94]

. . . on peace

אם אין שלום אין כלום . . . מכאן שהשלום שקול כנגד הכל. וכן הוא אומר, „עושה שלום ובורא את הכל״.

If there is no peace, there is nothing. . . . From here we derive that peace is equal to everything. So too does it say,[95] "He makes peace and creates everything."[96]

(92) Rashi, *Mishlei* 14:10.
(93) Rashi, Numbers 24:5.
(94) Rashi, Numbers 23:24.
(95) Benediction preceding the Morning *Shema.* Cf. Isaiah 45:7.
(96) Rashi, Leviticus 26:6.

. . . on G-d's eternal love for Israel

> „כעת יאמר ליעקב ולישראל מה פעל קל". עוד עתיד להיות עת כעת הזאת, אשר תגלה חבתן לעין כל. שהן יושבין לפניו ולומדים תורה מפיו, ומחיצתן לפנים ממלאכי השרת. והם ישאלו להם, „מה פעל קל"? וזהו שנאמר „והיו עיניך רואות את מוריך".
>
> *In time it will be said to Jacob and to Israel, "What has G-d wrought?"* There is yet destined to be a time like this, when [G-d's] love for them will be revealed to the eyes of all. For they will sit before Him and learn Torah from His mouth, and their position will be before that of the ministering Angels. And the Angels will ask of them, *"What has G-d wrought?"* And this is the meaning of the verse,[97] *And your eyes shall see your Teacher.*[98]

A Personification of Torah

Rashi was beloved for his profound humility, for his remarkable character traits, and for his love and concern for every fellow Jew, which are abundantly manifest throughout his writings. His disciples saw in him a living embodiment of Torah, and all that Torah represents. As one of his *talmidim* writes concerning him, רבנו הקדוש . . . כל מעשיו לשם שמים — "Our holy teacher . . . does everything for the sake of Heaven."[99]

It is for this reason that not only Rashi's responsa, but many of his customs in his household, as well, are cited by his disciples as a frame of reference for definitive halachic rulings and appropriate halachic stringencies.

In this vein, we find, for example, that a disciple makes the following remark.

> אין רבי מניח לאכול גבינה או חלב על שלחן אחד שהוא סועד עליו בשר . . . אלא אם כן נוטל מפה על ברכיו, ואוכל לצד אחר שלא על השלחן.
>
> Our teacher [Rashi] would not permit one to eat cheese or dairy foods on the same table upon which one is eating a

(97) Isaiah 30:20.

(98) Rashi, Numbers 23:23.

(99) *Sefer haOrah*, S. Buber ed. II:75, p. 205. See also Lipschutz, *op. cit.*, p. 28, n. 3, citing *Sefer haPardes*, 242.

> meat meal . . . unless he places a cloth upon his knees, and eats on the side, removed from the table.[100]

In regard to the kashering and preparation of liver on a spit, we are informed, Rashi instructed his household to observe certain stringencies, even beyond the actual halachic stipulations.

> אבל רבנו הקדוש נוהג בו איסור, שכל מעשיו לשם שמים.
>
> Our holy teacher observed halachic stringencies in this regard, for everything he does is for the sake of Heaven.[101]

On one occasion, a woman entrusted an expensive ring to Rashi's young daughter for safekeeping. When his daughter lost the ring, Rashi said, "Even though I am halachically not liable for an article lost by my young daughter,[102] I will nevertheless pay the woman the face value of the ring, since her loss was caused by a member of my household."[103]

Ravages of the First Crusade

Rashi lived to witness the ravages of the First Crusade of 1096. Some of Rashi's responsa reflect the terrible traumatic scars which the vicious bands of Crusaders inflicted upon the Jewish communities of the Rhineland and of Northern France. Regarding those who were forcibly baptized by the Crusaders, Rashi writes,

> חלילה לפרוש מיינם לביישם, שכל מה שעשו, עשו מפני אבחת חרב, וימהרו לפרוש בכל יכולתם.
>
> G-d forbid that we should prohibit their wine [as we would in regard to that of a non-Jew], thereby embarrassing them, for whatever they did was only because of the slaughter by the sword, and they hastened to separate themselves [from their forcible conversion] with all their might.[104]

Elsewhere Rashi writes,

(100) *Sefer haOrah, op. cit.,* II:76, p. 205.

(101) *Sefer haOrah* II:75, p. 205.

(102) See Mishnah, *Bava Kamma* 87a — חרש שוטה וקטן פגיעתן רעה.

(103) *Sefer haOrah* II:136, p. 221. See also *Machzor Vitri,* Sect. 156, p. 144; *Sefer haOrah,* II:47, p. 194.

(104) Rashi's responsa in *haPardes* (Likutim), as cited by Lipschutz, *op. cit.,* p. 32, n. 39.

כהן שהמיר דתו וחזר בתשובה, מותר לו לעלות לדוכן, ולקרוא בתורה ראשון.

A *Kohen* who was [forcibly] converted, and who later repented, is permitted to go up to recite the Priestly Blessing, and to be called up to the Torah for the first *aliyah.*[105]

"Beseech the Awesome One"

Rashi's heart was broken by the suffering which the Crusaders brought upon his people. He composed heartrending liturgical poems, which reflect his profound grief and pain for the wanton slaughter and destruction of the Jewish communities of Germany and France at the hands of the Crusaders, and which express his yearning for Israel's redemption.

תורה התמימה, אלפים קדומה.
חלי נא פני קל, בעד יונה תמה . . .

בקשי עלבון חסידיך, ושפיכת דם למודיך,
מיד בני זנונים, מכריתי תלמידיך.

אשר קרעו יריעותיך, ורמסו אותיותיך.
ושצף קצף, החריבו משכנותיך.

שאלי מאת הנורא, להתעיל מחץ ומוסרה,
מבין מכעיסיו, יקבץ עם מפזרה.

O' perfect Torah;[106]
Preceding [Creation] by two thousand years.[107]
Offer supplication to G-d,
For [Israel] the perfect dove.[108] . . .

Seek [to avenge] the humiliation of your pious ones,
And the spilled blood of your scholars,
At the hands of the children of harlotry,
Those who have destroyed your disciples.

(105) Rashi's responsa in *Shibbolei haLeket* 15, as cited by Lipschutz, p. 32, n. 40.

(106) See Psalms 19:8, תורת ד׳ תמימה.

(107) אלפים שנה קדמה תורה לבריאת העולם — "Torah preceded creation by two thousand years" (*Bereshis Rabbah* 88:2; *Vayikra Rabbah*, beg. Chap. 29; *Bamidbar Rabbah* 5:5).

(108) Israel is referred to allegorically as a dove (*Shir haShirim* 5:2). See *Midrash Tanchuma, Tetzaveh* 5.

They have torn your parchment,
They have trampled your script,
And in great fury,
Have they destroyed your dwelling places.

Beseech the awesome One
To eliminate the crushing blows and the fetters.
From among those who arouse His anger,
Shall He gather the scattered nation.[109]

Rashi's "Prophecy"

It is related that during the early years of the First Crusade a powerful nobleman, Count Godfrey of Bouillon, made preparations to lead a large army of Crusaders to Palestine, to wrest Jerusalem from Muslim control. Like many others, he had heard of Rashi's greatness, and he decided to seek Rashi's counsel.

The Count informed Rashi that he had assembled an army of one hundred thousand men and seven thousand cavalry, and he insisted that Rashi provide him with counsel regarding his undertaking. Rashi was very reluctant to reply, but finally informed the Count that he would conquer Jerusalem and rule over it for six days. On the seventh day, the Muslims would reconquer the city, and drive him out. He would return in ignominious defeat, with only two horsemen to accompany him. The Count was very angry. "If I return with even three horsemen," he said, "I will put you to death, together with all the Jews of France."

The Count embarked on his journey, and he laid siege to Jerusalem for four years. He conquered the city, and thereafter all that Rashi had foretold came to pass — with but one exception. The Count returned, together with three horsemen. Remembering his conversation with Rashi, he decided to return to Troyes, and to take his vengeance upon Rashi for his dire prediction. As the group of four approached the gates of the city, however, a large stone fell from the entrance tower and killed the fourth horse and its rider. The Count was amazed, and decided to return to Rashi and render him great honor, for he now realized how great Rashi really was. He returned to Rashi's home, only to learn that Rashi had already passed away.[110]

(109) Poetic eulogy by Rashi, as cited by Margolios, *op. cit.*, IV:1291.

(110) Rabbe Gedaliah b. Yosef Ibn Yachya (1515-1587), *Shalsheles haKabbalah* (Jerusalem, 1952), p. 113.

The Light Glows Ever Brighter

On 29 Teves 4865 (1105), two years after the Rif passed away in Spain, Rashi passed away. Yet, the light of his Torah wisdom did not diminish, but rather, it continues to grow ever brighter, and to cast its radiant glow upon each succeeding generation.

In truth, it was not only through his writings that Rashi exerted a lasting influence upon succeeding generations. Rashi established a Yeshiva in Troyes, and it was not very long before students flocked to his Yeshiva from all over France and Germany. Although Rashi had no sons, he had three daughters, who married three of his most distinguished disciples.

Rashi's first son-in-law, who married his eldest daughter, Miriam, was Rabbeinu Yehudah ben Nasan (Rivan). The Rivan completed Rashi's commentary on the last five pages of tractate *Makkos* after Rashi passed away.[111] His words are also frequently cited in *Tosafos.*

Another son-in-law, who married Rashi's daughter, Yocheved, was Rabbeinu Meir ben Shmuel of Ramerupt. Rabbe Meir studied under the *Chachmei Lutir* — the scholars of Lorraine — as the most outstanding students of Rabbeinu Gershom were known.[112] He was known as *Avi haRabbanim* — Father of Rabbis — and later in life was referred to as "the Elder."[113] His *Tosafos* are cited by his son, Rabbeinu Tam,[114] and his words are frequently cited by our *Tosafos.* Rashi's third daughter is believed to have married Rabbeinu Ephraim,[115] who may have been the father of Rabbeinu Shemaiah, one of Rashi's most outstanding *talmidim.*[116]

(111) See *Makkos* 19b; *Or haChaim,* no. 1031, p. 470.
(112) *Or haChaim,* no. 1101, p. 525.
(113) Urbach, *op. cit.,* p. 39.
(114) *Sefer haYashar* of Rabbeinu Tam, Chap. 255.
(115) *Or haChaim,* no. 1195, p. 584.
(116) See Urbach, *op. cit.,* p. 34, who maintains that Rabbeinu Shemaiah was not Rashi's grandson, but was the father-in-law of Rashi's grandson, the Rashbam.

A Father-Son Relationship

Rashi's relationship to his disciples was like that of a father to his son. He refers to his *talmidim* as חביבי — "my beloved friend," רעי — "my friend," and אחי — "my brother."[117]

תלמידו של אדם חביב עליו כגופו — "One's *talmid,*" Rashi writes, "is as beloved to him as himself."[118] This was the essence of Rashi's relationship with his *talmidim.* Master pedagogue that he was, he was interested always in training his *talmidim* to think independently. Rashi expresses this thought very beautifully in his commentary on *Mishlei.*

> תורתו של מורה, תחלה היא כמים המכונסין, וסוף נובעין והולכין.
>
> The Torah of a teacher is at first like a pool of still water. Later, it is like an ever bubbling fountain [for the student learns to think independently].[119]

Elsewhere Rashi writes,

> כשאדם מטעים דבריו לתלמיד, וממתיק דבריו בטעמים, יוסיף לקח.
>
> When a teacher clarifies his words for his student, and sweetens them with fine reasoning, the student will increase [his own] understanding.[120]

Moreover, Rashi observes, this will increase the teacher's own understanding, as well.

> הלכה בלב חכם סתומה, ובא תלמיד נבון ודלה אותה ממעיו.
>
> A halacha may be unclear to a Torah scholar, but the wise student will come along and draw it out [with clarity] from his teacher [with his incisive questions].[121]

(117) *Teshuvos Chachmei Tzorfas veLutir,* responsum 15, p. 9a. See Lipschutz, *op. cit.,* p. 46.

(118) Rashi, Deuteronomy 31:29.

(119) Rashi, *Mishlei* 5:15.

(120) Rashi, *Mishlei* 15:21.

(121) Rashi, *Mishlei* 20:5. This follows the dictum of the Sages, מתלמידי יותר מכלם — "I have learned much Torah from my teachers, even more from my colleagues, and from my *talmidim* more than all." (*Ta'anis* 7a; *Makkos* 10a.)

It is in this vein that we often find Rashi conducting halachic discussions and arguments with his *talmidim*, and even permitting them to render definitive halachic judgments in his presence.[122]

Rashi's Talmidim

In addition to his sons-in-law, who had a *talmid-chaver* or student-disciple relationship with Rashi, the following were among his most outstanding *talmidim*. Rabbe Shemaiah was Rashi's devoted disciple and scribe, who transcribed and arranged many of Rashi's halachic decisions in his *Sefer haPesakim*, which later became a primary source of the *Sefer haPardes*.[123] Rabbe Shemaiah wrote commentaries on tractates *Tammid* and *Middos*, "before Rashi," which are included in all standard editions of the *Shas*. His son, Rabbe Moshe, arranged the halachic decisions of Rashi in the *Sefer haOrah*.[124]

Another disciple of Rashi, Rabbe Simchah of Vitri, prepared and arranged the *Machzor Vitri*, which likewise contains many of Rashi's halachic decisions. Rabbe Simchah's son, Rabbe Shmuel, married Rashi's granddaughter, and was the father of Rabbe Yitzchak of Dampierre — the Ri haZaken.[125]

Some of the other halachic collections of Rashi which have been published under the heading *Sifrei de-Vei Rashi*, are: *Issur veHetter*, *Siddur Rashi*, *Sefer haSedarim*, and *Teshuvos Rashi*.

Among Rashi's other *talmidim* were his grandsons, Rabbe Shmuel b. Meir (Rashbam), who completed Rashi's commentary on *Bava Basra*, and Rabbe Yitzchak b. Meir (Rivam). Rabbe Yosef Kara, who wrote a commentary on *Tanach*, was also a *talmid* of Rashi.

When the great light of Israel was extinguished on 29 Teves 4865 (1105), Rashi was succeeded as *Rosh haYeshiva* of his Yeshiva in Troyes by his great disciple and grandson, Rabbe Shmuel ben Meir (the Rashbam). The light of Rashi's Torah wisdom is Israel's perpetual legacy — a beacon which illuminates the complexities of the Talmud, and which brings the warmth and radiance of Torah into the hearts and homes of Jews everywhere.

(122) See, for example, *Teshuvos Maharam of Rothenburg*, Vol. I, *Defus Krimona*, No. 152, citing Rashbam. For other references, see Lipschutz, *op. cit.*, p. 46.

(123) *Tosafos* in *Berachos* 25b, *s.v.* והרי, cites a halachic ruling of "Rabbeinu Shemaiah, the *talmid* of Rashi."

(124) See Urbach, *op. cit.*, p. 36, citing Assaf, *Sifran shel Rishonim*, p. 11.

(125) See *The Mordecai*, *Mo'ed Kattan*, *siman* 835, where the Ri haZaken refers to Rabbe Simchah miVitri as "my grandfather." See also Urbach, *op. cit.*, p. 195.

Bibliography and Indices

Subject Index 247
Sefarim Index 256
Name Index 259
Bibliography and Source Index 267
Glossary 273
Abbreviations 274

Subject Index

Achima'atz family, 13, 71-73; R. Achima'atz b. Paltiel, 71; R. Achima'atz the Elder, 72; Scroll of, 71

Aggadic literature, 25. *See also* R. Yaakov Ibn Chaviv, *Ein Yaakov*.

Ahavas Zion: R. Yehudah haLevi, 121 f

Akdamos Millin, 215, 217 f

Alexandria. *See* Egyptian School

Alfasi, R. Yitzchak b. Yaakov [Rif], 58t, 89t, 99t; and Ri Migash, 113 f; biog. 102-112; commentaries on, 107 f; dispute with R. Yitzchak Albalia, 101; dispute with R. Zerachiah haLevi, 175, 177, 184 f; elegies for, 111 f; expulsion, 91; halacha process, 57; *Hilchos Rav Alfas*, 103-107; overview, 116 f; *Ru'ach haKodesh*, 109 f; Sefer haEzer of R. Meir of Trinquetaille, 191; *Sefer haMa'or* of R. Zerachiah haLevi, 175, 177, 184 f;

Almohades, 85t, 99t; invasion, 114 f; Maimon family, 133 f; persecutions, 91, 129 f

Amidah, 49-55

Amoraim, 52

Anavim family, 13; R. Binyamin b. Avraham haRofei, 78 f; R. Tzidkiah, 78; R. Yechiel, 79; R. Yechiel b. Yekusiel, 79; R. Yehudah b. Binyamin haRofei, 77

Andulasia. *See* Iberian Peninsula.

Ani Ma'amin, 151

Anshei Knesses haGedolah, 25t

Anti-Maimunists: R. Avraham b. David of Posquires, 166; R. David Kimchi [Radak], 194; R. Meir b. Todros haLevi, 174; R. Shlomo Min haHar, 159, 191 f; R. Shlomo Petit of Acre, 165; R. Yehudah Alpachar of Toledo, 159 f. *See also* Maimonidean controversy; Book II, pp. 132, 154-157, 169

Anti-Semites: historical events, 85; roots, 84-89. *See also* Book II; Blood libels; Crusades; Disputes; Expulsions; Inquisition; Talmud burning.

Arab conquest, 34

Arba'ah Shevuyyim, 13, 85t; and Divine Providence, 56-58; R. Chushiel b. Elchanan, 67 f; R. Moshe b. Chanoch, 61 f; R. Shemariah, 66; R. Y.I. haLevi, 45 f; Ravad, 42-44

Arch of Titus, 70

Ashkenazic School, origins: and Charlemagne, 45, 47, 79 f; and Divine Providence, 56-58; eighth century, 47 f; Kalonymos family, 45, 47, 211-213; R. Amnon, 81 f; R. Leontin, 81, 211 ff. *See also* Franco-German School.

Assassination, of R. Yehosef haNagid, 98

Astronomer: Ralbag, 205

R. Avraham b. David Ibn Daud haLevi [Ravad I], 99t; biog. 89, 92, 128-130; re. R. Baruch Albalia, 101; re. Ri Migash, 114

R. Avraham b. David of Posquires Ba'al haHasagos [Ravad III], 89, 92, 187; and *Kabbalah*, 172; *Ba'alei haNefesh*, 179 f; biog., 176-183; critique on Rambam, 148, 166; critique on Rif, 107; death of, 182; disciples, 189-191; *Hasagos haRavad*, 177-179; re. R. Moshe b. Chanoch, 61; re. R. Yosef Ibn Plat, 176; re. Rif, 109 f, 185; *Ru'ach haKodesh* of, 180-182; Torah transmission, 56

R. Avraham b. Yitzchak Av Bes Din of Narbonne [Ravad II], 18, 26t, 187t; and R. Zerachiah haLevi, 183; biog., 171-173; re. R. Meshullam of Lunel, 174; re. R. Moshe b. Yosef b. Mervon haLevi, 173

Ba'alei haTosafos, persecutions of, 91-93. *See also* Book II
Babylonian Academies: *amidah* benedictions, 50; *Arba'ah Shevuyyim,* 45 f; customs, 54-57; Iberian Peninsula, 34 f
Bais HaMikdash: Arch of Titus, 70, 98; as "heart," 125; construction of, 228n
Ban. *See Cherem.*
Bechirah. See Free will.
Benedictions: during Rosh Hashanah, 49-53; of Eretz Yisroel Yeshivos, 46; of R. Natronai b. Hillel Gaon, 35
Betar, 70
Bigamy, 219
Bitachon: and happiness, 236; *Chovos ha-Levavos,* 119-121
Black Plague massacres, 85, 93, 208
Blessing of: Eliyahu haNavi to Rashi, 227f; Heaven re. Rashi's father, 227f; Moshe Rabbeinu to Rambam, 142; Moshe Rabbeinu to Rashi, 233; Rambam to Chachmei Lunel, 132, 167 f; Ri Migash to Rambam, 134 f
Blood libels: Bloyes, 85t; Mainz, 85t; Oberwessel, 85t; R. Yisroel Bruna, 94. *See also* Book II.
Burial, 182n
Byzantine Emperors, 87

Calendar: establishment of, 85n; of Eretz Yisroel Yeshivos, 46
Carolingian Dynasty, 34, 85t; Charlemagne, 79 f; Louis the Pious, 80
Chachmei Tzorfas, and Rambam, 158
Rabbeinu Chananel b. Chushiel [Rash], 14, 15, 26t, 56, 58t; and halacha process, 68 f
R. Chanoch b. Moshe, 15, 26t, 58t; and R. Chisdai, 38; and R. Yitzchak b. Reuven Al-Bargeloni, 102n; as *Rosh Yeshiva,* 62; poem, 60; re. greatness, 60; traditions of, 51, 54
Character traits: development of, 137; of R. Shmuel haNagid, 64 f; of R. Yehudah b. Yakar, 223; of Ri Migash, 114
Charity: rewards for, 200; spiritual fulfillment through, 145
Chaver, and Khazar King, 122-124
Cherem: during Maimonidean controversy, 165, 192; *takanos* of R. Gershom, 219 f
R. Chisdai b. Yitzchak Ibn Shaprut, 15, 16, 35-40, 58t; and Khazar King, 36 f; and lexicographers, 39 f; and R. Moshe b. Chanoch, 62; as leading figure, 35 ff; political intervention of, 37-39
Christian-Roman Emperors, 86
Christianity, and anti-Semitism, 84 ff
Chukim, 143
Churban: and origins of Sephardic Jewry, 33; date of, 33n
Church, and anti-Semitism, 84 ff, 87 f
R. Chushiel b. Elchanan, 14, 58t; *Arba'ah Shevuyyim,* 43 f; as leader, 67 f; disciples of, 68 f; disciples of, 68 f; eulogy for, 68; poem, 60; re. greatness, 60
Communal prayer, 125
Conflict: Yaakov and Esau, 84
Contentment, 164
Conversion, compulsory: Almohad Invasion, 115, 129 f; during Bishop Severus, 86; during First Crusade, 239 f; during Friederich II, 220; in Byzantine Empire, 72
Correspondence between: Ramban and *Chachmei Lunel,* 166-168, 189; Rambam and R. Shmuel Ibn Tibbon, 197 f; R. Yehudah Anav and R. Avigdor, 14, 78

Creation: and Torah faith, 123 f; *Chovos haLevavos,* 119 f; existence of, 151, 156
Critique: Glosses on Rif, 177; *Hasagos haRavad,* 166, 177-179; R. Zerachiah haLevi, 183-186; Ravad, 176-183; *Sefer haMa'or,* 184 f; *Sefer haTzava,* 185
Crusades, 85t, 213t; and Mainz, 225; and Rashi, 239 f; First, 85, 210, 225, 239-241; martyrdom, 93; Pastoreaux, 208; Second, 85; Torah leaders, 92-94
Customs: of Eretz Yisroel Yeshivos, 46 f; of Italian Torah masters, 47; of Rashi, 238 f; of Sephardic School, 49-53; re. Rosh Hashanah *Amidah,* 49-55; re. shofar, 52; *Sefer haManhig,* 191

Debates: and Talmud burning, 85, 92; Ramban vs Apostate Pablo Christiani, 85, 93
Decentralization: and Divine Providence, 31-33; *Arba'ah Shevuyyim*, 42-46; Babylonian and Eretz Yisroel Academies, 54-56; Early Ashkenazic School, 47; halacha process, 49-58; Italian School, 45-47; Sephardic School, 44, 48 ff
Disputes, halachic: *Dayyanim* of Alexandria and *Nasi* of Damascus, 103; *Hasagos haRavad*, 177-179; Maimonidean controversy, 150, 158 f, 165 f; R. Eliezer haLevi and Rashi, 230; R. Yaakov b. Yakar and R. Eliezer haGadol, 224; R. Yitzchak Albalia and R. Yitzchak Alfasi, 101; R. Yitzchak haLevi and Rashi, 230; R. Yosef Ibn Avitur and R. Chanoch b. Moshe, 62; Rambam and BaHaG, 139; Rambam and Rif, 109n; Rashi and R. Zerachiah Ba'al haMa'or, 185; Rif and *Geonim* re. *Tefillin* benediction, 110 f; Rif and R. Zerachiah Ba'al haMa'or, 182; Rosh Hashanah Mussaf *Amidah* controversy, 49-55; *Semichah-Sanhedrin* renewal controversy, 145 f. *See also* Book II, Disputes.
Divine Providence: and R. Moshe b. Maimon, 130; and Torah dissemination, 31-33; and transition of Torah, 30, 56-58, 130; in Thirteen Principles of Torah Faith, 151; Rashi, 226
Divorce, and *cherem* of R. Gershom, 219
Dreams: and halacha, 110, 185; of Kalonymos b. Meshullam, 213; of Rambam, 142

Egyptian School: R. Elchanan b. Shemariah, 66; R. Shemariah b. Elchanan, 66
Elegies by: R. Moshe Ibn Ezra, 112; R. Shlomo Ibn Gabirol, 42; R. Shmuel haNagid, 68; R. Yehudah haLevi, 111 f
Elegies for: R. Chushiel b. Elchanan, 68; R. Hai Gaon, 42; Rambam, 131, 162; Rif, 11 f
Eliyahu haNavi, and: Rashi, 227 f; Ravad II, 172; Ravad III, 181
Eretz Yisroel: *Kaftor vaPherach*, 207; love for, 121 f
Eretz Yisroel Academies: and *Arba'ah Shevuyyim*, 45 f; customs of, 54-57; Italian School, 46
Eternal life, 136
Ethical Bequest of Rambam, 153 f
Ethics: contentment, 164; humility, 153, 157; *Iggeres haMussar*, 153 f; in *Mishneh Torah*, 142-147; in *Pirkei Avos*, 137; in *Yad haChazakah*, 140; integrity, 153; kindness, 158, 200; morality, 144; of King of Israel, 147; of Rambam, 145, 153 f; of Torah scholar, 147; spiritual fulfillment thought, 200-202; truth, 157; *tzedakah*, 200; verbal, 157
Exile: and redemption, 237; by Almohades, 114-116; First Temple, 11; France [1306], 205-208; Maimon family, 92, 133, 135; of King Yechoniah, 11
Exodus, and faith, 123 f
Expulsions, 188t; Almohad Invasion, 114-116; French Expulsion of 1306, 205-208. *See also* Persecutions.

Faith: *Bechirah*, 129; *Chovos haLevavos*, 118-121; Creation, 157; G-d's existence, 151, 156; *HaEmunah haRamah*, 129; historical imperative, 123 f; Khazar King, 122-124; quest for, 122-124; *Sefer haKuzari*, 122-126; *Sefer Olam Kattan*, 117; strengthening, 158; Thirteen Principles, 151; through mitzvos, 119
Families: Achima'atz, 13, 71-73; Anavim, 13, 77-79; Ibn Tibbon, 21, 195-198; Kalonymos, 13, 45, 211 f; Kimchi, 21 f, 192-194; Maimon, 133-166
Fasting: as functional mitzvah, 119; R. Yaakov Moellin, 93 f; R. Yitzchak haLevi, 225; Rashi, 233
Father-son relationship: Rashi and *talmidim*, 243
Five Yitzchaks, 16, 58t, 97-112; R. Yitzchak b. Baruch Albalia, 100-102; R. Yitzchak b. Moshe, 102; R. Yitzchak b. Yaakov Alfasi, 102-112; R. Yitzchak b. Yehudah Ibn Ghayyas, 97-100

Fourth Lateran Council, 87
Franco-German School, 22 f, 215t; and Divine Providence, 56-58; earliest origins, 45, 47, 81 f; Kalonymos family, 211-212; R. Amnon, 81 f; R. Gershom, 217-221; R. Meshullam haGadol b. Kalonymos, 81, 213; R. Shimon haGadol, 81; R. Yehudah b. Meir haKohen Leontin, 81, 212 f; R. Yehudah b. Yakar, 222-224; Rashi, 226-244; Rashi's disciples, 242-244; Rashi's teachers, 222-225. *See also* Ashkenazic School.
Free will, 129

Greatness of: Italian Torah com., 71; R. Amnon, 82; R. Avigdor, 78; R. Avraham Ibn Ezra, 127; R. Baruch Albalia, 101; R. Chananel, 69; R. Chanoch, 60, 62; R. Chushiel, 60, 67, 68; R. Gershom Me'or haGolah, 217; R. Shmuel haNagid, 64, 65; R. Yaakov b. Yakar, 223 f; R. Yehudah haLevi, 126; R. Yitzchak Alfasi [Rif], 95, 109-112; R. Yosef Ibn Tzaddik, 118; R. Zerachiah haLevi, 185 f; Rambam, 131, 137, 150, 152-154, 158-162, 174; Rashi, 209, 229, 231, 233 f; Ravad III of Posquires, 169, 177, 178, 181 f; Ri Migash, 96, 113 f

Genealogy: Scroll of Achima'atz, 71
Genizah, 37n
Geonic era: and *Arba'ah Shevuyyim*, 42 f; close of, 31; customs during, 49-53
Geonic literature, 35, 50-53
Geonim: and Sephardic Jewish community, 54-57; R. Amram, 35, 50; R. Ashi, 32; R. Dosa, 39; R. Hai Gaon, 31, 50; R. Natronai, 35, 50; Torah transmission, 51-53
R. Gershom b. Yehudah Me'or haGolah, 22 f, 26t, 83, 90, 92, 215t; biog., 217-221; re. R. Yehudah b. Meir haKohen Leontin, 212 f; *takanos* of, 219 f; *talmidim* of, 217-219, 222-225; teachers of, 212;
Gezeros Tasnu, 93n, 215n; R. Kalonymos b. Shabse, 225; R. Nehorai's son, 218
G-d: existence of, 151; fear of, 124; gratitude to *HaShem*, 203 f; Heavenly decrees, 72, 78; joy for, 124; love for, 124; nearness to, 156; traits of, 151. *See also* Divine Providence; *Kiddush HaShem*.
Golden Age of Spain: Alomohad Invasion, 114; Five Yitzchaks, 97-112; R. Avraham b. David Ibn Daud haLevi, 128-130; R. Avraham Ibn Ezra, 126-127; R. Bachya Ibn Paquda, 118-121; R. Yehudah b. Barzilai haNasi, 116 f; R. Yehudah haLevi, 121-126; R. Yitzchak b. Yaakov Alfasi, 102-112; R. Yosef Ibn Tzaddik, 117 f; R. Yosef haLevi [Ri Migash], 112-114
Great Torah leaders, summary, 89 ff

Hachnasas Kallah, and *Arba'ah Shevuyyim*, 46n
R. Hai Gaon, 11, 25t, 26t, 58t, 85t, 215t; and *Amidah* benediction, 50; and Italian Torah Center, 74 f; and R. Matzliach, 74, 76; close of Geonic era, 31; disciples of, 68; re. R. Chushiel b. Elchanan, 67
Halacha process: development, of, 49-58; in *Hilchos Rav Alfas*, 104-106
Halachic decisions: and customs, 49-58; of Ashkenazic communities, 47 f; of Rashi, 230; of Rif, 109 f; of Sephardic communities, 46 f; *takanos* of R. Gershom, 219-221
Halachos: in *Mishneh Torah*, 140-147; *Min haShamayim* 110 f, 185
Halachos from Heaven: re. Razah, 185; re. Rif, 110
Haughtiness, 157
Heavenly decree re.: burning of Talmud, 78; Caesar Basil I, 72
Hebrew grammarians. *See* Lexicographers
Hilchos Rav Alfas: explanation of, 103-107
Historical imperative, 123 f
Holocaust, 87 f
Honoring parents. *See Kibud av va-em.*
Humility: and greatness, 236; in Ethical Bequest, 153; of R. Avraham b. haRambam, 162; R. Chushiel, 68; R. Yaakov b. Yakar, 223 f; R. Yehudah b. Yakar, 223; Ramban, 154, 167; Rashi, 229 f, 238; Ri Migash, 114; vs. haughtiness, 235

Iberian Peninsula: Arab-Muslim conquest, 34; as Torah center, 62; Babylonian Academies, 34 f; origins, 33; persecutions in, 34; under pagan rule, 33
Ibn Tibbon family, 21; R. Moshe, 198; R. Shmuel, 196-198; R. Yehudah, 195
Idol-worship, 123, 140
Iggaros haRambam: Iggeres haShmad, 151 f; *Iggeres Teiman*, 151 f
Integrity, of: R. Avraham b. haRambam, 163; Rambam, 153
Interpersonal relations, 202
Introductions of Rambam: contents, 137; to Mishnah, 137; to *Perek Chelek*, 137; to *Pirkei Avos*, 137
Italian School: Anavim family, 77-79; and Divine Providence, 73t; and Eretz Yisroel Academies, 45t, 71; *Arba'ah Shevuyyim*, 45-47; early origins, 45-47, 70; early Torah masters, 74-79; Kalonymos family, 70; Scroll of Achim'atz, 71; Ten Torah martyrs, 74
Italian School: Achima'atz b. Paltiel, 71; R. Abu Aharon b. Shmuel haNasi, 71-73; R. Matzliach Ibn Al-Bazak, 74; R. Nasan b. Yechiel, 75 f; R. Shephatiah b. Amitai, 73; R. Tzidkiyah Anav, 78; R. Yehudah b. Binyamin haRofei Anav, 77 f; R. Yeshayah b. Mali of Trani, 77; R. Yitzchak of Siponto, 76

Jewish badge, 87
Jewish Pope, 23; and R. Shimon haGadol, 216
Justinian code, 87
Justice, of R. Avraham haNagid b. haRambam, 163

Kabbalists: R. Abu Aharon, 71; R. Avraham of Narbonne, 172; R. Azriel, 183; R. David b. Ravad III, 181-183; R. Ezra, 183; R. Yitzchak Sagei Nahor, 181-183; Ravad II, 172; Ravad III, 181
Kaddish, 152
Kairouan. *See* North African School.
Kalonymos family, 13, 45, 70-73, 82, 211 f
Karaites, 129
Kashrus: controversy, 230; of Rashi, 238 f
Kedushah, 179 f
Khazar King, 15, 85t; and R. Chisdai, 36 f
Kibud av va-em, 106
Kiddush HaShem: and *Ani Ma'amin*, 151; during First Crusade, 210, 215, 225; *Gezeros Tasnu*, 93n
Kiddush Hashem of: R. Alexander Suslin haKohen, 93; R. Amnon, 81 f; R. Avraham Ibn Daud, 129 f; R. Chasdai Crescas' son, 94; R. Elazar Ba'al haRokeach's wife, 92; R. Elchanan b. Ri haZaken, 92; R. Eliyahu of York, 93n; R. Kalonymos b. Shabse of Rome, 225; R. Meshullam haParnes, 212; R. Mordecai b. Hillel, 93; R. Moshe's wife, 44; R. Moshe b. Chanoch's wife, 44; R. Nehorai's son, 218; R. Petter haKadosh, 93n; R. Uri, 93n; R. Yaakov of Orleans, 92; R. Yehudah b. Yitzchak, 225; R. Yitzchak b. Yehudah, 225; R. Yitzchak b. Yehudah's sons, 225; R. Yom Tov of Joigny, 93n; Ravad I, 92, 129 f; Ten Italian martyrs, 13, 74; Torah leaders, 91-94
Kimchi family, 21, 22; R. Moshe, 192; R. Yosef, 192; Radak, 192-194
Kindness, 200
Kings of Israel, 146 f
Kohanim: and Ravad III, 181 f; re. burial, 182n
Korbanos, 144
Kuntreisim, of: Magentz, 24, 219; Rashi, 24, 231 f

Lashon hara, 106
Laws. *See Halachos.*
Lexicographers, 58t, 99t; Dunash b. Labrat of Baghdad, 40,99; Kimchi family, 21 f, 192-194; later Kimchi family, 192; Menachem b. Yaakov Ibn Saruq, 39, 99; R. Shlomo Ibn Gabirol, 42, 99; Yehudah Ibn Chiyug, 40 f, 99; Yonah Ibn Janach, 41

Litigation, in non-Jewish court, 219
Liturgical poems. *See Piyyutim.*
Livelihood, 120 f
Love of G-d, 124, 140, 238
Lulav, 119

Maimon family: R. Avraham b. ha-Rambam, 162-165; R. David b. Avraham, 165 f; R. Maimon, 133 f; Rambam, 134-162, 166-168
Maimonidean controversy, 150, 158 f, 165 f, 174, 189, 191 f. *See also* Anti-Maimunists; Book II.
Manna, 123 f
Marriage, 144
Mashiach, 151
Meiri, R. Menachem b. Shlomo, 22, 27t, 188t; biog., 198-202; re. R. Meir of Trinquetaille, 190; re. R. Meshullam of Beziers, 175; re. Ravad II, 172; re. Rif, 110
Mesorah: and faith, 123 f; *Sefer ha-Kabbalah,* 128 f
Mezuzah, 119
Mishkan, 228n
Mishnah, 25t; redaction of, 32n
Mishneh Torah: as ethical-mussar compendium, 140-147; as halachic compendium, 140-142; ethical values, 145; contents, 139-149; fourteen *sefarim,* 140 f; King's role, 146 f; morality, 144; penitence, 146; preparation of, 141 f
Mishpatim, 143
Mitzvah observance: and perfection, 157; love of, 202
Mitzvos: equality in performance, 124; functional vs. conceptual, 118 f; observance of, 157, 202; performance of, 118 f, 143, 236 f; 613 positive and negative, 138 f; through love, 136; *Sefer haMitzvos,* 138 f
Modesty, 237
Morality, 144
Moreh Nevuchim, 17; contents, 149 f; Maimonidean controversy, 150, 158 f, 165, 174; translation of, 149 f, 189, 196; vindication of, 150
R. Moshe b. Maimon [Rambam], 17t, 26t, 99t; and BaHaG, 139; and R. Yehonasan haKohen, 189; and R. Yitzchak Sagei Nahor, 183; and Ramban, 196-198; and Ri Migash, 134 f; biog., 133-168; death of, 161 f; elegy for, 162; ethics of, 153 f; family of, 162-166; greatness of, 158-162; *Hasagos haRavad,* 177-179; humility of, 167; Maimonidean controversy, 150, 158 f, 165 f; on ethical traits, 144-147, 153 f, 157 f; on faith, 143, 156, 157, 158; performance of mitzvos, 137; persecutions of, 155 f; teachers of, 134; Torah transmission of, 56, 89, 90, 92; tragedies of, 155 f
R. Moshe b. Maimon, re.: R. Avraham Ibn Ezra, 127; R. Yosef Ibn Tzaddik, 117 f; Ravad III, 178, 185; Ri Migash, 113; Rif, 109; son, R. Avraham, 162 f
R. Moshe b. Maimon, works of: *Iggeres haMussar,* 153 f; *Iggeres haShmad,* 151 f; *Iggeres Teiman,* 151 f; Introductions of Rambam, 137; *Mishneh Torah,* 139-141, 166 f; *Moreh Nevuchim,* 149 f; *Sefer haMa'or,* 135 f; *Sefer haMitzvos,* 138 f; Thirteen Principles of Torah Faith, 151
R. Moshe b. Nachman [Ramban], 90; comment. on Rif, 107; debate of, 93; defense of BaHaG, 139; re. R. Avraham Ibn Ezra, 127; re. R. Yitzchak b. Reuven Al-Bargeloni, 102; re. Rashi, 233 f; re. Ravad III, 179; teachers of, 190; Torah transmission, 57
Moshe Rabbeinu: and Rambam, 131, 142, 162; and Rashi, 233; humility of, 146; Rambam's dream, 142; in Thirteen Principles of Torah Faith, 151; Torah transmission, 57n

Nesi'us, 87
North African School, 14; R. Chananel b. R. Chushiel, 68 f; R. Chushiel b. Elchanan, 67 f; R. Nissim b. Yaakov of Kairouan, 69-70; R. Yitzchak Alfasi, 102 f

Pastoreaux Crusade, 85 t, 208
Paytanim: Kalonymos family, 212; R. Amnon, 213; R. Eliyahu haZaken, 218 f; R. Gershom, 217-221; R. Meshullam b. Kalonymos, 213; R. Shimon haGadol, 213 f; Rashi, 240 ff
Peace, 237
Persecutions, 85t; Almohad Invasion, 114 f; 133 f; and Torah leadership, 89-94; *Ba'alei haTosafos,* 91-93; Black Plague massacres, 208; First Crusade, 210, 215, 225, 239-241; French Expulsion [13061, 205-208; *Gezeros Tasnu,* 212, 218; in Alexandria, Egypt, 66; in Byzantine Empire, 72; in Iberian Peninsula, 34; in Morocco, 134; of Kairouan community, 15; of R. Chisdai Ibn Shaprut, 38; of Rambam, 155 f; of Ravad III, 181; Pastoreaux Crusade [1320], 208; Ten Italian Martyrs, 74; throughout centuries, 84 ff; under Caliph Al Chakamim, 66. *See also* Inquisition.
Philosophers: R. Avraham b. David Ibn Daud haLevi, 129; R. Bachya Ibn Paquda, 118-121; R. Levi b. Gershon [Ralbag], 203-205; R. Moshe b. Maimon, 149-152; R. Yehudah haLevi, 121-126; R. Yosef b. Yaakov Ibn Tzaddik, 117 f. *See also* Anti-Maimunists.
Philosophy: *Moreh Nevuchim,* 149 f; Thirteen Principles of Faith, 151 f
Piyyutim of: R. Amitai, 13, 72; R. Gershom Me'or haGolah, 220 f; R.Meir Nehorai *[Akdamos],* 217 f; R. Shephatiah, 13, 72; R. Yehudah haLevi, 121 f; Rashi, 240
Poems. *See Piyyutim.*
Poetry: R. Avraham Ibn Ezra, 126 f; R. Yehudah haLevi, 121 f; *See Piyyutim.*
Pogroms, 91-94. *See also* Persecutions; Anti-semitism.
Political intervention of: R. Chisdai, 37 f; R. Shephatiah b. Amitai, 72; R. Yehudah b. Yosef haNasi Ibn Ezra, 115 f
Prayer: and Kalonymos family, 71; and *Korban Tamid,* 224; and nearness to G-d, 156; as climax, 124 f; as halacha, 140; communal, 125; for deliverance, 204; heartfelt, 202; of Eretz Yisroel Yeshivos, 46
Prophecy, 25t; and truth, 201; as principle of faith, 151; Introd. to Mishnah, 137; of Shmuel haNavi, 32n
Provencal School, 18-22, 187t, 188t; *Chachmei Lunel,* 117; Early School, 82; French Expulsion [1306], 205-208; Ibn Tibbon family, 195-198; R. Avraham b. Yitzchak [Ravad II], 171 f; R. David Kimchi [Radak], 192-194; Ibn Tibbon family, 195-198; R. Avraham b. Yitzchak [Ravad II], 171 f; R. David Kimchi [Radak], 192-194; R. Levi b. Gershon [Ralbag], 203-205; R. Moshe b. Yosef b. Mervon haLevi, 173; R. Moshe haDarshon, 83; R. Meshullam of Lunel, 173 f; R. Zerachiah haLevi Ba'al haMa'or, 183-186; Ravad Ba'al haHasagos, 176-183
Purim, 145

Rabbanan Savorai, 51
Rebbe-talmid relationship, 243 f
Rebuke, 106, 200 f
Reconquista, 85t
Redemption: and Exile, 237; everlasting, 194
Reindfleisch massacres, 85t, 93
Reish Kallah, 38n
Repentance, 146
Resurrection. *See Techiyas haMeisim.*
Revelation, 123 f
Reward and retribution, 151
Rosh Hashanah, 81 f, 213
Rosh Hashanah controversy, 49-55
Ruach haKodesh: and halacha, 110 f, 185 f; of Rambam, 160; of Rashi, 231, 241; of Rashi's father, 226-228; of Ravad, 180-182; of Rif, 109 f

Sanctity. *See Kedushah.*
Sandik, 227
Scroll of Achima'atz, 13, 81n, 85t
Secular studies, 179
Selichos, of R. Gershom, 220 f
Semichah-Sanhedrin renewal controversy, 145 f

Sephardic School, 58t, 99t; and Divine Providence, 56-58; Arab-Muslim conquest, 34; *Arba'ah Shevuyyim*, 42-44; development of, 48-53; Early, 59-94; Golden Age, 35 ff, 57-94; lexicographers, 39-42; origins of, 33-44; reliance on Geonim, 54-58; Achima'atz b. Paltiel, 71 f; R. Chananel b. R. Chushiel, 68-70; R. Chanoch b. Moshe, 61 f; R. Chisdai, 35-40; R. Chushiel b. Elchanan, 67 f; R. Moshe b. Chanoch, 61 f; R. Moshe of Paviah, 75; R. Moshe Kalfo, 75; R. Nasan b. Yechiel, 75 f; R. Nissim b. Yaakov, 69 f; R. Shemariah b. Elchanan, 66; R. Shephatiah b. Amitai, 72; R. Shmuel haNagid, 63-66; R. Yitzchak of Siponto, 76; *See also* Golden Age of Spain; Sephardic Torah Center
Sephardic Torah Centers: Egypt, 66; Italy, 70-79; North Africa, 67-70; Spanish community, 61-66
Seventh Crusade, 85t
Sexual relations, 140, 144
Shabbos laws, 76n, 105 f
Shavu'os, 217 f
Shema, 87n

R. Shlomo b. Yitzchaki [Rashi], 23 f, 25t, 26t, 215t; and Moshe Rabbeinu, 233; and R. Yaakov of Marvege, 185 f; biog., 226-244; birth of, 226 f; commentaries, 231-235; commentaries on, 232 f; comment. on Rif, 107; disciples of, 242-244; during First Crusade, 90, 92, 239-241; halachic decisions, 229 f; humility of, 229 f; on ethical traits, 235-238; re. Rabbeinu Gershom, 217; re. R. Yehudah b. Yakar, 222 f; teachers, 222-225, 228-230
Shmuel b. Yehudah Ibn Tibbon, 21, 188t; and Rambam, 196-198; biog., 196-198; translation of *Moreh*, 149 f, 166, 189
R. Shmuel b. Yosef haNagid, 15, 58t; and halacha process, 51; and R. Matzliach, 74; and Ritzag, 97-99; as Visier, 63-66; character traits of, 64 f; eulogy for R. Chushiel, 68; traditions of, 51n
Shofar, 52 f
Siddur, of R. Amram b. Sheshna Gaon, 35
Six hundred thirteen mitzvos, 138 f
Slavery, under Titus, 70
Spiritual fulfillment: through charity, 145, 200; through ethical behavior, 147; through *teshuvah*, 146
Spiritual perfection: attainment of, 157; in Eretz Yisroel, 125
Spiritual tenacity, despite persecutions, 89-94
Sukkah, 119
Suffering of: *Gedolei Yisroel*, 91-94; R. David haNagid, 165; R. Maimon, 133; R. Meir b. Ri Migash, 115; R. Yehosef haNagid, 68; Rambam, 155, 156, 167; Ravad I, 129 f; Spanish Jewish community, 115

Takanos of R. Gershom, 219-221
Talmid chacham, 147
Talmid-chaver relationship, 190, 244
Talmud Bavli 25t; vs. *Talmud Yerushalmi*, 88, 104-106
Talmud burning, 78, 85t, 92, 192
Talmud Yerushalmi, 25; close of, 86, 88n; vs. *Talmud Bavli*, 104-106
Taryag mitzvos, 138 f
Techiyas haMeisim, 44, 151
Tefillah. *See* Prayer.
Tefillin, 146; dispute re. 110 f
Teiman, Iggeres, 152
Ten commandments, 139n
Teshuvah. *See* Repentance.
Tetragrammaton, 156n
Thirteen Fundamental Principles of Torah Faith, 18t; contents, 151; Introd. to *Perek Chelek*, 137; *Rosh Amanah*, 160
Thirteen Hermeneutic Principles, 205
Tish'ah beAv: [1492], 94; and Rambam, 152 f
Tochachah. *See* Rebuke.
Torah benefactors: R. Chisdai b. Yitzchak Ibn Shaprut, 38 f, 62; R. David b. Maimon, 155; R. Meshullam of Lunel, 173 f; R. Paltiel, 74; R. Shmuel b. Paltiel, 74; R. Shmuel haNagid, 38 f, 62-66; Ravad III, 181

Torah centers. *See* Ashkenazic School; Babylonian School; Egyptian School; Eretz Yisroel School; Franco-German School; Golden Age of Spain; Italian School; North African School; Provencal School; Sephardic School.
Torah covenant, 193
Torah dissemination: and *Arba'ah Shevuyyim,* 42 f; responsibility for, 204 f
Torah study: and Divine Providence, 56-58; diligence in, 201; ever-new, 235 f; importance of, 144; Rebbe and *talmid,* 243 f; rewards of, 236
Torah transmission, 11-23; Divine Providence, 56-58; halachic rulings, 51 f; Rambam's Introd. to Mishnah, 137; *Sefer haKabbalah,* 128 f
Torah wisdom, in *Mishneh Torah,* 147 f
Torah wisdom, of: R. Ashi, 88n; R. Avraham Ibn Ezra, 127; R. Chisdai, 39; R. Chushiel b. Elchanan, 60, 67 f;. R. Moshe b. Chanoch, 61 f; Rambam, 134 f; Ri Migash, 96, 113 f; Rif, 109-112, 184; R. Shmuel haNagid, 64 f
Translators, 188t; Ibn Tibbon family, 195-198; R. Shmuel Ibn Tibbon, 196-199; R. Yehudah b. Shaul Ibn Tibbon, 195;

Travels: R. Benjamin of Tudela, 127; R. Estori haParchi, 207; R. Pesachiah of Regensburg, 128
Trust. *See Bitachon.*
Truth, 157; and prophecy, 201
Tzitzis, 140; as functional mitzvah, 119

U'nesaneh Tokef, 81 f, 213

Writing, accuracy in, 158

Yad haChazakah: contents of, 140 f. *See Mishneh Torah.*
R. Yehonasan b. David haKohen of Lunel, 20 f, 187t; and R. Shmuel Ibn Tibbon, 196; biog., 189; blessing of Rambam, 168; comment. on Rif, 107
R. Yehudah haLevi, 89, 99t, 195t; biog., 121-126; elegy for Rif, 111 f; re. Ri Migash, 113 f; *Sefer haKuzari,* 122-126
Yetzer hara, 144
R. Yosef b. Meir haLevi Ibn Migash, 26t, 99t; and Rambam, 134 f; biog., 112-115; Torah greatness of, 96

R. Zerachiah haLevi [Razah], 20t, 26t, 187t; and Shmuel Ibn Tibbon, 196; biog., 183-186; comment. on Rif, 107; customs of, 54, 56, 89; dispute with Rif, 175, 177; re. Rif, 110; teacher of, 173

Sefarim Index

[Listing All Sefarim Cited in Text]

Adkamos Millin, R. Meir b. Isaac Nehorai Shliach Tzibbur of Worms (11th c.), *piyyut for Shavu'os:* 217 f

Arba'ah Turim, R. Yaakov b. Asher Ba'al ha-Turim, 1270-1343), *halachic code:* 27t

Ba'alei haNefesh le-haRavad, R. Avraham b. David of Posquires, Ba'al haHasagos (Ravad III, 1120-1198), *Hilchos Niddah:* 179 f

Be'er Rechovos, R. Yitzchak Isaac b. haKadosh Yeshaya Reiss Auerbach (early 18th c.), *com. on Rashi's Torah com.:* 233

Chakmoni, R. Shabbatai Donnolo, *com. on Sefer Yetzira* (fl. 925): 74

Chibur haTeshuvah, R. Menachem b. Shlomo haMe'iri (1249-1315), *mussar:* 199

Chovos haLevavos, R. Bachya Ibn Paquda (fl. 1080), *mussar; hashakfah:* 16, 118-121, 173, 195

Divrei Malchus Yisroel baBayis haSheni, R. Avraham b. David Ibn Daud haLevi (Ravad I, 1110-1180), *Jewish history:* 129

Ein Mishpat, R. Yehoshua Bo'az miBaruch (d.1554), *Talmud index to Rambam's Mishneh Torah:* 108

Emunos veDe'os, R. Saadiah b. Yosef Gaon (882-942), *Jew. philos., hashkafah:* 195

Glosses of Ravad III. *See* **Hasagos haRavad (on Rif) (on Rambam],** R. Avraham b. David of Posquires Ba'al haHasagos (Ravad III, 1120-1198): 176f

Gur Aryeh, R. Yehudah Loew b. Bezalel (Maharal miPrague, 1512-1609), *com. on Rashi's Torah com.:* 232

HaEmunah haRamah, R. Avraham Ibn Daud haLevi (Ravad I, 1110-1180), *hashakfah:* 17, 129

Haggahos Maimuniyos, R. Meir haKohen of Rothenburg (13th c.), *Glosses on Mishneh Torah:* 148

Halachos Gedolos, R. Shimon Kayyara (BaHaG, fl.780 C.E.), *halachic code:* 25t

Halachos Kelulos, R. Yitzchak Ibn Ghayyas (Ritzag, 1038-1089), *halachic code:* 98

HaMafte'ach, R. Nissim b. Yaakov of Kairouan (d. 1050 C.E.), *Talmud com.:* 69

HaMa'or haGadol, R. Zerachiah b. Yitzchak haLevi Ba'al haMa'or (Razah, 1125-1186), *critique on Rif:* 184

HaMa'or haKattan, R. Zerachiah b. Yitzchak haLevi (Razah, Ba'al haMa'or, 1125-1186), *critique on Rif:* 184

Hasagos haRavad on Mishneh Torah, R. Avraham b. David of Posquires (Ravad III, 1120-1198), *critique on Mishneh Torah:* 19-20, 166, 177-179

Hasagos haRavad on Rif, R. Avraham b. David of Posquires (Ravad III, 1120-1198): 107, 177

Hilchasa Gavrasa, R. Shmuel haNagid (993-1055), *halachic code:* 63

Iggeres haMussar of the Rambam, R. Moshe b. Maimon (Rambam, 1135-1204), *mussar; hashkafah:* 153 f

Iggeres haShmad, R. Moshe b. Maimon (Rambam, 1135-1204), *mussar; hashkafah:* 151 f

Iggeres Nechamah, R. Maimon b. Yosef (12th c.), *mussar; hashkafah:* 134

Iggeres Teiman, R. Moshe b. Maimon (Rambam, 1135-1204), *mussar; hashkafah:* 151 f, 198

Kessef Mishneh, R. Yosef Caro (1488-1575), *Mishneh Torah com.:* 148

Kol Bo, R. Aharon haKohen of Lunel (fl. 1306), *halachic code:* 206, 219-221

Korban haEdah, R. David Fraenkel (1707-1762), *com. on Talmud Yerushalmi:* 25t

Lechem Mishneh, R. Avraham diBoton of Salonika (1560-1606), *Mishneh Torah com.:* 149

Lev Same'ach, R. Avraham Alegre (1560-1652), *com. on Sefer Mitzvos le-haRambam:* 138

Levush haOrah, R. Avraham b. Mordecai Yaffe (1530-1612), *com. on Rashi's Torah com.:* 232

Ma'amar Techiyas haMeisim, R. Moshe b. Maimon (Rambam, 1135-1204), *mussar; hashkafah:* 198

Machberes, Menachem Ibn Saruq (d. 970), *Heb. grammar:* 39

Maggid Mishneh, R. Vidal Yom Tov diTolossa (14th c.), *Mishneh Torah com.:* 148

Marganissa Tava, R. Aryeh Leib Zital Horowitz (fl. 1760), *com. on Sefer haMitzvos le-haRambam:* 138

Mavo haTalmud, R. Shmuel haNagid (993-1055), *introd. to Talmud:* 63

Me'ah She'arim, R. Yitzchak b. Abba Mari of Marseilles (Ba'al haIttur, 1122-1193), *glosses on Rif:* 186

Mechilta of R. Shimon b. Yochai, R. Shimon b. Yochai (2nd c. C.E.), *Tannaitic halachic Midrash:* 25t

Mechilta of R. Yishmael b. Elisha (beg. 2nd c. C.E.), *Tannaitic halachic Midrash:* 25t

Megillas Esther, R. Yitzchak deLeon II b. Eliezer Ibn Tzur (fl. 1546), *com. on Rambam's Sefer haMitzvos:* 138

Mekor Chaim, R. Shlomo Ibn Gabirol (1020-1057), *philosophy:* 42

Mesoras haShas, R. Yehoshua Bo'az mi-Baruch (d. 1554), *Talmud cross-reference index:* 106

Migdal Oz, R. Shem Tov b. Avraham Ibn Gaon (b. 1287), *Mishneh Torah com.:* 148

Milchamos HaShem, R. Moshe b. Nachman (Ramban, 1194-1270), *Rif com.:* 107

Mira Dachya, R. Mordecai b. Yechiel Michel (fl. 1613), *com. on Rashi's Torah com.:* 233

Mivchar Peninim, R. Shlomo Ibn Gabirol (1020-1057): 195

The Mizrachi, R. Eliyahu Mizrachi of Constantinople (Re'em, 1450-1525), *com. on Rashi's Torah com.:* 232

Ner Mitzvah, R. Yehoshua Bo'az miBaruch (d. 1554), *Talmud cross-reference to Tanach:* 108

Nimmukei Yosef, R. Yosef Chaviva (15th c.), *Rif com.:* 108

Olam Kattan, R. Yosef Ibn Tzaddik (1070-1149), *hashkafah:* 17, 98, 117

Onkelos, Onkelos haGer Tzedek (beg. 2nd c. C.E.), *Aramaic Torah translation:* 25t

Orchos Chaim, R. Aharon haKohen of Lunel (d. 1344), *halachic code:* 206

Pekudas haLevi'im, R. Aharaon haLevi of Barcelona (Re'ah, d. 1305), *Rif com.:* 108

Piskei Halachos, R. Yeshayah b. Eliyahu of Trani (Ri'az, d.c. 1280): 77

P'nei Moshe, R. Moshe Margolios (1710-1781), *Talmud Yerushalmi com.:* 25t

Seder Olam Zuta, R. Yosef Tov Elem (11th c.), *history of Torah transmission:* 222

Sefer Chasidim, R. Yehudah b. Shmuel heChasid (1150-1217), *minhagim; mussar:* 212

Sefer haAruch, R. Nasan b. Yechiel (d. 1106), *Talmudic lexicon:* 75

Sefer haDin, R. Yehudah b. Barzilai haNasi al-Bargeloni (end 11th-beg. 12th c.), *hal. code:* 116

Sefer haEshkol, R. Avraham b. Yitzchak, Av Bes Din of Narbonne (Ravad II, 1110-1179), *hal. code:* 172

Sefer haEzer, R. Meir b. Yitzchak of Trinquetaille (end 12th c.), *defense of Rif:* 191

Sefer haHashlamah, R. Meshullam b. Moshe of Beziers (d. 1238), *Rif com.:* 108, 175

Sefer haHashlamah, Yonah Ibn Janach (990-1050), *Hebrew grammar:* 41

Sefer haIttim, R. Yehudah b. Barzilai haNasi al-Bargeloni (end 11th-beg 12th c.), *hal. code:* 116

Sefer haIttur, R. Yitzchak b. Abba Mari (Ba'al haIttur, 1122-1193), *hal. code:* 186

Sefer haKabbalah le-haRavad, R. Avraham b. David Ibn Daud haLevi (Ravad I, 1110-1180), *hist. of Torah trans.:* 110, 128

Sefer haKuzari, R. Yehudah haLevi (1075-1141), *hashkafah:* 16, 122-126, 195

Sefer haManhig, R. Avraham b. Nasan ha-Yarchi (1155-1215), *halacha and minhagim:* 191

Sefer haMa'or, R. Zerachiah b. Yitzchak ha-Levi (Ba'al haMa'or, 1125-1186), *critique on Rif:* 184 f

Sefer haMaspik leOvdei HaShem, R. Avraham b. haRambam (1186-1237), *mussar; hashkafah:* 164

Sefer haMe'oros, R. Meir haKohen of Narbonne (d. 1263), *halachic code:* 176

Sefer haMichlol, R. David b. Yosef Kimchi (Radak, 1160-1235), *Heb. grammar:* 192

Sefer haMitzvos le-haRambam, R. Moshe b. Maimon (Ramban, 1135-1204), *Taryag mitzvos:* 138 f

Sefer haMussar, R. Shlomo Ibn Gabirol (1021-1057), *mussar:* 195

Sefer haPesakim, *Sifrei Devei Rashi (end 11th c); Piskei halachos:* 244

Sefer haRikmah, Yonah Ibn Janach (990-1050), *Heb. grammar:* 41, 195

Sefer haRokeach, R. Elazar b. Yehudah of Worms (Ba'al haRokeach, 1160-1237), *halachic code:* 211

Sefer haSharashim, R. David b. Yosef Kimchi (Radak, 1160-1235), *Heb. grammar:* 192

Sefer haSharashim, Yonah Ibn Janach (990-1050), *Heb. grammar:* 41

Sefer haTzava, R. Zerachiah haLevi, Ba'al haMa'or (Razah, 1125-1186), *Talmud methodology:* 185

Sefer haZechus, R. Moshe b. Nachman (Ramban, 1194-1270), *defends Rif:* 107

Sefer Kol Bo. *See* **Kol Bo.**

Sefer Tikun haMiddos, R. Shlomo Ibn Gabirol (1020-1057), *mussar:* 42

Sefer Yereim, R. Eliezer b. Shmuel of Metz (Re'em, 1115-1198), *halachic code:* 79

Sha'arei Tzedek, *Geonic responsa:* 205

Sha'arei Tzedek, R. Levi b. Gershom (Ralbag, 1288-1344), *com. on Baraisa deRabbe Yishmael:* 62

She'elos u'Teshuvos min haShamayim, R. Yaakov of Marvege (fl. 1203), *responsa:* 185 f

She'iltos, R. Achai miShabcha (680-760), *halachic-Midrashic Torah com.:* 25t

Shemonah Perakim le-haRambam, R. Moshe b. Maimon (Rambam, 1135-1204), *introd. to com. on Avos:* 137

Shibolei haLeket, R. Tzidkiyah b. Avraham haRofei Anav (fl. 1240), *hal. anthology:* 78

Shitas Rivavan, R. Yehudah b. Binyamin haRofei Anav (1215-1280), *Mishnah com. on Shekalim:* 78

Shulchan Aruch, R. Yosef Caro (1488-1575), *hal. code:* 28t

Sifrei Devei Rav, R. Chiyya Rabbah or Rav (beg. 2nd c. C.E.), *Tannaitic hal. Midrash:* 25t

Sifsei Chachamim, R. Shabse Meshores (d. 1719), *com. on Rashi's Torah com.:* 233

Targumim, Yonasan b. Uziel (beg. 1st c. C.E.); Onkelos Ger Tzedek (beg. 2nd c. C.E.), *Aramaic translations of Torah:* 25t

Temim De'im le-haRavad, R. Avraham b. David of Posquires (Ravad III, 1120-1198), *responsa:* 179

Teshuvos Geonei Mizrach u'Maarav, *anthology of Geonic responsa:* 62

Tiferes Yisroel, R. Yisroel Lipschitz (1782-1860), *Mishnah com.:* 25t

Tosafos, Ba'alei haTosafos (12th-13th c.), *Talmudic novellae:* 25t

Tosafos Rid, R. Yeshayah b. Mali of Trani (1180-1260), *Talmudic novellae:* 77

Tosafos Yom Tov, R. Yom Tov Lipmann Heller (1579-1654), *Mishnah com.:* 25t

Tosefta, *Tannaitic halachic source:* 25t

U'Nesaneh Tokef, R. Amnon of Mainz (10th c.), *Piyyut for Rosh Hashanah and Yom Kippur:* 81, 213

Yad haChazakah. *See* **Mishneh Torah.**

Yichus She'er Basar, R. Yehudah b. Barzilai haNasi (end 11th-beg. 12th c.), *hal. code:* 116

Yichusei Tannaim veAmoraim, R. Yehudah b. Kalonymos (13th c.), *anthol. of Tannaim and Amoraim; Talmudic lexicon:* 212

Torah Or, R. Yehoshua Boaz miBaruch (d. 1554), *Tanach sources for Talmud:* 108

Name Index

LEGEND: A—Acharon; Am:B-1—Amora, Bavel, 1st gen. Amora; Ash — Ashkenaz; Aus—Austria; B—Bavel; b.—born; beg.—beginning; c.—century; c.,ca.—approximately; C.E.—Common Era; com.—commentary; Con.—contemporary; d.—died; Eg—Egypt; Emp—Emperor; Eng—England; EY—Eretz Yisroel; F—France; ff—and following pages; fl.—flourished; G:P-3—Gaon, Pumbedisa, 3rd c. Geonic era; gen.—generation; Ger—Germany; Gr—Greece; Heb—Hebrew; It—Italy; Jew—Jewish; J—Judges; Jud—Judah; K—King; Lexicog—Lexicographer; Mac—Maccabbee; N—Navi; NA—North Africa; P—Patriarchal era; pP—pre-Patriarchal era; Q — Queen; R—Rishon; Rom—Roman; Seph—Sephardic School; SF—Southern France; Sp—Spain; T-1—Tanna, 1st gen. Tanna; t—Table; Turk—Turkey; Z-1—1st gen. Zugos.

Abad al-Rachman III (Caliph of Cordoba, fl. 950 C.E.), 36

Abohav, R. Yitzchak I (R:Seph, beg. 15th c.), *Menoras haMa'or:* 27

Abohav, R. Yitzchak II (R:Seph, 1433-1493), 27t

Abrabanel, R. Don Yitzchak (R:Seph, 1437-1508), *Tanach com.; Rosh Amanah:* 27t, 91, 94, 160

R. Abu Aharon b. Shmuel haNasi (R:Bav-It, beg. 9th c.), *Kabbalist:* 71-73

Abudraham, R. David b. Yosef (R:Seph, fl. 1340), *Sefer Abudraham:* 27

Abulafia, R. Meir b. Todros haLevi of Toledo [Ramah], *Yad Ramah:* 26, 99

R. Achai of Shabcha (G.era-P2, 680-760), *Sheiltos:* 25

R. Achima'atz the Elder (R:It, beg. 9th c.), 72-73

Achima'atz b. Paltiel (R:It, fl.1052), 71, 73

Achima'atz family (R:It, 9th-11th c., or 840-1040 C.E.), 71-73. *See also* Subject Index.

Adres, R. Shlomo b. Avraham [Rashba] (R: Seph., 1235-1310), *Mishmeres haBayis; Toras haBayis; Responsa:* 27, 57, 90, 165

R. Aharon b. Meshullam of Lunel (R:SF, d. 1210), 19, 26, 174, 187

R. Aharon b. Yosef haLevi of Barcelona [Re'ah] (R:Seph, c.1235-1300), *Bedek haBayis; Sefer haChinuch; Sefer Pekudas haLevi'im:* 27, 108

R. Aharon haKohen of Lunel (R:SF, d. 1334), *Orchos Chaim:* 22, 27, 90, 93, 188, 205, 206

R. Akiva b. Yosef (T-3, beg. 2nd c.), 25, 32

Albalia, R. Baruch b. Yitzchak (R:Seph, 1077-1126), 99, 101, 113

Albalia, R. Yitzchak b. Baruch (R:Seph, 1035-1094), 16, 26, 58, 98 f, 112

Albo, R. Yosef (R:Seph, fl.1425), *Sefer ha-Ikkarim:* 27

Alegre, R. Avraham of Constantinople (A: Turk, 1560-1652), *Lev Same'ach:* 138n

R. Alexander Suslin haKohen of Frankfort [Maharzach] (R:Ger, d.1349), *Sefer ha-Agudah:* 27, 90, 93

Alfasi, R. Yitzchak b. Yaakov [Rif] (R:Seph, 1013-1103). *See* Subject Index.

Alphonso VII of Castile [King] (K:Sp, c.1148 C.E.), 115

Alshech, R. Moshe [Alshech haKadosh] (A: EY, 1508-c.1600), *Toras Moshe:* 28

R. Amittai b. Shephatiah (R:It, 9th c.), *Piyyutim:* 13

R. Amnon of Mainz (R:Ger, 10th c.), *U'nesaneh Tokef:* 81 f, 213, 215t

R. Amram b. Sheshna Gaon (G:Sura-3, 858-876), 50, 350

Anav, R. Binyamin b. Avraham haRofei (R: It, fl.1240), 73t, 78 f

Anav, R. Tzidkiyah b. Avraham haRofei (R: It. fl.1240), *Shibolei haLeket,* 12, 26t, 73t, 78

Anav, R. Yechiel b. Yekusiel (R:It, fl.1314), *Tanya Rabbati:* 73t, 79

Anav, R. Yehudah b. Binyamin haRofei [Rivavan], (R:It, 1215-1280), *Shitas Rivavan:* 14, 73t, 77 f

Anavim family (R:It, 1215-1315), 13, 73t, 77-79. *See also* Subject Index.

Arama, R. Yitzchak b. Moshe (R:Seph, 1420-1494), *Akedas Yitzchak:* 27

Ari haKadosh. *See* Luria, R. Yitzchak b. Shlomo.

R. Asher b. Meshullam [Rosh miLunel] (R: SF, d.1210), *Hilchos Yom Tov:* 19, 174 f, 187

R. Asher b. Yechiel [Rosh]] (R:Seph, 1250-1327), *Hilchos Rabbeinu Asher:* 26, 55, 57, 90, 108

R. Ashi (Am:B-6, 371-427), *Redacted Babylonian Talmud:* 25, 32, 52, 88

Ashkenazi, R. Bezalel b. Avraham (R-A:EY, c.1520-1592), *Shitah Mekubbetzes:* 28
Aspian [King] (K:Sp, c.3338 [68 C.E.]), 33
R. Avigdor b. Elijah haKohen of Vienna (R: Ger, 13th c.), 14, 78
R. Avraham b. David Ibn Daud haLevi [Ravad I] (R:Seph, 1110-1180, *Sefer haKabbalah. See* Subject Index.

R. Avraham b. David of Posquires Ba'al haHasagos [Ravad III] (R:SF, c.1120-1198). *See* Subject Index.

R. Avraham b. Meir Ibn Ezra (R:Seph, 1090-1164), *Tanach comment.:* 26, 99, 126 f
R. Avraham b. Nasan haYarchi (R:SF, 1155-1215), *Sefer haManhig:* 26, 188t, 191
R. Avraham b. Yechiel of Rome (R:It, 11th c.), 13, 73t, 75
R. Avraham b. Yitzchak Av Bes Din [Ravad II] (R:SF, d.1158), Sefer haEshkol. See Subject Index.

R. Avraham b. Yitzchak of Montpelier Min haHar (R:SF, d.1315), 188t, 203
R. Avraham haNagid b. haRambam (R:Seph, 1186-1237), *Birchas Avraham:* 18, 99, 162-165
R. Azriel (R:SF, end 12th c.), *Kabbalist:* 183

Ba'al haIttur. *See* R. Yitzchak b. Abba Mari of Marseilles.
Ba'al haTurim. *See* R. Yaakov b. Asher.
Bacharach. R. Yair Chaim (A:Ger, 1638-1702), *Chavos Yair:* 28
R. Bachya Ibn Paquda (R:Seph, fl.1080), 26t, 89, 99, 118-121, 173
BaHaG. *See* Kayyara, R. Shimon.
Bar Kochba (Jew. commander, fl.130 C.E.), 70
R. Baruch b. Shmuel of Magentza (R:Ger, d. 1237), *Sefer haChachmah:* 26t
Basil I [Caesar] (Rom. Caesar, 867-886), 72 87
R. Benjamin of Tudela (World traveler, 12th c.), *Sefer Masa'os:* 99, 127, 175
Benvenista, R. Chaim b. Israel (A:Turk, 1603-1673), *Knesses haGedolah:* 28t
Berav, R. Yaakov of Safed (R-A:EY, 1475-1546), *Semichah renewal:* 28t
Bertinoro, R. Ovadiah [R'av] (R-A:EY, c. 1445-1510), *Mishnah Commentary:* 25t, 27t
Blau, R. Yehudah (Contemp.), 203
Boton, R. Avraham (A:Gr, 1560-1606), *Lechem Mishnah:* 28t, 149
Bruna, R. Yisroel b. Chaim (R:Ger, c.1400-1480), 27t, 90, 94
Bulan [King] (K:Khazars, 8th c.), 36, 122 f

Canpanton, R. Yitzchak (R:Seph, 1360-1463), *Darkei haGemara:* 27t
Caro, R. Yosef [The Mechaber] (R-A:EY, 1488-1575), *Bais Yosef; Kesef Mishnah; Shulchan Aruch:* 27t, 28t, 91, 94, 148

Chabbus [Emir] of Granada (Emir:Span, beg. 11th c.), 63 f
Chachmei Lunel (R:SF, fl.1190 C.E.), 155, 166-168, 187t
R. Chafetz b. Yatzliach (R:NA, 10th c.), 58t
R. Chaim b. Yitzchak Or Zaru'a (R:Aus, end 13th c.), *Simanei Or Zaru'a:* 26t
R. Chananel b. Chushiel [Rach] (R:NA, d.c.1055).*See* Subject Index.

R. Chanina b. Akashiah (T-4, c.135-170 C.E.), 136
R. Chanoch b. Moshe (R:Seph, 10th c., d.c. 1025). *See* Subject Index.

Charlemagne [Charles the Great] (Ger Emperor, 742-814), 79 f, 81n, 85, 211
R. Chasdai the Elder (R:It, d.925 C.E.), 13, 73t, 74
Chaviva, R. Yosef. *See* R. Yosef Ibn Chaviv.
R. Chisdai b. Yitzchak ibn Shaprut (915-970 C.E.). *See* Subject Index.

R. Chiyya b. Abba (T-5:end 2nd c.), 25t
R. Chizkiah b. Manoach (R:F, 13th c.), *Chizkuni:* 26t
R. Chushiel b. Elchanan (R:NA, end 10th c.). *See* Subject Index.

Constantine [King] VIII (Rom. Emperor, 307-337 C.E.), 38n
Constaninus II (Rom. Emp. 337-361), 86
Cordovero, R. Moshe [Ramak] (R-A,EY, 1522-1570), *Kabbalist:* 28t
Crescas, R. Chasdai b. Avraham (R:Seph, 1340-1412), *Or HaShem:* 27, 91, 94

R. Daniel b. Yechiel of Rome (R:It, end 11th c.), 13, 73t, 75
DaSilva, R. Chizkiah b. David (A:It, 1659-1695), *P'ri Chadash:* 28t
David [King] (K:Jud, 2884-2924), 147
R. David b. Avraham haNagid [grandson of Rambam] (R:Eg, 1213-1301), 27t, 99, 165

R. David b. Ravad III of Posquires (R:SF, end 12th c.), *Kabbalist:* 181, 182, 183
R. David b. Shlomo Ibn Avi Zimra [Radvaz] (R-A, Seph, 1480-1574), 28t, 91, 94, 149

R. David b. Shmuel haLevi [Taz] (A, 1586-1667), *Turei Zahav:* 28t
Donin Nicolas (Apostate, fl.1240), 92
Donnolo, R. Shabbetai (It, fl.930), *Chakmoni:* 73 f
R. Dosa b. Saadiah Gaon (G era, fl.940), 39
Dunash b. Labrat haLevi (Heb. lexicog., Seph, 920-970), 15, 58, 99
Duran, R. Shimon b. Tzemach [Rashbatz] (R: NA, 1361-1444), 27t

Edels, R. Shmuel Eliezer b. Yehudah haLevi [Maharsha] (A, 1555-c.1631), 28t
R. Elazar b. Yehudah b. Kalonymos of Worms Ba'al haRokeach (R:Ger, 1160-1237), *Sefer haRokeach:* 26t, 85t, 90, 92, 211, 212.
R. Elchanan b. Shemariah (R:Eg, 11th c.), 15, 58
R. Elchanan b. Shimon (Jewish "Pope," 10th c.), 214, 215t
R. Elchanan b. Yitzchak [son of Ri haZaken] (R:F, d.1184), 92
Eli haKohen (J, d.2871), 32
R. Eliezer b. Nasan [Ravan] (R:Ger, c.1090-1170), *Even haEzer:* 26t
R. Eliezer b. Shmuel of Metz [Re'em] (R:F, 1115-1198), *Sefer Yereim:* 26
R. Eliezer b. Yitzchak haLevi [Rabboseinu haLevi'im] (R:Ger, end 11th c.), 225
R. Eliezer b. Yoel haLevi [Raviah] (R:Ger, 1140-1225), *Avi Ezri:* 26t
R. Eliezer haGadol (R:Ger, 10th c.), 23, 215, 216, 222 f
R. Eliezer of Touques (R:F, d.c.1291), *Tosafos Touques:* 26t
R. Eliyahu b. Shlomo Zalman [Vilna Gaon] (A, 1720-1797), 126, 160
Eliyahu haNavi (N, fl.c.2960-3043). *See* Subject Index.
R. Eliyahu haZaken (R:F, fl.1000), 215t, 218 f
R. Eliyahu of York (R:Eng, d.1190), 93n
R. Ephraim [talmid Rashi] (R:F, end 11th c.-beg. 12th c.), 242
R. Ephraim b. Yaakov of Bona (R:Ger, 1133-1196), 82n
R. Ephraim Qua'alat Hammad (talmid haRif, R:NA, end 11th c.-beg. 12th c.), 99t, 108
Esau (P era, 2108-2255), 84
R. Estori haParchi (R:SF, 1280-1355), *Kaftor vaPherach:* 207 f
Eved al-Rachman Alnazzar of Cordoba [Caliph] (fl, 960 C.E.), 43
R. Ezra (R:SF, end 12th c.), *Kabbalist:* 183

Falk, R. Yehoshuya [S'ma] (A, 1550-1614), *Sefer Me'iras Einayi .n:* 27t, 28t
Friederich II (Ger King, fl.1012), 220

Gallus (Rom. Caesar, fl. 350 C.E., 86
R. Gershom b. Yehudah Me'or haGolah (R: Ger, 965-1040). *See* Subject Index.
Godfrey [Count] of Bouillon (fl.1280), 241
Gombiner, R. Avraham Abeli (A, 1637-1683), *Magen Avraham:* 28t

R. Hai Gaon (G:P-4, 939-1038). *See* Subject Index.
Harun Al-Rashid [Caliph] of Baghdad (764-809), 80
Helena [Queen] (Queen, Byzantine Emp., c. 950 C.E.), 38
Heller, R. Yom Tov Lipmann (A, 1579-1654), *Tosafos Yom Tov:* 28t
Heraclitus (Rom Caesar, 632 C.E.), 87
Heschel, R. Yehoshua (A, d.1648), *Meginnei Shlomo:* 28t
R. Hillel b. Eliakim of Greece (R:Gr, 12th c.), *Peirush Sifra:* 26t
Hillel haZaken (Z-5, 3728-3768; 32 B.C.E.-8 C.E.), 25t
R. Hillel of Verona (R:It, fl.1242), 159
Hillel the Second (Am:EY-5, fl.360 C.E.), *Established calendar:* 87n
Horowitz, R. Aryeh Leib Zital (A, 1550-1615), *Chesed Avraham:* 138n
Horowitz, R. Yeshayah b. Avraham haLevi [Shilah haKadosh] (A, 1560-1630), *Shnei Luchos haBris:* 28t

Ibn Alarif (Granada, 1030 C.E.), 63
Ibn Tibbon family (Translators, R:SF, 1120-1280), 21, 195-198
Ishbili, R. Yom Tov [Ritva] (R:Seph, 1250-1330), *Talmud novellae:* 27t
R. Israel of Krems (R:Aus, fl.1350), *Haggahos Ashiri:* 27t
Isserlein, R. Yisroel b. Pesachiah (R:Ger, 1390-1460), *Terumas haDeshen:* 27t
Isserles, R. Moshe [Rama] (R-A: Poland, 1530-1572), *Darkei Moshe; Mapah:* 27t, 28t, 91

Joseph [King] (K:Khazars, c.950 C.E.), 36, 37n

Kalfo, R. Moshe of Bari (R:It, 11th c.), 13, 73t, 75
Kalonymos family (R:Ger, 9th c.-12th c.), 13, 70, 71, 72n, 72, 211 f. *See also* Subject Index.
R. Kalonymos b. Meshullam haGadol (R: Ger, 10th c.), 82, 187t

R. Kalonymos b. Moshe of Lucca, Italy (R: Ger, fl.787 C.E.), 22, 45, 47, 80, 83, 211, 215t
R. Kalonymos b. Shabse of Rome (R:Ger, d. 1046), 225
R. Kalonymos b. Todros haZaken (R:SF, 9th c.), 18, 83
Katzenellenbogen, R. Meir [Maharam Padua] (R-A:It, 1473-1565), 28t
Kayyara, R. Shimon [BaHaG] (G.era, S-2, fl. 780 C.E.), *Halachos Gedolos:* 25, 139
Kimchi family, 21 f, 192-194. *See also* Subject Index
Kimchi, R. David [Radak] (R:SF, c.1160-1235), 21, 26t, 188, 192-194
Kimchi, R. Moshe (R:SF, 12th c.), 21 f, 188t, 192
Kimchi, R. Yosef (R:SF, 12th c.), 21, 188t, 192
Klausner, R. Avraham (R:Aus, d.1407), *Sefer Minhagim:* 27t
Krochmal, R. Menachem (A, d.1661), *Tzemach Tzedek:* 28t

Landau, R. Yaakov (R:Ger-It, 15th c.), *Sefer haAgur:* 27t
Leo III (Rom. Emp., 721 C.E.), 87
Leo IV (Rom. Emp, c.890 C.E.), 87
Leontin, R. Yehudah b. Meir haKohen (R: Ger, 10th c.), 22, 212 f
R. Levi b. Gershon [Ralbag; Gersonides] (R: Seph, 1288-1344), *Tanach com.; To'aliyos Ralbag* 21, 27t, 188t, 203-205
R. Levi Ibn Chaviv of Jerusalem [Ralbach] (R-A:EY, 1483-1545), 28t
Lima, R. Moshe (A, 1605-1658), *Chelkas Mechokek:* 28t
Louis the Pious (K:Ger, 814-840), 34, 80
Luria, R. Shlomo [Maharshal] (R-A: Poland, 1510-1573), *Yam shel Shlomo:* 28t
Luria, R. Yitzchak b. Shlomo [Ari haKadosh] (R-A:EY, 1534-1572), 28t

R. Machir [brother of R. Gershom] (R:Ger, 10th c.), 215t, 217
R. Machir [Kalonymos family] (R:SF, 8th c.), 18, 45, 80, 83, 187t
Maharaf. *See* R. Peretz b. Eliyahu of Corbeil.
Maharam. *See* R. Meir b. Gedaliah of Lublin.
Maharam Baruch of Rothenburg. *See* R. Meir b. Baruch of Rothenburg
Maharam Padua. *See* Katzenellenbogen, R. Meir.
Maharam Sal [Maharam Segal]. *See* R. Meir b. Baruch haLevi.
Maharash. *See* R. Shalom b. Yitzchak Zekel of Austria.
Mahrashdam. *See* Medina, R. Shmuel.
Mahari Mintz. *See* Mintz, R. Yehudah.
Maharil. *See* Moellin, R. Yaakov b. Moshe.
Maharit. *See* Trani, R. Yosef b. Moshe.
Maharitz Ghayyas. *See* R. Yitzchak b. Yehudah Ibn Ghayyas.
Maharsha. *See* Edels, R. Shmuel Eliezer b. Yehudah.
Maharshal. *See* Luria, R. Shlomo.
Maharzach. *See* R. Alexander Suslin haKohen of Frankfort.
Maimon family, 133-168
R. Maimon b. Yosef [father of Rambam] (R: Seph, d.c.1165), 99t, 133 f
Maimuni, R. David haNagid. *See* R. David b. Avraham haNagid.
R. Matzliach b. Eliyahu Ibn Al-Bazak (R:It, 10th c.), 13, 73t, 74, 76
Medina, R. Shmuel [Maharashdam] (A:Gr, d. 1589), 28t
R. Meir b. Baruch of Rothenburg [Maharam Baruch] (R:Ger, 1220-1293), *Extensive responsa:* 27t, 78, 85, 90, 93, 219
R. Meir b. Baruch haLevi [Maharam Sal; Maharam Segal] (R:Ger, d.1404), 27t
R. Meir b. Gedaliah of Lublin [Maharam] (A: Poland, 1558-1616), 28t
R. Meir b. Isaac Nehorai (R:Ger, 11th c.), 215t, 217 f
R. Meir b. Ri Migash (R:Seph, 1148), 91, 115
R. Meir b. Shmuel of Ramerupt [Rashi's son-in-law] (R:F, 1060-1135), 26t, 215t
R. Meir b. Todros haLevi Abulafia (R:Seph, 1170-1244), *Yad Ramah:* 174
R. Meir b. Yitzchak of Trinquetaille (R:SF, end 12th c.), *Sefer haEzer:* 21, 187, 189-190
R. Meir haKohen of Narbonne (R:SF, d. 1263), *Sefer haMe'oros:* 176, 188t
R. Meir haKohen of Rothenburg (R:Ger, 13th c.), *Haggahos Maimuniyos,* 148
Meiri, R. Menachem b. Shlomo (R:SF, 1249-1315), *Bais haBechirah. See* Subject Index.
R. Menachem b. Aharon b. Zerach (R:Seph, c.1310-1385), *Tzedah laDerech:* 137, 231
R. Menachem b. Chelbo [teacher of R. Yosef Kara] (R:SF, 11th c.), 83, 187t
Menachem b. Yaakov Ibn Saruq (Heb. lexicog.:Seph, d.970), 15, 39, 58t, 99t
R. Menachem of Merseburg [ReMaM] (R: Ger, beg. 14th c.), 27t
R. Meshullam b. Kalonymos (R:F, 10th c.), 213
R. Meshullam b. Moshe of Beziers (R:SF, 1175-125), 19, 108, 175, 176, 188t
R. Meshullam b. Yaakov of Lunel [Rebbe of Ravad of Posquires] (R:SF, d.1170), 18, 173-176, 183, 187t, 195

Mintz, R. Moshe (R:Ger, 15th c.), 27t

Mintz, R. Yehudah [Mahari Mintz] (R:It, 1408-1506), 27t

Mizrachi, R. Eliyahu b. Avraham [Re'em] (R-A,Turk, c.1450-1525), *HaMizrachi:* 27t

Moellin, R. Yaakov b. Moshe [Maharil] (R: Ger, 1360-1427), 27t, 90, 93 f

R. Mordecai b. Hillel haKohen (R:Ger, 1240-1298), *The Mordecai:* 90, 93, 224

R. Moshe b. Chanoch (R:Seph, 10th c.), 16, 43 f, 58, 61 f, 80

R. Moshe b. Ibn Ezra (Heb. poet:Seph, 1055-1135), 98

R. Moshe b. Kalonymos (R:Ger, 8th or 9th c.), 22, 73t, 211, 215t

R. Moshe b. Maimon [Rambam; Maimonides] (R:Seph, 1135-1204), *Yad haChazakah. See* Subject Index.

R. Moshe b. Meshullam haParnes (R:Ger, d. 1096), 212

R. Moshe b. Nachman [Ramban; Nachmanides] (R:Seph, 1194-1270). *See* Subject Index.

R. Moshe b. Shmuel Ibn Tibbon (R:SF, d.c. 1283), 188t, 198

R. Moshe b. Yaakov of Coucy (R:F, d.1260), *Sefer Mitzvos Gadol/Semag:* 26, 90, 92

R. Moshe b. Yehudah of Lunel (R:SF, 12th c.), 175

R. Moshe b. Yosef b. Mervon haLevi [Rebbe of Ravad III of Posquires] (R:SF, d.1165), 18, 173, 183, 187t

R. Moshe haDarshon of Narbonne (R:SF, 11th c.), 18, 73t, 76, 83, 187t

R. Moshe of Paviah (R:It, 10th c.), 73t, 75

Moshe Rabbeinu (N, d.2488). *See* Subject Index.

R. Moshe the Parnes (R:SF, 9th c.), 18t, 83, 187

R. Nasan b. Meir of Trinquetaille (R:SF, beg. 13th c.), *Sefer haEzer:* 21, 188t, 190 f

Nasan b. Yechiel of Rome (R:It, 1035-1106), *HeAruch:* 11, 26t, 73t, 75, 83, 87t

R. Nasan haDayyan (R:Seph, 10th c.), 61 f

R. Natronai b. Hilai Gaon (G:Sura, 853-858), 35, 50

Nebuchadnezar (K:Bavel, d.3364), 33, 48

R. Nissim b. Reuven of Gerondi [Ran] (R:Seph, d.c.1380), Rif Commentary: 27, 90, 108

R. Nissim b. Yaakov of Kairouan (R:NA, d.c. 1056), *Talmud com.:* 14 f, 26, 58, 68 f

R. Paltiel (Torah patron:It, 10th c.), 74

R. Paltoi b. Mar Abbaye (G:Pumb, 841-857 C.E.), 35

R. Peretz b. Eliyahu of Corbeil [Maharaf], (R:F, d.1298), *Tosafos Rabbeinu Peretz:* 26t

R. Pesachiah of Regensburg (world traveler: Ger, fl.1170-1175), *Sefer Sivuv:* 128

Philip IV [King] (K:Fr, fl.1306), 205

Phoebus, R. Shmuel (A, c.1650-1700), *Bais Shmuel:* 28t

Pollack, R. Yaakov b. Yosef (A: Poland, d. 1530), 28t

Rach. *See* R. Chananel b. Chushiel.

Radak. *See* Kimchi, R. David.

Radvaz. *See* R. David b. Shlomo Ibn Avi Zimra.

Ralbach. *See* R. Levi Ibn Chaviv.

Ralbag. *See* R. Levi b. Gershon

Rama. *See* Isserles, R. Moshe.

Ramah. *See* Abulafia, R. Meir b. Todros haLevi of Toledo.

Ramak. *See* Cordovero, R. Moshe.

Rambam. *See* R. Moshe b. Maimon.

Ramban. *See* R. Moshe b. Nachman.

Ran. *See* R. Nissim b. Reuven of Gerondi.

Rashba. *See* R. Shlomo b. Adres.

Rashbam. *See* R. Shmuel b. Meir.

Rashi. *See* R. Shlomo b. Yitzchak.

R'av. *See* Bertinoro, R. Ovadiah.

Rava (Am:B-4, 338-352), 32

Ravad I. *See* R. Avraham b. David Ibn Daud haLevi.

Ravad II. *See* R. Avraham b. Yitzchak Av Bes Din.

Ravad III [Ba'al haHasagos]. *See* R. Avraham b. David of Posquires.

Ravan. *See* R. Eliezer b. Nasan.

Raviah. *See* R. Eliezer b. Yoel haLevi.

Ravina II b. R. Huna [Ravina Zuta] (Am: B-6, beg. 5th c.), 25t

Razah. *See* R. Zerachiah haLevi.

Re'ah. *See* R. Aharon b. Yosef haLevi of Barcelona.

Rebbe. *See* R. Yehudah haNasi; Rabbeinu haKadosh.

Re'em. *See* R. Eliezer b. Shmuel of Metz.

ReMaM. *See* R. Menachem of Merseburg.

R. Reuven b. Chaim [Rebbe of Meiri] (R:SF, end 13th c.), 188t, 198

Ri haZaken. *See* R. Yitzchak b. Shmuel of Dampierre.

Ri Migash. *See* R. Yosef b. Meir haLevi Ibn Migash.

Richard the Lion-Hearted (K:Eng, fl.1189), 92

Rif. *See* Alfasi, R. Yitzchak.
Ritva. *See* Ishbili, R. Yom Tov.
Ritzag. *See* R. Yitzchak b. Yehudah Ibn Ghayyas.
Ritzva. *See* R. Yitzchak b. Avraham of Dampierre.
Rivam. *See* R. Yitzchak b. Meir.
Rivash. *See* R. Yitzchak b. Sheshes.
Rivavash. *See* Anav, R. Yehudah b. Binyamin haRofei.
Rogers III (K:SF, fl.c.1180), 181
Romamus I (Rom. Emp., 932 C.E.), 87
Rosanes, R. Yehudah (A:Turk, 1657-1727), *Mishneh laMelech:* 149
Rosen, R. Yosef [Rogatchover Gaon] (A, 1858-1936), 150
Rosh. *See* R. Asher b. Yechiel.
Rosh miLunel. *See* R. Asher b. Meshullam.
Rudolph I of Hapsburg [Kaisar] (Ger, fl.1186 C.E.), 93

R. Saadiah b. Yosef Gaon (G:Sura-4, 882-942), *Emunos veDe'os:* 57
Sangari, R. Yitzchak (Kuzari "Chaver", 8th c.), 123
Schiff, R. Meir of Fulda [Maharam Schiff] (A:Ger, 1605-1641), 28t
Schor, R. Ephraim (A, d.1633), *Tevu'os Shor:* 28t
Semak. *See* R. Yitzchak b. Yosef.
R. Shabse b. Meir haKohen [Shach] (A, 1622-1663), *Sifsei Kohen:* 28t
Shach. *See* R. Shabse b.Meir haKohen.
Shachna, R. Shalom (A, d.1558), 28t
Schor, R. Ephraim (A, d.1633), *Tevu'os Shor:*
R. Shalom b. Yitzchak Zekel of Austria [Maharash] (R-A, end 14th c.), 27t
Shaprut. *See* R. Chisdai b. Yitzchak.
R. Shem Tov b. Avraham Ibn Gaon of Gerondi (R:Seph/EY, b.c. 1287), *Migdal Oz:* 27t, 148
R. Shemaiah (R:F, beg. 12th c.), 215, 234, 242
R. Shemariah b. Elchanan (R:Eg, d.1011 C.E.), 15, 43 f, 58t, 66
R. Shephatiah b. Amitai (R:It, d.886 C.E.), *Piyyutim:* 13, 72
R. Sherira Gaon (G:P-4, 968-1006), *Iggeres R. Sherira Gaon:* 14, 42, 50
Shilah haKadosh. *See* Horowitz, R. Yeshayah b. Avraham haLevi
R. Shimon b. Yochai (T-4, 2nd c.), 25t
R. Shimon haGadol I (R:Ger, 10th c.), 213-215
R. Shimon haGadol II [Rashi's uncle] (R:Ger, 11th c.), 214, 215, 216n, 219
R. Shimshon b. Avraham of Sens [R. Shimshon miShantz] (R:F, d.c.1230), *Tosafos Shantz:* 26t, 85t, 90, 92
R. Shimshon b. Yitzchak of Chinon (R:F, 14th c.), *Sefer haKrisus:* 27t
R. Shlomo b. Avraham min haHar (R:SF, fl. fl. 1230), 20, 159, 188t, 191 f
R. Shlomo b. Yitzchak [Rashi] (R:F, 1040-1105). *See Subject Index.*
R. Shlomo Ibn Gabirol (Poet/philosopher: Spain, 1020-1057), 42, 99t, 195
R. Shlomo Petit of Acre (Kabbalist, R:EY, end 13th c.), 165
R. Shmuel b. Kalonymos [Chasidei Ashkenaz] (R:Ger, 12th c.), 26t, 212
R. Shmuel b. Meir [Rashbam] (R:F, 1080-1158), 26t, 90, 215, 244
Shmuel b. Paltiel (Torah patron: It, 10th c.), 74
R. Shmuel b. Yehudah Ibn Tibbon (R:SF, c.1160-1230), *Translator. See* Subject Index.
R. Shmuel b. Yosef haNagid (R:Seph, 993-1055), *Mavo haTalmud. See* Subject Index.
Shmuel haNavi [haRamassi] (N, 2832-2884), 32
R. Shmuel b. Kalonymos heChasid [Chasidei Ashkenaz] (R:Ger, 12th c.), 212
R. Shmuel haKohen (Rosh Yeshiva: Baghdad, fl. 1285), 165
R. Shmuel Shlettstadt (R:Ger, 14th c.), *HaMordecai haKattan:* 27t
R. Simchah b. Shmuel of Vitri (R:F, 12th c.,, *Machzor Vitri:* 215t, 234, 244
Sir Leon. *See* R. Yehudah b. Meir haKohen Leontin.
Sirkes, R. Yoel (A, 1561-1640), *Bayis Chadash:* 27t
S'ma. *See* Falk, R. Yehoshua.
Spiro, R. Nasan b. Shlomo (A, 1585-1633), *Megaleh Amukos:* 28t

R. Tam. *See* R. Yaakov b. Meir of Ramerupt.
Taz. *See* R. David b. Shmuel haLevi.
Theodosius (Byzantine Emp., 378-395 C.E.), 86
Theodosius II (Byzantine Emp., 408-450 C.E.), 86
Tiktin, R. Menachem David [Maharam Tiktin] (A, 16th c.), 28t

Titus, Flavius (Roman Emp, d. 81 C.E.), 70, 77, 98
R. Todros b. Machir (R:SF, 9th c.), 18, 83
R. Todros b. Moshe haParnes (Parnes, R:SF, beg. 12th c.), 172, 187t
Trani, R. Moshe b. Yosef [Mabit] (R-A:EY, 1500-1580), 28t
Trani, R. Yeshayah I haZaken b. Mali di (R: It, c.1180-1260), *Tosafos Rid:* 13, 26t, 73t, 77
Trani, R. Yosef b. Moshe [Maharit] (A:Eng-Turk, 1568-1639), 28t
Trani, R. Yeshayah II b. Eliyahu di (R:It, d.c. 1280), *Chidushei haRi'az:* 14, 73t, 77
Tyrnau, R. Yitzchak (R:Aus, d.1470), *Sefer haMinhagim:* 27t
R. Tzemach b. Paltoi Gaon (G:P-3, 871-880), 35, 76n

Ula (Am:Ey-3, beg. 4th c.), 105

R. Vidal Yom Tov diTolosa (R:Seph, d.1357), *Maggid Mishneh:* 27t, 148
Vilna Gaon. *See* R. Eliyahu b. Shlomo Zalman.
Vital, R. Chaim b. Yosef (A, 1542-1620), 28t

Weil, R. Yaakov b. Yehudah [Mahariv] (R: Ger, d. before 1456), 27t

Yaakov Avinu (PN, 2108-2255), 57, 84, 175n
R. Yaakov b. Asher [Ba'al Turim] (R:Seph, 1270-1343), *Arba'ah Turim:* 27t, 90, 93
R. Yaakov b. haRif (R:Seph, beg. 12th c.), 99t
R. Yaakov b. Meir of Ramerupt [Rabbeinu Tam (R:F, 1100-1171), 26t, 71, 85t, 90, 92, 116
R. Yaakov b. Shlomo Ibn Chaviv (R:Seph-Gr, 1445-1516), *Ein Yaakov:* 27t
R. Yaakov b. Yakar [Rashi's Rebbe,] (R:Ger, d.1064), 23, 26t, 215t, 219, 222-224
R. Yaakov b. Yitzchak haLevi [Rabbosenu haLevi'im] (R:Ger, end 11th c.), 225
R. Yaakov of Kairouan (R:NA, end 10th c.), 58t
R. Yaakov of Marvege (R:F, fl. 1203), *She'elos U'Teshuvos min haShamayim:* 110, 185 f
R. Yaakov of Orleans (R:SF, d.1189), 90, 92

Yaffe, R. Mordecai b. Avraham [Ba'al haLevushim] (A, 1530-1612), 28t
R. Yechiel b. Yosef of Paris (R:F, d.1268), 26t, 90. 92
R. Yechiel of Rome (R:It, 10th c.), 11, 73t, 75
Yechoniah [King] (K:Jud, 3327), 11
R. Yehonasan b. David haKohen of Lunel (R:SF, 12th c.), *Comment. on Rif. See* Subject Index.
R. Yehosef haNagid (R:Seph, d.1067) 5, 58, 66, 69, 98
R. Yehoshua Boaz miBaruch (A, d.c.1554), *Mesoras haShas; Ein Mishpat; Torah Or:* 108

Yehudah [b. Yaakov Avinu] (P, c.2195-2330), 58
R. Yehudah [b. R. Moshe haDarshon] (R:SF, 11th c.), 83
R. Yehudah b. Barzilai of Barcelona (R:Seph, 12th c.), *Sefer haIttim:* 26t, 99, 102, 116 f, 171 f
R. Yehudah b. Binyamin haRofei [Rivavan] (R:It, beg. 13th c.), 26t, 78f
Yehudah b. David Ibn Chiyug (Heb Lexicog: Seph, fl.1000), 15, 40 f, 58t, 99t
R. Yehudah b. Kalonymos b. Meir of Speier (R:Ger, 13th c.), *Yichusei Tannaim veAmoraim:* 212
R. Yehudah b. Meir haKohen Leontin [Sir Leon] (R:Ger, 10th c.), 212 f, 215t
R. Yehudah b. Moshe haDarshon (R:SF, 11th c.), 83, 187t
R. Yehudah b. Nasan [Rivan] [Rashi's son-in-law] (R:F, beg. 12th c., 26, 215, 242
R. Yehudah b. Shaul Ibn Tibbon (translator, R:SF, 1120-1190), 18, 21, 42, 118, 173 f, 188t, 195
R. Yehudah b. Shmuel heChasid [Chasidei Ashkenaz] (R:Ger, 1150-1217), *Sefer Chasidim:* 26t, 212
R. Yehudah b. Yechezkel (Am:B-2, 257-299), 32
R. Yehudah b. Yosef Nasi Ibn Ezra (Nasi: Seph, fl.1148), 115 f
R. Yehudah al-Charizi [Tachkemoni] (poet: Spain, 1165-1225), 39
R. Yehudah Alpachar of Toledo (R:Seph, 13th c.), 159 f
R. Yehudah haLevi (R:Seph, 1075-1141), *Kuzari. See* Subject Index.
R. Yehudah haNasi [Rebbe; Rabbeinu haKadosh] (T-5, end 2nd c.), 25t, 32n
R. Yehudah Loew b. Bezalel [Maharal of Prague] (A, 1512-1609), 28t
R. Yehudai Gaon [b. Nachman] (G:S-2, 757-761), *Halachos Pesukos:* 25t

R. Yekusiel b. Moshe b. Kalonymos of Lucca (R:Ger, 8th or 9th c.), 22, 211, 215t

R. Yerucham b. Meshullam (R:Seph, d.1350), *Sefer Mesharim:* 27t

R. Yeshayah b. Chizkiah (Exilarch:Damascus, fl.1285), 165

R. Yeshayah I b. Mali haZaken of Trani. *See* Trani, R. Yeshayah II b. Mali haZaken.

R. Yeshayah II b. Eliyahu the Younger of Trani. *See* Trani, R. Yeshayah II b. Eliyahu di.

R. Yishmael b. Elisha II (T-3, beg. 2nd c.), *Mechilta of R. Yishmael:* 25t

R. Yitzchak b. Abba Mari of Marseilles [Ba'al haIttur] (R:SF, 1122-1193), *Ittur Soferim:* 20, 26t, 107, 172, 186, 187f

R. Yitzchak b. Asher hLevi of Speyer [Riva] (R:Ger, fl.1150), 26t, 215

R. Yitzchak b. Avraham of Dampierre [Ritzva] (R:F, d.1205), 26t, 190

R. Yitzchak b. Elazar haLevi of Worms [Rashi's Rebbe] (R:Ger, d.c.1070), 23, 26t, 215t, 219, 222, 225, 229

R. Yitzchak b. Meir [Rivam] (R:F, 12th c.), 26 215t, 244

R. Yitzchak b. Meir of Dueren (R:Ger, end 13th c.), *Sha'arei Dura:* 27t

R. Yitzchak b. Melchizedek of Siponto (R:It, c.1090-1160), *Mishnah com.:* 14, 73t, 76

R. Yitzchak b. Mervon haLevi of Narbonne (R: SF, beg. 12th c.), 171, 187t

R. Yitzchak b. Moshe of Baghdad (R:Baghdad, 11th c.), 16, 58t, 99t, 102

R. Yitzchak b. Moshe of Vienna (R:Aus, 1180-1250), *Or Zaru'a:* 26t

R. Yitzchak b. Reuven of Barcelona (R:Seph, 1043-1100), 16, 26t, 58t, 99t, 102

R. Yitzchak b. Reuven [Rif's grandson] (R: Seph, 12th c.), *Esrim Sha'arei Shevu'os:* 104

R. Yitzchak b. Sheshes Perfet [Rivash] (R: Seph, 1326-1407), 27t, 91, 94, 231

R. Yitzchak b. Shmuel of Dampierre [Ri haZaken] (R:F, d.c.1185), 26t, 90, 109

R. Yitzchak b. Yaakov of Bohemia [R. Yitzchak haLavan] (R:Bohemia, 12th c.), 128

R. Yitzchak b. Yehudah Ibn Ghayyas [Ritzag] (R:Seph, 1038-1089), 16, 23, 50-52, 56, 58t, 97 f, 99t

R. Yitzchak b. Yehudah of Mainz [Rashi's Rebbe] (R:Ger, 11th c.), 26t, 75, 215t, 219, 224 f

R. Yitzchak b. Yosef of Corbeil [SeMaK] (R: F, d.1280), *Sefer Mitzvos Kattan/SeMaK:* 26t

R. Yitzchak deLeon I [HaAri haGadol] (R: Seph, d.1492), 27t

R. Yitzchak deLeon II b. Eliezer Ibn Tzur (A, fl.1546), *Megillas Esther (com. on Sefer haMitzvos:* 138n

R. Yitzchak haKohen of Narbonne (R:SF, beg. 13th c.), 188t, 198

R. Yitzchak Sagei Nahor b. haRavad III of Posquires (Kabbalist, R:SF, 12th c.), 181, 182, 183

R. Yochanan b. Zakkai (T-1, T-2, 1st c.), 152n

R. Yom Tov b. Yitzchak of Joigny (R:Eng-F, d.1190), 93n

R. Yonah b. Avraham heChasid of Gerondi (R:Seph, 1200-1263, *Sha'arei Teshuvah:* 26t, 90, 93, 108, 159, 183, 191

Yonah Ibn Janach (Heb Lexicog: Seph, 990-1050), 41, 58t, 195

Yonasan b. Uziel (T-1, beg. 1st c. C.E.), *Targum Yonasan:* 25t

R. Yosef b. Meir haLevi Ibn Migash [Ri Migash] (R:Seph, 1077-1141). *See* Subject Index.

R. Yosef b. Yaakov Ibn Sahal of Cordoba (R: Seph, d.1124), 98

R. Yosef b. Yaakov Ibn Tzaddik (R:Seph, 1070-1149), *Olam Kattan:* 98, 99t, 117 f

R. Yosef b. Yehudah Ibn Aknin (R:Seph, 1150-1220), 99t, 153 f, 156, 162, 163n

R. Yosef b. Yehudah Ibn Shimon (R:Seph, 12th c.), 162, 163n

R.Yosef Ibn Avitur (R:Seph, beg. 11th c.), 58t, 62

R. Yosef Ibn Chaviv (R:Seph, d.beg. 15th c.), *Nimmukei Yosef:* 27t, 108

R. Yosef Ibn Plat (R:SF, 12th c.), 176

R. Yosef Kara of N. France (R:F, 11th c.), *Comment. on Nach:* 83, 244

R. Yosef Tuv Elem (R:F, fl.c.1070), *Seder Olam Zuta:* 26t, 215t, 221 f

R. Zerachiah haLevi [Razah] (R:SF, 1125-1186). *Sefer haMa'or. See* Subject Index.

Bibliography and Source Index

[Listing All Sefarim Cited in Footnotes, as Source References]

Anvil of Sinai [N.Y.: Hashkafah Pub., 1985, 3rd ed.], R. Zechariah Fendel, *Hashkafah:* 124, 129

R. Avraham b. haRambam (1186-1237), **Sefer haMaspik leOvdei HaShem** [Jerusalem, 1973]: 164

R. Avraham b. haRambam, Responsa, as cited in appendix section to Shulsinger Rambam [N.Y.: Shulsinger Bros., 1947]: 164

Azulai, R. Chaim Yosef David [Chida]. *See* **Shem haGedolim.**

Ba'alei haTosafos [Jerusalem: Mosad Bialik, 1968], Ephraim Urbach: *History:* 231

Bahag. *See* **Halachos Gedolos.**

Bais haBechirah. *See* **Me'iri.**

Bais Yosef, R. Yosef Caro (1488-1575), *Tur com.:* 103, 148

Bigdei Yesha, *Com. on Mordecai:* 224, 300

Caro, R. Yosef. *See* **Bais Yosef; Shulchan Aruch.**

Chakmoni, R. Shabbatai Donnolo (b. 913 C.E.): 74

Chayyei Adam, R. Avraham Danzig (1748-1820), *Halachic code:* 225

Chovos haLevavos [Warsaw: Y. Goldman, 1875], R. Bachya Ibn Paquda (c. 1080), *Hashkafah; mussar:* 119, 120, 121

Derech Tamim: 111

Doros haRishonim [Frankfort-on-Main, 1901-1918], R. Yitzchak Isaac haLevi Rabinowitz (1847-1914), *History:* 42, 43, 44, 46, 47, 48, 49, 54, 56, 57, 86

Encyclopedia Judaica [Jerusalem: Keter Pub., 1973], Cecil Roth, ed.: 86

Encyclopedia leToledos Gedolei Yisroel [Jerusalem: Chachik Pub., 1969], Mordecai Margalios (1909-1968), *Biog. Enc.:* 41, 43, 65, 66, 67, 77, 78, 81, 102, 114, 225

Encyclopedia Talmudis [Jerusalem, 1971], R. Shlomo Yosef Zevin, ed., *Talmud. Enc.:* 104, 105

Fendel, R. Zechariah. *See* **Anvil of Sinai; Legacy of Sinai; Masters of the Mesorah: Later Rishonim; The Torah Ethic; Torah Faith: The Thirteen Principles.**

Halachos Gedolos, R. Shimon Kayyara (c. 780 C.E.), *Halachic code:* 139

HaMe'iri. *See* **Me'iri.**

HaMoreh laDoros [Jerusalem: Mosad haRav Kook, 1968], Meir Uryan, *Biog.-Rambam:* 159

Hilchos Alfasi, R. Yitzchak Alfasi (Rif, 1013-1103), *Halachic code:* 104, 106, 111

Hilchos Rabbeinu Asher (Rosh, 1250-1327), *Halachic code:* 50, 52, 53, 117

Iggeres Kena'os, R. Yehudah Alpachar of Toldedo: 160

Iggeres Rabbeinu Sherira Gaon (906-1006) [Haifa, 1921], ed. Dr. Menasheh Lewin (1879-1944), *Historical source:* 35

Introd. to HaMa'or haKattan, R. Yitzchak b. Zerachiah haLevi (fl. 1144, father of Ba'al haMa'or), *Introd. to critical Glosses on Rif:* 184

Introductions in Vilna Shas, end, tractate Berachos (before the Rif), 111, 112, 184, 185

Kaftor vaPherach, R. Estori b. Moshe ha-Parchi (1280-1355)), *Encyc. work on all aspects of Eretz Yisroel:* 207

Korei haDoros, 79

Kuzari [Warsaw: Y. Goldman, 1880], R. Yehudah haLevi (1075-1141), *Torah hashkafah and mussar:* 37, 123, 124, 125

Legacy of Sinai [New York: Hashkafah Pub., 1985, 2nd ed.], R. Zechariah Fendel: *History of Mesorah:* 32, 33, 38, 45, 46, 51, 52, 66, 75, 89

Ma'amar haIttim: 233

Machzor, Selichos: *Penitential prayers:* 72

Machzor Vitri, R. Simchah b. Shmuel of Vitri [12th c.], *hal. and resp.:* 215, 234, 244

Machzor Yom Kippur, "Seder haAvodah": *Yom Kippur Mussaf service:* 81

Masters of the Mesorah: Later Rishonim [New York: Hashkafah Pub., 1990], Rabbi Zechariah Fendel, *History of Torah transmission:* 78, 90, 91, 92, 93, 107, 108, 128, 145, 148, 149, 150, 159, 165, 182, 186, 190, 191, 207

Matzreif leChachmah [Paris Ms., No. 772], Joseph Delmedigo: 72

Mechokekei Yehudah [New York: Reinman Pub.,], R. Yehudah Leib b. Yitzchak Krinski, *Com. on Ibn Ezra Torah Com.:* 126

Megillas Achima'atz, Achima'atz b. Paltiel (fl. 1052), *Hist. Poetic narrative:* 71-74

ME'IRI, R. Menachem b. Shlomo (1249-1315), **Bais haBechirah** [Jerusalem: S. Wachsman, 1944), **Avos:** 116, 172, 179, 190, 199, 201, 205

Me'iri, Bais haBechirah [New York: R. Chanoch Albeck, 1947], **Preface to Yevamos:** 179, 182, 199

Me'iri, Bais haBechirah: 182, 200, 201, 202

Me'iri, Mishlei: 201, 202

Melo Chofnayim: 230

Meshech Chachmah, R. Meir Simchah ha-Kohen of Dvinsk (1843-1926), *Torah com.:* 144

Midrash haChachmah, R. Yehudah b. Shlomo haKohen (fl. 1080): 129

Midrash haGadol [Jerusalem: Mosad haRav Kook, 1967], R. David b. Amram haEdni, [13th c.], ed. Mordecai Margalios, *Midrashic anthology on Torah:* 181

MIDRASH RABBAH: *Amoraitic Aggadic Midrash on Pentateuch and the Five Megillos:*
Bamidbar Rabbah: 240
Bereshis Rabbah: 240
Vayikra Rabbah: 240

Midrash Rabbeinu Bachya, R. Bachya b. Asher (d. 1340), *Torah com.:* 183

Midrash Tanchuma, *Homiletical Midrash on Torah:* 138, 139, 240

Mishnah Berurah, R. Yisroel Meir haKohen (Chafetz Chaim, 1839-1933): 225

The Mordecai, R. Mordecai b. Hillel (1240-1298), *Halachic code:* 224, 244

R. Moshe b. Maimon. *See* **Rambam.**

R. Moshe b. Nachman. *See* **Ramban.**

Nachlas Shadal: 223

Olam Kattan, R. Yosef Ibn Tzaddik of Cordoba (d. 1149), *Hashkafah; mussar:* 117, 118

Or haChaim [Jerusalem: Mosad haRav Kook, 1965], R. Chaim Michel (1792-1846): 40, 68, 79, 102, 104, 111, 112, 116, 129, 134, 152, 161, 172, 173, 181, 183, 186, 191, 224, 225, 228, 242

Orchos Chaim, R. Aharon haKohen of Lunel (d. 1334), *Halachic code:* 170, 181, 205, 206

Otzar haGeonim, Chagigah: *Geonic lit. and resp.:* 35

Otzar Meforshei Mishneh Torah [New York: Shulsinger Bros., 1947], Rabbi Y. Rubinstein: 148

Rabbeinu Tam. *See* **Sefer haYashar.**

Radak (R. David Kimchi, c. 1160-1235), *Nach commentary:* 193, 194

Ralbag, To'aliyos Ralbag [Tel Aviv: Netzach, 1961], R. Levi b. Gershon (1288-1344), *on Torah parshiyos:* 204, 205

RAMBAM (R. Moshe b. Maimon, 1135-1204), **Iggaros haRambam** [Jerusalem: Mosad haRav Kook, 1960], Mordecai Dov Rabinowitz, ed.: 48

Rambam, Iggaros u'Teshuvos haRambam [Jerusalem: haAchim Levin-Epstein]: 154

Rambam, "Iggeres haMussar," Iggarosav ve-Toledos Chayyav [Tel Aviv: Mordecai Inst., 1970], M. Bar Joseph, ed., *Ethical Bequest:* 127, 153, 158

Rambam, Iggeres haShmad: 152, 157, 158

Rambam, Iggeres Teiman [Tel Aviv: Mordecai Inst., 1970], Bar Joseph, ed.: 158

Rambam, Introd. to Mishnah [Tel Aviv: Hotza'as Rishonim, 1948], in *Otzar haHakdamos,* ed. M.D. Rabinowitz: 109, 113, 134, 135, 137, 157

Rambam, Introd. to Sefer haMitzvos [Jerusalem: haAchim Levin-Epstein, 1956]: 138, 139

Rambam, Mishnah Commentary: 135, 136

Rambam, MISHNEH TORAH **(Hilchos Aveil)** 182; **(Bais haBechirah)** 180; **(De'os)** 147, 154; **(Kiddush haChodesh)** 142; **(Lulav)** 180; **(Megillah)** 145; **(Melachim)** 147; **(Niddah)** 180; **(Sanhedrin)** 146; **(She'elah u'Pikadon)** 134; **(Shemittah veYovel)** 142; **(Ta'anis)** 153; **(Teshuvah)** 145, 146; **(Yesodei haTorah)** 156

Rambam, Moreh Nevuchim: 156, 157

Rambam, Rabbe Moshe ben Maimon [Jerusalem: Mosad haRav Kook, 1969], R. Yehudah Leib Maimon, *Biog.:* 65, 118, 134, 135, 162

Rambam, Rabbeinu Moshe ben Maimon, Iggarosav veToledos Chayyav [Tel Aviv, 1970], ed. M. Bar Joseph, *Biog.:* 141, 150, 154, 155, 156, 163, 167, 168, 178, 197

RAMBAN (R. Moshe b. Nachman, 1194-1270), **Chidushei haRamban:** 117

Ramban, Commentary on Torah: (Introd.) 127, 234

Ramban, Hilchos Nedarim: 102

Ramban, Iggeres haRamban to Chachmei Tzorfas: 150, 152

Ramban, Introd. to Milchamos HaShem: 185

Ramban, Sefer haZechus: 177

Ramban, Rabbeinu Moshe ben Nachman [Jerusalem: Mosad haRav Kook, 1967], Heb. edit, R. Chaim Dov Chavel, *Biog.:* 159, 160, 190

Ramban: His Life and Teachings (Eng. edit.) [New York: Feldheim, 1960], R. Charles B. Chavel, *Biog.:* 150

RASHI (R. Shlomo b. Yitzchak, 1040-1105), **Sifrei deVei Rashi, "Chofes Matmonim,"** *Halacha and Resp.:* 229

Rashi, Sifrei deVei Rashi, "Sefer haOrah," S. Buber ed. [Benei Berak, 1980], *Halacha and Responsa:* 238, 239

Rashi, Sifrei deVei Rashi, "Sefer haPardes," ed. H.L. Ehrenreich [Benei Berak, 1980], *Halacha and resp.:* 223, 225, 229 f, 238

Rashi, Peninei Rashi laTorah, R. Moshe Chesed (d. 1989) [Jerusalem: Hotza'as Reuven, 1989]: 235

Rashi [Jerusalem: Mosad haRav Kook, 1966], R. Eliezer M. Lipschutz [Jerusalem: Mosad haRav Kook, 1966], *Biog.:* 223, 229, 230, 238, 239, 240, 244

Rashi, Yalkut Rashi, R. Shmuel Kleiman [Kansas City, 1942]: 235

Ravad I. *See* **Sefer haKabbalah.**

RAVAD III (R. Avraham b. David of Posquires, Ba'al haHasagos, 1120-1198), **Ba'alei haNefesh le-haRavad,** *Hilchos Niddah:* 179, 180, 181

Ravad III, Hasagos haRavad, *Critical glosses on Rambam, Mishneh Torah:* 148, 178

Ravad III, Hasagos haRavad le-haRif, *Critical Glosses on Hilchos Rav Alfas:* 110, 177, 178, 180

Ravad III, Temim De'im le-haRavad [Jerusalem: Mosad haRav Kook, 1974], *Halacha; Responsa:* 173, 176, 179

Rivash (R. Yitzchak b. Sheshes Perfet, 1326-1407), [Jerusalem, 1968], *Resp.:* 104, 231

Rosh Amanah [Tel Aviv: Hotza'as Sifreisi, 1958], R. Don Yitzchak Abrabanel (1437-1508), *Clarifying Thirteen Ikkarim:* 160

Seder haDoros [Warsaw: Y. Goldman, 1882], R. Yechiel Halpern (1660-1747), *History of Torah transmission:* 142, 228

Seder Olam Zuta haShalem [Jerusalem: Toras Chesed, 1957], attrib. to R. Yosef Tov Elem (fl. c. 1070), ed. R. Moshe Yair Weinstock, *Hist. of Torah transmission:* 33, 222

Sefer Abudraham [New York: Saphograph Pub.], R. Yosef Abudraham (fl. 1340), *Hil. u'Minhagei Tefillah:* 161

Sefer haAruch [Tel Aviv: Bais Rafael], R. Nasan b. Yechiel of Rome (1035-1186), *Talmudic Aramaic dictionary:* 234

Sefer haChinuch, attrib. to R. Aharon haLevi (Re'ah, 1235-1300), *Commentary on Taryag Mitzvos:* 144

Sefer haEmunos: 172

Sefer haGalui, R. Saadiah b. Yosef Gaon (928-942 C.E.): 31, 57

Sefer haKabbalah, R. Avraham b. David Ibn Daud haLevi (Ravad I, 1110-1180), *Historical source:* 42, 44, 62, 63, 64, 66, 68, 97, 98, 102, 103, 110, 113, 114, 115, 116, 118, 129, 130

Sefer haManhig, R. Avraham b. Nasan ha-Yarchi (1155-1215), *Halacha:* 98

Sefer haMa'or, R. Zerachiah b. Yitzchak ha-Levi (Razah, Ba'al haMa'or, 1125-1186), *Critique on Hil. Rav Alfas:* 41, 53, 54, 56, 110, 184

Sefer haMasa'os, Benjamin of Tudela (12th c.), *Travel observations:* 175, 181

Sefer haYashar of Rabbeinu Tam (R. Yaakov b. Meir of Ramerupt, 1100-1171) [Berlin, 1898; Jerusalem, 1972], S. Rosenthal, ed., *Responsa:* 46, 54, 59, 71, 242

Sefer Moznaim, R. Avraham Ibn Ezra (1090-1164): 40

Sefer Yuchsin haShalem [Jerusalem: Vardi, 1963], R. Avraham Zacuto (1442-1515): 80, 161, 162, 182

Sha'ar Tzion, R. Yitzchak diLatish: 189

Shalsheles haKabbalah [Jerusalem: HaDoros haRishonim, 1962], R. Gedaliah b. Yosef Ibn Yachya (1515-1587), *Hist. of Torah transmission:* 126, 227, 241

She'elos u'Teshuvos min haShamayim, R. Yaakov of Marvege (fl. 1203), [Jerusalem: Mosad haRav Kook, 1967], ed. Reuven Margalios, *Responsa:* 110, 111, 185, 186

Shem haGedolim [Warsaw: Y. Goldman, 1876], R. Chaim Yosef David Azulai (Chida, 1724-1806), *History of Torah transmission:* 186, 228, 233

Shevet Yehudah [Jerusalem, 1947], Solomon Ibn Verga (fl. c.1492), *Hist. of Jewish persecution:* 33, 48, 182, 189

Shibbolei haLeket, R. Tzidkiyah b. Avraham haRofei Anav (fl. 1240), *Hal.:* 240

Shulchan Aruch, R. Yosef Caro (1488-1575), *Halachic code:* 105, 110, 232

Siddur Rav Amram, R. Amram b. Sheshna Gaon (858-876), *Siddur:* 35

Sifra deVei Rav [Toras Kohanim], red. either by R. Chiyya (c.200 C.E.), or Rav (c.220 C.E.), *Tannaitic halachic Midrash on Leviticus:* 143

Sifran Shel Rishonim [Jerusalem, 1935], ed. Simchah Assaf, *Halacha and responsa:* 174, 176, 244

Tachkemoni, R. Yehudah Al-Charizi (1165-1225): 39

Tashbetz, R. Shimon b. Tzemach Duran (1361-1441), *Responsa:* 102, 116, 179

Tekufas haGeonim veSafrusah [Jerusalem: Mosad haRav Kook, 1955], Simchah Assaf (1889-1953), ed. Mordecai Margalios, *History, Geonic era:* 35, 43, 46, 56, 87

Teshuvos Chachmei Tzorfas veLutir (11th c.) [Vienna: ed. J. Mueller, 1881], *Responsa:* 229, 230, 243

Te'udah Chadashah leToledos Reshis ha-Kabbalah [Tel Aviv: Sefer Bialik, 1934], G. Scholem, *History, Kabbalah:* 183

Tibbon, R. Yehudah Ibn (d. 1190), **Ethical Bequest,** *Mussar:* 195, 196

Tibbon, R. Yehudah Ibn, Introd. to Chovos haLevavos: 195

Toledos Tannaim veAmoraim [Jerusalem: Kiryah Ne'emanah, 1964], R. Aharon Heiman (1862-1937), *Hist.; Biog.:* 86

The Torah Ethic [New York: Hashkafah Pub., 1988], R. Zechariah Fendel, *Hashkafah, mussar:* 146, 153

Torah Faith: The Thirteen Principles [New York: Hashkafah Pub., 1985], R. Zechariah Fendel, *Hashkafah:* 151

Tosafos Ma'asei Rav, R. Eliyahu b. Shlomo Zalman of Vilna (Vilna Gaon, 1720-1797): 126

Tzedah laDerech [Warsaw: C. Kelter Pub., 1881], R. Menachem b. haKadosh R. Aharon b. Zerach (d. 1389), *Halacha and hashkafah:* 109, 137, 231

Zacuto, R. Avraham. *See* **Sefer Yuchsin ha-Shalem.**

R. Zerachiah b. Yitzchak haLevi. *See* **Sefer haMa'or.**

TORAH, NVI'IM, KESUVIM

TORAH

GENESIS:
(5:24) 82 (17:21) 111 (22:1) 236 (24:26-27) 203 (25:27) 175 (25:31-34) 84 (Ch.27) 84 (27:33) 111 (27:41) 84 (28:5) 229 (32:10-12) 204 (33:4) 84 (46:28) 58

EXODUS:
(11:9) 160 (18:1) 172 (19:1) 236 (19:21-22) 143 (20:1) 124 (20:2-3) 139 (28:39) 224 (30:7) 224 (31:8) 234 (32:26) 39 (33:10) 160

LEVITICUS:
(1:9) 144 (18:5) 143, 144 (19:37) 143 (26:6) 237 (26:14-46) 161

NUMBERS:
(11:12) 146 (12:8) 160 (19:1) 78 (23:23) 238 (23:24) 237 (24:5) 237 (27:17) 57 (28:4) 224

DEUTERONOMY:
(4:4) 146 (5:6-7) 139 (5:20-24) 139 (6:6) 236 (8:18) 121 (11:13) 236 (12:19) 126 (21:17) 234 (22:8) 119 (26:16) 236 (27:9) 236 (28:68) 70 (31:29) 243 (33:4) 139 (33:10) 204 (34:10) 160 (34:12) 139

NVI'IM

Ezekiel:
(36:27) 193

Isaiah:
(2:3) 59 (28:8) 234 (29:14) 205 (30:20) 238 (40:11) 147 (45:7) 237 (49:3) 147 (51:2) 111 (57:1) 115 (57:16) 145 (59:2) 146 (59:21) 193 (65:24) 146 (66:22) 194

Jeremiah:
(3:17) 122 (15:2) 130 (31:30-33) 193 (31:32) 168

Joshua:
(1:1) 161

Judges:
(1:2) 77 (5:31) 197 (5:10) 206

I Kings:
(5:26) 228

II Kings:
(23:25) 113

Malachi:
(2:7) 65, 160

I Samuel:
(3:3) 32 (3:4-10) 33 (4:22) 161 (14:6) 121

KESUVIM

I Chronicles:
(28:2) 146

Daniel:
(9:23) 160

Ecclesiastes:
(1:5) 32, 130, 226 (9:7) 146

Job:
(11:9) 116

Proverbs:
(5:15) 243 (5:19) 234 (14:10) 236 (15:21) 243 (16:19) 235 (16:20) 236 (19:1) 240 (20:5) 243

Psalms:
(1:2) 234 (8:7) 119 (19:13) 167 (25:14) 181 (68:23) 44 (78:71) 147 (102:15) 122 (112:4) 185

Shir haShirim:
(2:8) 199 (5:2) 240

TALMUD BAVLI

Redacted ca. 500 C.E. [*Tosafos; **Me'iri]

Avodah Zarah: (9a) 69 (11b) 84 (57b) 222 (75a) 227

Avos: (1:2) 144 (1:17) 164 (2:2) 201 (3:17) 194 (4:8) 201 (4:13) 64

Avos deRabbe Nasan: (41:1) 64

Bava Basra: (9b) 200** (10b) 202** (12a) 160

Bava Kamma: (64a) 175* (87a) 239

Bava Mezia: (31a) 106 (59a) 202**

Beitzah: (24b) 222, 225, 230

Berachos: (10a) 204 (17b) 117* (25b) 229* (34b) 236

Chagigah: (14b) 152

Chullin: (139b) 76

Eruvin: (56a) 75 (83b) 49 (104a) 105, 117*

Gittin: (36b) 154 (57b) 44 (59a) 89 (59b) 182, 228

Kesuvos: (6a) 76* (50a) 200** (103a) 182

Kiddushin: (31a-b) 106 (37b) 127* (72b) 32, 226

Makkos: (5a) 49 (10a) 243 (19b) 242 (23b) 138, 139

Megillah: (6a) 68 (12b) 234

Menachos: (20b) 59*

Pesachim: (8a) 152 (112a) 202**

Rosh Hashanah: (4:14) 51, 52, 56 (13a) 127* (34a) 53 (4:10) 106 (13a) 127*

Sanhedrin: (7a) 201**

Shabbos: (8a) 49 (33a-b) 106 (59b) 228 (92a) 75 (118b) 106 (123b) 49 (130a-b) 106 (137b) 227*

Sukkah: (35b) 228

Ta'anis: (7a) 243 (12b) 224 (20b) 127* (27b) 144

Yevamos: (117a) 117

Yoma: (16b) 228 (23a) 154 (48a) 93*

Zevachim: (14b) 93*

Yerushalmi, Beitzah: (5:2) 105

Glossary of Hebrew Terms

Acharonim. Later Torah scholars [after 16th c.].
Al Kiddush HaShem. In sanctification of G-d's Name.
Al yichud HaShem. For Unity of G-d's Name.
Amidah. The Eighteen Benedictions.
Amoraim. Sages, Talmudic era [beg. 3rd c.-5th c. C.E.].
Arba'ah Shevuyyim. The "Four Captive" scholars
Aron. The Torah Ark; a coffin.
Av Bes Din. President of Bes Din.
Bas Kol. Heavenly Voice.
Birkas haMazon. Grace after Meals.
Bitachon. Trust in G-d.
Chukim. Inscrutable Torah statutes.
Churban. Destruction of Temple.
Dayyan. Judge.
Din Torah. Litigation by a Bes Din.
Emunah. Faith.
Galus. Exile; Diaspora.
Geonim. Sages, post-Talmudic era [589-1038 C.E.]
Get. Bill of divorce.
Golah. Exile; diaspora.
Haftorah. Weekly reading from Nvi'im [Prophets].
Hashkafah. Torah outlook.
Kabbalah. Esoteric Torah study.
Kohen Gadol. High Priest.
Korban[os]. Ritual sacrifice[s].
Kunteres [Kuntreisim]. Unstructured notes and glosses.
Maran. Our master.
Mashiach. The Messiah.
Mekubal. A student of Kabbalah.
Nagid. Prince; exilarch.
Neshamah. Soul.
Nusach haTefillos. Text of tefillos.
Paytan. Author of liturgical poems.
Piyyut. Liturgical poems.
Poskei Ashkenaz. 15th-16th c. German scholars.
Poskim. Halachic authorities.
P'shat. Basic meaning of text.
Rabbanan Savorai. Sages, post-Talmudic era [475-589 C.E.].
Reish Kallah. Head of the Academy.
Rishonim. Early Torah scholars [11th-15th c.].
Rosh Yeshiva. Head of a Yeshiva or Torah academy.

Ru'ach haKodesh. Divine Spirit.
Sandik. Holds infant during circumcision.
Sedarim. Six Orders or Divisions of the Mishnah.
Selichos. Penitential Prayers.
Semichah. Rabbinic ordination.
Shali'ach tzibbur. Leader of congregational prayer service.
Shas. Entire Talmud.
Sugya. Unit of Talmudic discussion.
Talmid[im]. Disciple[s].
Talmid-chaver. Disciple-colleague relationship.
Tannaim. Sages, Mishnah era [3rd c.B.C.E.-end 2nd c. B.C.E.].
Taryag mitzvos. 613 primary Torah commandments.
Techiyas haMeisim. Resurrection of the Dead.
Tefillah. Prayer.
Tekufah. Era.
Tochacha. Admonishment in Parshas Bechukosai.
Tosafist. Author of Tosafos [12th and 13th c.].
Tosafos. Incisive Talmudic Novellae.
Tum'as Kohen. Defilement of sanctity of Kohen.
Tzaddik. Righteous indivdiual.
Yir'as Shamayim. Fear of Heaven.
Zal; zatzal. Of blessed memory.
Zekenim. [The seventy] Elders.

Abbreviations

ad. loc. on this passage
b. born
B.C.E. before Common Era
c. century
c., ca., circa. approximately
C.E. Common Era
Cf. compare
Ch., Chap. Chapter
d. died
ed. editor, edition
e.g. for example
f., ff. and the following page[s]
fl. flourished
ibid. in the same place
i.e. that is
infra below
introd. introduction
loc. cit. in the place cited
n. footnote
op. cit. in the work cited
p., pp. page[s]
R. Rabbe, Rabbeinu, Rabbi
supra above
s.v. under the word or heading
v. see
vol. volume

תם ונשלם שבח לקל בורא עולם.
ברוך הנותן ליעף כח, ולאין אונים עצמה ירבה.